EATING ARCHITECTURE

Eating Architecture

edited by Jamie Horwitz and Paulette Singley

THE MIT PRESS   CAMBRIDGE, MASSACHUSETTS   LONDON, ENGLAND

This book was set in Avenir and Clarendon by Graphic Composition.
Printed and bound in the United States of America.

Library of Congress Cataloging-in-Publication Data
Eating architecture / edited by Jamie Horwitz and Paulette Singley.
    p. cm
  Includes index.
  ISBN 0-262-08322-1 (hc : alk. paper)
  1. Food. 2. Architectural design. 3. Space (Architecture) I. Horwitz, Jamie. II. Singley, Paulette, 1960–
TX355.5.E28 2004
641.5—dc21

              2003054053

DEDICATED TO OUR MOTHERS

For Marjory Rosen Horwitz, who shows us how artistry
and grace can heal better than chicken soup.

And for Therese Daniels, who inspired this book with
the piquant scenarios for her Sexy Sauces and Recipes.

CONTENTS

ACKNOWLEDGMENTS

This book is the result of much generosity. We are especially grateful to Roger Conover, Lisa Reeve, Alice Falk, Derek George, and Matthew Abbate of the MIT Press for their dedication to transforming our manuscript into a book. We wish to thank the Graham Foundation for Advanced Studies in the Fine Arts, Iowa State University, Woodbury University, and Kenneth R. Nielsen for providing substantial financial support for this publication; without them, this project would not have been possible. And, along with all of the contributors, we gratefully acknowledge the following individuals whose presence and assistance carried this project forward: Kevin Lippert of Princeton Architectural Press, David W. Hall, Lynn Paxson, Norman Millar, Deborah Fausch, Catherine Ingraham, Elisabeth Sandberg, Georges Teyssot, Alessandra Ponte, Alice Friedman, Fern Kupfer, Mark Jarzombek, Clare Cardinal-Pett, M. Victoria Liptak, Jane Zaring, Mikesch Muecke, Roberta Feldman, Cal Lewis, and Jonathan Bober, who edited his mother's unfinished essay for this collection after her death.

Eating Architecture

PROLOGUE: CUISINE AS
ARCHITECTURAL INVENTION

PHYLLIS PRAY BOBER

To consider cookery through an architectural lens summons up a host of images at the same time culinary and art historical. First to come to some minds will be the romantic creations by the founder of modern French *grande cuisine*, Antonin Carême, following his dictum: "Most noble of all the arts is architecture, and its greatest manifestation is the art of the pastry chef." Others, more resolutely postmodern, will admire or decry current obsession on the part of certain chefs with "plated" constructions that owe more to inspirations from Frank Gehry's imaginative craft of novel materials and visual delights than to gustatory pleasure.

My own thoughts, since I am currently working on a Renaissance/baroque sequel to my *Art, Culture, and Cuisine: Ancient and Medieval Gastronomy* (1999), turn to those wondrous *apparati* and *intermezzi* that punctuated the courses of formal banquets and other *feste* of these inventive epochs when famous artists, like Leonardo at the Milanese court, did not shrink from turning their gifts to festive dining display. Ephemeral by their very nature, castles and other edifices created with their landscapes as table *trionfi* by the confectioner's art, as well as full-scale structures composed of edibles, their descriptions awaken a wistful sense of loss and wonder.

Who would not yearn to imitate Mark Twain's Connecticut Yankee at King Arthur's court and be transported back to early-sixteenth-century Florence to share in communal dinners put on by Giovanfrancesco Rustici and his sodality "of the Cauldron," artists and craftsmen all, each bidden to use his ingenuity in contributing a dish? A splendid architectural one was presented by Andrea del Sarto on one occasion of which Vasari tells, "an octagonal church like San Giovanni [the Baptistery], but resting on columns":

> The pavement was made of gelatin, seemingly compartments of variously colored mosaic; the columns, which looked like porphyry, were large sausages; their base and capitals were parmesan cheese; the cornices were formed of sugar paste, and the tribune of marzipan. In the center was a choir-stall made of cold veal, with a book shaped of pasta [lasagne], its letters and notes formed in peppercorns. The singers were roasted thrushes with open beaks, wearing surplices of thin, cooked pig's caul, and behind these were two large pigeons for the counterbass, and six ortolans for the soprano part.

Giovanfrancesco and Andrea belonged to another, larger "Company of the Trowel" that also drew Vasari's attention in his biography of the former. A different theme for its feasts was set by each month's "president," while the participants became actors in some ingenious fantasy. I have written of one fertile invention, suggesting its classical model and tracing its later imitations.[1] On the occasion in question, guests endured a fearsome banquet in Hell as witnesses to the torments of the damned and imitations of hideous foods before more congenial regalement. But for edible architecture, one feast organized by Rustici and Giuliano Bugiardini truly matches the name of the company.

All the members came dressed as master builders and laborers, bearing their trowels and hods, to find the plan of a building provided by the hosts.

> The laborers began to bring in the materials for laying the foundations, that is, vessels full of cooked pasta and ricotta for mortar; sand made of cheese, spices and pepper, and for gravel, coarse confetti and crumbs of cake. The bricks and

0.1

Arch of vigilance, celebrating the rule of the Duke of Alba, Naples, June 23, 1629. From Francesco Orilia, *Il Zodiaco, idea di perfettione di prencipi . . .* (Naples, 1630); courtesy of the Warburg Institute.

tiles brought in baskets on wheel-barrows were of bread and buns. A plinth was
brought in and judged unsatisfactory by the masons; it was decided to break it
up, and they found the interior full of tarts, livers, and the like. . . . They brought
in a great column wound round with calf's tripe; pulling this to pieces, they ate
poached veal, capons, and other things of which it was composed. They next at-
tacked its base of parmesan cheese and its marvelous capital of roast capon and
slices of veal with moldings of tongue [a pun on tongue-and-dart molding?]. . . .
A very ingenious architrave next entered on a cart, with frieze and cornice, com-
posed of too many viands to relate [alas!]. When it was time to leave, there came
up mimic rain and thunder, and all left work and fled back home.

The three-dimensional equivalent of paintings by Arcimboldo, Andrea's baptistery was merely a model, while the Company of the Trowel seems to have devoted its energies more to eating the materials than to construction. But just as postprandial theater spectacles of the period anticipate the grandiose effects of opera staging in the seventeenth century, these early-sixteenth-century fantasies presage the full-scale, edible architecture of the baroque. As one particularly fetching example, more ambitious than the usual pyramids, I reproduce a woodcut rendering of a triumphal arch erected of cheeses, hams, sausages, and whole roast piglets for a Neapolitan *festa* on St. John the Baptist's Day, 1629. No problem in cleaning up after such a parade! Townsfolk were simply invited to carry off what they could of the ephemeral bounty.

NOTE

1. In *Oxford Symposium on Food and Cookery, 1990: Feasting and Fasting: Proceedings* (London: Prospect Books, 1991), 55–57.

PHYLLIS PRAY BOBER

1

INTRODUCTION

PAULETTE SINGLEY AND JAMIE HORWITZ

From the fanciful art of shifting scales to the logic of measurement promised by a teaspoon or an inch arises the secret architecture of food, or perhaps the secret food of architecture. This quiet apposition of form and substance, found in a plate of tomatoes more Pompeian red than any wall fragment, enunciates the central questions of this collection. What can be learned by examining the intersections of the preparation of meals and the production of space? What can be made from the conflation of aesthetic and sensory tastes in architectural design and what is disclosed by their dissociation? Such questions guide this work toward an architecture found in the gestures, artifacts, and recipes that belie any distinction between art and life. Rather than elaborating solely on the more facile comparison of "like an architect, so too the chef," we propose that the rituals of dining, the design of meals, and the process of cookery form and inform a distinctly expressive architecture. Drawn from the meal, sited on the table, and constructed from both appetite and conversation, *Eating Architecture* collects together in one volume a series of essays and images that interrogate the boundary between the culinary and design arts and linger over the sensational and inspirational properties of cookery.

This book insinuates itself into an architecture redolent with the aroma of dessert, say a lemon cake, followed by an unexpected line of poetry: "I have measured out my life with coffee spoons," writes T. S. Eliot in "The Love Song of J. Alfred Prufrock" (1917). The rhythms that govern our daily cadences suggest the dreamy metamorphoses of cooking utensils into drafting equipment. How do we translate these moments into words about architecture? Luce Giard, in *The Practice of Everyday Life*, asks:

> How can one choose words that are true, natural, and vibrant enough to make felt the weight of the body, the joyfulness or weariness, the tenderness or irritation that takes hold of you in the face of this continually repeated task where the better the result (a stuffed chicken, a pear tart), the faster it is devoured, so that before a meal is completely over, one already has to think about the next.[1]

This state of imaginative distraction that accompanies cooking or cleaning up after a meal may provoke bursts of intensive creativity—a sort of "euphoric idleness" that Flaubert once called "marinating."[2] If sometimes we find our best ideas when washing dishes or chopping onions, then the trajectory of a habitual reach for that slightly burned slotted spoon, the rapid-fire choreography of stops and starts involved in the final preparations of a holiday meal, or the plastic modeling of dough into a basket crust also inspires design.

CULINARY FORMALISM

Someone seeking further evidence of culinary architecture might instead turn to the cookbook, an essential manual of home economics, subject to the rifling of stained fingers or the filing of family secrets. Filled with diagrams explaining the cuts of beef or how to arrange a proper place setting, the cookbook offers a quick insight as to what we hope our book will deliver. In *Eating Architecture* the improvisational hand that turns the pages of the cookbook or pours a cup of tea also traces the dimensions of architecture into a space that is part ritual, part circumstance, part theory, part lunch.

Consider the projects of Italian designer Aldo Rossi (1931–1997), who draws his architecture, at least in part, from a uniquely culinary dimension of analogous form. Inspired by what he terms *apparecchiare la tavola*—meaning "to set the table, to prepare it, to arrange it"—his numerous drawings of concurrent scales and spaces blur the distinction between table settings and cities.[3] In the "Coffee and Tea Piazza" that Rossi designed for Alessi he enclosed a coffeepot and teapot in a glass pavilion, as if these utilitarian objects conceal inhabitable rooms within a larger enclosure. The title of the project suggests that a serving tray may function as a small piazza, a comparison that Robert Venturi makes visible, in still another Alessi design, with his "Campidoglio Platter." These shifts in position and scale transform cups and saucers into Lilliputian buildings that we move about on tabletop cities or render more abstractly onto nearby napkins.

Rossi's description of entering the colossal statue of San Carlo at Arona inversely parallels the scale-shifting he experiences through the visual and physical consumption of objects on a table:

> This first impression of the interior-exterior aspect has become clear more recently, at least as a problem: if I relate it to the coffeepots, it is also bound up with food and with the objects in which food is cooked; the true meaning of the manufacture of utensils and pots, which often, annoyingly, is obscured when they are accumulated and displayed in museums, is something that is continually present to us.[4]

Projecting ourselves inside the space of the statue or the coffeepot rather than simply gazing at these objects from behind a glass case opens up the tabletop or the kitchen counter into a delirious landscape of possibility.

Consider another urban moment defined by Frank O. Gehry's signature fish, a built reference to the live carp that his grandmother stored in her bathtub before she prepared gefilte fish. The giant form rising next to the Vila Olímpica (1992) in Barcelona, Spain, or the Fishdance restaurant in Kobe, Japan (1986), serves as a hieroglyph for unlocking the raw or uncooked materiality of Gehry's undulating curves. The titanium or stainless steel skins covering the Guggenheim Museum in Bilbao, Spain, or the Disney Concert Hall in Los Angeles, California, display the complex geometry of nonuniform, rational B-spline curves. While these forms may rely on the aeronautical computer application CATIA, they also evoke the preparatory motion of folding and creaming necessary to produce the sectional meringue of their curvature.

Biglie con ricotta e wurstel

Aragosta vellata alla Sleazy Dora

Spaghetti al cartoccio Frankie Toronto

Lettere di pollo

1.1
Claes Oldenburg and Coosje van Bruggen, drawings for a collaborative performance with Frank Gehry titled *Il corso del coltello (The Course of the Knife)*.

PAULETTE SINGLEY AND JAMIE HORWITZ

Greg Lynn quite specifically develops these culinary techniques in his own practice of computer-generated form. He describes architectural folding as "the ability to integrate unrelated elements within a new continuous mixture." According to Lynn,

> Culinary theory has developed both a practical and precise definition for at least three types of mixtures. The first involves the manipulation of homogeneous elements; beating, whisking and whipping change the volume but not the nature of a liquid through agitation. The second method of incorporation mixes two or more disparate elements: chopping, dicing, grinding, grating, slicing, shredding, and mincing eviscerate elements into fragments. The first method agitates a single uniform ingredient, the second eviscerates disparate ingredients. Folding, creaming and blending mix smoothly multiple ingredients "through repeated gentle overturning without stirring or beating" in such a way that their individual characteristics are maintained. For instance, an egg and chocolate are folded together so that each is a distinct layer within a continuous mixture. Folding employs neither agitation nor evisceration but a supple layering.[5]

Lynn, Gehry, and Rossi remind us that a small perceptual shift—in scale, position, or process—can locate design strategies in uncanny proximity to the kitchen. In particular, Gehry's fish and Lynn's curvilinear forms disturb distinctions between animate and inanimate objects. These sculptural architectures appear frozen in parabolic jumps and liquid sine curves that simultaneously underscore their exanimate reality.

Gehry's fish, then, serves as edible architecture, formal hieroglyph, memory trace, and performative medium. The trajectory of this culinary formalism extends to his 1985 collaboration with Claes Oldenburg and Coosje van Bruggen, titled *Il corso del coltello* (*The Course of the Knife*; figure 1.1). Artists and architect staged a performance on Venice's Grand Canal that culminated in a public meal set in the Piazza San Marco—a scenography that evokes the opening scenes of Peter Greenaway's 1987 film *The Belly of an Architect*, which took place in Rome's Piazza del Panteon. Providing a direct precedent for *Il corso del coltello*, Filippo Tommaso Marinetti's aesthetics of tactility and cannibalism of form likewise lead to an understanding that food might stand in for architecture and that architecture might be edible. Thus P. A. Saladin's *Cubist Vegetable Patch*—"little cubes of celery from Verona fried and sprinkled with paprika" and "little cubes of fried carrot sprinkled with grated horseradish"—also performs as the building blocks of miniature culinary structures, even imaginary cities (figure 1.2).[6] In Gehry's Venice, full-scale objects of cookery—knife, radish, escarole—float past confectionery facades while a publication about this event includes recipes for dishes such as "lettere di pollo" and "calzone con pattini." Gehry's work displays a deep awareness of and affinity with the conventions of formal analysis derived from studying *nature morte*, Cézanne, and cubism, while his Venice performance adds a twist of dada to the mélange.

As the artifacts and advocates of modern architecture report, still life painting and collage served as generative processes in the exploration of space. The former, also known as *nature morte*, allows artists and architects to study the oppositional play of overlapping geometry in an open field that draws from the table's order or composed disarray. The latter relies on the collection, distribution, and eventual reconstitution of the remainders of the day—newspaper clippings, chair caning, box labels, and so on—into an articulate spatial composition that might approximate the orchestrated disorder of a table after the meal has ended.

Where modern architects would look to painting as a means to interrogate composition and generate form, more recently postmodernists have looked to the text as a way to problematize this naïve teleology leading from the tabletop to the paraline drawing. Such a paradigm shift from object to text, one that questions the taste (aesthetics/connoisseurship), the hunger (body/libidinal systems), the ingredients (materiality/tectonics), and the recipes (history/theory) that go into the making of building, space, or landscape, nonetheless left us hungry. While critiques of the formally compelling but theoretically empty container of modern architecture gave way to methods of inquiry that sought to extract content at the expense of form, the theoretically compelling but formally empty site of contemporary theory has accomplished the opposite. Given such choices, the subject of cookery offers the possibility of comprehensive and intelligent study. An understanding of the form and space of cookery provides a site to rethink and reorder the material and metaphysical, empty and full, high and low, or dirty and clean into mutually inclusive investigative categories.

CULINARY PERFORMANCE

The intersection of food and architecture also finds expression in the performative spaces that the preparation and consumption of a meal imply. This is a process, from

PAULETTE SINGLEY AND JAMIE HORWITZ

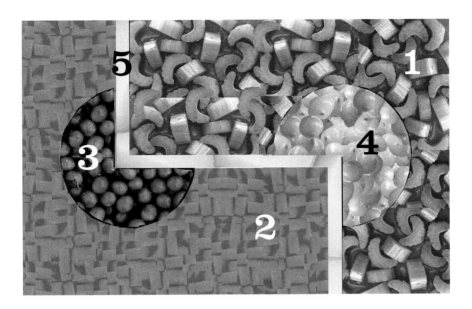

1.2

Cubist Vegetable Patch by
Paulette Singley, after P. A.
Saladin's description in Filippo
Tommaso Marinetti's *The Futurist
Cookbook*. (1) Little cubes of
celery from Verona fried and
sprinkled with paprika; (2) little
cubes of fried carrot sprinkled
with grated horseradish; (3) boiled
peas; (4) little pickled onions from
Ivrea sprinkled with chopped
parsley; (5) little bars of Fontina
cheese. N.B.: The cubes must
not be larger than one cubic
centimeter.

set table to abandoned disorder, that Sarah Wigglesworth quite literally drew into 9 Stock Orchard Street, a London terrace house based on the clinical mapping of a dinner party (figure 1.3).[7] A chef's pyrotechnic juggling of knives at Benihana's chain of Japanese restaurants, cable television's food network, and numerous films about cooking and eating offer ample evidence to support Barbara Kirshenblatt-Gimblett's argument for "food as a performance medium." She writes that "to perform is to do, to execute, to carry out to completion . . . all that governs the production, presentation, and disposal of food and their staging." According to Kirshenblatt-Gimblett, performance encompasses social practices—whether customs or laws, ritual or etiquette—and thus composes what Pierre Bourdieu calls the *habitus* of everyday life. When doing and behaving are displayed, when participants are invited to exercise discernment and appreciation, "food events move towards the theatrical," a convergence of taste as a sensory experience and taste as an aesthetic faculty.[8] Like the table itself, food stages events, congregating and segregating people, and food becomes an architecture that inhabits the body.

Among the several vocations that Marcus Vitruvius Pollio recommends for the training of an architect in *De architectura,* cooking is not included and setting the table never enters the discussion. And yet, his discussion of the origins of architecture around fire certainly implicates the culinary arts in the production of space. On the

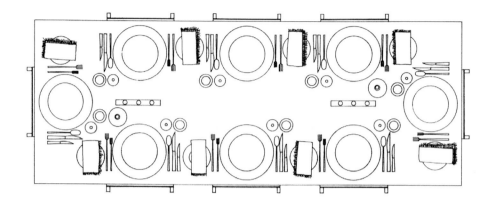

THE LAY OF THE TABLE

An architectural ordering of place, status, and function. A frozen moment of perfection. This is how architects see.

1.3
Sarah Wigglesworth Architects,
9 Stock Orchard Street, London.

PAULETTE SINGLEY AND JAMIE HORWITZ

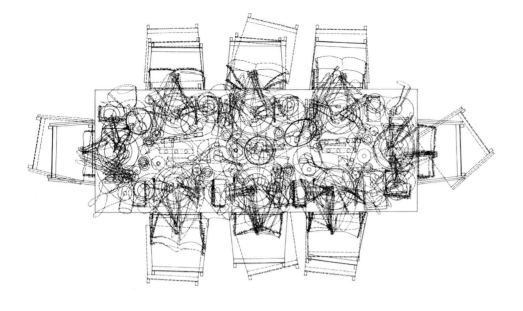

THE MEAL

Use begins to undermine the apparent stability of the (architectural) order. Traces of occupation in time. The recognition of life's disorder.

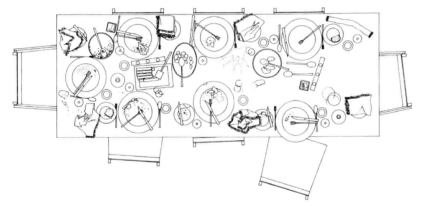

THE TRACE

The dirty tablecloth, witness of disorder. A palimpsest. This is the reality of domestic life.

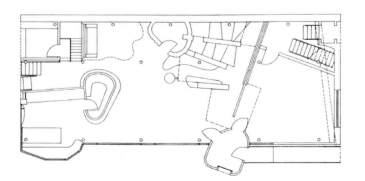

THE LAY OF THE PLAN

The trace transformed into the plan of our house. Clutter filling the plan(e). Domestic difficulties interrupting the order of the grid.

other hand, where Titus Petronius Arbiter will describe in *The Satyricon* a spectacular Roman banquet—featuring a sow stuffed with live quail—he does not consider the architecture of this space. If not precisely *De architectura* or *The Satyricon*, Marco Frascari's essay "*Semiotica ab Edendo,* Taste in Architecture" (reprinted in this volume) stands as a foundational text in the history of architecture and food. Frascari turns to other sources, to "the etymological visions of Isidore of Seville," in writing this history: "the ancients used the word *aedes* (i.e., dwelling), in reference to any edifice. Some think that this word was derived from a form of the term for 'eating,' *edendo*, citing by way of example a line from Plautus: 'If I had invited you home (in *aedum*) for lunch.' Hence we also have the word 'edifice' because originally a building was made for eating (*ad edendum factum*)."[9]

Even though Frascari cautions us that "Isidore's interpretation is probably incorrect," that "edibles and edifices are not the same, etymologically speaking," the false etymologies nonetheless tempt us like dessert.[10] In seeking out culinary architecture's foundational moments, we also might turn to George Hersey's troping of the origins of classical architecture in ritual practices. Hersey argues that the ancients saw "their temples as assemblages of materials, including food, used in sacrifice."[11] Dalí had earlier offered a more intuitive observation about surrealism's "cannibalism of objects," famously writing that "beauty will either be edible or not at all."[12]

In the years since Frascari's 1986 publication of his essay in the *Journal of Architectural Education,* a substantial amount of interdisciplinary research has been devoted to the culinary arts. Indeed, a number of recent publications and exhibitions within the disciplines of art and culture interrogate the aesthetics, form, and content of cuisine, which is increasingly seen as a legitimate site for the discussion of aesthetics. The periodicals *Gastronomica: The Journal of Food and Culture* and *Slow: The Magazine of the Slow Food Movement,* like Copia, the American Center for Wine, Food and the Arts in Napa, California, are examples of mounting interest—and a similarly rising level of sophistication among a broad reading and cooking public—in artisanal agriculture, culinary history, and regional cuisine, which has helped blur the distinctions between culinary arts and other forms of art and architecture.

Food has become not only a powerful cultural obsession but also an alternative art form, scholarly domain, and literary industry. Likewise, the growth of the food movement within the United States and beyond has confirmed cookery as a significant subject for interdisciplinary research into the many dimensions of material culture that can be teased out of diverse architectures—both metaphorical and actual—through a panoply of theoretical positions and methodological approaches. Rather than dogmatically adhering to one theory or method, this collection of essays presents a mélange of approaches and scholarly positions. Studies of quotidian culture, for example, may merge with environmental psychology, landscape architecture with postcolonial politics, poststructuralism with conventional iconography, culinary arts with the history of science, or formalism with feminism, producing in this mix a cohesive set of diverse perspectives that adhere to each other through a singular and highly probative focus on architecture's culinary dimensions.

CULINARY TOPOGRAPHY

Translating culinary practices into the design arts—as the aforementioned examples of architecture imply—might suggest that they be removed from their kitchen origins and repositioned in nondomestic contexts. But they could just as plausibly return to or remain in the domestic sphere. The exchange and transformation of generative practices in food and architecture may provide an insight into domestic space and, in turn, reflect social change that further validates this typically female domain. If the study of food implicates and questions the domestic sphere, then it also contaminates this ground even as it builds upon it.

As the architectural historian Elizabeth Cromley notes, at any given time, the conventions that constitute the relationships between cooking, storing, serving, eating, and disposing operate as a food axis in the social production of space.[13] *Eating Architecture* elaborates on the inherent spatiality of all that goes into the preparation and consumption of meals while it simultaneously discusses the desiring mechanism of architecture within the realm of appetite. Within these two areas of investigation, we identify social and historical transformations as well as the formal and aesthetic implications of conflating food and architecture. These two emphases, which quite naturally betray our editorial biases and strengths, form the compass points that aid in navigating the topographical field we have constructed in our section divisions, leading from the sites of production to the space of consumption. We have thus organized this collection around a food axis similar to that which Cromley proffers, dividing the essays into a loose arrangement of four spaces that lead from the land-

Photomontage of Le Corbusier's culinary axis, composed by Paulette Singley. Commercial glassware and crockery from *The Decorative Art of Today; Still Life, Flask and Glasses* (1922); *Table Objects, Still Life* (1920); Bernhard Hoesli's diagram showing layers in painting (1968); axonometric drawings of Villa Stein from Kenneth Frampton's *Modern Architecture;* Le Corbusier's drawing of Villa Stein; kitchen of Villa Stein with fish.

scape to the kitchen, to the table, and finally to the mouth. The four topoi parallel our section divisions: "Place Settings," "Philosophy in the Kitchen," "Table Rules," and "Embodied Taste."

We begin with "Place Settings," a group of essays that question the fundamental relationship between food and locale as it emerges both inside and outside the theoretical context of modernity. Each story problematizes the relation between culinary regionalism, colonialism, and the global economy of tourism. Next we turn to the site of thinking and making. "Philosophy in the Kitchen" is where the cleansing, cutting, and cooking of food form a routine that also doubles as a site for aesthetic experimentation. By drawing gastronomy out of the kitchen, the essays that follow shift the discussion toward the performative space of eating—a site that is inherently unstable, mutable, mobile, and memorable. "Table Rules" locates the intersections between food and architecture in the slow transformations of cultural practice and in the apparent speed with which artists and designers represent and fabricate these changes in their own highly personal formal language. Finally, the smelling, the tasting, the sighting, and ultimately the ingestion of food offer a rare opportunity to literally consume a work of art. Such "Embodied Taste" marshals all of the senses in an apprehension and absorption of the beautiful as well as the disgusting.

In addition to these essays, we are publishing a set of projects solicited in direct response to the question of the architectural recipe. This "Gallery of Recipes" derives from the irresistible temptation to propose an evolutionary sequence of design production—replete with all the positivist baggage that taints such an analysis—from Le Corbusier's *Table Objects, Still Life* to Bernhard Hoesli's diagram of this painting and then finally to a plan oblique drawing of the Villa Stein (figure 1.4). Such formalism proposes that Le Corbusier derived the shapes and figures of his architecture from his paintings of wine bottles, guitars, plates, and sundry objects placed on a tabletop. Indeed, one might hazard the assertion that for modern architecture and urbanism, the production of architecture moved from the tabletop—loaded with its scattered debris

PAULETTE SINGLEY AND JAMIE HORWITZ

of crockery and foodstuffs—to the canvas without ever having looked at the site. While this claim is something of a hyperbole, it serves well to describe the still life painting as an essential and generative interlocutor with the modern architect in the production of his or her spatial alchemy.

We thus have gathered together a series of essays and images that adapt the generative exercise of cooking and performative spaces of the food axis to the imperatives of contemporary architecture and its potential to engage the issues of identity, ideology, taste, conviviality, memory, and loss that cookery evokes. Based upon this *architecture à la carte,* we offer the parallels between the preparation of meals and the production of space.

NOTES

1. Luce Giard, "Gesture Sequences," in *The Practice of Everyday Life,* by Michel de Certeau, Luce Giard, and Pierre Mayol, vol. 2, *Living and Cooking,* ed. Luce Giard, trans. Timothy J. Tomasik, rev. ed. (Minneapolis: University of Minnesota Press, 1998), 199.
2. Anson Rabinbach, *The Human Motor: Energy, Fatigue, and the Origins of Modernity* (1990; reprint, Berkeley: University of California Press, 1992), 28.
3. Aldo Rossi, *A Scientific Autobiography,* trans. Lawrence Venuti (Cambridge, Mass.: MIT Press, 1981), 5.
4. Ibid, 3.
5. Greg Lynn, "Architectural Curvilinearity: The Folded, the Pliant, and the Supple," in *Folding in Architecture,* [ed. Greg Lynn], special issue of *Architectural Design,* vol. 63, nos. 3–4 (London: Academy Editions, 1993), 8.
6. Saladin, quoted in F. T. Marinetti, *The Futurist Cookbook,* trans. Suzanne Brill, ed. Lesley Chamberlain (San Francisco: Bedford Arts, 1989), 155.
7. We are grateful to Dora Epstein for pointing us to the Wigglesworth project.
8. Barbara Kirshenblatt-Gimblett, "Playing to the Senses: Food as a Performance Medium," *Performance Research* 4, no. 1 (spring 1999): 1–30; an earlier version is available at <http://www.nyu.edu/classes/bkg/issues/food-pr6.htm> (accessed March 2003).
9. Marco Frascari, "*Semiotica ab Edendo,* Taste in Architecture," *Journal of Architectural Education* 40, no. 1 (1986); reprinted in this volume.
10. Ibid., 194.
11. George L. Hersey, *The Lost Meaning of Classical Architecture: Speculations on Ornament from Vitruvius to Venturi* (Cambridge, Mass.: MIT Press, 1988), 2.
12. Salvador Dalí, "Art Nouveau: Architecture's Terrifying and Edible Beauty," *Architectural Design,* nos. 2–3 (1978): 139.
13. Elizabeth Collins Cromley, "Transforming the Food Axis: Houses, Tools, Modes of Analysis," *Material History Review,* no. 44 (fall 1996): 8–20.

PLACE SETTINGS

2

CULINARY MANIFESTATIONS
OF THE *GENIUS LOCI*

ALLEN S. WEISS

*Wine is truly a universal that knows how to make itself singular, but only if it finds
a philosopher who knows how to drink.*

GASTON BACHELARD

We may imagine—as in dreams and nightmares, fairy tales and hallucinations, and especially in those marvelous Christmas window displays
on the great Fifth Avenue department stores in New York—a forest
where all mushrooms have faces, differing one from another as do caricatures by
Daumier or Hogarth and showing the arrogant bourgeois repletion of *Boletus edulis*,
the nearly obscene, priapic pride of the poisonous *Amanita phalloides*, the dubious
bewitchment of *Boletus satanas*; where trees are humanized skeletons grasping at us
with their gnarled hands; where birds sing the songs of Messiaen, and a mixed chorus
of crickets, cicadas, frogs, and rain chants a stochastic dirge by Xenakis; where snails
dance with slowness imperceptible to our all-too-quick vision; where houses are edible and rainbows drinkable—all in a scene lighted by the diaphanous luminescence

of fireflies. Fairy tales reveal the lineaments of our desires; the enchantment of the edible world not only sets a mood but also offers the sort of poetic personification that reminds us that foodstuffs indeed lead their own lives before ever attaining their culinary apotheosis. Culinary style begins as natural form.

In *The Interpretation of Dreams* Freud describes an unreachable, uninterpretable, originary nexus of significations in the dreamwork. The ungraspable profundity of the symbolic is a function of the pure contingency of our bodies, of local, historicized situatedness. This nexus is precisely the point where the symbolic enters into history, where the particularization and the communalization of the individual are accomplished as contemporaneous events. Though there is always a signifier at this unattainable point, that signifier can be *anything* whatsoever. But it remains unknown: not because repressed, but because ineluctably real. Might we not discover here the formal efficacy of the symbolism of the earth, in all its polyvalent splendor and terror? As Nietzsche teaches, the soul is something of the body, and the body is something of the earth. This is the point where the organizational pivot of the symbolic is no longer a *floating signifier* but rather a *lost signifier* that is, however, fully localized. Both for dream interpretation and culinary judgment, this site—unstable, ungraspable, ephemeral—which determines the radical individuality of personal taste, must be placed within the limits of an empirical and symbolic nexus. Subjectivity is charted on the map of the objective, where the soul is silently rooted while the body is sublimated into its desires. One begins to understand that all true gastronomy, like all metaphysics after Nietzsche, can be written only in the first-person singular.

Such enchanting, oneiric moods still grace certain secluded country inns, archetypal locales for dishes that both induce reverie and remain close to their earth. For example, the chef Régis Marcon's L'Auberge des Cimes, at the town with the unlikely and suggestive name of Saint-Bonnet-le-Froid in the depths of the Haute-Loire, offers such produce culled from the surrounding woods: *tuile de noisette aux grenouilles et aux mousserons, crème d'orties* (hazelnut wafer with baby frogs' legs and fairy-ring mushrooms, with a cream of nettle sauce) harmonizes local forest flavors with great delicacy, ideally set to the counterpoint of a simple, spicy wine such as syrah de l'Ardèche. How this fantasy harmonizes with our dreams and expectations is another matter . . .

First impressions used to be filtered through mythology or history; now they are inflected by advertisements and guidebooks. Yet it is often initially through cuisine

ALLEN S. WEISS

that we know the nature of a given part of the earth, as gastronomic culture is inextricably mixed with travel. Traveling by train from Lyon, I arrived for the first time in the Bourbonnais at noon, the perfect hour, under that particular sky characterized by *le bleu d'Allen*—a sky neither mystical and transcendental, like the celestial vaults of Renaissance Tuscan and Umbrian painting, nor manifesting the pure pictorial surface of modernism as in Matisse's niçois oceanic cobalt blues modulating turquoise and his mirage-filled aquamarines, but an active sky, windswept, with well-formed cottony clouds; a sky proffering the all-too-earthly qualities of the region, from the dark volcanic masses delimiting the southern horizon to the lush, rich, vegetal green everywhere else apparent. And the sky was a blue made all the bluer by contrast with the seemingly endless fields of sunflowers covering the landscape—not a sign of torment and harsh faith, as in van Gogh, but the incarnation of summer and life, marked by an aestival solar exuberance. It was as if the sun had escaped from the clouds to spill down from the celestial orb and descend upon the earth—a sun transformed into the very flowers strewn upon the land to celebrate the arrival of some long-lost god. The omens were propitious.

What I did not know is that in the reality, as well as in the imagination, of the Bourbonnais, this sight would evoke not a terrestrial simulacrum of the sun but rather oil in its floral form. My immediate, extreme, and unqualified delight at this sublime vision (underwritten, it must be said, by expectations of tastes I would soon be experiencing) was quickly rebuked by my host, Jean-Claude Bonnet, who is, among other things, a specialist on nineteenth-century gastronomic texts. He explained that in fact sunflowers are not part of the traditional agriculture of the Bourbonnais, and that their sudden appearance that year was due to market pressures from the European Economic Community. As increasing health consciousness caused more demand for low-cholesterol oils, farmers uprooted traditional crops, hoping for greater profit. Needless to say, this lack of coherent agricultural politics can result only in the degradation of regional crops, with the consequent danger to regional cuisines (not to mention the risk to what little remains of small farmers and the peasantry, ever more subject to the unstable, irrational, and countergastronomic economics of international markets).

The traditional geographic-culinary butter/oil frontier that sets Provence, with its myriad styles of olive oil, apart from the rest of France is menaced by a choice of nearly tasteless, internationally standardized oils, available in any supermarket, that threaten previously unimaginable uniformization. This extreme example is but a sign of the standardization that is further and further besetting the cultivation and distribution of foodstuffs. What used to constitute the natural, regional basis of French cuisine is slowly disappearing; what used to be "natural" is now available as "deluxe." One may hope that a combination of culinary regionalism and the ever-increasing profitability of deluxe products will save the earthly basis of French gastronomy in a sort of "trickle-down" culinary economy; yet a certain pessimism must reign if the economic pressures are such that cuisine must be saved from the top down rather than from the very roots that traditionally fed and informed taste.

The cautionary tale is not meant to support what may appear to be a traditionally French culinary xenophobia. For developments in twentieth-century French cuisine were intricately linked to the continual influx of exotic foods and cultures, spurred by a series of cultural events: the Universal Exposition of 1900, the Colonial Exposition of 1931, the great disruptions of World War II and the nascent "Americanization" of Europe by the Marshall Plan, the Indochinese war and Vietnamese emigration, the Algerian conflict and the North African exodus, and the weakening of traditional cultural and social relations in 1968 that ironically paved the way for the influx of international capital, hastening the decentralization and internationalization of world culture. Commentators reacted to these events as signs of loss, motivating a false nostalgia for a culinary purity that never really existed. Yet they were in fact signs of increasing complexity, openness, and richness.

Establishments like Hédiard, as well as chefs such as those who invented the nouvelle cuisine, took advantage of these opportunities and added to the complexity of French cuisine. The dialectic between the indigenous and the exotic is a key factor in both modernist and postmodernist art, cuisine included. Consider one of the creations of Alain Senderens, who was instrumental in helping to establish the nouvelle cuisine, by integrating foreign techniques and recipes into French cuisine, and by rediscovering long-lost recipes from ancient, medieval, and Renaissance sources. At his former Parisian restaurant, L'Archestrate, one of his masterpieces was a particularly luscious salade composée: salade de homard aux mangues et basilic (lobster and mango salad with basil). The question of whether this dish was inspired by, or merely homologous to, the traditional Vietnamese papaya and shrimp salad with lemonweed is beside the point. Senderens's salad is rendered deluxe by substituting lobster for shrimp; it is Gallicized (via Provence) by substituting basil and vinaigrette for lemon-weed and the fermented fish sauce *nuac mam*. Crucial is the manner in which such salads transform the nature and stretch the limits of what constitutes a "salad" in France, as well as the inspiration that such an influx of exotic flavors offers for other creations, such as Senderens's fabulous *homard à la vanille* (vanilla lobster).

In contradistinction to the domestication of the exotic, we may also consider the issue of typicality in terms of the renovation of the indigenous. Dominique Le Stanc, formerly head chef at the Chantecler of the Hôtel Negresco in Nice, foreshadowed his brilliant transformations of regional cuisine—such as the *risotto aux artichauts, parmesan et truffes noires* (risotto with artichokes, Parmesan, and black truffles), or the *fricassée de St-Jacques et langoustines au basilic* (fricassee of sea scallops and scampi with basil)—with the offering of an appetizer: a Lilliputian *pan bagnat*, small as the tip of one's thumb, with all the authentic flavors of this niçois sandwich (tuna, vegetables, olives, oil) condensed into one bite. It was all the more amusing because once a year, on the beach opposite the hotel, one of the popular, if grotesque and carnivalesque, attractions of this city is the creation of a gargantuan *pan bagnat* one kilometer long!

Modernist art and modern cuisine have a central trope in common: *invention*. Indeed, even simplification is a mode of invention. If there were to be a theory of cuisine, it would constitute a theory of exceptions, nuances, refinements. Culinary taste would transform aesthetics by redefining the limits of art within the human sensorium, and in doing so transform all previous relationships between the arts—and between aestheticizations of the senses. The gastronomic must no longer serve as mere metaphor for the arts, but must take its place among the muses.

The modernist conditions of cuisine may be placed in a historical context insofar as they reveal a startling coincidence between the nouvelle cuisine and the discourse of postmodernism in the arts, both of which share several central tenets: self-conscious reflexivity (experimentation to reveal the primary qualities of the component materials of a work), questioning of origins (the realization that all inventions are but variations, transmutations, or inspirations based on previous works), regionalism (the decentralization and relativization of techniques, materials, and styles), and exoticism (the juxtaposition and incorporation of foreign elements on an equal footing with native material). Indeed, if we consider postmodernism to have emerged after the 1970s movements of minimalism and conceptualism, then we may date the nouvelle cuisine, originating in the late 1960s, as a true aesthetic avant-garde that (along with dance) preceded the postmodern discourse by a decade. We must remain attuned to such stylistic innovations and conceptual complications, to these coincidences and intersections, if we are to enhance our appreciation of contemporary cuisine.

In *The Unanswered Question,* a study of music that may serve as an allegory for an aesthetics of cuisine, the composer-conductor Leonard Bernstein wrote: "I believe that from Earth emerges musical poetry, which is by the nature of its sources tonal. . . . And by that metaphorical operation there can be devised particular musical languages that have surface structures noticeably remote from their basic origins, but which can be strikingly expressive as long as they retain their roots in earth."[1] In that "musical poetry" which is cuisine, such "tonality" may be understood as the principal flavor of a dish; the metaphorical operations would consist of the various modes of cooking; the musical languages are constituted by different regional cuisines; and expressivity would be the style of each chef.

Cuisine is a function of the *genius loci,* the spirit of the place. And one who says "place" also says "season," one who says "earth" also says "heaven." The *goût de terroir* (the taste of the earth, meant in the literal and not the pejorative sense) that typifies so many wines and foodstuffs is only the most immediate manifestation of this gastronomic specificity. On the metaphorical level, it inspires infinite possibilities of transformation and sublimation. This is why it is commonly claimed that regional cuisines don't travel; this is why there is no such thing as "French cooking" but only a mosaic, palimpsest, or collage of regional cuisines and specialties, many of which inspire and are consequently abstracted into urban, national, and international cuisines. For example, we can imagine many variants on chicken in honey sauce harking back to medieval recipes; yet the chicken in lavender honey with *herbes de Provence* of the restaurant Les Santons at Moustiers-Sainte-Marie—eaten after passing through Grasse, the perfume center of France; after traveling through the Var amid the lavender fields and mountain wildflowers that are garlands to the savage gash of the Gorges du Verdun—is an inimitable taste, intimately linked to the region. Sitting on the terrace of the restaurant under the ex-voto star suspended on a chain stretched between two peaks dominating the village, and feeling the very same mistral that dried the herbs—an always varying and mysterious combination of basil, chervil,

ALLEN S. WEISS

tarragon, parsley, thyme, sage, savory, rosemary, bay leaf, wild thyme, marjoram, oregano—feeling that wind blow across the land, I find it impossible to abstract the dish from its environment. The odor of lavender in the air and the taste of lavender in the honey are part of one meta-bouquet, inextricably, harmoniously, and seductively mixed with the lemon-scented perfume from Menton worn by my companion. . . .

These very specificities and differences, these contingencies and essences, reveal the traditional French social tensions between Paris and the provinces, centralization and regionalism, nouvelle and ancienne, popular and savante, academicism and avant-garde, unconscious and conscious, collective and individual, closed and open. The fact is that both sides of these polarities exist in constant exchange and renewal. To valorize the earth is not to denigrate the techniques and complexities of haute cuisine. We need not espouse, à la lettre, the iconoclasm of a Jean Dubuffet—creator of diverse series of paintings, such as the *Pâtes battues, Texturologies, Géographies, Topographies,* and *Eléments botaniques,* and inheritor of the family wine business—who once wrote to his friend, Jacques Berne: "I was enchanted by the crayfish, which pleased me greatly, and I thank you. It is a very rich food. Almost too rich. Too rich! I often tell Lili that her cooking is too rich—cream, butter, etc. I much prefer grass, or earth, which seems to me to be much more sumptuous. To eat earth, now there's a rich dish!"[2] Such is a joyous twist on the theme of the meals of stones suffered by Don Juan, however unlikely its attraction, however sardonic its metaphor!

Nor need we reduce cuisine to its simplest and most archaic elements and techniques, valorizing the mythical and millennial simplicities of peasant cooking, as Joseph Delteil does in *La cuisine paléolithique.* Following the motto "Live simply," he espouses—in a sort of culinary ecologism, written at a time when the truly "natural" was already in the process of becoming a gastronomic luxury—the myth of a *naturel,* instinctive cuisine, a sort of *cuisine brut:* "It is necessary to *resist,* to rediscover the *earth,* to become wild again, virgin in sense and spirit as on the first day." He celebrates the single dish, and proposes only fourteen recipes, just enough for one week, "but all the weeks in the world are similar, and here is the breviary for the rest of your life." He knows of only three dishes (soup, fricassee, roast) and he revels especially in the regional specificity of patois "because it is closest to origins, richest in sperm, and the most sacred."[3] Might we suggest that this romantic extreme, rich in its simplicity, need not become a norm in order to be appreciated? What if we were to read Delteil against the letter, and suppose that this purity must be the symbolic, or at least imaginary, precondition of all gastronomic appreciation? What if each and every bite and thought of food must be filtered through this sort of basic specificity and simplicity before entering into a "higher" level of culinary consciousness, a higher state of cuisine?

The *genius loci* establishes the essence of cuisine. Consider the restaurant Michel Bras, situated near the remote town of Laguiole in the Aubrac region of France's Massif Central. One of Michel Bras's signature dishes is the *gargouillou,* whose ingredients grace the cover of his book *Le livre de Michel Bras.*[4] The term evokes the verb *gargouiller,* the bubbling or gurgling sound of a liquid—an onomatopoeia for both the cooking process and the streams that run through the Aubrac. But *gargouillou* also refers to one of the principal regional dishes, an elementary ragout of potatoes in bouillon. Yet rather than strive for a nostalgic and restrictive regionalist "authenticity," Bras raises the simplest of dishes to the summits of the culinary art. His vision consists of an everchanging combination, culled from the daily market choices, of as many as three dozen vegetables and grains chosen from nearly a hundred possibilities that constitute this "virtual" recipe; each ingredient necessitates a separate preparation, and all are mixed and moistened in a light butter sauce emulsified with vegetable broth flavored with ham essence, then decorated with herbs, crystallized leaves, edible wildflowers, wild mushrooms, and pearls of parsley oil.

This dish, offered as the overture to his tasting menu, effectively articulates many of the major dichotomies informing contemporary French cuisine—peasant/haute, simple/refined, traditional/nouvelle, regional/international, raw/cooked, wild/cultivated—all the while stressing the primacy of the seasons, revealing the gustatory specificity of the region, and ambiguously straddling the butter/oil line that had long separated "French" cooking from its Provençal other. The synthesis of contradictions in Bras's *gargouillou* partakes of a gastronomic symbolic system typifying Jean-François Revel's claim that "the summits of the art are attained precisely in those periods when the refinement of recipes associates a complexity of conception with a lightness of results."[5] Complexity of conception provides the range of variations on a theme that permits continual inventiveness; the lightness of realization ensures the presentation of the essential, primal qualities of foodstuffs, harking back to a nostalgia for simple flavors raised to their quintessential powers, as stressed by the nouvelle cuisine. Essence dominates appearance.

ALLEN S. WEISS

Bras, an erudite autodidact, is concerned not only with the history of cuisine (French and foreign) but also with ancient and modern botany. One of his major contributions to contemporary French cuisine is precisely the rediscovery and creative use of many long-forgotten vegetables, wildflowers, and aromatic and medicinal herbs. Among those used in the *gargouillou* (besides numerous more common varieties) are giant amaranth, orach, basella, ironwort, white and blue borage, comfrey, vetch, hops, pimpernel, rape, purslane, and rue. The cuisine of such chefs as Michel Bras, Régis Marcon, Marc Veyrat (of the Auberge de l'Eridan in Annecy, Haute Savoie), and Jean-Paul Jeunet (in Arbois, Jura) is often mentioned in an ecological context, owing both to its intimate and erudite relation to the environment and to its restitution to French cuisine of many lost or unknown plants. Although this sensibility often gives rise to a tendentious, stereotyping, and mythicizing discourse of authenticity and nostalgia for the earth[6]—at its worst resulting in culinary reincarnations of ancient and medieval dishes better destined for the museum than the table—it has at its best provided a crucial source for the regeneration of French cuisine. The tendencies of this so-called *cuisine verte* help articulate the often antithetical styles of the nouvelle cuisine and the sundry *cuisines de terroir*. On the spiritual level, this culinary transformation is expressed by Bras's claim that "The great interest of this approach is that through this cuisine I live body and soul with my region [*pays*]"; yet there is a strict corollary on the practical level, as Marcon states: "I try to support organic agriculture, so as to encourage those artisans who maintain quality."[7] The symbolic articulation of cuisine necessitates a hybrid discourse of body and soul, food and style, pleasure and technique.

These issues are usually limited in the gastronomic press to a description of the dishes in question. Yet their broader symbolic significance can be ascertained only by considering the total context which gives rise to the recipes, and within which the dishes are presented. In the case of Michel Bras, at first glance his subtle regionalism is apparently belied by the architecture of his restaurant-hotel, set high on the west side of a hill located approximately 6 kilometers outside Laguiole. The Aubrac is one of the most remote and least populated regions of France, with vast, rolling, boulder-strewn vistas of some austerity, and huge open skies that often resemble Turner watercolors.

In contrast to the landscape, the hotel, designed by the Bordeaux architect Eric Raffy, is built of basalt, steel, and glass, a high modernist structure materialized as if accidentally in the natural setting. The lounge area offers glass walls that open upon the splendid vistas; but the long, rectangular, glass-walled restaurant offers what is at first a rather frustrating surprise. The westward view, often approaching the sublime, is cut off at the horizon by the roofline of one of the hotel buildings, letting only the sky appear. Between the windows of the restaurant and the initially exasperating wall is a narrow rectangular garden that runs the length of the restaurant, open at the northern end to visually flow into the countryside. As one looks obliquely northward, the unmarked extremity of the garden flows into and is indistinguishable from the landscape beyond; looking directly westward, the garden is framed by the windows and delimited by the wall. This garden is stylistically equivocal, not unlike many of Bras's dishes. With several rugged stones placed as if randomly on its low grass field, highlighted by wild grasses and wildflowers, it simulates the very Aubrac landscape that is hidden by the facing wall; yet it also refers stylistically to the green Japanese Zen garden. Microcosm replaces macrocosm; international syncretism enriches symbolic regionalism.

But this simple setting offers a complex theatricality. For upon the appearance of the first dish—the *gargouillou,* in the case of the "Découverte & Nature" menu—the relation between the garden and what appears on the plate (the most condensed microcosm in this scenario) is apparent. One is occasionally even served the same sorts of flowers growing in the garden before one's gaze. As for the outer Aubrac scenery, of which only the skyscape is visible, the summer sun initially prohibits much appreciation, as the light is particularly brash, necessitating protective shades on the glass walls to soften its effect. But as the sun reaches the horizon, the waiters, in choreographed synchronicity, raise the shades, revealing the Turneresque sky with the added surprise of double sunsets (in ancient times a portentous cosmic sign), created by the double plate glass of the windows. The symbolic, indeed metaphysical role of the sun has played a major part in the constitution of French landscape architecture ever since Versailles, where the garden's central axis marks the solar trajectory, culminating at the vanishing point where the sun sets at infinity, all in homage to the Sun King.[8] This tradition is continued at Michel Bras, where the artificial horizon of the rooftop doubles and dissimulates the natural horizon, articulating outer sky with inner garden landscape, all framed by the glass walls that also enclose the sun in a "captured view."

As the sun sets, artificial lighting replaces natural light, with highlights created by spotlights; the disappearance of the sky into night condenses the world into the space of the garden and the restaurant, progressively narrowing the field of visibility and concentration. The only activity in the garden is the "performance" of the light—first natural, then artificial—establishing a theatricality whose gastronomic function is to condense the scene inward, toward the pictorial and performative space of the table. In another context, this effect is explained, mutatis mutandis, in *Looking at the Overlooked*; there Norman Bryson writes of the "anti-Albertian," that is, antiperspectival, genre of still life:

> Instead of plunging vistas, arcades, horizons and the sovereign prospect of the eye, it proposes a much closer space, centered on the body. Hence one of the technical curiosities of the genre, its disinclination to portray the world beyond the far edge of the table. Instead of a zone beyond one finds a blank, vertical wall, sometimes coinciding with a real wall, but no less persuasively it is virtual wall. . . . That further zone beyond the table's edge must be suppressed if still life is to create its principal spatial value: nearness. What builds this proximal space is gesture: the gestures of eating, of laying the table.[9]

In a site that provides a profoundly symbolic dining experience, one fully orchestrated in relation to the surrounding environment and its culinary riches, the restaurant Michel Bras meets the aesthetic conditions of this anti-Albertian genre. In doing so, it provides a paradigm for the culinary arts, one that should also help renew our meditations on landscape and the art of gardens.[10]

NOTES

This text first appeared in *Uncertain Ground*, ed. Martin Thomas (Sydney: Art Gallery of New South Wales, 1999). Portions appeared in Allen S. Weiss, *Flamme et festin: Une poétique de la cuisine* (Paris: Editions Java, 1994), and Allen S. Weiss, *Unnatural Horizons: Paradox and Contradiction in Landscape Architecture* (New York: Princeton Architectural Press, 1998).

1. Leonard Bernstein, *The Unanswered Question* (Cambridge, Mass.: Harvard University Press, 1976), 424. On the geographic specificity of French cuisine, see Jean-Robert Pitte, *Gastronomie française: Histoire et géographie d'une passion* (Paris: Fayard, 1991); for an intimate appreciation of the rela-

tions between food, the seasons, and the earth, see Patience Gray, *Honey from a Weed: Fasting and Feasting in Tuscany, Catalonia, the Cyclades, and Apulia* (New York: Harper and Row, 1986).

2. Jean Dubuffet, "Letter of 15 May 1949," in *Prospectus et tous écrits suivants,* vol. 2 (Paris: Gallimard, 1967), 433–434.

3. Joseph Delteil, *La cuisine paléolithique* (1964; reprint, Montpellier: Arléa/Presses de Languedoc, 1990), 15, 19, 21.

4. Michel Bras, *Le livre de Michel Bras* (Rodez: Editions de Rouergue, 1991).

5. Jean-François Revel, *Un festin en paroles: Histoire littéraire de la sensibilité gastronomique de l'Antiquité à nos jours,* rev. ed. (Paris: Editions Suger, 1985), 21.

6. For a discussion of one such reactionary myth in the context of the discourse of regionalist cooking, see my "The Ideology of the Pot-au-feu," in Allen S. Weiss, *Feast and Folly: Cuisine, Intoxication, and the Poetics of the Sublime* (Albany: State University of New York Press, 2002), 39–58.

7. See Jean Maisonnave, "La cuisine des champs," *Gault-Millau,* May 1991, 47–52.

8. See Allen S. Weiss, "Versions of the Sun: The Fearful Difference," in *Mirrors of Infinity: The French Formal Garden and Seventeenth-Century Metaphysics* (New York: Princeton Architectural Press, 1995), 52–77.

9. Norman Bryson, *Looking at the Overlooked: Four Essays on Still Life Painting* (Cambridge, Mass.: Harvard University Press, 1990), 71.

10. This was written before the recent renovation of the restaurant, which entailed raising the level of the floor so that the landscape beyond has become visible. What is gained in picturesque visibility is not, in my opinion, sufficient compensation for the loss of a brilliant aesthetic and symbolic effect.

3

TASTE BUDS: CULTIVATING A CANADIAN CUISINE

SUSAN HERRINGTON

The Latin idiom *genius loci* is a common stock for theories of landscape gardens and debates concerning regionalism. It is also a trope for local dishes and ingredients. Regional cuisine, gardens, and landscapes knead natural history with material history as their constituent features are manipulated by the cultivation of taste. To many a connoisseur, the agreeableness of this blending relies on both a deep understanding of the raw ingredients of a locale and a cook's or gardener's ability to transform these materials into an aestheticized experience for the eye, the mind, and the tongue.

The chefs Alice Waters (Berkeley), Lydia Shire (Boston), and Daniel Boulud (New York) refer to the *genius loci* in their culinary endeavors, noting that their menus inspire "a sense of place" and an evolving "gastronomic heritage" that "works with a region's bounty."[1] Boulud proffers a meal that mimics the chain of predators in a region. He suggests that you should conclude a main course of wild game with "fruits of the forest, like chestnuts, food consumed by the hunter, or serve grapes with game, since birds love to eat grapes. Then whatever the birds eat becomes the relation."[2]

Julia Child reminds gastronomes that those succulent duck livers for sautéed scallops of fresh duck foie gras must be of European stock, and for less eloquent dishes like Rhode Island johnny cakes, Child insists that to produce the "authentic" cakes, "you must have Rhode Island stone-ground white cornmeal."[3] Even CuisineNet claims that "the chef knows not only from which region come the finest *petits pois* (small, young green peas), but from which town," continuing with a toponomy of ingredients that include "Pessac for strawberries, the peas of Saint-Germaine, Macau artichokes, the Charolais steer, butter of Isigny."[4]

This detailed knowledge of diverse landscapes and their associated foods and cuisine is confusing to the average postmodern. Fortunately, books like *Canadian Food Words* provide an etymological lexicon of the gastronomic isoglosses for expansive countries like Canada. Equipped with this book, you can readily discern a range of culinary delicacies such as *herbes sâlées,* a preserved seasoning of vegetable herbs and brine from Quebec; *madouèce rôti,* a roasted porcupine dish from New Brunswick; or *ciselette,* a pork and molasses dessert sauce from Acadia.[5] These dishes say as much about gastronomy in Canada as they do about the invention of landscape as a narrative system that situates the hybrid histories of cuisine and garden design with connoisseurship. Looking beyond the explanation of the *genius loci,* Allen Weiss contends that the culinary arts provide rich counterparts to the paradoxes found in landscapes.[6] My essay traces the spatiotemporal gastrography of gardens, landscapes, and cuisine from their mediatory and mimetic value to their use by the gardener Elsie Reford as a leitmotiv that heightens their inherent contradictions.

The spatial and pictorial vivacity common to the culinary arts, gardens, and landscapes has a long yet uncharted history that dates to Horace and Pliny. The vine-covered triclinia in the peristyle gardens and oporthecas (outdoor fruit houses) of villas are sites where the necessity of food and the art of life intersect amid the fecund sensualities of the Roman Campagna. Pliny's descriptions of the unswept floors in both indoor and outdoor dining areas and their representation in mosaic floors, the statuettes of pastry vendors and fruit bearers that adorn peristyle gardens, and the topiary that would eventually move from the garden proper to the outdoor table for decorative effect reveal an al fresco composition where exigency and luxury exude compatibility. The oporthecas accommodate fruit production while simultaneously providing aesthetic retreats for dining guests, who, according to Sarah Petersen, use the "ingenious pomology to enhance the scene by constructing still lifes of fresh fruits."[7] The trompe l'oeil of the frescoed walls allude to a garden, while still lifes, as complements to dinner tables and represented on garden walls, illuminate the exquisite details of the external landscape, freshly plucked and brought to the inward-looking eye of Roman pictorial consciousness.[8]

When this eye is opened during the Renaissance, cuisine, gardens, and landscapes make a synecdochic cassoulet that heightens the ambiguities of the spiritual and material world. The Medici, ardent patrons of Renaissance gardens where heroic sculptures are placed in a symmetrical humanist narrative, extend this aesthetic to a culinary pageantry across the Mediterranean landscape. In 1589, during the two-month-long wedding celebration of Grand Duke Ferdinando I de' Medici to Christine de Lorraine (whose grandmother Catherine introduces her Italian pastry chefs and the fork to France), a sequence of spectacular meals are orchestrated during Christine's ceremonial passage through several Tuscan cities and her triumphal entry into Florence. As one art historian notes, these meals are characterized by "the amount of labor expended to exploit basic bodily needs as a pretext for decorative artifice."[9] Such extravagant displays of courtly spectacle might entail thirty-two courses for 280 guests; and at one such meal, the sideboards are enshrined by four-foot-high mythological sculptures made of melted sugar. Giovanni da Bologna, who sculpted the figures of Ferdinando I and Cosimo I and two fountains in the Boboli gardens in Florence, created confectionery follies for dynastic weddings in 1600 and 1608.[10]

While the final disposition of these figures is not known, the relegation of the sweet sculptures to the margins of the banquet table adheres to the Renaissance conviction that refined sugars ruin the appetite. Pastries and other sugar-laden food are not consumed until the end of the meal, "where it was provided in an abundance to check the appetite that had been so artfully stimulated."[11] The use of sugar as a material for sculptural ornaments, sometimes adorned with moss, participates in the topos of the Italian Renaissance that ushers in modern myths counterpoising the state of nature with that of culture. The mimetic devices of the Italian Renaissance gardens present ephemeral, organic material such as plants as artifice (topiary), while ornaments made of inert material (concrete and stone) mimic organic forms. Honey, produced by the natural inclinations of the bee, is the relished sweetener of the ancients. Refined sugar, introduced by Arabic cookery, and a substance that both allures and raises the suspicion of Petrarch,[12] is a highly processed ingredient requiring the sophistication of Renaissance technology and trade to produce and distribute. When refined sugar, the artifice of raw food, is fabricated as a rosette of *Rosa canina*, a double inversion is invoked. This play on the ambiguity of the realms of nature and culture plagues even modern myths in which science is employed to decipher their discursive classifications.

For example, gardens and the culinary arts provide sustenance to positivist explorations of mythic thought that seeks to distinguish culture from nature. The origins of cultivating plants and cooking food are the subject of Lévi-Strauss's writings on the structural role of myths, and further evoke an intimate relationship between cooking and gardening. In *The Raw and the Cooked,* the transformative operations of food preparation manifest the problematic dialectic of distinguishing natural processes from cultural products through the degree of human effort, an exertion directly proportional to the amount of natural materials expunged.[13] Edible plant parts plucked fresh from the wilds of Brazil are raw nature, while the cooking of these plants is a cultural process. Lévi-Strauss hypothesizes that a key myth

> belongs to a set of myths that explain the origins of the cooking of food (although this theme is, to all intents and purposes, absent from it); that cooking is conceived of in native thought as a form of mediation; and finally, that this particular aspect remains concealed in Bororo myth, because the latter is in fact an inversion, or a reversal, of myths in neighboring communities which view culinary operations as mediatory activities between heaven and earth, life and death, nature and society.[14]

In this structural relationship, any attempt to garden or cook will entertain its rhetorical opposite; the exotic or domesticated, hunted or cultivated, synthesized or naturalized, included or excluded. The raw is raw because it is not cooked, the cooked is cooked because it is not raw. The pattern of interpermeable oppositions in Bororo and other tropical South American cultures underlies the gastronomy of numerous culinary endeavors, including sweet and sour pork, surf and turf, chaud-froid sauce, soup-and-salad lunches, or "for here or to go?" Weiss notes that the particular contradictions of "peasant/haute, simple/refined, traditional/nouvelle, regional/international, raw/cooked, wild/cultivated" are central to contemporary French cuisine.[15]

SUSAN HERRINGTON

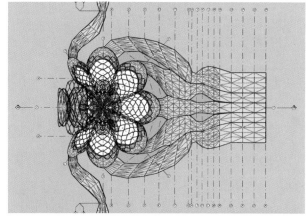

THE ARK OF THE WORLD is conceived as an institution that celebrates the ecological diversity, environmental preservation, ecotourism, and cultural heritage of Costa Rica. A tourist destination situated in the heart of the mountainous primary rain forests of the country's interior, it is a mixture of natural history museum, ecology center, and contemporary art museum. The architectural design is inspired in its form, color, and symbolism by the tropical flora and fauna indigenous to the country. The site is designed to accommodate a primary entry through a garden of water-filled columns that keep the site cool and moist. From the entry lobby, the three types of exhibit are both visible and accessible. In a central vertical space, a helicoidal stair rises three stories and terminates in a glass-fiber-reinforced fabric-covered canopy from which visitors can look into the canopies of the surrounding rain forest. This central vertical space is filled with representations of the Costa Rican environment and serves as an orientation zone for ecotourists. Galleries for exhibiting contemporary art inspired by the natural environment surround this vertical space in a circular fashion; these exhibitions will be drawn from local as well as international artists. The ground floor of the building extends as a single-story natural history exhibition designed around E. O. Wilson's concept of consilience. The Consilience Museum contains exhibitions of the global environment and of natural history and ecology. This ground-floor museum unfolds into the landscape and terminates in a stage and amphitheater where music can be performed outdoors in the evening and where the Ark of the World Awards in ecology, being launched along with the building, will be presented annually.

Mitchell Squire, CULTUREWARE: IMPLEMENTS OF DESIRE; OR, EAT THIS!

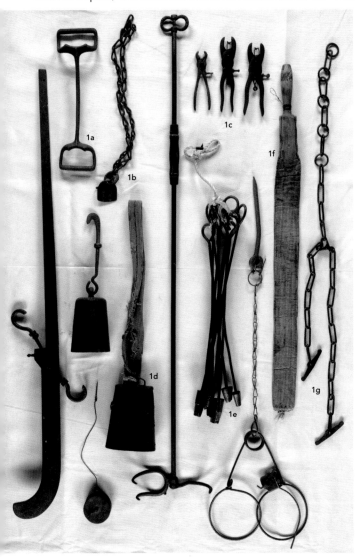

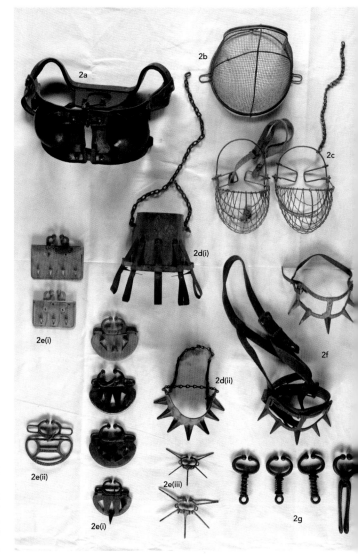

1. BLACKENING

Marking: the "GRAPHIC meridian"

- **1a** Hog Catcher. For easy catching and holding of hogs.
- **1b** "Maytag" Cow Tag.
- **1c** Hog Ringers. Cast iron, with adjustable side stop. One ring in nostrils discourages rooting and fence lifting.
- **1d** Cow Bell.
- **1e** Branding Irons.
- **1f** Hog Whip, Scott Mfg. Co., Omaha, Nebraska. Inscription reads, "Prevent Bruises."
- **1g** Cow Kicker.

2. PRESSURE COOKING

Managing: "theMANage . . ."

- **2a** Bull Blinder, Russell Mfg. Co., Platteville, Wisconsin. Pat. No. 1912-53. Prevents a bull from charging.
- **2b** Horse Nose Basket.
- **2c** Calf Weaner—Basket Type.
- **2d** Calf Weaners. Prevents calf from "stealing" milk. (i) "NU-WAY WEANER," Austin Mfg. Co., Round Grove, Illinois. Pat. No. 2341072. (ii) "SO-BOSS," Simonsen Iron Works, Sioux Rapids, Iowa.
- **2e** Calf Weaners: (i) Plate Type; (ii) Gate Type, "KANT SUK" brand Pat'd Aug. 16, 1910; (iii) Prong Type.
- **2f** Calf Weaners, "DAISY" brand, Pat'd Oct 11, 1932.
- **2g** Bull Leads. Spring-loaded lead closes in animal's nose. Useful in transport of animal. 2" x 3" across center dia.

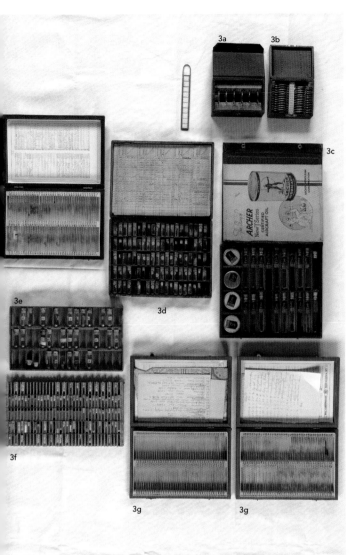

3. REDUCING

Arranging: "smallBOXES/high numerical CONTENTS" **or** "Handling Matters"

3a Microscopic Lens Trial Set. A.O. [American Optical]. 6 lenses, black box [opened]; 5.75" W x 2" H x 8" D.

3b Untitled Lens Set. 12 pair lenses; 5" W x 1.25" H x 8" D.

3c Archer Lubricants Sample Case, ca. 1955–1956. Archer Petroleum Corporation, Omaha, Nebraska. Includes sales pamphlet featuring "5 Steps to a SALE."

3d Untitled Vial Set. 100 slots; 11.5" W x 0.75" H x 17" L.

3e Untitled Vial Set. 48 slots, 12.5" L x 7" W x 1" D.

3f Untitled Vial Set. 175 slots, 119 bottles; purple velvet-lined tray [opened]; 13" L x 7" W x 0.5" D.

3g Microscopic Slide Sets. 100 count; Veterinary Medicine Animal Disease samples and notes. Approx. 11" L x 7.75" W x 1" H.

4. U.S. MEASUREMENTS

Measuring: "dirty WHITE devices"

4a Health-o-Meter Scale [Bath Type]. Capacity 300 lbs.

4b Dietetic Scale, Pelouze Manufacturing Co., Chicago.

4c "COMPUTING" Scale [Candy]. Pelouze Mfg. Co., Chicago and Evanston, Illinois. Style: "Supreme." May 25th 1915; June 28th 1927; Pats. Pend'g.

4d Health-o-Meter [Bath Type]. Continental Scale Works, Chicago, Illinois. Reg. TM. Pat'd Dec. 1917, June 1921.

4e Universal Scale [Kitchen Type]. Landers, Frary & Clark, New Britain, Connecticut.

4f Pediatric Scale [Nursery Type]. Inscription on tray reads "WHAT A GIRL SHOULD WEIGH!" and "WHAT A BOY SHOULD WEIGH!"

4g Mascot Egg Grader. Prospectus Mfg. Co., Minneapolis, Minnesota (nonpatented).

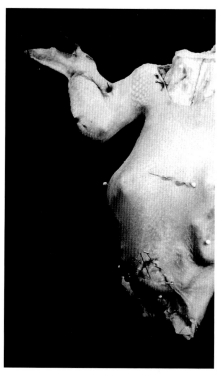

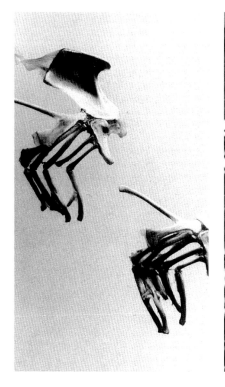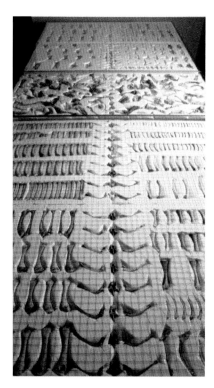

FOR SEVEN YEARS she saves the bones of every animal she eats. Every restaurant meal, every barbecue at a friend's house, every time she cooks meat at home, the bones are retrieved—rescued from their fate as refuse. Away from home she wraps them in a napkin or doggy bag. At home she sets them aside. After dinner she washes the dishes, then she washes the bones with a toothbrush—meticulously. The bones are set to dry in the dish rack alongside the dishes. Clean and dry. Later, when she puts the dishes back in the cupboards, she will prepare the bones for storage like a taxidermist, and file them by type, like a nineteenth-century naturalist.

This becomes a regular part of her domestic chores.

An astounding transformation occurs through this labor. By these painstaking yet simple acts of devotion, she transforms what would have been garbage into a growing collection of small miracles. A radical recategorization. These bones, no less beautiful than those displayed in a museum of natural history, have been redeemed. Instead of being scraped off the plate as garbage, they have been made into precisely what they are. Like museum specimens, they exude through their form both the miracle of life and the presence of mortality.

For seven years she saves and prepares the bones from her meals without knowing what she is preparing them for. Then she decides to make her family's dining room table. She chooses only the chicken bones (she prefers chicken).

The bones are gently cradled below the surface of the table like a landscape, like an excavation, like an archaeological dig. The table is set. Sitting at the table waiting to eat, we look back in time. Mother's meals. The flesh that is not there becomes mother's flesh. The flesh she prepares for dinner is made emphatically present. Life and mortality, the miracle inside us, the fundamental sacrifice, is made beautiful, comic, and creepy.

Mark Robbins, **JUST ADD WATER**

Friendship, 2001, collage

Tang and Country Time, 2001, collage

THE AMERICAN SUPERMARKET is a museum. The mix of products on the shelves is fantastic both in quantity and kind. The foods of a nation are sold with faces, slogans, and graphic designs with mass and niche appeal, from the nouvelle bottles of Glaceau water to the homely, irregular shapes of shrink-wrapped salt pork.

The Quaker with white hair and blue eyes selling grits shares shelf space with an unnamed black man in a white chef's hat and a red bow tie (the image ca. 1940), beaming approvingly at the steaming bowl of cream of wheat ("Since 1893") below. Both men smile broadly: a diptych, the Quaker and the freedman. The familiar Land O' Lakes beauty holds an image of herself holding the image of herself holding a pound of butter, with the recursivity of a '60s black-light poster. Next to her a tub of margarine with a dewy blonde worthy of Miss Clairol offers "Homestyle," the adjective substituting for the noun: a spread of soybean oil and propylene glycol.

The postwar era was a boon to food science and suburbia—every wife a modern chef, liberated with speed, convenience, and labor-saving ease: Minute Rice in '49; deluxe processed cheese slices, perfectly square orange panels individually wrapped in plastic, in '52. Imagine the later shock of Stilton after a childhood of *cheese food*, pasta after Chef Boyardee, or the hard, resistant texture of cooked long grain after Minute Rice. In the face of this abundant doubling, we were encouraged not to notice the difference.

In 1957 General Foods introduced the iconic Tang, in its distinctive ribbed glass jar, not as orange juice but as "breakfast beverage crystals." It was a modern product—even the name is quick, clipped, abstract—sold on the basis of its new tech, developed for NASA, "as drunk by the astronauts." By 1975, in the midst of the future forecast in the '50s, the dew of the modern was off the rose, and Kraft introduced Country Time Lemonade. The current TV commercials feature images of a misty summer morning, on a backlit porch overlooking a farm with grandpa and the kids. To take a drink of this beverage is to grab for a transitory moment of balance and harmony.

Both Tang and Country Time are now made by Kraft, which was itself acquired by Philip Morris, now the neutralized Altria. Each comes in identical white, induction-molded plastic containers, efficient for stacking and shipping, with shrink-wrapped "Endura" labels. The tubs are ergonomically designed with a central furrow in the middle for ease of handling; the caps are designed as built-in measuring cups for mixing on the go.

Country Time makes an appeal to its softened vision of nature, Tang perhaps to science. The problem is not the mild fantasy of either—the consumption of fantasy in all forms is our birthright—but the righteous insistence on confusing "flavor crystals" with the lemon, masking the thing with a cartoon. It's part of a larger wave of nostalgia that keeps us moving forward with our eyes fixed firmly behind.

Homestyle 48% Soybean Oil Spread, 2001, collage

Urban Rock Design (Jeanine Centuori and Russell Rock), **NO SUBSTITUTIONS ALLOWED**

METAPHORS MATTER. The conventions of style conveyed through the delectable photograph, a clean yet consumable artifact, helped promote and codify modern architecture, cleansing the palate of preconceptions and inviting the viewer into a delicious new world. The style and composition of these photographs foregrounded reforms in taste.

The quick 1950s meal composed of a hamburger, french fries, and soda pop, followed by a slice of chocolate cake and breath mints, symbolizes a new and unique American contribution to culture—the pleasure of the immediate and disposable. The burger strives to claim an individuality among meals as an essential piece of Americana with casual edibility. Such heroic reform addresses a new manner of domestic living: mobile, compact, and efficient.

In contrast to the burger, the smooth European aperitif or *digestif*—filled out as an assortment of cheeses, pastries, fruit, or handmade bread—provides slower, deeper fulfillment. These foods take time to eat and absorb; their varied flavors fill the mouth and appropriately bracket a meal. And yet their modern availability promises us new, novel, and rich satisfaction delivered by the simplest of ingredients. It assumes the mantle of the spiritually heroic.

The photograph focuses our desires while tempting us with a clarity of purpose. We want to be where we see, we want to take these visions inside and ruminate on their special flavors.

BENEATH THE LAYER of rational organization and focus implicit in place/design practices and the professional realm exist the perpetual, invisible, and diffuse patterns of the quotidian; a recipe of familial, social, and mundane events, duties, and joys, which continually threatens to go awry.

These tiles make physical the routines of domesticity and the centrality of food in everyday life. The diminutive scale of the panels echoes Gaston Bachelard's profound writings on the "intimate immensity." They depict the minutiae of daily events, tiny in themselves but significant, and the omnipresent sensual stimuli that come from preparing and sharing food. The constraint of using a limited palette of white, where the form and detail are essentialized, derives from architectural theory that examines whiteness as a metaphor for modernity and purity, and from contemporary culture which associates good housekeeping with cleanliness.

These pieces literally imprint and trace mementos of modest eating rituals, demonstrating the resource that is to be found in a close reading of the (extra)ordinary.

Gina Ferrari, **MAKING POLENTA**

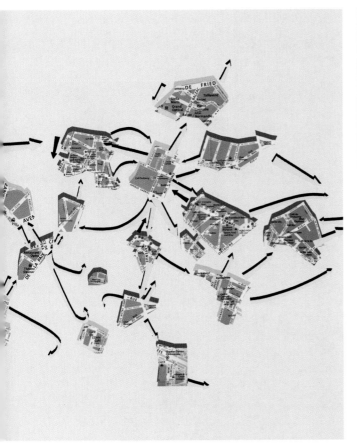
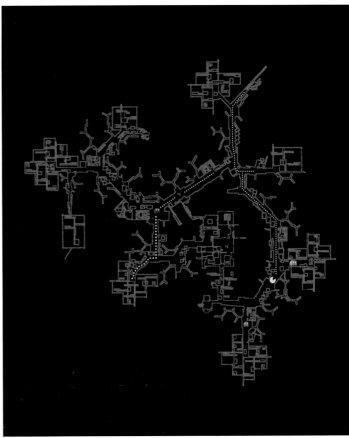

KONSUMTERROR IS A CONCEPT coined by Ulrike Meinhof in defense of the Red Army Faction's use of terrorism. For Meinhof, the real terror is late capitalism's constant demand that we always consume more.

Pac-Man demonstrates the relentless logic of Konsumterror. Like the late-capitalist subject, Pac-Man feels no hunger but can't stop consuming. Pac-Man opens and closes his mouth insipidly, eating everything in his path. Everything tastes the same for him; his mouth is his only organ. The point of Pac-Man is to consume enough that the game never ends.

Urban Konsumterror is a critique of the condition of architecture in the contemporary city. The use of signature architecture to draw in tourist dollars is nothing more than a game of architectural Pac-Man. Signature architecture begins by consuming the museum: in order to build more and more, funds for exhibits or even routine maintenance are cannibalized. When buildings fall apart as a result, they can be torn down and new ones can be built. Cities also become consumed.

When you say "Bilbao," you refer to a building by Frank Gehry. The city's identity no longer matters. All imaginative and financial capacity for real urban interventions is consumed by signature architecture.

Konsumterror creates a perpetual crisis both for the individual and for architecture: like Pac-Man, the game can end only when you lose. You can play again, but you will lose again. Eventually you run out of quarters or get bored and give up.

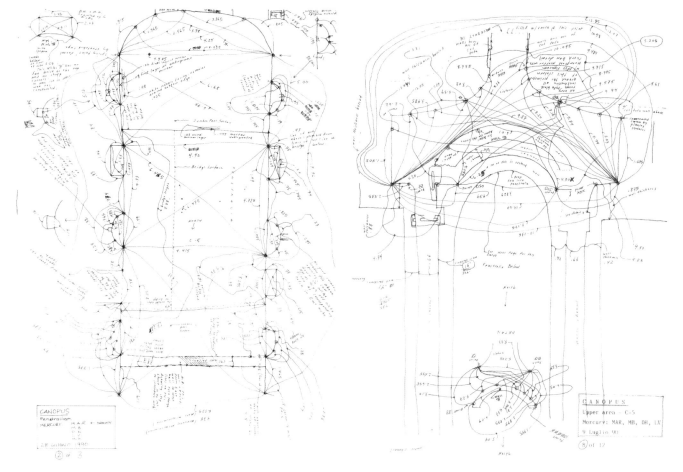

THE CANOPUS, built between 118 and 134 C.E. by the Emperor Hadrian at his villa near Tibur (modern Tivoli, 30 kilometers east of Rome), is a construction that formalizes an existing topographical feature of a waterfall and ravine.

The apsidal dining pavilion is a tremendous retaining wall with a semicircular *triclinium* (dining area) in which sits a semicircular sloped *stibadium* (dining couch or bed) of masonry that originally would have been shrouded with cushions and linens for the reclining diners. It was said to have been the site of extravagant banquets and parties of the sort described by Petronius in *Satyricon* and portrayed in Federico Fellini's film.

An elongated extension behind the *stibadium* that pushes into the hill was named the Penetralium by Piranesi. Le Corbusier drew it in 1910 and later developed this space as a reference for the light monitors of Ronchamp.

The natural watercourse was elaborately reconfigured into a set of choreographed waterworks that included water jets, a continuous semicircular basin behind the *stibadium* for washing feet, small waterfalls in the niches behind the diners, and a 119-meter-long *euripus* or reflecting pool that, through the Egyptian and classical sculpture found there (Amazons, crocodiles, river gods, and more), is identified with both the Nile and Tiber rivers. Most dramatically, a tremendous curtain of water could be raised and lowered through the simple operation of wooden gates in miniature aqueducts above. When the curtain was "drawn" at the beginning of an afternoon dining party, with perhaps hundreds of diners on couches lining the *euripus*, the guests would have seen a sparkling vertical surface backlit by a mysterious light source. The raising of the water curtain would have revealed a deep grotto space serving as the backdrop for the most honored guests—including Hadrian the host—as the meal moved toward twilight.

Because of our measuring work at Hadrian's villa over more than a decade, we became intimately familiar with this and the other (roughly) sixty buildings on the site. With the help of nearly 200 graduate students of architecture acting under the name of "Atelier Italia," a new plan of the villa is in the making. (The last substantial plan was produced by Piranesi and published under the name of his son, Francesco.)

We inhabited the Canopus for many days as we measured. We also dined upon the *stibadium* on many occasions—mostly for summer picnic lunches, as we took time out from the long hot days of work, but also on several occasions at twilight and into the night accompanied by candles in the niches to light up the pumpkin dome and by a tape recording of water to simulate the missing waterworks. It is through experiences of habitation like these that the history of architecture becomes not simply history but a living presence.

Opposite, top: Atelier Italia photographs of the Penetralium; subfloor pattern found in the floor of the pool of the Penetralium; the stibadium or masonry dining couch, 1990.

Opposite, bottom: Atelier Italia field measurement sheets of the Canopus Penetralium, 1990.

Below left: "Anatomy of the Canopus," drawing by Atelier Italia.

Below center: Le Corbusier's 1910 drawing of the Penetralium from his travel sketchbooks.

Below right: detail of the Canopus by Giovanni Battista Piranesi, from Pianta delle fabbriche esistente nella Villa Adriana (1781).

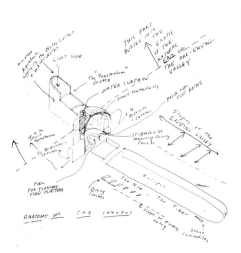

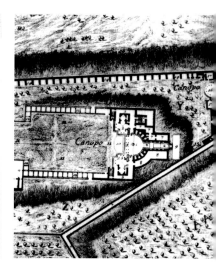

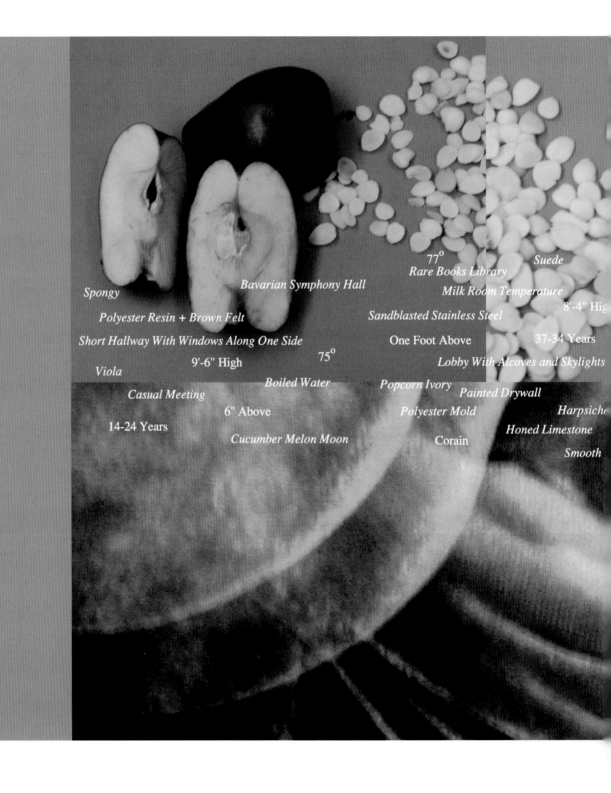

Spongy

Bavarian Symphony Hall

77°
Rare Books Library
Suede

Milk Room Temperature

Sandblasted Stainless Steel

8'-4" Hig

Polyester Resin + Brown Felt

Short Hallway With Windows Along One Side

One Foot Above

37-34 Years

Viola

9'-6" High

75°

Lobby With Alcoves and Skylights

Boiled Water

Popcorn Ivory

Painted Drywall

Casual Meeting

6" Above

Polyester Mold

Harpsiche

14-24 Years

Cucumber Melon Moon

Honed Limestone

Corain

Smooth

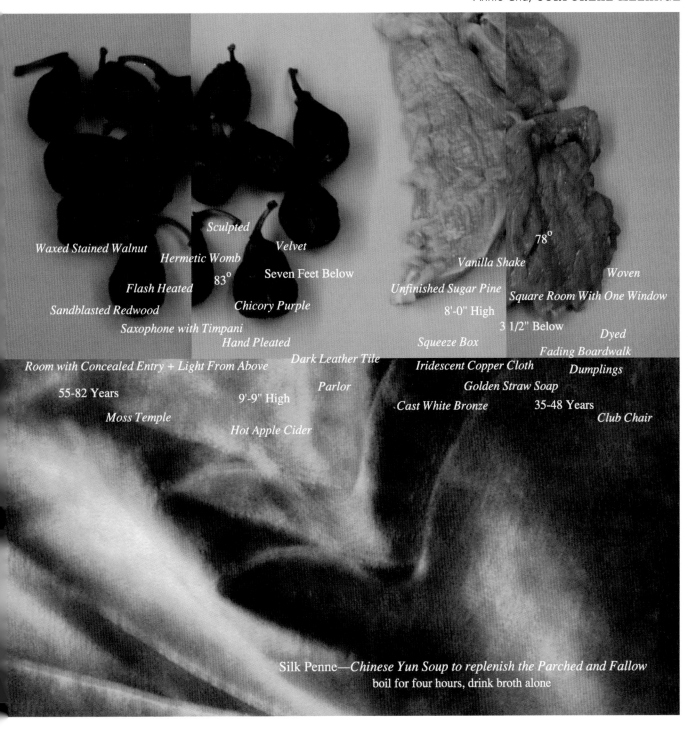

Waxed Stained Walnut

Sculpted

Hermetic Womb

Velvet

83°

Seven Feet Below

Flash Heated

Sandblasted Redwood

Chicory Purple

Saxophone with Timpani

Hand Pleated

78°

Vanilla Shake

Woven

Unfinished Sugar Pine

Square Room With One Window

8'-0" High

3 1/2" Below

Dyed

Squeeze Box

Fading Boardwalk

Dark Leather Tile

Iridescent Copper Cloth

Dumplings

Room with Concealed Entry + Light From Above

55-82 Years

9'-9" High

Parlor

Golden Straw Soap

35-48 Years

Moss Temple

Cast White Bronze

Club Chair

Hot Apple Cider

Silk Penne—*Chinese Yun Soup to replenish the Parched and Fallow*
boil for four hours, drink broth alone

Carisima Koenig, **PROSCIUTTO MAP OF ROME**

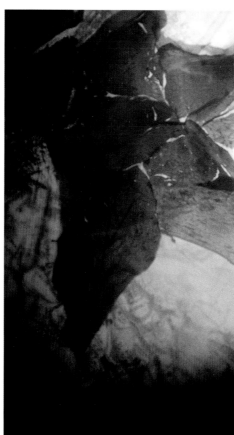

STATES OF DISCOVERY. Cut, who has cut? Is a cut not a wound, a slice, something to be dressed? The eroticization of the cut. The "pure cut"—the pureness of this cut produces vague beauty versus adherent beauty. Where is Rome, Roma, not a series of cuts? Cuts place and frame; they position object to object, view to view. The section cut—to section the ground, to mark off as Romulus incised the site—creates slices, or wounds. Remus died. Remus killed. The section cut of flesh, translucent weak flesh bound by hard edges. The density within the flesh, within the fat and tissue section . . . if the section is too thin it fails, the muscle falls from the fat and dries. The muscle stretches, distorts, and changes views. A map in the process of incorporation, making a move from the errant to the adherent.

Many of the great garden traditions can be structured through a juxtaposition and synthesis of opposites. Gardens and landscapes mediate, and by reconstituting what they are, they refer to what they are not. Simply by adding water, Islamic gardens prepare a raw, desiccated landscape as a succulent oasis cultivated in a series of rectilinear fourfold gardens. At the sixteenth-century Safavid Isfahan, irrigation tunnels below grade saturate the sands of the Persian desert. The garden recontextualizes the pragmatic irrigation system on the symbolic plane of the ground surface, where a geometry of tranquil pools and vegetative bosques align with Mecca. This salubrious and orderly garden reproduced from sand is also contrary to its surrounding city, which offers what theorists of the garden call an "exploratory pilgrimage, twisting between close walls, amidst the noise of artisans and merchants, the aroma of spices, and the dust and jostle of crowds."[16]

Knife skills, a fundamental component of French haute cuisine, inform the baroque gardens by Le Nôtre. Carved from their dense medieval woodlands, the infinite avenues of Versailles, which display the elegant slicing techniques described by Julia Child as employing the full length of the knife,[17] contradict the fragmented and domestic intimations of the remnant woodlands. An acute knowledge of scales and proportions is crucial to the practice of slicing geometric figures into the surface of land and thereby composing the experience of these landscapes. Likewise, the exactness and congruency of cutting julienne or macédoine ensure a uniform cooking process and appearance, and also a consistency in the experience of its taste. In the julienne avenues and macédoine parterres, fêtes, divertissements, and other collations in the French baroque garden are codified in playacting and feasting. The garden and cuisine are condiments to these spectacles of pervasive authority; Chandra Mukerji describes how they "move from the extraordinary to the ordinary, [from] allegorical dramas to carefully choreographed rituals of everyday life, from realms of the fictive to political regimen, from mythology to history, where the enactment of power could be rawly presented."[18] These "rituals of submission" and seduction suspend life in the animation of their play and in the excessiveness of the food that is demolished by guests.[19]

For the English Enlightenment gardens, these dichotomies of the culinary landscape become deliciously dissimulated. A compatible mixture of rough and smooth textures is key to the picturesque gardens of the eighteenth and nineteenth centuries,

SUSAN HERRINGTON

3.1
The picturesque landscape at
Blenheim Palace in galantine
presentation. Photo by author.

and it is of cardinal importance to menu planning as identified by Antonin Carême (1784–1833). Carême revolutionizes *pièces montées*, extravagant wedding-cake-like table decorations. Prior to Carême's creations, the landscape critic Horace Walpole condemns *pièces montées* as culinary anathemas of vulgar taste that might include "wax figures that moved by clockwork" and "castles made of pies filled with live frogs and birds."[20] By giving his edible fortifications a visual sensibility that embraces the elite's fascination with antiquity and classical ruins, and by accurately translating classical designs to the scale and proportion of the table, Carême relocates confectionery to the level of connoisseurship shared by landscape architecture and the fine arts.[21]

Edmund Burke's 1757 psychological treatise, *A Philosophical Enquiry into the Origins of Our Ideas of the Sublime and the Beautiful,* presents coarseness as epitomizing the state of the sublime and smoothness as the most salient source of beauty.[22] While Burke's insights foreshadow debates on whether to preserve the mixture of smoothness and roughness in landscape aesthetics (arguments that conflate politics with garden design), picturesque landscapes, like Uvedale Price's Foxley estate in Herefordshire, mask the synthetic act of artistry. Dissolving the difference between designed landscapes and lands free from human intervention, the picturesque indulges in the aesthetics of galantine presentation. Galantine calls for the chef to debone and restuff poultry, fish, or fowl. It is a reassembly of the animal so that it can be displayed as its cultured sign.[23] Consider Julia Child's reformed lettuce heads, for which "washed and dried salad greens are loosely arranged in the bowl to look again like a large head of Boston lettuce."[24] Likewise, the raw conditions of the site are reassembled in the picturesque landscape (figure 3.1). Streams are dammed, earth is moved, and trees are added or subtracted to re-present the landscape as the cultured sign of nature. Charles Bridgeman went as far as to invent the first ha-ha at Stowe in Buckinghamshire, where the manicured lawns of the estate and coarse pastureland meld into one unified field of vision from the house.

Burke's *Sublime and the Beautiful* also whets "the growing taste for ruins and melancholy terror, for graveyard poetry, for wild and desolate scenery."[25] Lévi-Strauss further expands this structure of myth by noting that "the raw/cooked axis is characteristic of culture; the fresh/decayed one of nature, since cooking brings about the cultural transformation of the raw, just as putrefaction is its natural transformation."[26] While his anthropological postulate concerns nature and culture, the more tantalizing question for any cook or gardener is to cook or not to cook, to garden or not to garden. This question is more central to gardens, landscapes, and cuisine than to any of the design arts. To not garden or cook is a cultural act; yet the oozing cucumber forgotten in the refrigerator or the overgrown garden inundated with weeds blurs these cultural states of nature and culture, as it occupies the territory of the rotten.

An aesthetic of ruins is cultivated as early as 1499 in Francesco Colonna's *Hypnerotomachia Poliphili*, and climaxes in the emotional excesses and imaginative embellishments of Gothic literature. From Roussea's advice to study botany instead of minerals and animals that will surely involve "stinking corpses, livid running flesh, blood, repellent intestines" to Mary Shelley's protagonist, whose academic proclivities compel him to investigate "how the worm inherited the wonders of the eye and the brain,"[27] decay is the synecdoche for the processes of nature. Embedded in the garden, the associative effects of ruins or actual tombs such as Rousseau's at Ermenonville invoke the ethereal, fleeting, and fragmentary meiosis of the living, a prerequisite for Romantic thinking (figure 3.2). Indeed, the fabrication of ruins in the picturesque landscape does for gardening what mold does for blue cheese; and by the early nineteenth century this penchant for decay is reified in bourgeois instruction manuals on the picturesque, featuring "ragged peasants, shaggy livestock of all kinds, ruins, and decaying cottages" as essential accompaniments to the garden scene.[28]

An appreciation of decay is further fortified by an exposure to Eastern sensibilities encouraged by British imperialism. Japanese aesthetics probe the depths of the fresh/rotten axis with a diet of raw fish and an intense feeling for the *wabi sabi* of dead trees and edifices strewn with mosses that speed their decay (figure 3.3). The prevalence of tea from China and India at English garden parties and London coffeehouses is only one example of British consumption of the East.[29] In his 1757 *Designs of Chinese Buildings, Furniture, Dresses, Machines, and Utensils*, William Chambers introduces a Chinese garden and its ability to evoke the "appellation of the horrid." His descriptions of the garden portray it as a consequence of nature as much as artistry:

> In their scenes of horror, they introduce impending rocks, dark caverns, and
> impetuous cataracts rushing down the mountains from all sides; the trees are
> ill-formed, and seemingly torn to pieces by the violence of tempest; some are
> thrown down, and intercept the course of torrents, appearing as if they had been

3.2
Lichen consumes the Pantheon at Stourhead. Photo by author.

3.3
The wabi-sabi of a moss-coated garden at Saihoji. Photo by Lisa McNiven.

brought down by fury of the waters; others look as if shattered and blasted by the force of lighting; the buildings are some in ruins, others half-consumed by fire, and some miserable huts dispersed in the mountains serve at once to indicate the existence and wretchedness of the inhabitants.[30]

Later that year Chambers begins his design for Kew Gardens, foreshadowing another import from China—exotic plants. As one of the most zealous of entities collecting exotic specimens, Kew finances an ambitious series of plant-hunting expeditions into the remote mountain ranges of Tibet, Burma, and China. Venturing into the wild terrains of the snow leopard, hostile weather conditions, yak butter, buckwheat, and tsamba balls,[31] plant hunters from both England and France radicalized the *fonds de cuisine* of plants cultivated in Europe and North America. Rhododendrons, azaleas, primula, gentians, asters, chrysanthemums, and the elusive blue poppy are the jewels of the garden, and they even make their way onto the table as decorations of an ornate meal.[32] It is no surprise that these exotic delicacies intrigue Joris-Karl Huysmans's protagonist in *Against the Grain (A Rebours).* In his search for natural flowers imitating the false, Des Esseintes ponders the exotic flowers at the hothouses of the Avenue de Châtillon and the valley Aunay, noting their "blossoms dazzling and cruel in their brilliance" and observing that "Nature is by herself incapable of producing species so morbid and perverse; she supplies the raw material, the germ and the soil, the procreative womb and the elements of the plant, which mankind rears, models, paints, carves afterwards to suit his caprice."[33]

Exotic flowering plants combine with native plantings to provide a heady mixture of tastes in the ornamental gardening dear to suburban homeowners in the nineteenth century. By the 1850s dining is à la Russe in Europe and North America. Each dish is presented at separate times, the sequence of meals is predicated on the middle-class work schedule, and the size of the servings is directly proportional to the smallness of the newly emerging suburban lots. Gardening authors, such as Jane and John Claudius Loudon, translate the codes and conventions of estate landscape designs and ornamental farming to small suburban gardens. Producing an exhaustive and comprehensive collection of gardening books and periodicals in a vein of academic eclecticism, they believe, as David Stuart explains, that in the garden "everything should be included, from soursop to calbash, cocoa to cashaw (the latter then

SUSAN HERRINGTON

with medicines, as well as culinary use), pawpaw (both for fruit and for the papain even then used for tenderizing meat), cinnamon, vanilla, and the rest."[34] Among their accomplishments, John authors the bible of Victorian gardening, *Encyclopedia of Gardening* (1822), and Jane spearheads *The Ladies' Companion* (1849), one of the earliest periodicals to spread domestic wisdom from the garden to the kitchen.

In both the landscape and culinary worlds, cookbooks, gardening manuals, and magazines reinforce the dominance of bourgeois tastes. The acceptance of women studying Linnaean nomenclature coupled with the novels of Jane Austen gives rise to a sex newly educated in the social morality of landscape gardening. Likewise, the collapse of spatiotemporal gastrographies because of the increased use of trains connects cuisine with the site where, in the words of one nineteenth-century observer, "fresh kills may be obtained,"[35] thereby disordering the relationship of landscape with cuisine. This cocktail of social and technological transformations heightens the interpenetration of popular and high culture, giving an ideological edge to the culinary and garden arts that seek vainly to justify and sustain their differences. As the privileged apparatus of symbolic capital, cuisine, garden, and landscape not only articulate the facile distinctions between social identities but also, by combining nature with class, elaborate elite culture as a natural act. Genetics aside, pedigree is naturalized through the acquisition of taste, a cultural practice that becomes widespread in the twentieth century.

The powers of allusion embedded in the act of naturalization give Roland Barthes much to complain about when it comes to cooking. Among his many explications concerning food is the 1955 essay "Ornamental Cookery," in which Barthes describes how valorized images of prepared dishes in *Elle* magazine are "unbridled beautification" ornamented with "chiselled mushrooms, punctuation of cherries, motifs of carved lemon."[36] Barthes is reacting to the barrage of media images that manipulate something as foundational as food; according to Jill Forbes and Michael Kelly, he finds that "food ceases to be the staff of life and becomes a prop of life-style, 'une cuisine du revêtement et de l'alibi' (cookery which is about covering up, which is a pretext), an elaborate metonymy."[37] This ornamental cookery "is based on coatings and alibis, and is for ever trying to extenuate and even to disguise the primary nature of foodstuffs, the brutality of meat or the abruptness of sea-food. A country dish is admitted only as an exception (the good family boiled beef), as the rustic whim of jaded city-dwellers."[38]

The gap between Barthes's raw food and the "unbridled beautification" of food promoted by *Elle* journalists indicates instability in this signifier. There is no literal meaning in food, and *Elle*'s "foodstuffs" could relate only to something other than "primary nature"—hence a postmodern desire for chicken fingers and lettuce heads. Yet Barthes closely aligns the food fashioned by *Elle,* which he never tastes, and the moral character of *Elle*'s producers and consumers. While Barthes criticizes ornamental cookery as "fleeing from nature," he finds much comfort in the "real cookery" of the middle class, exemplified in the readers of *L'Express,* who enjoy "a comfortable purchasing power."[39] The desire to seek a correspondence between a group's socioeconomic standing and the material artifacts produced for and consumed by that group can be found in numerous critiques aimed at designs ranging from cities to teacups. But such a critique is complex when applied to materials that are constructed by culture as raw or immutable.

Barthes detects depravity in the slippery layers between the power of allusion and the economic power situated in a second-order nature. Both cooking and gardening have the ability to collapse the differences between nature and the culture that captures, contains, and displays nature. Whether it takes the form of ornamental gardening or ornamental cooking, bedding-out or baking, cutting or beheading, the manipulation of these materials engages a second order of power. Dean MacCannell argues, "It transcends any individual expression and appears not as power, but as natural order. It is operative only to the extent that all believe that their place within its hierarchies, however grand or humble, is proper"; and if it violates this order it is identified as immoral.[40]

It is this second order of power that MacCannell finds pervasive in landscapes and gardens: "Gardens and landscaping are situated with sex and cuisine precisely in the gap between nature and culture, idea and event, cause and effect."[41] They are particularly potent because they are produced and consumed through both the metaphoric language and the hegemonic discourse of evolutionary science. The extensive presence in literature of women who have created and described gardens is also significant to MacCannell's theories. Rousseau's heroines, in *Julie, ou La Nouvelle Héloïse* and elsewhere, suggest that the garden is the territory where issues concern-

3.4

Elsie Reford in her garden, ca.
1930. Photo by Robert Wilson
Reford.

ing gender, race, and politics are played out. Julie's description of her garden as a place where "nature has done everything, but under my direction, and there is nothing here that I have not ordered"[42] underscores that the garden serves as a living tableau where power relations are reconstructed to reappear as natural.

Consider the extensive gardens that the Canadian debutante Elsie Reford (1872–1967; figure 3.4) designs and builds in the remote wilds of Quebec. During the first quarter of the twentieth century, she transforms the raw conditions of her wilderness lodge, Estevan,[43] into a garden retreat replete with the civility and conviviality of her Montreal home. Reford invokes the unfolding of a number of mythic dichotomies at Estevan. She dresses in delicate Parisian frocks to navigate the rugged waters of the St. Lawrence; they fish at twilight, not dawn; the raw fish and game are prepared as lavish spectacle that guests eat with civility to heighten the taste of the wild; Reford ships to England many of the salmon who faithfully returned to Estevan; and she brings tender plant specimens to a decadent forest that, although it has climaxed, is sterile.[44]

In 1918 Reford inherits the 1,000-acre Estevan property, containing a thirty-seven-bedroom camping lodge, two working farms, and large tracts of boreal forests.[45] Canada's forest is vast, five times the size of western Europe, and a favorite destination for those wishing to wrest subsistence from the raw wild, a prerequisite for ascending into elite society. As Emile, another of Rousseau's characters, is told as a young man, "If I wanted to taste a dish from the ends of the earth, I would, like Apicus, go and seek it out rather than have it brought to me. For the most exquisite dishes always lack a seasoning that does not travel with them and no cook can give them the air of the climate which produced them."[46] Reford is fanatical about catching salmon, sometimes catching a hundred a day, and she often outcompetes her male guests. Fresh salmon is a highly prized food in Reford's time, and she regularly ices and boxes her catch for shipment to England as gifts. According to a London paper in the late nineteenth century, "to the epicure, a fresh salmon caught in the gulf of the St. Lawrence, especially early in the season, will always afford a rich treat."[47] The desire to catch, present, and consume salmon arises not only because of its undeniably wild taste but also because of the distinct nature of *Salmo salar* itself. Though it roams great distances, the Atlantic salmon migrates from salt water to spawn every year in the same fresh waters as its ancestors. This loyalty to a specific geographic location, passed down genetically in salmon despite their wanderings, is emblematic for many British Canadians, who are far away from home yet still loyal to Britain.

Estevan is situated at the confluence of the St. Lawrence River and the Grand Métis River, and its ownership includes the seigneurial fishing rights to those waters. The right to fish salmon in this aquatic zone, where fresh waterways intersect with salt water, is a valuable privilege. Reford continues Estevan's international reputation as a retreat for rising industrialists and politicians from Montreal, New York, and London who partake of its wealth of fish and fowl and enjoy the camaraderie of its salubrious waters and forests. Yet she not only makes the raw materials of Estevan into an instrument of elite cultural allegiance but also furthers that enterprise by transforming these materials into the defining episode of a day's consumption, dinner. Each morning Reford meets with her chef to establish the day's meals and orchestrate lavish dinners—haute cuisine made with local ingredients—for select guests.

Salmon features abundantly in the exhibitions, cooking schools, and cookbooks of Reford's day. For example, to prepare a freshly caught male as *saumon à la*

SUSAN HERRINGTON

Humbert Ier,[48] the fish must be disemboweled, filled with mousse, and then poached in a mixture that calls for four bottles of white wine from Capri. Once cooked and cooled for three hours, it is coated with several glazes and cooked crayfish are inserted into its back, giving this perceptibly two-dimensional vertebrate a third dimension. A miniature crown with jewels adorns its head. The Concours Culinaire in Paris recommends making the eyes "look natural with mayonnaise"; more specifically, "the center of the eye can be made with a cooked egg white. In the mouth of the fish put a camellia made out of a beet."[49] The double metonymy of dead fresh fish reified as the cultured sign of fish referring to the late Italian ruler and of the placement of the vegetable as flower in its mouth, a practice common in primitive funerary ceremonies, dissolves the proximity of the raw within the elaborate decorum of the meal. This aestheticized presentation of cultural syncretism in a menu of raw delectation foreshadows the creation of yet another recipe, that for Reford's gardens at Estevan.

In 1926 Reford is advised by her doctor to engage in gardening as an alternative to her aggressive salmon fishing. Canada is an absurd place to garden. The majority of the country lies above the 50th parallel, in the frigid zone. The average growing season runs two months, and in Quebec frozen snow covers the ground well into June. The *Oxford Companion to Gardens* notes that "Canada cannot be said to have developed a great gardening tradition" and that any artistic development "belongs to those islands of human culture where nature had been brought under control."[50] Yet over the following thirty years, Reford creates 40 acres of gardens at Estevan, cultivating 50,000 ornamental plants, many grown from seed. An aficionada of exotic plants and a member of the Royal Botanical Society, she avidly collects hundreds of rare species hunted on expeditions for Kew Gardens or directly from sources in Asia and Europe. Reford's most prized feat is her successful domestication of *Meconopsis betonicifolia*, the blue poppy.[51] Discovered in 1926 by the British plant hunter F. Kingdon Ward in Tibet, the blue poppy is the crème de la crème of the horticulture world. *Meconopsis betonicifolia* is desired for its "unnatural" azure color, a hue that is difficult to reproduce in food as well as flowers, and a sight that would surely have stimulated the ruminations of Des Esseintes.

Reford's success in transplanting and cultivating these exotics in Canada ensures her participation in the wider production of gardens as an art form. In her garden designs at Estevan, Reford mixes hardy plants and exotics whose fecundity contradicts their backdrop, the decadent forest. A typical composition includes English primrose and ferns alongside *Primula sieboldii* from Japan and veronica from Armenia. Garden treatises such as *The Wild Garden* (1870) by the Irish gardener William Robinson strengthened this cultural endeavor by promoting the use of hardy exotics in irregularly shaped planting beds. The *Wild Garden* would appeal to Reford, a British descendant living in the newly emerging nation of Canada. By the 1920s the Victorian era, during which Britain had unified its subjects in many disparate lands, is ending, and gardening and cooking are ideal endeavors to display England's superior ability to domesticate the wild and cultivate the exotic.

Reford's Estevan gardens include a 300-foot "Long Walk" (the only straight line in the estate gardens) flanked by dense perennial borders, a series of swaled glade gardens, an upper terrace garden and lawn, and linear woodland gardens that penetrate the forest. The formal qualities of these gardens do not conform to the geometric patterns promoted for ornamental plants or to the whimsical, kidney-shaped planting beds used for natives. Rather her strategy is strikingly modern, as she uses the microclimatic needs of plants as a guide to their location. The gardens are free of any eye-catchers or follies; the abstract workings of climate provide a template for her design. The shapes of the planting areas follow the lines of the topography with the exotic plants in the lower swales, where they are protected from the wind, and the hardier local plants at the crest. Her functionalist design is predicated on the biophysical processes of the site, predating Ian Hamilton Finlay's dictum that "weather is the chief content of a garden."[52]

As she extracts raw elements and cultivates them as culinary riches and horticultural gems, Reford deems the lands and waterways of her estate "magical."[53] Estevan is Reford's cultural enterprise from the order of wilderness, landscape, garden, to table—a project where she procures wild salmon from unruly waters to enhance the civility of her table, and where she cultivates species from exotic landscapes within the confines of her garden. *Genius loci* is only one of many tropes. The reciprocal influences between cuisine, landscape, and garden offer a provocative avenue for studying episodes of aesthetic contradiction, mediation, and simulation. Where the irreducible ingredients of symbolic order and cultural fact classify nature and artifice, pleasure and power arbitrate taste. Sweet, sour, salt, and spice may have reservations on the tongue, but their flavors are savored in the garden.

SUSAN HERRINGTON

NOTES

1. Andrew Dornenburg and Karen Dornenburg, *Culinary Artistry* (New York: Van Nostrand Reinhold, 1996), 230–232.

2. Ibid., 232.

3. Julia Child, *The Way to Cook* (New York: Alfred A. Knopf, 1989), 344.

4. CuisineNet, "Diner's Digest: French Cuisine Introduction," 1998, <http://www.cuisinenet.com/digest/region/france/index.shtml> (accessed January 2003).

5. Bill Casselman, *Canadian Food Words* (Toronto: McArthur and Company, 1998).

6. Allen S. Weiss, *Unnatural Horizons: Paradox and Contradiction in Landscape Architecture* (New York: Princeton Architectural Press, 1998), 126.

7. Sarah T. Petersen, *Acquired Taste: The French Origins of Modern Cooking* (Ithaca: Cornell University Press, 1994), 121.

8. Wilhelmina F. Jashemski, *The Gardens of Pompeii: Herculaneum and the Villas Destroyed by Vesuvius* (New Rochelle, N.Y.: Caratzas Brothers, 1979), 55.

9. James M. Saslow, *The Medici Wedding of 1589* (New Haven: Yale University Press, 1996), 163.

10. Ibid., 159–160.

11. Petersen, *Acquired Taste,* 201.

12. Ibid., 45.

13. Claude Lévi-Strauss, *The Raw and the Cooked: Introduction to the Science of Mythology I,* trans. John and Doreen Weightman (New York: Harper and Row, 1969).

14. Ibid., 64–65.

15. Weiss, *Unnatural Horizons,* 133.

16. Charles W. Moore, William J. Mitchell, and William Turnbull, *The Poetics of Gardens* (Cambridge, Mass.: MIT Press, 1993), 150.

17. Child, *The Way to Cook,* 232.

18. Chandra Mukerji, *Territorial Ambitions and the Gardens of Versailles* (Cambridge: Cambridge University Press, 1997), 217.

19. Ibid., 218.

20. Horace Walpole, quoted in Craig Claiborne and Pierre Franey, *Classic French Cooking* (New York: Time-Life Books, 1970), 75.

21. Weiss, *Unnatural Horizons,* 126–132. Also see Claiborne and Franey, *Classic French Cooking* (73–82), for a discussion on scale adaptations.

22. J. T. Boulton, "Editor's Introduction," in *A Philosophical Enquiry into the Origins of Our Ideas of the Sublime and the Beautiful,* by Edmund Burke, ed. J. T. Boulton (London: Routledge and Kegan Paul, 1958), xcv.

23. Amy B. Trubek, *Haute Cuisine: How the French Invented the Culinary Profession* (Philadelphia: University of Pennsylvania Press, 2000), 136.

24. Child, *The Way to Cook,* 352.

25. Boulton, "Editor's Introduction," lvii.

26. Lévi-Strauss, *The Raw and the Cooked,* 142.

27. Jean-Jacques Rousseau, *Reveries of the Solitary Walker* (1782), trans. Peter France (Harmondsworth: Penguin Books, 1979), 21; Mary Shelley, *Frankenstein: or, The Modern Prometheus* (1818; reprint, Cologne: Könemann, 1995), 45–46.

28. David C. Stuart, *Georgian Gardens* (London: Hale, 1979), 162.

29. Philippa Pullar, *Consuming Passions, Being an Historic Inquiry into Certain English Appetites* (Boston: Little, Brown, 1970), 154–155.

30. William Chambers, "Designs of Chinese Buildings, Furniture, Dresses, Machines, and Utensils" (1757), in *The Genius of the Place: The English Landscape Garden, 1620–1820,* ed. John Dixon Hunt and Peter Willis (New York: Harper and Row, 1975), 284.

31. See Kingdon F. Ward, *The Land of the Blue Poppy: Travels of a Naturalist in Eastern Tibet* (1913; reprint, Cambridge: Cambridge University Press, 1971).

32. Tom Carter, *The Victorian Garden* (London: Cameron Books, 1984), 185.

33. Joris-Karl Huysmans, *Against the Grain (A Rebours),* trans. Havelock Ellis (New York: Hartsdale House, 1931), 186–187.

34. Stuart, *Georgian Gardens,* 132.

35. Peter Simmonds, *The Curiosities of Food, or, The Dainties and Delicacies of the Different Nations Obtained from the Animal Kingdom* (1859; reprint, London: Ten Speed Press, 2000), 266.

36. Roland Barthes, "Ornamental Cookery," in *Mythologies,* trans. Annette Lavers (New York: Hill and Wang, 1972), 78.

37. Jill Forbes and Michael Kelly, *French Cultural Studies* (New York: Oxford University Press, 1995), 239.

38. Barthes, "Ornamental Cookery," 78.

39. Ibid., 79.

40. Dean MacCannell, "Landscaping the Unconsciousness," in *The Meaning of Gardens,* ed. Mark Francis and Randolph T. Hester (Cambridge, Mass.: MIT Press, 1990), 95.

41. Ibid., 94.

42. Rousseau's *Julie, or, The New Héloïse* (1761), is quoted in ibid., 100.

43. The name *Estevan* was a telegraph code used by its original owner, Lord Mount Stephen.

44. *Decadent forest* is a forestry term for a stand losing volume because of decay that will continue to decay because it is left untouched.

45. Elsie inherited Estevan from her uncle, Lord Mount Stephen, who established it as a fishing retreat in the nineteenth century.

46. Jean-Jacques Rousseau, *Emile or On Education* (1762), trans. and annot. Allan Bloom (New York: Basic Books, 1979), 345.

47. The London paper is quoted in Simmonds, *The Curiosities of Food,* 266.

48. The actual menus for Estevan are not extant. *Saumon à la Humbert Ier* was a popular dish of that day, but Reford may not have served it.

49. Trubek, *Haute Cuisine,* 118–119.

50. Michael Hough, "Canada," in *The Oxford Companion to Gardens,* ed. Sir Geoffrey and Susan Jellicoe (Oxford: Oxford University Press, 1986), 89.

51. Reford also excelled in domesticating thirty-five species of *Lilium,* including temperamental varieties such as *Lilium martagon "album."*

52. John Beardsley, "Artists' Statements," in his *Earthworks and Beyond: Contemporary Art in the Landscape* (New York: Abbeville Press, 1984), 133.

53. I am grateful to Elsie Reford's great-grandson, Alexander Reford, for this information.

4

CONSUMING THE COLONIES

PATRICIA MORTON

The Negro restaurant opens, with its terraces and basements. Squadrons of blacks clothed in white—Bambaras, Toucouleurs—maneuver among the tables under the guidance of French maîtres d'hôtel. Their singing voices emit raucous accents and they laugh with all their white teeth. We enter and choose our menu. Today, it is Guinea's day, and Senegal's tomorrow. I notice the hors-d'œuvres in Conakry fashion, mutton with Mamou rice and, oh marvel! next to the fruits of Guinea and the Senegalese rice, the name of a dish that leaves me dreaming: Saint-Louis calf brains with a Faidherbe sauce. Through the minor arts, introducing us to regional dishes, we have discovered culinary France. Is the Colonial Exposition going to reveal to us a worldwide gastronomy? We hope, nevertheless, that there will be no restaurant reserved for cannibals[.][1]

The 1931 Colonial Exposition in Paris was a cornucopia of strange sights, tastes, smells, drink, and food.[2] A "bouquet of local color" flavored by vanilla, rum, saffron, and coffee, the Exposition proffered olfactory and gastronomic delights amid a visual efflorescence of exotic architecture. The Exposition promised an easily digested taste of the colonies, a processed and domesticated sensory experience that swallowed up the visitor in a temporary wonderment that was

4.1
Café at the French West Africa
section, 1931 International Colonial
Exposition, Paris. From *L'Illustration*,
special issue (July 1931), n.p.

easily sloughed off outside the fairgrounds. Food and architecture at the Exposition reinforced the differences between the colonizing French and their subject peoples and demonstrated the alien quality of other cultures. For the commentators of the time, the very taste of a rum cocktail or a couscous evoked the foreign nature of indigenous civilization.

Paul-Emile Cadilhac's account of the Exposition's food might seem to foreshadow today's fusion cuisines—food fashions melded by the global, multicultural migrations of the recent past—but in 1931, there was little endorsement of mixing ingredients or cultures into new hybrids. Whatever blending occurred was usually considered beneficial only to the colonized people, taking the form of "civilization" and economic development, or was ignored. The colonies were meant to be assimilated and absorbed into France and the other colonial empires under the colonizers' dominance. Spicy flavors and native huts were equally incompatible with the great cuisines and edifices of Western civilization. Official events such as the Colonial Exposition disregarded the reciprocal relationship and mutual influence of France and her colonies. My essay will look at this gap and provide some reasons for it.

The guest at the Colonial Exposition could safely sample exotic delicacies and stroll through faraway places without fear of compromised taste. Food and drink aided the visitor's immersion in a colonial environment fabricated out of monumentalized native buildings. According to Maurice Tranchant, the railroad circumnavigating the Exposition traversed "a great setting featuring elephants or tigers. . . . Negro waiters in the cafés, and exotic restaurants where one savors the food of all colonies" (figure 4.1). The novelist Paul Morand described the Guadeloupe pavilion as set "among guavas, parallel to gems set with crystallized sugar, among the odors of vanilla in braids, cola powder, balls of snowy cotton, sacks of Basse-Terre coffee, jars of liquor, [where] a rum shop retails small glasses of tafia rum." In the view of Paul-Emile Cadilhac, the Grand Avenue of the Colonies, the Exposition's main axis, was a panoply of sensual stimuli: "One strolls along the Grand Avenue of the French Colonies . . . [when] constructions spring up to the right and the left, topped by a radiant dome while the muffled roll of the tambourines, backing up the piercing Arab flutes, mixes the nostalgia of the old Orient with the stamping of the crowd, the guttural cries of the merchants, the odors of cooking drenched with oil."[3]

As the "Tour of the World in One Day," the Colonial Exposition inventoried the cultures and peoples of the world without the inconvenience and danger of global travel. In his description of a "promenade across the five continents," Cadilhac counseled travel-weary visitors to try the Exposition: "I advise those travelers who dread voyages around the world to pass by the Exposition. There, neither rolling nor pitching; sea sickness is unknown. . . . Distances are abolished, the oceans suppressed, and this is not the least of the miracles realized by Marshal Lyautey."[4] The Exposition also reproduced touristic sites and attractions, such as the Tunisian section, where one could find "Moorish cafés, sellers of fritters and *rahat-lokoum,* a reconstitution of the souks of the Madiva, a fort from the time of Charles-Quint, a minaret, an Arab house, and a *marabou* under an olive tree"[5] (figure 4.2). Separated from Paris and the subversive influences and politics found there, the Colonial Exposition was a hermetic world constructed within its own synchronous time. Contemporary realities in the colonies, such as the anticolonial riots and famine in Indochina, were ignored in favor of a "timeless," deracinated picture of indigenous cultures and peoples, carefully isolated within the Exposition precinct.

The colonial sections offered flavors, smells, and sights unavailable in Paris proper. The visitor could experience a relocation of ordinary taste toward the forbidden and the excluded (figure 4.3). For example, contemporary accounts emphasized the tropical drinks and exotic dances found in the Caribbean pavilions, which accentuated the torrid atmosphere that the French associated with Creole culture: "Tired, we sit down in front of the Martinique pavilion. They mix there cold punches of a taste infinitely superior to the brutal cocktails of Anglo-Saxon America. Mulattos, quadroons of a slightly copper tint dance and sing delicious dances and songs."[6] The theme of rum-induced intoxication, seductive music, and sensuous dance appeared repeatedly in articles about the Exposition, echoing popular myth and the Exposition's own press releases. Odors and sounds were particularly potent means for stimulating sensual responses from French observers: "A strong odor of vanilla! Under walls of violent stains of red, green, yellow, blue. We are in the Martinique pavilion, so gay, so spruce. . . . Sounds of its snuffling fifes and accordions attract visitors to a bar where the rum and coffee of the Antilles run in profusion, while on the floor of a neighboring room move black dancers well known in the *bals nègres* of rue Blomet."[7]

PATRICIA MORTON

Exposition Coloniale Internationale de Paris 1931.

2078. SECTION TUNISIENNE. Le Café Maure.

V. Valensi Architecte D.P.L.G.

4.2
Moorish Café at the Tunisian
section, 1931 International
Colonial Exposition, Paris,
postcard. Collection of the author.

4.3
Bar at the Martinique pavilion,
1931 International Colonial
Exposition, Paris. From *L'Illustration*,
special issue (July 1931), n.p.

One observer asserted, however, that the Colonial Exposition's North African food would only make visitors fonder of French cuisine. "Visitors will have . . . couscous, *méchouis* (sausage), *tajine (tadjiu)* with olives, which will complete their impression of the Magreb and perhaps even make them, on their return, appreciate the cuisine of France better."[8] Paul-Emile Cadilhac's narrative of the Colonial Exposition rehearsed this preference for familiar, bourgeois cuisine:

> *Dead beat, exhausted, dazzled, I can no longer distinguish where I am: China, Tonkin, Africa? My eyes burn, my head wobbles. Only smell still remains and it works well. An aroma of garlicky sausages titillates me and makes me sneeze. I open an eye. Where am I? In a clearing, some people sit on the grass—a whole family of petit bourgeois or workers—eating with an appetite that gives me pleasure. Cooked meats circulate, liters [of wine] travel, a flowering of papers blooms among the trees. This familiar spectacle reassures me: it is Paris, it is Vincennes, and classic in such a place.*[9]

The food, drink, and entertainment offered at the Colonial Exposition were necessary supplements to its sober, didactic pavilions and exhibits, constructed to give an inspiring lesson of French colonialism's benefits. Previous expositions had included pavilions devoted to colonial or foreign food and drink, such as the tea hut at the 1867 Universal Exposition in Paris. But unlike its predecessor expositions and colonial sections, which were largely carnivalesque entertainments of exotic titillation, the Colonial Exposition purported to convey information to the French public in a serious manner. As the Exposition's organizers stated, "This is why the pavilions of the French and foreign colonies are, in their principal aspects, authentic reproductions of monuments of a characteristic exoticism, stylizations of an excellent taste, capable of offering vibrant syntheses to the gaze and the mind."[10] The Exposition's architecture was to demonstrate the "facts" of French colonization and of the racial hierarchies and cultural divisions between the colonizing nations and their native subjects.

The premise that architecture can explain the past and future evolution of a society was central to the discipline of human geography, which influenced the Exposition's architectural program. Paul Vidal de la Blache, the principal theoretician of French human geography, believed that architecture and food could be read as evidence of a society's *genre de vie* (mode of life), its level of evolution, the physical resources available to it, and its social "character" and structure. In his view, everything from religion to the intelligence of a people is visible in its *genre de vie*. According to Vidal's theory, each society (or civilization, in his terms), developed through the interaction of the racial characteristics of its people and their response to their *milieu* (environment). For example, "The equipment that the Kirghiz devised to meet the requirements of his unsettled life—the shape of his tent and the cut of his clothes—is a perfectly integrated whole, in which everything has its place, the materialization of a mode of life."[11] The most fruitful *milieu* provided its occupants frequent contact with other peoples, life in a temperate climate, and the natural resources with which to develop high-level technology and agriculture.

Vidal maintained that non-European societies' intellectual and cultural development were retarded or arrested by the limitations inherent in their race, their physical isolation from other societies, or by a lack of natural resources or a beneficial climate in their milieu: "The African village whose site may be changed by a mere accident, and the European village whose history is traceable for thousands of years, are widely different as the city of antiquity and the immense metropolis of today. The distance is that between a rudimentary and an advanced stage of civilisation."[12] The relative hierarchy of races and their evolutionary capacities could not change, in this view—a conception represented at the Colonial Exposition. Geographers assumed that the physical and social conditions producing *genres de vie* were static, although they acknowledged historic, distant contacts.[13] Human geography, and therefore the Colonial Exposition, failed to account for the mutual influences sponsored by centuries of European exploration and colonization.

The proliferation of exotic food at the Colonial Exposition was, in fact, evidence of the extensive culinary and cultural exchange effected by imperialism. Hybrid cuisines (curry, chutney, chop suey, gumbo, "French" fries) resulted from global colonization and diasporic movement, along with other forms of cultural mixture. Couscous is cooked with tomatoes and potatoes brought from the New World; corn appears in Italian polenta; and American manioc, peanuts, and peppers are staples of African cuisine. Consuming the exotic—their ingredients, spices, and condiments—has been a favored method for assimilating other cultures. Bland Western taste has been improved by addition of savage flavors from distant sources, an imperial attitude that survives in "multicultural" appreciation for exotic cuisine. The international taste for

4.4
Belle Jardinière advertisement.
From *L'Illustration*, special issue
(July 1931), n.p.

PATRICIA MORTON

sugar, for example, transformed modern trade; produced diasporas of Africans, central Asians, and Europeans; and created new types of wealth and poverty. The anthropologist Sidney Mintz asserts that the plantation products of coffee, rum, tobacco, and especially sugar formed part of "a complex of 'proletarian hunger-killers,' and played a crucial role in the linked contributions that Caribbean slaves, Indian peasants, and European urban proletarians were able to make to the growth of western civilization."[14]

Colonization encouraged the dissemination of foods from colonized areas to Europe and to other colonies—tomatoes, corn, potatoes, and chocolate originated in the Americas, for example—and, simultaneously, stimulated colonizers to import food and goods from their home countries in an effort to distinguish their eating habits from those of the natives (figure 4.4). This reciprocal exchange of foodstuffs and methods did not generate an "international cuisine" during the age of conquest; instead, it accentuated European awareness of national identities and created new culinary hierarchies. One food historian notes, "Formerly, the patterns of eating had been divided horizontally. The food of the rich in Europe, like that of the poor, had a great deal in common, regardless of country. But a vertical division now also emerged, and the cuisines of individual countries began to take on consciously individual characteristics."[15] The rise of nation-states and the emergence of separate national identities increased the importance of what had been regional culinary traditions and their distinction from other food cultures.

The refinement of both classic French food and architecture mirrored such developments and was a buttress against the insidious effects of foreign influences. The French were concerned to preserve the "Frenchness" of their products against inferior races and degenerate cultures. By the nineteenth century, a reaction against the adoption of exotic ingredients caused chefs and architects alike to eradicate "non-French" aspects from their work. From the Enlightenment until World War II, classicism dominated French architectural training and practice, codified at the official school of architecture, the Ecole des Beaux-Arts, and patronized in state commissions.[16] Exotic architectural vocabularies, borrowed from Asian, North African, and Middle Eastern sources, appeared in French civic and commercial structures only if they had a "colonial" association, such as the Ecole Coloniale, or were entertainment buildings, such as theaters, cinemas, zoos, casinos, or park kiosks.[17]

In French food practices, spices fell out of favor as too "foreign," a symbol of cultural difference, and a vestige of the medieval aristocratic taste for excessively spiced dishes. François Pierre de La Varenne, author in 1651 of the first modern French treatise on food, frowned on the use of spices, and the famous gastronomic critic Jean Anthelme Brillat-Savarin (1755–1826) did not even mention the use of spices in his treatise.[18] After World War I, local French food was recorded and preserved as a valuable part of France's distinctive character, as opposed to the dangerously cosmopolitan cuisines influenced by foreign cultures. This French character was enshrined in regional folklores, which were recorded in the interwar period in an effort to preserve and celebrate local, oral customs outside the national culture.[19]

The French obsession with food and its nationalist connotations forms a critical example of what Roland Barthes called a "commemorative impulse":

> Food permits a person (and I am here speaking of French themes) to partake each day of the national past. In this case, this historical quality is obviously linked to food techniques (preparation and cooking). . . . They are, we are told, the repository of a whole experience, of the accumulated wisdom of our ancestors. . . . [T]hrough his food the Frenchman experiences a certain national continuity. By way of a thousand detours, food permits him to insert himself daily into his own past and to believe in a certain culinary "being" of France.[20]

Barthes held that food encapsulates national character and allows access to the essential "French character" guarded in contemporary food as well as in folkloric studies. In his view, French food was a constitutive ingredient in French civilization as the result of historical experience. Like Proust's famous madeleine, which evoked a whole world and the past simultaneously, Barthes's construction of French food in general could summon the collective memory of the French nation. The nation did not encompass the colonies, in this case, but was confined to l'Hexagone, the historic French provinces.

In French culture, a simple taste in food and a gluttonous appetite were obvious signs of a lack of civilization. Gluttony, excessive consumption, and an unrefined palate revealed an absence of civilized training and were anachronistic vestiges of earlier practices and the aristocratic privilege of excess. The "civilizing of appetite," according to the food historian Stephen Mennell, was related to better food supplies, colonial conquest, and such civilizing processes as the transformation of table manners: "The increased security of food supplies was made possible by the extension of trade, the progressive division of labour in a growing commercial economy, and also by the process of state-formation and internal pacification."[21] Through the civilizing of appetite, delicacy, discrimination, and self-restraint became bourgeois values in the seventeenth and eighteenth centuries.

In its description of the Colonial Exposition, the daily *Le Matin* gave an account of life at the Exposition among the West African natives that featured food and its appreciation.

> *In the corner of a cabin, a Toucouleur woman, the headband of her coiffure in the form of a diadem, prepares the evening meal. Her name is Dalanda Diallo.*
>
> *A great devil of a gendarme from the Sudan, with the barred dolmen of the military medal and many other decorations, serves us as interpreter. Miss Dalanda Diallo is very shy with whites. She made the amusing faces of a schoolgirl.*
>
> *—"Yes, yes. Very happy to have come to France. But is there no sun here? It would be so amusing if it didn't rain!"*
>
> *—"Good food! Better meat than back home . . . More abundant . . . good fish also . . . But no manioc flour . . . Instead, rice, potatoes, split peas, tomatoes . . . And the peppers! . . . And the oil! . . ."*
>
> *And Miss Dalanda Diallo, who must be a* gourmande *in her own way, passed a very red tongue over her lips in thinking of the peppers and the oil.*
>
> *—"In the morning, sweet coffee!" the gendarme explained to me while clicking his heels.*
>
> *And he laughed to himself the good laugh of the infant* gourmand *in dreaming of the sweet coffee of tomorrow morning.*[22]

This description of Ms. Diallo's uncultivated palate demonstrated her naïveté, even gullibility, regarding food and her budding taste for "better" (French) flavors. The description of her "schoolgirl" charm and the gendarme's infant *gourmandisme* reiterated the French conception that natives, especially Africans, were childlike, unfit to govern themselves. Food and taste, therefore, were indicators of civilization predicated on race, education, and level of evolution.

The use of *gourmand(e)* when describing Ms. Diallo's and the soldier's tastes pertained to the association of *gourmandise* with gluttony.[23] Brillat-Savarin defined *gourmandise* as "a passionate, rational and habitual preference for all that flatters the palate."[24] The *gourmand* is, however, an amateur, not an expert practitioner of the culinary arts, as is the *gastronome*. Brillat-Savarin claimed he could detect the true *gastronome* by means of "les éprouvettes gastronomiques," little gastronomic tests: "We mean by this expression food renowned for their flavor and of such indisputable excellence that their mere appearance must evoke, in a man of well-ordered character, all the powers of the palate." Those in whom these dishes provoked no "spark of desire" or "ecstatic radiance" could be marked as unworthy of the occasion and its pleasures. The little test is "a power-gauge which must be differently calibrated for different levels of society." It could identify what Brillat-Savarin labeled the "false *gastronome*," who is "almost always a gross eater, fat and proud of it, who is almost totally ignorant in matters of cookery."[25] Dalanda Diallo and the Sudanese gendarme could be *gourmands* but never *gastronomes*, since they lacked the refinement of palate and discernment required and they were not trained in the delicate eating habits of French culture and cuisine.

Other descriptions of the Exposition echoed the dominant French view that native culinary practices and culture revealed a crude appreciation of food and a fundamentally lower evolutionary development among the natives. Their excessive consumption of food and drink, along with unrestrained bodily movement and a general lack of corporeal control, indicated a lower degree of civilization. For example, Tranchant wrote: "The noise of tambourines troubles the peace of the Negro village. Around a statue of a divinity, the fanatics dance until falling with exhaustion. The sorcerers, disappearing under their bizarre ornaments, shake their fetishes. The chief of the tribe assists these choreographic and sacred revels with his watching; and the ceremony ends with a sumptuous feast and copious libations."[26] The Colonial Exposition displayed such spectacles as part of its entertainment programs, complements to the primitive architecture of the colonial pavilions (figure 4.5). Housed in hybridized reproductions of native architecture, natives exhibited their essential degeneracy and distance from French civilization.

At the Exposition, however, native architecture could not achieve quite the same level of uncivilized unrestraint as food, since it was the inauthentic fruit of French

4.5
Dance performance, French West
African section, 1931 International
Colonial Exposition, Paris. From M.
Cloche, *60 aspects de l'Exposition
Coloniale* (Paris: Studio Deberny
Peignot, 1931), n.p.

architects' imagination. The Exposition pavilions were designed by French, Beaux-Arts-trained architects, many of whom had no experience with or direct knowledge of native architecture in the colonies. Their training militated against the pure reproduction of native degeneracy, since French architecture was founded on Enlightenment disinterest and a metaphysical mission. The highest level of architecture was more than the mere provision of shelter or physical comfort, according to Pierre Lavedan, architectural historian at the Ecole des Beaux-Arts: "All architecture worthy of the name therefore consists of more than answering a physical need; it is a spiritual as much as a material work."[27] Architecture was part of the taste institutions that had maintained French greatness, the classical systems of distinction established during the Sun King's reign.

During the nineteenth century and early twentieth century, the discourse of restraint and civilization developed such that distinctions between races and cultures were gauged by eating habits, tastes, and table manners. In *Princess Tam-Tam* (1935), for example, Josephine Baker enacted the French fear of gluttony or excess as a marker of degeneracy and savagery. As Alwina, the primitive Algerian girl, Baker initially exhibited the unrestrained appetite characteristic of the uncivilized. In an early scene, Alwina eats couscous without control, showing her "natural" appetite and absence of manners—excesses that are tamed by her gradual adherence to a civilized schedule of meals and her superficial adoption of proper manners. Alwina's transformation is one of gustatory regulation; as the cultural historian Elizabeth Ezra notes, "The shepherdess Alwina's first lesson in civilization sets the stage for all those to come: after marveling that the French are able to discipline their appetites to correspond with mealtimes, she is told, 'A stomach can be civilized.'"[28] Alwina's white, male sponsors transform her into a princess from mythical "Parador" with the manners and appetites appropriate to royalty. She is accepted into Parisian society until her origins betray her when she cannot keep from dancing wildly to the tam-tam drums played at a Parisian party, a debacle anticipated in the title of the film. Her abandon of bodily control signals her redescent into an atavistic state of primitivism that her recent civilizing could not resist.

Such manifestations of cultural degeneracy justified colonialism's "civilizing mission": the eventual transformation of the colonies into extensions of French civilization. French food, especially bread, was introduced in colonies like Algeria as part of this colonization process.[29] While the colonies needed French civilization and technology to advance beyond their rudimentary level of evolution, according to the doctrine of the time, the French believed that their culture and food could learn little from the colonies. Neither French cuisine nor French architecture could accommodate the infiltration of outside flavors, which might adulterate the fragile integrity of French taste. The inability to tolerate foreign cooking echoes in every French discussion of their attitudes toward foreigners, argues the historian Theodore Zeldin: "Food isolates the French almost as much as their language."[30]

Some critics echoed this xenophobia in a hostile attitude toward "colonial" art and architecture that combined French traditions with native forms. There were those who asserted the quintessential incompatibility of indigenous and French cultures. Raymond Cogniat's critique of the Colonial Exposition's architecture, for instance, equated native styles with an intoxicating and indigestible cocktail:

> There is in the art of Asia something that escapes our sensibility, a refinement that we understand but that does not suit our temperament. In African art, there is a spontaneous force, an instinct that we will never assimilate. Both remain strangers to us: their refinement is perceptible to us, but we do not accept it with serenity. It is like a too strong drink whose merits we appreciate but that leaves us stupefied.[31]

Others more sympathetic to indigenous culture viewed Europe's dominion as inherently corrupting. The Orientalist writer and amateur of the exotic Pierre Mille likened the results of Western influence on native architecture to rotten produce that would sicken both its native and French progenitors: "Indigenous architecture disappears or only gives mediocre, unhealthy fruits. We cannot profit by it. But our architecture arrives, still full of energy. It makes a graft with this indigenous architecture, or it hybridizes with it."[32] While some palatable fruit had been produced in Morocco, Mille believed, most such hybrids were not fertile. He maintained that indigenous and European styles became mixed when the native woman grew fascinated by department store fashions. She repudiated the simple, chaste traditions of Arab architecture in favor of unsavory, inappropriate rooms and interior decoration.[33]

Although these critics were cool to the idea of a hybrid architecture based on French absorption of indigenous art and architecture, other thinkers, like former

4.6

Cartoon. From Jean Camp and
André Corbier, *A Lyauteyville,
Promenades sentimentales et
humoresques à l'Exposition
Coloniale* (Paris: Société nationale
d'éditions artistiques, 1931).

Minister of the Colonies Albert Sarraut, advocated a rejuvenating draught from the colonies as a cure for a decadent, enervated Europe. Sarraut rejected explicitly "Orientalizing" or "Africanizing" the art of the Occident—or the reverse operation on indigenous art—but perceived possible beneficial effects from the vitality of the colonies. Like a reviving potion, the colonies could provide Europe the means for its rebirth: "Our antique and illustrious Europe, having burned with too many ardors in matters of art and the spirit, has need of an influx of young vigor in its desiccated arteries." The originality, inspiration, observation of nature, and sumptuous technique of the arts of these "minor brothers" could result in "a splendid renaissance" for European culture.[34]

The Colonial Exposition repeated this consumption of other cultures: France, as host nation, used her colonies as a foil for her political, cultural, and culinary ascendancy. By displaying the cultures of subject peoples—which turned out to be overflavored, tasteless, or repugnant to the "civilized" observer—the colonizing states absorbed them into their empires and created renewed chains of being.[35] Alphonso Lingis observes, "But in traveling from country to country, being served like the emperor by every alien culture in restaurants where any substance, any living plant or animal, is laid out for our consumption, each of us situates ourselves in the food chain at the top, making self the uneaten one, the unexchangeable value, the cosmic dignity."[36] As a substitute for travel, the Exposition provided the average visitor with the elite's experience of colonial difference, a precursor of Club Med and Disneyland. Packaged to place the visitor in the *sahib's* shoes, the Exposition enabled the ontological reorientation of the viewer without responsibility or discomfort (figure 4.6). This consumption was a kind of cannibalism, since the colonies were ostensibly absorbed into the body of *La Plus Grande France* (Greater France). Sarraut's image of a roguish Europe ingesting her younger brothers is just one example of the consumption of the colonies. Europe assimilated her possessions with an ambivalence expressed in metaphors of excess, revulsion, and regret, clearly unable to digest the colonies whole and unable to subsist without them.

NOTES

1. Paul-Emile Cadilhac, "Promenade à travers les cinq continents," *L'Illustration* (May 1931), n.p. Bambaras and Toucouleurs are ethnic groups in West Africa. Conakry (Conakri) is the capital of Guinea, and Mamou is a region in Guinea. Louis Faidherbe, a general in the French army, was governor of Senegal (1854–1861, 1863–1865), where he "pacified" native groups and transformed the colony into the dominant political and military power in West Africa. See André Demaison, *Faidherbe* (Paris: Librairie Plon, [1932]).

2. For a full account of the Exposition, see my *Hybrid Modernities: Architecture and Representation at the 1931 International Colonial Exposition in Paris* (Cambridge, Mass.: MIT Press, 2000).

3. Maurice Tranchant, *Le tour du monde en un jour à l'Exposition Coloniale* (Paris: Studio du Palmier Nain, 1931), [20–21]; Paul Morand, "Rien que la terre à l'Exposition Coloniale," *La Revue des Deux Mondes* 101 (July 15, 1931): 336; Paul-Emile Cadilhac, "Une heure en Tunisie," *L'Illustration* 89, no. 4603 (1931): n.p.

4. Cadilhac, "Une heure en Tunisie," n.p. Louis Hubert Gonzalve Lyautey was the *commissaire général* of the 1931 Colonial Exposition and had been governor of Morocco, as well as a participant in colonial military conquests in Indochina and Madagascar. See Louis Hubert Gonzalve Lyautey, *Lyautey l'africain—textes et lettres du Maréchal Lyautey,* ed. Pierre Lyautey, 4 vols. (Paris: Calmann-Lévy, 1962), and Alan Scham, *Lyautey of Morocco: Protectorate Administration, 1912–1925* (Berkeley: University of California Press, 1970).

5. Jean Gallotti, "L'Afrique du Nord," *L'Art Vivant* 7, no. 151 (1931): 394.

6. Pierre Mille, "A l'Exposition Coloniale: Vue d'ensemble," *La Revue des Deux Mondes* 101 (May 15, 1931): 284.

7. Henri Cossira, "Martinique, Guadeloupe, Réunion, Madagascar, Indes Françaises," *L'Art Vivant* 7, no. 151 (1931): 397. The Bal Nègre, located on rue Blomet in Montparnasse, featured orchestras from the French West Indies rather than the American jazz popular at other venues. See Tyler Stovall, *Paris Noir: African Americans in the City of Light* (Boston: Houghton Mifflin, 1996), 97–98.

8. Pierre Paraf, "L'Afrique du Nord," *L'Illustration* 89, no. 4603 (May 23, 1931): n.p.

9. Cadilhac, "Promenade," n.p.

10. "Considérations générales sur l'esthétique de l'Exposition Coloniale," ed. Marcel Olivier, *Rapport Général* 5, no. 1 (Paris: Imprimerie Nationale, 1932), 390.

11. Paul Vidal de la Blache, *Principles of Human Geography,* trans. Millicent Todd Bingham (New York: Henry Holt, 1926), 163, 323 (quotation).

12. Ibid., 183, 186, 255, 272; quotation, 163.

13. See Anne Buttimer, *Society and Milieu in the French Geographic Tradition* (Chicago: Rand McNally, 1971).

14. Sidney W. Mintz, "The Caribbean as a Socio-cultural Area," *Cahiers d'Histoire Mondiale* 9 (1966): 916–941; quotation, 917.

15. Reay Tannahill, *Food in History* (New York: Stein and Day, 1973), 242.

16. See Arthur Drexler, ed., *The Architecture of the Ecole des Beaux-Arts* (New York: Museum of Modern Art; Cambridge, Mass.: MIT Press, 1977).

17. See Nadine Beauthéac and François-Xavier Bouchart, *L'Europe exotique* (Paris: Chêne, 1986).

18. Tannahill, *Food in History,* 283. See François Pierre de La Varenne, *Le cuisinier françois* (1651); Jean Anthelme Brillat-Savarin, *Physiologie du gout, ou Méditations de gastronomie transcendante* (Paris: Sautelet, 1826).

19. See Shannan Peckham, "Consuming Nations," in *Consuming Passions: Food in the Age of Anxiety,* ed. Sian Griffiths and Jennifer Wallace (Manchester: Mandolin, 1998), 174.

20. Roland Barthes, "Toward a Psychosociology of Contemporary Food Consumption" (1961), in *Food and Culture: A Reader,* ed. Carole Counihan and Penny Van Esterik (New York: Routledge, 1997), 24.

21. Stephen Mennell, "On the Civilizing of Appetite," in Counihan and Van Esterik, eds., *Food and Culture,* 326.

22. "A la veille de l'ouverture de l'Exposition Coloniale: Une visite aux noirs de l'Afrique occidentale française," *Le Matin,* May 5, 1931, 1–3.

23. The food historian Jean-Louis Flandrin describes an earlier distinction between *gourmandise,* the deadly sin of gluttony, and *friandise,* the love of good food and the art of recognizing it. See Flandrin, "Introduction: The Early Modern Period," in *Food: A Culinary History from Antiquity to the Present,* under the dir. of Jean-Louis Flandrin and Massimo Montanari, English ed. Albert Sonnenfeld, trans. Clarissa Botsford [et al.] (New York: Penguin, 2000), 364–365.

24. Brillat-Savarin, quoted in Prosper Montagné, *Larousse gastronomique: The Encyclopedia of Food, Wine, and Cooking,* ed. Charlotte Turgeon and Nina Froud, trans. Nina Froud [et al.] (New York: Crown, 1961), 472.

25. Ibid., 457–458.

26. Tranchant, *Le tour du monde,* [15].

27. Pierre Lavedan, *French Architecture* (London: Penguin, 1956), 51.

28. Elizabeth Ezra, *The Colonial Unconscious: Race and Culture in Interwar France* (Ithaca: Cornell University Press, 2000), 113, 115.

29. In a study of Algerian food consumption before and after French rule, Willy Jansen finds that bread has been an important arena for colonial domination, resistance to colonial repression, and Algerian nationalism (Jansen, "French Bread and Algerian Wine: Conflicting Identities in French Algeria," in *Food, Drink, and Identity: Cooking, Eating, and Drinking in Europe Since the Middle Ages,* ed. Peter Scholliers [Oxford: Berg, 2001], 195–218).

30. Theodore Zeldin, "Expensive v Cheap," in *The Faber Book of Food,* ed. Claire Clifton and Colin Spencer (London: Faber and Faber, 1993), 67.

31. Raymond Cogniat, "L'Exposition Coloniale (Les palais métropolitains, les colonies étrangères, les pays sous mandat)," *L'Architecture* 44, no. 9 (1931): 339.

32. Pierre Mille, *Au Maroc: Chez les fils de l'ombre et du soleil* (Paris: Firmin-Didot, 1931), 94.

33. Ibid.

34. Albert Sarraut, "L'Exposition Coloniale," *L'Art Vivant* 7, no. 151 (August 1931): 373.

35. "Race was defined through the criterion of civilization, with the cultivated white Western European male at the top, and everyone else on a hierarchical scale either in a chain of being, from mollusc to God, or, in the later model, on an evolutionary scale of development from a feminized state of childhood (savagery) up to full (European) manly adulthood" (Robert J. C. Young, *Colonial Desire: Hybridity in Theory, Culture, and Race* [London: Routledge, 1995], 94).

36. Alphonso Lingis, "Appetite," in *Eating Culture,* ed. Ron Scapp and Brian Seitz (Albany: State University of New York Press, 1998), 127.

5

LOCAL FOOD PRODUCTS, ARCHITECTURE, AND TERRITORIAL IDENTITY

FERRUCCIO TRABALZI

Much of the built environment is designed around food: producing, storing, transporting and selling, serving, and eating it. Recently, plans to regenerate sectors of the urban economy have also been organized around the production and consumption of food. In many cities, the socioeconomic base of old neighborhoods has been revamped in large measure around the opening of new cafés, restaurants, and specialty food shops.[1] Combining architecture with food has indeed become a favorite development strategy of many city planners, developers, and architects around the world. My interest in the crossover between food and architecture especially concerns the issue of economic identity of places and, in particular, how food traditions, local food products, and architecture can be deliberately combined and recombined to foster economic development in rural areas.

As the case of the wine-producing regions of France and Italy amply shows, anchoring local food products and food tradition to culture and place generates locational advantages that reverberate positively throughout the regional economy (e.g., Champagne, Valle del Chianti). Indeed, European policy makers explicitly recognize that the promotion of food products having specific characteristics may be the "trumpcard" for the rural world.[2] To this end, the European Union has instituted designations guaranteeing the origins and typicality of food products: Protected Designation of Origin (PDO), Protected Geographical Indication (PGI), and Traditional Speciality Guaranteed (TSG). Such labels identify products whose qualities are due essentially or exclusively to the geographical environment of production, including natural and human factors.[3] The certification of origins does not create local traditions from scratch, even though the use of these labels could help in recovering lost traditions and products. Instead, these labels invest local culture and know-how with a market value that can be exploited for development purposes.

Tuscany provides a classic example of how to create a successful regional identity with a formidable market appeal by conjoining local culture, architecture, food products, and simple food traditions. A careful restoration of the built environment (churches, historical centers, towers, villas), a well-orchestrated series of actions to protect the natural and agricultural landscapes, and worldwide promotion have transformed what were essentially isolated rural backwaters into destination spots for art and food lovers from around the world.[4] Tuscany is not the only region that has combined local food products with architecture to promote local development. Apart from the much-heralded wine and cheese regions of France, one could mention the success of the Napa Valley in northern California and of Stellenbosch in South Africa's Western Cape. In both instances, the blend of local resources and know-how, such as wine production, and architecture—modern in the Napa Valley, seventeenth-century Dutch colonial in South Africa—has created an economically viable regional identity with an international appeal.

Indeed, not every rural area is endowed in the same way and not all regions have proactive local institutions and entrepreneurs such as Tuscany has had since the 1960s. It is therefore very difficult to create marketable local identities by simply imitating successful cases from other regions; as a result, the process of identity creation through architecture and food can be fairly slow and inefficient. Such has been the case for many rural areas in southern Italy. Today, thanks to the EU policies of product certification as well as to a new entrepreneurial mentality among many local producers, these same areas are witnessing a period of economic renaissance. In the Sele River Plain south of Salerno—a region famous for its production of buffalo mozzarella, its natural beauty, and its archaeological sites—identity building has proceeded through at times conflicting dimensions. The creation of a territorial identity in this region pivots around the idea of the rural world not only as a space of production but also as a space for consumption; it starts with the promotion of local food traditions, products, and methods of production and ends with the reevaluation of rural ways of life more generally.[5] Central to such a process is the transformation of the working farm—*azienda agricola*—from a utilitarian into a polyvalent site of production as well as of intensive cultural life.

The architectural historian Kurt Forster hints at local traditions when he examines the origins of the Renaissance villa in northern and central Italy during the quattrocento.[6] In his analysis, Forster looks at the transformation of the farmhouse—*fattoria, casa colonica*—into a villa and criticizes the argument that such an innovation was based solely on "painstaking reconstruction of late antique models." In fact, he highlights the central role played by vernacular typologies and territorial building practices as frames of reference for architects and patrons alike. In particular, he points out that the achievements of fifteenth- and early-sixteenth-century architects should be seen as a "realization of vernacular building configurations in terms of neo-antique vocabulary."[7] Forster does not consider if and how the new building type reflected changes in the organization of production or in the perception of the countryside during the quattrocento. His perspective is that of the architectural historian interested in the evolution of building types and planning configurations isolated from the wider productive context. Thus he, like other architectural historians such as James Ackerman,[8] is disinclined to analyze the economic, cultural, and territorial connections between transformations at the level of single building types within the regional agricultural system. In other words, the analysis remains focused on the form and aesthetics of rural buildings and not on their function in the wider agricultural landscape.

As the agricultural historian Emilio Sereni notes, the Renaissance-style villa "was visibly tied to the need born from the evolution of new techniques and new agricultural relationships" and emerged in close relationship with the birth of the "bel-paesaggio" whereby Tuscan farmers and artisans begin to imprint more consciously elaborated forms on the agricultural landscape—rows of vines, avenues of cypresses.[9] When we consider rural architectures not by themselves but as part of a larger productive context, it is possible to understand change and continuity in building practices and typologies from a more complex perspective. Bringing the farmhouse back into such a productive context demonstrates the role that local typologies and building traditions can play today in shaping the economic and cultural identity of rural areas.

Rural architecture in the Sele River Plain, unlike that in north-central Italy, shows hardly any innovation at all. Yet the economic function of this seemingly homogeneous and monotonous architecture has produced innovation. The *azienda agricola* has become the distinctive feature in an emerging artistic and cultural landscape. The two cases presented here—a site of agrotourism, consisting of a buffalo farm and a cooking school, and an organic cheese farm with a museum and a cultural center—will help shed light on how territorial identities can be built and will highlight the specific role of local food and vernacular architecture in this process.

SHAPING THE ECONOMIC IDENTITY OF PLACES

Of the two major districts in Campania where it is produced, the Sele River Plain is where the production of buffalo mozzarella has maintained a closer association with traditional methods. From a production standpoint, such an association is possible today—that is, traditional methods are efficient and economically feasible—primarily because good-quality milk is available. Several factors are responsible for the milk's quality; not least is the capacity of buffalo breeders to contain contagious diseases such as brucellosis, a virus borne by air and water that moves from herd to herd and makes the milk unsuitable for human consumption unless pasteurized. Susceptibility to the devastating virus—infected herds have to be eliminated—is increased by intensive breeding. Everywhere in Campania intensive breeding has become the norm, but in the Sele Plain there is an important difference. While elsewhere the number of buffalo in production is increasing exponentially and farm sizes are shrinking, in the Sele Plain the number of buffalo is increasing at a lower rate and the average farm size remains the largest in the region. This translates into larger paddocks, with more space available for buffalo to roam, and therefore better sanitary conditions. The ability to produce milk unaffected by brucellosis is critical to keeping artisanal methods of production, because traditional buffalo mozzarella calls for the use of raw milk. It is thus no accident that a higher percentage of cheese makers who produce buffalo mozzarella with unpasteurized milk are located in the Sele Plain.

Also contributing to the maintenance of traditional methods in the Sele Plain are lower rates of urbanization and industrialization, which in other areas of the region have eroded the land available for breeding livestock. The determining factor, however, has been the approach taken to implementing the 1960s land reform. Unlike the rest of the region, in the Sele Plain land reform did not fragment the old baronial properties into small pieces of privately owned parcels. Though the reform allowed many farmers to buy land, the average size of these plots was not sufficient to sustain independent farming; therefore many of them were immediately resold to the previous owners, who were able to reconstitute their properties. As a direct consequence, many of the original buildings that were part of the old properties—farmhouses, baronial palaces, stables, and cheese houses—have not been lost. Rather, they have been maintained by the heirs and in many cases restored. This distinctiveness, missing from other areas of buffalo mozzarella production, has helped preserve sections of the agricultural landscape from land speculation.

Preservation of the agricultural landscape and its built environment is one proven method for developing a healthy tourist industry. In the Sele Plain, tourism is the second most important source of income after agriculture. During the summer, the population of the Sele Plain increases many times. An uncontaminated coastline attracts tourists from all over Europe, while the magnificent Greek temples of Paestum—the largest and best-preserved examples of Greek architecture outside the Valley of the Temples in Agrigento, Sicily—make the area a destination for art lovers from around the world. Likewise, the natural beauty of the mountainous Cilento region and the closeness to the famous Amalfi coast add luster to a tourist industry with a well-developed infrastructure—hotels, campsites, B&Bs, agrotourism. The tourist industry, even if only seasonal, is an incentive for local buffalo mozzarella producers to maintain or, more precisely, to believe in the economic viability of local traditions. Tourists, in fact, strengthen the market for local, especially fresh, food products. During the summer, hotels, restaurants, roadside kiosks, supermarkets, and grocery stores increase the demand for buffalo mozzarella to the point that some cheese houses are hard-pressed to satisfy it. It is not uncommon, in fact, for those visiting a cheese house at midday from June to September to find that the daily production has already sold out. Being able to sell on the spot mitigates the need of cheese makers to produce for distant markets; and a strong local market exists all year round, as mozzarella is considered a staple among locals.

When it comes to shaping the economic identity of rural areas, the target market—whether local or distant—makes all the difference in the world. Cheese makers who operate for export markets by necessity have to distance themselves from local conventions such as using raw milk, to ensure that their product will still be safe to eat when it reaches their intended customers. Export producers have to work within industrial parameters, processing larger batches of pasteurized milk by mechanized means. Furthermore, they have to address the problem of time and distance, which is usually resolved by putting the cheese in a sealed package filled with a stabilizing liquid. The end result is a standardized product removed as far as one can imagine from the "original," which not only is made for immediate consumption but also tastes different from cheese house to cheese house. In the case of buffalo mozzarella, targeting local rather than distant markets is the sine qua non for maintaining or, conversely, discarding local traditions of production.

Environmental, historical, and technological factors alone are not enough to guarantee a successful territorial identity, however. The local populations, in this case the network of food producers, must be able to take advantage of their resources—and to sense institutional opportunities—to create a coherent development project with market appeal. What follows are two cases of buffalo milk and mozzarella producers, chosen because they illustrate different strategies that such an agroproducer might adopt to deliberately pursue a territorial identity. The first case is that of Seliano, a family-run farm, agrotourism center, and culinary school; the second is Vannulo, a family-operated cheese house and buffalo farm that has become world famous by producing organic buffalo mozzarella in a perfectly restored rural setting.[10]

STRATEGY #1: DIVERSIFICATION INTO AGROTOURISM AND FOOD MAKING

The Seliano-Eliseo estate is located south of the Sele River between Capaccio Scalo and the temples of Paestum. The property is divided into two separate entities: Seliano proper, where the Bellelli family operates an agrotourism center, and Eliseo, where they have a farm with more than 600 buffalo. Although this is not the only agrotourism in the province of Salerno, and the Bellelli are not the only buffalo milk producers that are hoteliers as well, Seliano is indeed unique in having developed directly from a buffalo farm. Other agrotourism centers in the province of Salerno, particularly those located within the natural park of Cilento, have appeared as a direct consequence of the new EU agricultural policies, but the families who operate them are not necessarily farmers or buffalo breeders.[11]

Cecilia and her two sons, Ettore and Ernesto Massimino, manage Seliano and Eliseo using modern techniques profoundly rooted in local conventions. A functional division of labor allows the family to take advantage of the individual strengths of each of its members. Ettore is the most involved with the farm and is responsible for contacts with suppliers and with the cheese houses, while Massimino works mostly at Seliano as manager as well as evening cook. Cecilia also participates actively in the agrotourist business. She meets and greets her guests, coordinates the work in the kitchen, and at times prepares elaborate dishes such as *timballo di maccaroni*. Ettore and Massimino have been particularly shrewd in promoting Seliano as a place not only for taking summer vacations but also for celebrating weddings, baptisms, confirmations, graduations, and family reunions. Tapping into the "ceremonial" circuit and cultural habits of southern Italian families complements the activity of receiving tourists from all over the world. First, these particular ceremonies and events, unlike the tourist business, usually do not involve overnight stays. Second, they occur all year long, keeping Seliano open during the low season.

Cecilia does not fit the stereotype of the classic southern Italian mother. As she points out, "I am not at all *tutta casa e chiesa* (all house and church)." Indeed, she is not. Independent, eclectic, and well-educated (she speaks English and French), Cecilia has transformed her personal interests into a sustainable activity and in so doing has been able to strengthen the economic foundations of her family. She came up with the idea of transforming the underutilized rural compound at Seliano into an innovative project centered on promoting the history and tradition of local cuisine. With the help of a local architect, they adapted the old stables into a first-class restaurant and the nineteenth-century circular cheese house into a store displaying local food products. With the help of a Belgian tourist guide who decided to stay in Seliano more than fifteen years ago after his work brought him there, Seliano offers its visitors the option of visiting Naples, Capri, the Amalfi coast, and the ruins of Pompeii and Herculaneum. Local guides are hired for those wishing to visit the nearby Greek temples. Today,

Seliano's agrotourism is well known both within the circuit of food lovers in Italy and internationally, and the number of tourists who spend a few days there during the summer increases annually.

The estate produces its own extra virgin olive oil, liquors such as *limoncello* and *nocino* made with locally grown lemons and walnuts, and a wealth of jams and fruit preserves from their orchard. These products are served to guests for breakfast and also sold, according to availability. A staff of three local women, employed full-time, rigorously prepare homemade food. Seliano is also an enterprise of the extended family. Cecilia's sister, *signora* Anna, excels in desserts inspired by local traditions. She and her two daughters, who occasionally wait tables together with Ettore, prepare most of the elaborate cakes and sweets served. Working side by side with their employees until late at night, though their own origins are noble, is a laudable characteristic of this family and definitely one of the secrets of their growing success. As of 2002, about nine years after opening, Seliano agrotourism generates almost 40 percent of the family's gross income; the remaining 60 percent is derived from the sale of buffalo milk. As Ettore points out: "Now we are doing OK, but in the beginning it was very hard for all of us. Mamma knew how to produce buffalo milk in theory and we had to learn everything from scratch."

Indeed, the beginnings were not easy. Cecilia lost her husband when Ettore and Massimino were small; she was left alone to manage the family business, which until then had been largely the responsibility of her husband's partner. As she explains, "I had little familiarity with buffalo" and hands-on management of the estate was a new experience for her. By her own admission, Cecilia learned "the dangers of cooperation." As Ettore points out, "many people external to the family came forward to assume control of the farm and leave Mamma on the margin. This was a thing that she could not allow to happen, for herself and for us." They had a vast network of relatives employed in the business of agriculture and milk production, but—as is true in all famililes—such connections do not always lead to mutual help, especially in times of need. Massimino and Ettore recall, "Some relatives, rather than help us, stood there waiting for Mamma to fail, hoping that eventually she would give up so that they could assume the control of the property." Eventually Cecilia found help from Umberto, her late husband's foreman, whose loyalty and sense of responsibility toward the Bellelli family enabled Cecilia to maintain the business.

Umberto, who is now 81 years old, began working at Seliano when he was a small boy. As he explains: "The first day I was sent by the old baron to the mountain with the others to get the *bastoni* (wooden sticks with a 'hook,' or spur, used to guide buffalo)." Since then, Umberto has never left the estate and has never taken a day off. A few years ago Ettore gave him a piece of prime property along the *statale* from Battipaglia to Agropoli large enough for Umberto to build a new house for his family. Ettore told me, "I could have used the land to open my own cheese house but I do not care, he deserves it."[12]

The commercial success of Eliseo is grounded in Umberto's knowledge and experience. More than seventy years spent raising buffalo have given him a wealth of practical knowledge. He is able to judge when an animal is worth keeping not only by measuring the quantity of milk produced but also by looking at how it walks, eats, sleeps, and behaves with the other buffalo in the herd. Each heifer and bull has its own name (a practice that is being phased out, replaced by the use of an impersonal number); and even if it is difficult for him to remember them all, once he recognizes the animal he still can recite his or her genealogy by heart. Umberto's knowledge of the business of producing buffalo milk made it possible for the family to concentrate their efforts on the business of tourism and cooking. In the past two years Cecilia has renovated the old compound at the Eliseo farm and has transformed it into a second agrotourism facility that she is managing personally. The new structure contains only five rooms (Seliano has about twelve rooms now) and functions also as a cooking school, with Cecilia personally teaching courses on regional cuisine.

The new enterprise will promote food products made on the farm and those made by small producers in the region who are riding on the success of buffalo mozzarella to revamp the food traditions of the plain. Cecilia embarks in long and exhausting field trips by car and on foot to the most remote corners of the region, searching for what she calls "old flavors." These can be goat and sheep cheeses made by herders on a secluded mountain top, or *caciocavallo*, a semifresh cheese made from the milk of the long-forgotten *podolica*, a local breed of cow that is enjoying a renaissance thanks to people like Cecilia. She is not interested only in cheese. On request, she takes the most adventurous guests in search of hams and sausages made from swine fed with a type of acorns that grow only in small oak groves two hours from the closest road. Also, she targets bread makers and fruit growers as well as restaurants located in offroad villages that serve homemade pasta prepared with local herbs and forgotten spices. These newly established networks not only enable Cecilia to increase her agrotourism and her international fame as food connoisseur but also permit small producers, at times very small, to find a direct market for their products without the hassle, and costs, of marketing. Cecilia is a paradigmatic example of someone refashioning a territorial identity built on a mix of food traditions, material culture, and aesthetic sensibility, which helps not only the individual entrepreneur but also, by virtue of culinary networking, a host of local producers and, indirectly, the territory at large.

STRATEGY #2: HIGH-QUALITY PRODUCTS AND LOCAL MARKETS

The *azienda agricola* Vannulo is located along the main road between Battipaglia and Agropoli. Paddocks containing buffalo are visible on the left side of the road, while the view on the right reveals fields planted with alfalfa and, in the far background, the mountains of Salerno. The cheese shop is an extension of the cheese house that is one of the buildings on the property. A barn close to the cheese house recently has been rebuilt to accommodate a small laboratory for producing yogurt and ice cream made with buffalo milk. Behind the barn, the old cheese house has been transformed into a small museum dedicated to the history and culture of peasant labor in the Sele Plain; it contains tools and memorabilia used in lowland agriculture before mechanization. Olive trees outline the parking lot, while the owner's residence, an eighteenth-century baronial house separated from the areas dedicated to visitors, provides the stately background.

Antonio Palmieri, the grandfather of today's proprietor, his namesake, established Vannulo in 1907 with only eight buffalo. Today the farm consists of about 350 heifers that deliver enough milk to produce about 400 kilos of mozzarella daily. Besides mozzarella, Vannulo also produces a small quantity of ricotta and, as milk is available, semifresh varieties of cheese such as *provola*. These quantities place Vannulo at the border between being a very small producer and a small producer. At Vannulo there are thirteen full-time employees, including a cheese master and two young women who work at the cheese shop. The remaining workers rotate between the cheese house, the stables, and the fields. Unlike most employers, Antonio the grandson does not discriminate between an experienced and inexperienced workforce. In fact, he prefers to employ inexperienced workers because, he says, "Not all cheese houses operate in the same way. Workers pick up bad habits that I do not want transferred here. I like to train my workers personally and I want them to learn my way."

All the workers are local people known to the owners even before they apply for jobs; often they are the sons and daughters of workers previously employed in the *azienda*. It goes without saying that individual reputation is all that counts in the world of buffalo breeding and cheese making. Personal character, skills, and manner of conducting oneself in the workplace and in the community at large are qualities that are most appreciated.

A former bank director, Antonio Palmieri is the reincarnation of Kurt Forster's stereotypical gentleman farmer, a pragmatic competitor yet open to change and renewal; this model of enlightened bourgeoisie is quite common in the Sele Plain among buffalo breeders. In keeping with the market-oriented tradition of the region, Antonio was among the first in Italy to experiment with new breeding techniques and to adapt production to the contemporary market. As he points out:

> I do not like to follow what other people are doing around me. I prefer to go my own way and, rather than a follower, I like being a model for others to follow. I was the first in this area to change the shape of the manger from chipped on the edge to square and to build couchettes with stones for my buffalo. They thought I was crazy to spend money on these particulars. Now everybody is doing the same thing.

Indeed, Vannulo is a model of creative and efficient entrepreneurship, and Antonio is seen as the prototype of the local innovator. Highly respected among his peers both as an individual and as an entrepreneur, known throughout the region and even Italy among buffalo breeders, he provides an ideal exemplar, especially to young entrepreneurs who only now are entering the market. As he observes, his philosophy of production is "simplicity and recovery of the techniques of the past." Consistent with this motto, the method of cheese production is manual and the milk is not pasteurized. The use of raw milk and the hand process are characteristic of the production of mozzarella in the Sele Plain in general, particularly of the left bank of the river in the triangle formed by the towns of Capaccio, Paestum, and Altavilla Silentina. From this point of view Vannulo is not different from La Contadina, Barlotti, Torricelle, La Perla,

Salati, Rivabianca, equally successful cheese houses within the district that have adopted similar techniques of production. What separates Antonio from the rest of the competition is not simply a revamping of local traditions; rather, it is the extent to which new technologies have been incorporated while re-creating a context of production as close as possible to traditional knowledge and practices. In this respect, Vannulo is unique.

Since 1996, the farm has converted from conventional methods of production to new methods of organic agriculture. This is a revolutionary approach: as of 2002, Vannulo and L'Albero della Vita, a cooperative of lay monks near Rome, are the only organic producers of buffalo mozzarella in Italy. Antonio, however, downplays the significance of his choice, which he describes as "nothing more than an attempt to reintroduce some of the characteristics of cheese making as it was before the 1960s." Yet his decision was a difficult one to make, because the conversion from conventional to organic methods influences the practices of breeding (feeding, reproduction, etc.), the quantity of milk produced, and the cheese making itself. As the only organic producer in the area, Antonio cannot use milk from other farms where buffalo consume feed treated with chemicals. Understandably, making decisions that will limit production is difficult at any time; the difficulty is heightened for buffalo breeders, whose profit margins are narrow and subject to change throughout the year. Even more challenging is deciding to produce less when the demand for buffalo mozzarella seems inexhaustible. Shifting from conventional practices to more environmentally sensitive (i.e., traditional) ones goes against not only the immediate interests of milk producers but also market forces, as organic feed is twice as expensive. This fact alone automatically doubles the costs of milk production.

At Vannulo, the shift away from conventional methods has been possible in part because the owner works within certain parameters of scale and quality. The question of capital is not an issue; Antonio declares, "I have enough land that if I wanted to increase the number of my buffalo I could still produce sufficient organic fodder for all my animals." In fact, what makes the conversion from conventional to alternative methods and practices economically feasible, allowing the recovery of traditional methods and practices, is a particular scope of production. The purpose of producing mozzarella in the first place eventually shapes the economic strategy of entrepreneurs such as Antonio Palmieri.

During the course of several interviews I had with him, his wife, and his children, it became clear that family, and his responsibility toward the familial core, was central to Antonio's worldview. He told me that for him, the point of making mozzarella was to give a future to his children. Most cheese producers have a sophisticated understanding of family well-being, an understanding rarely expressed solely in materialistic terms but couched in terms of total quality of life. Clearly, the social and economic background of each entrepreneur influences how such quality is judged and the decisions about how such a state of well-being should be achieved. Nonetheless, it is safe to say that the majority saw making mozzarella not as an end in and of itself but as a means toward higher goals. For Antonio, those goals are to provide for his wife and children and, most important, to be a good husband and a good father. He explains, "I try to spend as much time with my family as possible. I like to be able to accompany my children to school, to go with them to the movies, and to eat together with the family in the evening. Expanding production would increase my worries and subtract time that I prefer to spend with my family." Small-scale production dedicated to local markets (Antonio's mozzarella can be purchased only at his farm) can indeed be a conscious economic strategy. In this particular case, limiting production is consistent with the entrepreneur's view of how life in general and his life in particular ought to be spent. Clearly, Antonio also is an ambitious individual constantly searching for new economic opportunities that will increase his profits. How does he do it? What are the sources of his inspiration? How does he understand the market?

The farm's commercial motto is "quality, cleanliness, and courtesy." A good part of Antonio's activity, in fact, is devoted to talking to his clients. By establishing an interpersonal relation with clients, the entrepreneur can achieve two important economic objectives: maintaining a loyal clientele and refining his or her "feeling" for the market. The first objective is particularly important here because customers can choose among different cheese houses; one client lost means one gained for the competition. Because he listens to what customers have to say, Antonio is constantly informed about their level of satisfaction with his products and about how they are performing in the market. Moreover, it allows him to save on advertising. As he points out, "I do not advertise my product; I have never done so. I let my product speak for itself. My clients do the advertising for me. I believe in the *passaparola* (word of mouth)." This emphasis on the interpersonal helps Antonio understand that producing more is not the only way to increase his profits—producing high-quality products can also do the trick. He is happy with the results: "When I decided to produce organic mozzarella, I knew that I had to increase the price and I was not sure how the market would react. Now I sell my mozzarella at a higher price than the others but by noon I have sold it all out, even in winter."

Diversifying production into activities not necessarily connected directly with mozzarella also produces an economic return. Recently, Antonio Palmieri has started to produce a small amount of buffalo yogurt and ice cream in addition to his mozzarella business. Production is completely automatic, thanks to a custom-made machine designed by an artisanal firm from Parma that specializes in dairy technologies. The yogurt is packaged in small glass containers shaped like little amphoras with a twist cap on top. A worker then ties an attractive label with information about the product and the company to the container with a string, and the product is ready to sell. Production has been located in the old barn close to the cheese house, which has been renovated to accommodate the expansion. As he likes to emphasize, the work was all done legally—that is, with the approval and necessary licenses from the local commune and under the technical supervision of an architect. "The idea was to create a *yogurteria*," he explains, "a new kind of cheese house where customers can sit in a comfortable environment and have breakfast if they want." The production room is protected by transparent glass, rendered effectively invisible from the outside by a preexisting partitioning wall made of solid bricks. The remaining area is furnished with small tables and chairs on one side, a few stools along the wall, and a functional bar at the opposite side serving ice cream, yogurt, and, of course, coffee. Antonio jokes, "Do you want to know why I bought the espresso machine? I was tired of going out to get my coffee or of asking my wife to make coffee at home for my clients." In fact, in the same way that he considers his workers to be collaborators, he treats his clients as guests. The possibility of offering them coffee, yogurt, or ice cream on the spot makes things friendlier; at the same time, it highlights products other than cheese.

Wooden stairs lead to the second floor of the barn. Originally, this was the place where farmers stacked hay. After the reconstruction it has been transformed into a vast room used for cultural events such as book presentations and conferences that the owner and his wife had previously held in the old stable adapted for the purpose that was located under the villa. The whole environment is rendered even more comfortable by the quality of the restoration process, which uncovered and exposed the original texture and materials of the barn wall and roof.

Vannulo is a multifunctional dairy farm where it is possible to purchase a high-quality mozzarella produced by methods as close to the traditional ideal as possible—and also something more. On request, visitors can tour the dairy farm, the paddocks, and the cheese house to see for themselves how the products are made and to view the conditions in which buffalo are kept. It is important to note that most breeders and cheese makers are proud of their activities and have no problem showing their buffalo and methods of production to those interested. In fact, it is common to meet local schoolchildren (mostly sixth to ninth graders) visiting farms and cheese houses, where they are introduced to the "secrets" of buffalo breeding and mozzarella making. The difference at Vannulo is that such visits are formally organized and led by personnel specially trained for the purpose. Antonio is among the first entrepreneurs to have incorporated public relations into the everyday activities of the farm. Aside from visiting the sites of production, customers seeking deeper knowledge can tour a small museum, located in a former cheese house, that is dedicated to the technology of farming; there they can get a sense of how things were done not so long ago in the Sele Plain.

Antonio Palmieri is also conscious of Paestum's resources for tourism, both national and international. The dairy farm is close to the ruins of Poseidonia, the Greek name of a city dedicated to Poseidon, god of the sea, that was founded about the middle of the seventh century B.C.E. and "rediscovered" in the 1700s by scholars in search of the roots of European art, European architecture, and the classical sense of aesthetics. The archaeological and ecological significance of the territory was recognized at the international level when UNESCO declared the area a World Heritage site in 1997. Inserting the activity of making mozzarella into such a lucrative circuit was simply natural for Antonio. Vannulo has now become a destination point; often there are buses in the parking lot filled with baffled Japanese tourists intrigued by seeing buffalo for the first time in their life and by viewing the dexterity of the cheese master.

GLOBAL VALUES, LOCAL PRACTICES

As the local food historian Howard Marshall notes, "Like dialect and architecture, food traditions are a main component in the intricate and impulsive system that joins culture and geography into regional character."[13] In this sense, food and architecture are processes "located" in the core of the individual as well as at the center of communal culture. As such they incorporate as well as reflect an intrinsic territorial identity or character that is not fixed but can change over time. Technology, business culture, demography, consumers' tastes, class differences, political ideology, and globalization are just a few of the factors that, together with countless other circumstances, influence the direction and meaning of such change and hence the economic identity of a specific territory or region. We can appreciate how the practices of constructing identity in the Sele Plain, as implemented by local food producers in their everyday economic activities, lead to a reevaluation of the role and function of vernacular architecture: an architecture that is rooted in the material culture of the place but also open to the global spectrum of commerce. This is also a sustainable architecture that responds to new economic imperatives using existing resources such as local materials and building traditions without alterations in scale, materials, or general appearance, a "regional" architecture in which the built environment is viewed as part of a larger landscape that is regional, cultural, and physical as well as economic and, as we have seen, gastronomic.

Most of all, the ways in which local food producers in the Sele Plain have carved out a new economic identity for themselves and for their territory suggest the limitations in how the notion of identity has been discussed and analyzed within the social sciences in the past.[14] Anthropologists, psychologists, and sociologists have argued that people build their personal identities out of the culture they live in and that cultural practices and rituals are used by local societies to maintain, or struggle to maintain, their identity amid change.[15] Erik Erikson, for example, underlines the notion of identity as stability and continuity when he defines patients suffering from an "identity crisis" as those who "had lost a sense of personal sameness and historical continuity."[16] Mary Douglas is even more explicit about the regressive role played by ritual practices of identity, observing that these rituals should be seen "as an attempt to create and maintain a particular culture, a particular set of assumptions by which experience is controlled."[17] But the economic strategies of buffalo mozzarella producers in the Sele Plain instead show that personal and territorial identities have an intrinsic market value—not only symbolic value—and thus can be changed and reorganized to suit a historical moment and ideology.

The ways in which food and architecture come together to shape the economic identity of places is a culture-producing process that enables the appropriation of global meanings and values in the local context (e.g., the countryside as a place for consumption). Such a process is possible when a culture breaks, rather than reinforces, the territorial links between contextual knowledge and local context. At the base of the new territorial identity of the Sele Plain is the success of buffalo mozzarella in the world market; but such success was possible only because local producers were able to avoid the trap of particularism. They have done so by infusing elements of a cosmopolitan identity into an original, local food tradition and architectural practice, thereby making such traditions accessible to a wider audience. The transformation of the working farm from a place of production closed to the public into a multifunctional structure open to a variety of uses and customers is an example of this process. Territorial identity thus does not exist apart from and outside such practices; hence it pertains more to the blending and mixing of local and global cultural boundaries than to unproblematic geographical and cultural origin (location).[18]

NOTES

1. Examples include Faneuil Hall, Boston; Third Street Promenade, Santa Monica; and Ghirardelli Square, San Francisco.

2. European Union, Committee of the Regions, *Promoting and Protecting Local Products—A Trumpcard for the Regions* (Brussels: Committee of the Regions, 1996); B. Ilbery and M. Kneafsey, "Niche Markets and Regional Specialty Food Products in Europe: Towards a Research Agenda," *Environmental Planning A* 31 (1999): 2207–2222.

3. PDO (Protected Designation of Origin) is the term used to describe foodstuffs that are produced, processed, and prepared within the boundaries of a given geographical area using recognized know-how. In the case of the PGI (Protected Geographical Indication), the geographical link must occur in at least one of the stages—production, processing, or preparation. Furthermore, the product can benefit from a good reputation. TSG (Traditional Speciality Guaranteed) does not refer to a food's origin but highlights its traditional character, either in the composition or means of production.

4. Robert Leonardi and Raffaella Y. Nanetti, eds., *Regional Development in a Modern European Economy: The Case of Tuscany*, 2nd ed. (Washington, D.C.: Pinter, 1998).

5. David Goodman and Michael Watts, "Reconfiguring the Rural or Fording the Divide? Capitalist Restructuring and the Global Agro-Food System," *Journal of Peasant Studies* 22, no. 1 (October 1994): 1–49.

6. Kurt Forster, "Back to the Farm: Vernacular Architecture and the Development of the Renaissance Villa," *Architettura* (1974): 12.

7. Ibid., 9

8. James S. Ackerman, *The Villa: Form and Ideology of Country Houses* (Princeton: Princeton University Press, 1990).

9. Emilio Sereni, *History of the Italian Agricultural Landscape*, trans. R. Burr Litchfield (Princeton: Princeton University Press, 1997), 148.

10. The quotations contained in these two case studies come from a series of interviews I conducted in the Sele Plain from 2000 to 2002.

11. Conversely, families of buffalo breeders who have expanded their activity into tourism do not necessarily opt for agrotourism. The Barlotti family in Paestum, for example, recently purchased a preexisting hotel rather than adapting rural structures on their property as the Bellelli family did. The two families are thus two different kinds of hoteliers; more important, they work with different types of tourists.

12. Having a piece of land along a busy road with easy automobile access is the dream of any cheese maker. Most farms in fact are located far from main roads, and finding the cheese houses often requires some time for those unfamiliar with the area. Moving to a site visible from the main road can clearly boost sales. Mainly for this reason, many cheese houses located in the interior open outlets along the road from Battipaglia to Agropoli.

13. Howard Marshall, "Meat Presentation on the Farm in Missouri's Little Dixie," *Journal of American Folklore* 92 (1979): 400; quoted in George H. Lewis, "The Maine Lobster as Regional Icon," *Food and Foodways* 3, no. 4 (1989): 303.

14. Ken Plummer, "Identity," in *The Blackwell Dictionary of Twentieth-Century Social Thought*, ed. William Outhwaite and Tom Bottomore (Oxford: Basil Blackwell, 1993), 270–272.

15. See George H. Mead, *Mind, Self, and Society*, ed. Charles W. Morris (Chicago: University of Chicago Press, 1962); Anselm L. Strauss, *Mirrors and Masks: The Search for Identity* (San Francisco: Sociology Press, 1969); Peter L. Berger, *Invitation to Sociology: A Humanistic Perspective* (Garden City, N.Y.: Doubleday, 1963), Roy F. Baumeister, *Identity: Cultural Change and the Struggle for Self* (Oxford: Oxford University Press, 1986).

16. Erik H. Erikson, *Identity: Youth and Crisis* (New York: W. W. Norton, 1968), 17.

17. Mary Douglas, *Purity and Danger: An Analysis of Concepts of Pollution and Taboo* (1966; reprint, Harmondsworth: Penguin, 1970), 153. For a thorough analysis of the contribution of Mary Douglas to the topic of food and identity, see Phyllis Passariello, "Anomalies, Analogies, and Sacred Profanities: Mary Douglas on Food and Culture, 1957–1989," *Food and Foodways* 4, no. 1 (1990): 53–72.

18. Jonathan Friedman, "Global System, Globalization, and the Parameters of Modernity," in *Global Modernities*, ed. Mike Robertson, Scott Lash, and Roland Robertson (London: Sage, 1995), 72–74.

6.1

6

TOO MUCH SUGAR

CLARE CARDINAL-PETT

Treading blindly for what seemed aeons in oppressive darkness on an unstable mush of fermenting sugar cane stalks, nearly overcome by the sickly sweet smell, you approached a faint ray of hope: the dim glow of a TV hanging overhead. On it was a video collage of Castro's life. And as you turned back, all senses on total alert, you faintly perceived the presence of bare living bodies, endlessly rubbing their mouths or slapping their thighs. Some viewers saw a man and a woman, others insisted there were four males. Like Cuba itself, it was a total sensory experience—contradictory, illusive, and hard to fathom. It summed up the invisibility, the toxic presence, the history of exploitation, and the heart of darkness.[1]

"It's like Cuba," the artist Tania Bruguera said to the *Artforum International* critic Nico Israel of her installation in a tunnel at La Fortaleza de San Carlos de la Cabana during the VII Bienal de la Habana.[2] "It's sweet. It can be dangerous. It's intoxicating." According to Israel, the work presented "a philosophy of (national) history in which people journey through a collective experience that can only be comprehended once they've reached its end, whereupon 'the past' reveals itself as having consisted of repeated rituals and empty gestures."[3]

Bruguera's attempt to overwhelm her audience with the odor of decay and the neurotic gestures of caged animals can obviously be read as an obituary for the Cuban revolution. Unlike many contemporary Cuban artists, she did not joke about it. Her piece lamented the death of what many Cubans call the "dream with no name." On the streets of Havana, decay is unavoidable. Buildings have dissolved, like wedding cakes in rain. Havana, so it appears, was made of sugar (figure 6.2).

At the end of the twentieth century, as the Soviet Union unraveled, Cuba's economy collapsed; extreme material shortages endangered everyday life. In Havana, where food shortages were especially severe, individuals joined in finding practical responses to the disaster, efforts to sustain the dream with no name—most notably urban farming, the *mercado mixto,* and the *paladar.* These particular urban improvisations created environments where food and architecture fraternized in a distinctly Cuban way; and, when examined collectively, they prefigure the resolution of Cuba's current struggle with globalization.

It is important to remember that Cuba's recent crisis is inextricable from its history as a producer of agricultural products with negligible nutritional value. The luxury commodities of Europe's aristocracy, later the staple ingredients of a middle-class lifestyle—sugar, coffee, tobacco, and rum—were first made market-ready by ill-fed slaves. In 1898, when Spain surrendered its port of entry into the Americas, U.S. corporations "modernized" the island's plantations. Rank-and-file Cubans cut cane, harvested coffee, and rolled cigars for the emerging international marketplace while a series of puppet governments threw elaborate parties for furloughed tycoons, celebrities, gangsters, and pimps. The hotels and casinos built by the Mafia boss Meyer Lansky during the 1950s served imported food along with domestic cigars, rum, and prostitutes. Working-class Cubans ate what could be gleaned from a landscape devoted to growing crops that were not life sustaining. The *comida tipica* of Cuba, its "cuisine," owes much to the survival tactics devised in colonial and imperial times. It is the diet we tend to associate with manual laborers and the poor: heavy on carbohydrates, meat, fat, and simple sugars. Traditional Cuban coffee is served exceptionally sweet.

In 1959 widespread poverty and human rights abuse fueled a revolution against the Batista government. Speaking on behalf of Cuba's indigent and illiterate, Fidel Castro, Che Guevara, and their comrades set out to remake Cuba from the ground up.

CLARE CARDINAL-PETT

6.2
Partially occupied tenement
in Central Havana, May 2001.
Photo by Steve Klocke.

They destroyed the casinos, prostitution rings, and tourism industry, but they did not burn the sugar fields and mills. The revolutionary government commandeered this perceived source of the country's economic freedom. Che himself set an example for the entire world when he went to work cutting the people's cane. A notoriously inefficient and unprofitable industry, sugar cane production was not an adequate economic base. It failed to cure the island's poverty, despite the free labor of thousands of well-wishers from around the world who traveled to Cuba to work at Guevara's side.

In 1961 Castro declared, opportunistically, the revolution a "socialist project" and struck a Faustian deal with the Soviet Union. In this bargain, Cuba gained access to the means of improving its educational and health-care systems but was subjected to planning theories that promoted a brutal industrialization of the rural landscape and produced "solutions" to housing, school, and hospital shortages that only a mediocre graduate of Hannes Meyer's Bauhaus could defend.

In 1989, when the Soviet Union collapsed, Cuba's heavy dependence on imported oil, fertilizers, and pesticides mirrored its dependence on its own sugar cane production. Having spent decades trading sugar well above global market values, Cuba was stranded. Cubans called the situation "The Special Period in Peacetime." It is a curious euphemism, given that the United States has continued to wage economic and political war against the Castro government. Cubans continue building bomb shelters throughout the countryside.[4] Invasions are still widely anticipated, and many Cubans stand ready to resist.

In the 1990s, however, defending the revolution often meant simply finding something to eat. During the Special Period, Cubans resurrected recipes from colonial times, such as the infamous *sopa de gallo* (rooster soup), which consists of *agua con azucar preita* (water with brown sugar).[5] They invented new variations on a similar theme, such as *pollo al bloqueo* (blockade chicken):

> *Day 1: Take a chicken, skin it, boil it, make soup from the stock . . . adding viandas: potatoes, tomatoes, carrots, yuca, boniato, tamale, maybe some pasta, corn or rice. Day 2: golden brown the actual pieces and parts of the chicken and serve it in a salsa criolla ade of tomato, red pepper, onion, aji. Day 3: take the chicken skin and sautee it until it's crackly hard—chicharrón de pollo, serve with white rice. Day 4: crack the chicken bones and suck out the marrow.[6]*

Like Castro, most Cubans have an extraordinary ability to improvise, to make do in the face of adversity. Christina Garcia, a U.S. writer whose first novel was *Dreaming in Cuban* (1992), describes this fundamental aspect of the Cuban character in "Simple Life," an essay about visiting her relatives in Cuba:

> *Cubans are masters at making the best out of any difficult situation. "Resolver," to resolve, is probably the most commonly used verb in the language on the island. "Resolver" can mean resuscitating a twenty-year-old Russian Lada for a ride to the beach or tracking down a single out-of-season sweet potato for a dessert offering to Yemaya, goddess of the seas. . . . In Cuba "resolver" means to survive, to overcome all obstacles with inventiveness, spontaneity, and most important, humor.[7]*

The lack of humor in Tania Bruguera's installation may indicate how severely the Special Period tested Cuba's resolve. Faced with no easy answers, Cuba became more open to global capitalism and, consequently, less egalitarian. By sending invitations to the largest industry in the global market, tourism, and by legalizing the currency of its enemy—the U.S. dollar—in 1992, the state opened a door to economic privilege and social advantage.[8] Tips from tourists, "remittances" from relatives abroad,[9] and other sources of dollar-based income now constitute a significant part of many households' economy. But many Cuban professionals do not work in the tourist sector or have family living in exile. In the emerging dollar economy, the government's peso-based salary for teachers, doctors, architects, and so on is no longer a living wage.

Many Cubans still can find comedy in this tragedy. Such recent films as *Guantanamera, The Waiting List,* and *Honey for Oshun* are good examples of how scarcity can be laughed at. Many contemporary Cuban artists have exploited the lack of materials by recycling refuse into art. And there are the ubiquitous jokes on the street; one features a Cuban "girl who dumps her boyfriend. 'He swore he'd struck it rich at the Hotel Nacional,' she gripes, 'claimed he'd actually landed the job of doorman.' But she dropped him when she learned the bitter truth, that he was just another Cuban neurosurgeon—a state job, that is, with no ties to the dollar economy."[10]

Tania Bruguera throws her "food" on the floor in protest. She also literally strips her neighbors (the "actors" in the piece) and makes them dumb. Their neurotic gestures are emblematic of the enormous waste of human capital that defiles Cuba's public space. Bruguera's lament is a wake-up call to those responsible for turning well-educated Cubans into cooks, waiters, and chambermaids. International tourism, the government's sugar-substitute, is the island's *pharmakon*.[11]

The mood in much of Cuba's professional community is also more somber. Mario Coyula, an architect in Havana and a member of an urban planning think tank, the Group for the Integral Development of the Capital, expressed his misgivings about the effect of the dollar economy on the city's neighborhoods in his 1996 essay "Havana Forever, Forever Havana":

> *A recent variant associated to a relatively higher income level of a pathetic nouveau riche projects into the streetscape with a Peerless type of chain-link fence two meters high that separates a passer-by from the salivating fangs of a well-fed Doberman pinscher, plus a front garden turned into a car porch covered with undulating green Fiberglas, where the owner's 1950's well-kept Chevrolet stands side by side with a 1990's Nissan rented by a foreign paid guest. The ubiquitous fencing sadly reflects the rising increase of thefts, which ten years ago were few.*[12]

He is optimistic, however, that his group's promotion of new planning methods that are "flexible, decentralized, cautious and regenerative" will help Havana recoup its losses: "This path could lead to the construction of a new paradigm, that of a *sustainable socialism,* if able to achieve and maintain the difficult equilibrium between the built, natural and social environment and a supportive economy; that is, a creative socialism, viable and deeply participatory."[13] In Havana, where blackouts are part of everyday life, hitching a ride is an art form, and banana peels are used as a meat substitute, the word *sustainability* merely means survival, one day at a time. The country is deeply scarred by scarcity, particularly in Havana, where the crisis hit hardest. While there is now more food on the table and there are buildings under construction or restoration, the city remains a cold-war zone. Neglected buildings collapse daily. The tabula rasa appears, here and there, overnight.

Coyula's "sustainable socialism" derives its theoretical armature from subaltern survival practices and betrays his faith in Cuba's improvisational skills. Shifting responsibility from the state to the individual, his sustainable socialism calls for a "integral transformation of the neighborhood" into a "workshop." The means of production are decentralized:

> In such a place, dwellings will stop being a mere refuge and become microworkshops, the basis of a neighborhood economy which could be organized much like the recently established rural co-operatives. Perhaps in this way, the old Marxist dream of erasing the difference between the city and countryside would follow a different path, away from the simplistic approach of building five-story apartment blocks in the middle of the countryside and small, squalid detached houses in the inner city.[14]

After more than four decades of a "proletariat dictatorship," it appears as if the state may be withering and the people challenged to fend for themselves.

It is in this context, then, that urban farming, the *mercado mixto,* and the *paladar* appeared. In the examination of these three provisional constructions that follows, I have arranged them in order, from benign to toxic, so that the *pharmakon* might be deconstructed. In the end I hope it is clear that, like Tania Bruguera's installation, this essay is a lamentation. I acknowledge Gayatri Spivak's declaration that "There is no state on the globe today that is not part of the capitalist economic system or can want to eschew it fully."[15] Cuba's entry into the global market place is inevitable. Like Bruguera, however, I cannot forgive global capitalism for (or joke about) its proclivity to waste human and natural resources.

A PIG IN EVERY BATHTUB

As is the case in many cities, farm animals are "unauthorized" in Havana. During the worst of the Special Period, a severe shortage of gasoline and diesel fuel cut supply lines from farms to markets. The city health inspectors looked the other way as rules were broken. Pigs inhabited the bathtubs of many apartments and were taken out to the sidewalks on leashes. Around the city you can still hear squealing from open windows and balconies. Laundry shrouds the slaughterhouses. Animal husbandry became unofficially sanctioned when the state rationed chicks to each family and every tenement incubated its future suppers[16] (figure 6.3).

A similar situation arose when fruits and vegetables failed to arrive in the city. Farms appeared in vacant lots. Cubans piled compost over the rubble in their neighborhoods and planted seeds. There were no pesticides or fertilizers so these gardens went "green" out of necessity. A spontaneous and unauthorized activity at first, the organic urban farm has now become a Havana fixture, with well-educated specialists tending the rows with scientific precision and efficiency. Early in the process the state

6.3
A pig in transit, May 2001.
Photo by Jorge Encarnación.

sent professionals to the various neighborhoods to train novices, some of whom are now experts themselves and conduct on-site research.

The current system of *organoponicos*, as they have been dubbed, is now integrated with Havana's Institute of Physical Planning, the governmental organization in charge of urban land management. The institute "lends" available space to one of several agricultural organizations that grow food in the city. The distribution is planned with future construction in mind and takes into account neighborhood accessibility. Some *organoponicos* are linked to particular schools or factories, providing food for the students, teachers, and workers. Areas of underutilized land such as the airport have been converted to edible landscapes.[17] Vegetables are sold on location, with some produce redistributed or traded with other gardens. The neighborhood produce stands have become new community centers, similar in function to the more historic bodegas, or corner grocery stores, that were eliminated by state planners:

> An ambitious program for building an extensive supermarket network promoted in the eighties intended to ease food distribution for the sake of the state agency in charge of that task, reducing the number of distribution points. This program aimed to eliminate the small corner groceries, combining several under one single roof of a new building. Actually, the concept of a supermarket—meant to compel people into buying goods that they do not really need—did not fit with the purpose of a socialist country where the state's concern was to ensure a fair supply of basic food to everybody. These ersatz supermarkets concentrated the negative impacts of storage and mass assembly of consumers, forcing people to walk longer distances with often heavy loads; and squandered valuable corner lots while leaving several previously well-shaped city corners adrift.[18]

The *organoponicos* that have sprouted in the urban decay have the potential to change traditional Cuban cuisine. While what we think of as traditional Cuban foods are global in their origins (all of the world's cuisines now reflect some history of global trade), there has been a curious predictability and invariability in the typical Cuban meal. But now *vegetales raros*, such as broccoli and bok choy, are grown and sold in the neighborhood stands. Recipes are posted for exotic vegetables; neighbors swap tales of what they did with the daikon radish bought yesterday. Many of these so-

CLARE CARDINAL-PETT

called weird vegetables are available because seeds have been donated by humanitarian organizations from abroad or come cheaply from China.[19] Havana's numerous *organoponicos* add color to a city short of paint. They provide affordable access to imported food, defying the U.S. trade embargo. They are a source of diversion and information about other countries.

Successful farming in Havana—raising city pigs, chickens, and produce—could not be reproduced in the United States. To be sure, vegetable gardens do exist in many U.S. cities and are a particularly vital element of many poor and immigrant neighborhoods. Supporting urban farming in the United States at the scale and efficiency of those in Havana, however, would take cooperation among all socioeconomic classes and would demand knowledgeable participation of the educated elite. Although Cuba now maintains a 75 percent urban population—as does most of North America—the revolution has made a point of educating its urban dwellers in rural values and knowledge. A long-standing and significant element of the Cuban educational system is an exchange of students and teachers between rural and urban schools. Students in city schools spend part of the year at schools in the countryside, where they learn agricultural and construction skills through service-learning-type activities. Students from rural areas are taken to the city on a periodic basis for cultural exposure. Even the most urbane *habanero* knows how to ride a horse, slaughter a chicken, harvest bananas, and cut sugar cane, and most can probably fix a tractor.[20] Unlike most North American city dwellers, all Cubans know where their food comes from. It is no surprise that urban farming in Havana has been so productive.

While much has been reported about Cuba's new "green revolution," there is little sign that the country's rural agricultural practices are radically shifting away from the industrialized and mechanized methods of production invented in the United States and embraced with a vengeance by the Soviet Union.[21] Sugar cane is especially difficult to cultivate organically. There are small institutes working on the problems of large-scale organic farming, but many people involved in this work fear that as the country gets back on its feet, support for green approaches will fall out of favor and that much of Havana's urban farming will be replaced with new construction.[22] When you can no longer hear roosters crow in Old Havana, you will know that tourists have completely occupied and consumed the neighborhood.

6.4
Farming in the shadow of the monument to José Martí, May 2000. Photo by author.

6.5
An "auto-supplier" markets his meat in Vedado, May 2001. Photo by author.

CLARE CARDINAL-PETT

One especially clear sign that the subaltern survival practices that created Havana's current agri-urban pattern will not survive is the lack of edible landscaping in the city's new housing development plans.[23] Cuba's more cosmopolitan design professionals apparently see the same dissonance that many visitors from the United States do when they encounter rural elements within the urban core. One member of the Institute for Physical Planning told me that since a few of the urban farms have been granted permanency, planners are discussing ways they might "design" the edible landscapes as if they were urban parks.[24] While this might be read as evidence of acceptance, it betrays the conventional urban designer's impulse to make natural processes "picturesque." Yet Havana's planners would accomplish an achievement of global significance if they produced a new model of urban design from the provisional farming now taking place in Cuba's capital city. Such a model would exemplify the sort of thinking Kenneth Frampton proposed in his keynote address at the 2002 Association of Collegiate Schools of Architecture (ACSA) International Conference in Havana, "Globalization and Its Discontents: Can Eco-Philosophy Serve as a Ground for Contemporary Environmental Design?" (figure 6.4).

MERCADO MIXTO

In Havana the distinction between city and countryside has been temporarily erased by the necessity to eat. The boundary also dissolves at the numerous farmers' markets and agricultural supply shops that have opened up throughout Havana's neighborhoods during the Special Period. Shops selling agricultural supplies—seeds, tools, and organic fertilizers and pesticides—are state-run enterprises. Supply stores also dispense advice to residents wanting to make their city yards and rooftops more edible. The proliferation and widespread distribution of agricultural supply stores and farmers' markets in the city brings rural Cuba deep into the heart of Havana (figure 6.5).

The farmers' market is a thriving microcosm of Cuba's newly mixed economy. For example, the market at the corner of Nineteenth and B in Vedado, a neighborhood bordering the city center that was built in the first half of the twentieth century, comprises—under one rambling roof—a ration distribution center, a state-subsidized meat and produce counter, and areas for "auto-suppliers" (private entrepreneurs selling their own pork and produce). This particular market is one of several around the city.

The market is a busy neighborhood gathering spot, a place to buy dinner and a cheap place to eat lunch. The building is a rambling shed fashioned out of concrete blocks and corrugated metal. In Vedado, where the architecture ranges from neo-classical stucco to early modernist glass and steel, the market does not fit in. Though it is made from prefabricated parts, its functionalism is not self-conscious. The structure seems appropriate to the food, raw and straightforward. Tourists do turn up at Havana's markets, but they are not of the travel-and-leisure class. The food is simply too raw and the flies too numerous.

Selling food as a private enterprise in Havana is lucrative. The auto-suppliers at the market in Vedado charge a higher markup on their goods than does the state. They can get away with it because the state's supplies of subsidized meat and produce are limited and often of a poorer quality. The prices on the state's rationed goods are even less than on its subsidized goods, but the shelves in that area of the market are empty more often than they are full and shipments rarely arrive on schedule. All prices in the three areas of the market are unbelievably low by U.S. standards. (My box lunch of squash and "salad" with beer on tap was the equivalent of 25 cents.) Minute differences, however, segregate Cuban shoppers. Under one deceptively simple roof, a once classless society buys its groceries at separate counters—each according to income in a multilayered economy. Foreigners do not see the true architecture of the Vedado market because everything in the rambling shed is bought and sold with Cuban currency. While the official exchange rate between the peso and the U.S. dollar is one to one, it actually takes 21 pesos to buy a dollar. Most Cuban salaries are the equivalent of about $15 a month. The shoppers buying dinner from auto-suppliers have simply arrived with more pesos in their pockets, having exchanged their dollars elsewhere (figure 6.6).

ROOM SERVICE

In Havana, as is the case all over the island, a Cuban national is not allowed into the rooms of foreigners at hotels that cater to tourists unless he or she is an employee. Barring Cubans from going to a tourist's hotel room is the government's attempt to prevent prostitution—the means justifying the ends. The rule reflects the country's paranoia about the corrupting effect of its rapidly expanding tourist population.

CLARE CARDINAL-PETT

6.6
My box lunch in Vedado,
May 2001. Photo by author.

6.7
Dinner in a private house,
Central Havana, May 2001.
Photo by author.

(Cuba's invitation to visit its unspoiled beaches was a dramatic and desperate move given the exploitative reality of tourism prior to 1959.) This law is broken frequently, however. When I took a Cuban friend with physical disabilities up to my hotel room to use the phone, he shrugged and joked, "Well, I guess I don't look like a hooker." After that icebreaker, I simply got in the elevator with locals and went upstairs—none of the lobby staff ever paid any attention.

Another form of human degradation can be found all over Havana, and the state is trying its best to address it. During the mid-1990s, many Cubans were allowed to turn their homes into means of economic production. Guest houses and small restaurants called *paladares* proliferated around Havana. Everyone in Havana knows someone who supplements his or her government salary with this form of second job. Some have abandoned their careers to become full-time hosts to tourists. While the government is now trying to curb this type of entrepreneurship through fines and taxes, it persists. Havana had nearly 1,000 *paladares* in the mid-1990s, but government regulations have whittled the official number down to around 120.[25] Many continue to operate clandestinely. Cuban law restricts private restaurants to twelve tables, a limit that makes them less profitable. Some *paladar* owners hide extra tables in their houses, giving over their bedrooms to more lucrative activities[26] (figure 6.7).

The occupation of the colonial and imperial city by the revolution has produced an urban landscape that is hard for visitors from consumer societies to comprehend. It is, to borrow Dana Cuff's description of Los Angeles, the ultimate "provisional city."[27] There are dwellings built on rooftops of bodegas, bodegas transformed into houses, houses occupied by day-care centers, and villas subdivided into a myriad of unrelated functions. In Old Havana, some palaces are now moneymaking museums; and because there is not enough money to support the construction and rehabilitation of neighborhood schools, classrooms occupy rooms in the museums. A lack of signage, advertisements, and other capitalist iconographies of architectural function distinguishes Havana's provisionality from that of Los Angeles. Beyond the new hotels and the tourist district of Old Havana, there are few familiar cues to guide those fluent in the language of most twenty-first-century cities. In this dense and misleading urban fabric, the typical tourist has a difficult time finding a *paladar* or guest house without a savvy cabdriver.

CLARE CARDINAL-PETT

Outside Cuba, however, the travel press aggressively promotes the *paladar*. For example, Marian Burros begins a recent *New York Times* article titled "Havana's Not for Eating, but Eating Can Be Fun,"

> *"PSSST! Want to go to my mother's restaurant?"*
>
> *Havana is the only city I have ever visited where going out to dinner sometimes takes on the cloak and dagger trappings of meeting with dissidents in Myanmar.*
>
> *Tourists are often approached on the streets around mealtime by local touts asking, sotto voce, if they would like to try the marvelous food at certain restaurants. These restaurants pay the touts a fee for every customer they bring to the door.*[28]

And a writer in the June 2001 issue of *Cigar Aficionado* similarly observes:

> [Paladares] *are completely different from the large restaurants designed for tourists that are run by the government or hotels, which are usually overpriced and offer dull food. A good paladar can be anything from a handful of tables in the dining room patio of a family's 1950s-era Miami Deco house in the quiet neighborhood of Nuevo Vedado, to a cluster of round wrought-iron tables in the garden of a manor house in the posh area of Miramar. They not only please your taste buds but also satisfy your general well-being with their distinctly Cuban atmosphere.*[29]

Both authors are quick to judge the food in government-run tourist facilities substandard: "In other countries choosing a restaurant based on information from a stranger on the street doesn't seem like a smart idea. In Cuba your chances of getting a decent meal at one of these often illegal private restaurants are better than what you will find in most state-run establishments, where the service tends to be indifferent and the food often barely edible."[30] Cuba is bereft of culinary sophistication, according to one European "who worked as a chef for a few months in a number of well-known Havana restaurants," because

> *the Cubans he worked with just didn't care, or simply couldn't understand, what good food was about—from the dishwashers to the head of the restaurant group. "I once asked my second what his favorite dish was and he said, 'Scrambled*

eggs with avocado and ketchup.'. . . I knew that someone like that would have problems appreciating the subtleties of cooking for educated people from around the world."[31]

In 1993, during the worst of the economic crisis, the average daily caloric intake for Cubans went from over 3,000 to just over 1,000. The whole country lost weight. The food shortage was more severe in Havana than other parts of the country because it was nearly impossible to transport supplies into the city from the countryside. Food trickled in, usually in large batches of one particular variety—a truckload of grapefruit on Wednesday, another of bananas on Saturday. Nitza Villapol, Cuba's Julia Child, began to broadcast alternative recipes on her weekly television show.[32] She offered Cubans ideas for adding variety to a diet of, say, nothing but grapefruit. As the primary ingredient of an especially stubborn cuisine, meat substitutes were invented from whatever was at hand. During the mid-1990s Cubans sliced the inner rinds of grapefruit, boiled out the bitterness, then breaded and fried it. They boiled banana peels and ground them like hamburger.

The so-called "educated people from around the world," people with habits of overconsumption, simply don't get it. The neighborhood *paladares* or guest houses, particularly those run by former professionals and those desperate illegal businesses that supply a growing demand, are a waste of human capital. Young people are dropping out of medical school and leaving their teaching jobs to help their parents run the family bed-and-breakfast. Christina Garcia recalls, "One Saturday afternoon in Havana, I casually mentioned to my uncle Tio Jorge that I was yearning for a piece of cake. About four hours later a prim man appeared at our door carrying an enormous coconut layer cake topped with fluffy pink meringue. It turned out that the delivery-man was, in fact, a heart surgeon who bakes cakes on weekends for extra cash."[33]

Havana's neighborhood "workshops" create wealth but undermine the education and health-care systems; they put food on the dining room table but erase the bedroom. In a country with a severe housing shortage, giving up one's precious domestic space to gain a tourist's dollar is a serious sacrifice of dignity. Cubans may be eating more, but they are still crowded in a crumbling infrastructure with their families and friends. The oldest parts of the city suffered extreme abuse and neglect under both Batista and Castro. The area had been rapidly deteriorating since the suburbanization

CLARE CARDINAL-PETT

6.8
A temporary fix in Old Havana,
May 2000. Photo by author.

of the city in the early twentieth century. Weathered roofing tiles from Old Havana's Spanish colonial buildings were removed and shipped to Miami in the 1920s to add authenticity to the Coral Gables subdivision.[34] By the time Batista came to power, the leaking buildings had already begun to disintegrate. After 1959, the revolutionary government, in an effort to rebalance wealth and social services, shifted its attention to the countryside, developing agricultural and industrial production facilities, worker housing, schools, and hospitals. The current efforts to restore Old Havana are possible only because it is a tourist attraction. In other areas of the city, the proprietors of *paladares* have been able to repair their crumbling properties with their profits. In the new tourism-based economy, some areas of the city are unlikely to be a restoration priority: no foreigner on vacation would want to eat lunch in a Soviet-inspired apartment building (figure 6.8).

Mario Coyula acknowledges the toxic properties of tourism and believes that the "neighborhood workshops" must somehow "rescue from degradation and cynicism a human capital amassed with endeavors, successes, mistakes, hardships and illu-

6.9
"In each neighborhood, revolution," Obispo Street in Old Havana, May 2001. Photo by Jorge Encarnación.

CLARE CARDINAL-PETT

sions." The rescue is "related to the necessity of empowering the economy of the city, neighborhood and family, with more productive activities than the elaboration of home-made sweets; thus avoiding to recreate step by step the long and tedious path from the earliest street vendors in the seedy environs of the port at the start of the 17th century."[35]

EPILOGUE

The Special Period's scarcity of food may have been a temporary phenomenon, but it has had a transformative effect on the Cuban political economy and Havana's urban fabric. Though the *comida tipica* is back on the daily menu, a taste of the global marketplace is available in every neighborhood.

Cuba's *pharmakon*, tourism, will probably cure the island of its dependence on sugar cane production, but the side effects will be lamentable. Perhaps the ancient locomotives that still haul the harvest will be assigned a more lucrative task, hauling nostalgic visitors through Cuba's history of exploitation. Perhaps there will be "living history" museums installed in the fields and mills with former engineers and teachers cutting and grinding and boiling—giving the tourists what they had in mind before they bought their tickets. Perhaps, as Tania Bruguera suggests, history will repeat itself (figure 6.9).

NOTES

1. Kim Levin, "Cuba Libre: Art and Contradiction at the Havana Bienal," *Village Voice,* December 20–26, 2000 <http://www.villagevoice.com/issues/0051/levin.php> (accessed January 2003).

2. The Bienal de la Habana was inaugurated in 1984 as a forum for artists outside the Western culture industry. The theme of the Seventh Bienal was "Closer to the Other."

3. Nico Israel, "VII Bienal de la Habana," *Artforum International* 39, no. 6 (February 2001): 147.

4. In May 2000 and May 2001, I traveled throughout the island with a Cuban national who pointed out the new shelters in towns and countryside.

5. Nitza Villapol, *Cocina cubana* (Habana: Instituto Cubano del Libro/Editorial Cientifico-Technica, 1997), 120.

6. George Semler, "Cuban Cuisine" <http://www.georgesemler.com/cubancuisine.html> (accessed January 2003).

7. Christina Garcia, "Simple Life," in *Cuba: True Stories,* ed. Tom Miller (San Francisco: Travelers Tales, 2001), 15.

8. For two of many published discussions of this opening to global capitalism, see Jon Glazer and Kurt Hollander, "Cuba's New Economy: Working for the Tourist Dollar," *Nation,* June 15, 1992, 820–824, and Thad Dunning, "Internal Bleeding," July 2001, Resource Center of the Americas <http://www/americas.org/> (accessed January 2003).

9. *Remittances* are transfers of money from abroad, legalized in the 1990s. In "Internal Bleeding," Dunning writes: "To make ends meet, roughly a third of Cubans can rely on the overseas remittances. The government collects no data on the income, which has reached an estimated $1 billion per year. But many economists speculate that remittances only worsen Cuba's inequity. Most of the money, they say, comes from the pre-revolutionary elite that fled to the United States four decades ago. These Cuban Americans, overwhelmingly white, tend to support light-skinned families in a country where most people have African ancestry."

10. The joke is recounted in a PBS *Newshour* segment by Paul Solman, "Capitalism in Cuba," July 17, 2001. A transcript of the entire report is available at <http://www.pbs.org/newshour/bb/latin_america/july-dec01/cuba_71-17.html> (accessed January 2003).

11. I borrowed the term *pharmakon* from Gayatri Spivak, who herself borrows it from Derrida when she writes, "Capitalism is thus the *pharmakon* of Marxism" (Spivak, *A Critique of Postcolonial Reason: Toward a History of the Vanishing Present* [Cambridge, Mass.: Harvard University Press, 1999], 83). Her footnote to Derrida reads: "For *pharmakon,* poison that is medicinal when knowingly administered, see Derrida, 'Plato's Pharmacy,' in *Disseminations,* tr. Barbara Johnson (Chicago: Univ. of Chicago Press, 1981), pp. 61–172."

12. Mario Coyula, "Havana Forever, Forever Havana," Grupo para el Desarrollo de la Capital (Havana, August 1996); the article is available online at <http://www.louisville.edu/org/sun/sustain/articles/1999/cuba/havanaforever/index.html> (accessed January 2003).

13. Ibid.

14. Ibid.

15. Spivak, *A Critique of Postcolonial Reason,* 84.

16. Interview with Eneide Ponce de Leon, Grupo para el Desarrollo de la Capital (GDIC), Havana, May 2001.

17. Interview with representatives from the Ministry of Agriculture, Havana, May 2001.

18. Coyula, "Havana Forever, Forever Havana."

19. Interview with Eneide Ponce de Leon.

20. Interview with Eduardo Miranda Cribeiro, Rumbos, Havana, May 2001.

21. See, for example, Stephen Zunes, "Cuba's New Revolution," *Designer/Builder,* August 2000, 5–8.

22. Interview with Egidio Paez, president of ACTAF, Havana, May 2001.

23. Interview with Mario Coyula, GDIC, Havana, May 2001.

24. Interview with Enrique Lanza, Havana, May 2001.

25. James Suckling, "Eating Well in Cuba," *Cigar Aficionado,* June 2001, 92.

26. Solman, "Capitalism in Cuba."

27. Dana Cuff, *The Provisional City* (Cambridge, Mass.: MIT Press, 2000).

28. Marian Burros, "Havana's Not for Eating, but Eating Can Be Fun," *New York Times,* August 5, 2001, Travel section.

29. Suckling, "Eating Well in Cuba," 92.

30. Burros, "Havana's Not for Eating."

31. Suckling, "Eating Well in Cuba," 92.

32. Tom Miller, *Trading with the Enemy* (New York: Basic Books, 1996), 136–137.

33. Garcia, "Simple Life," p. 15.

34. Jonathan Lerner, "The Future of Havana's Past," *Hemispheres*, June 2001, 92.

35. Coyula, "Havana Forever, Forever Havana."

PHILOSOPHY
IN THE KITCHEN

7

CUISINE AND THE COMPASS OF ORNAMENT: A NOTE ON THE ARCHITECTURE OF *BABETTE'S FEAST*

DANIEL S. FRIEDMAN

Beware of too much good staying in your hand.

—EMERSON, "Compensation"

The incomparable gourmand and architect Michael Brill liked to tell a story about the owner and chef of a famous Chinese restaurant in Fort Erie, Ontario, reputed to be among the best kitchens on the Niagara Frontier. After years of success, the venerable chef decided that it was time to find an apprentice. He would dine anonymously at Chinese restaurants in nearby Toronto until he encountered a dish to his liking. If the author of the dish proved willing and of appropriate age, he would invite the cook back to Fort Erie for an interview. The interview consisted of two tests. First, the older chef would give the younger cook an unfeathered duck, pointing to a small incision under the wing: "Remove all the bones through this hole." Next, the venerable chef would hand the candidate a raw carrot: "Prepare as though for a feast."

Through these two tests the senior chef seeks to observe the candidate's understanding of structure and decoration.[1] Each test exercises the question of good form: the first test, which requires knowledge of anatomy, enables the master chef to measure technical understanding and imagination; the second, which requires knowledge of custom, enables him to evaluate ethical disposition. Whether the carrot blossoms into a flower or evanesces into a cloud of weightless orange straw, its transformation embodies a pair of analogical proportions—carrot to not-carrot, and not-carrot to the occasion it elevates. The older chef needs someone who can do more than transform food from a fact into a poem. This latter test therefore demonstrates not so much artistic skill as suitability to context. He knows that however imaginative or unwieldy the ratio of carrot to festivity, culinary art always elaborates the immutable criterion, "fit to be eaten." The question this essay asks is, what part of "fitness" belongs to ornament?

Babette's Feast offers another good story that may help illuminate some of these distinctions. The film, which Gabriel Axel adapted from a short story by Isak Dinesen, tells the tale of a French dinner that disrupts life in a small Scandinavian fishing village.[2] The circumstances surrounding the culinary production at the heart of Dinesen's narrative bear some resemblance to the aforementioned dialectic between necessity and surplus. The story revolves around two middle-aged sisters, Martine and Philippa, who spend their days tending to the remnants of their father's austere religious community, delivering meals and ministering to his aging congregation. In the film, only two village residents operate outside the sphere of the pastor's influence: the grocer, who occasionally wears the hat of the mailman, and a French servant, a mature woman of grace and pleasant disposition named Babette.

In giving an account of how this cosmopolitan Frenchwoman came to live in such an unlikely place, both film and story flash back to the early adulthood of the sisters, who as younger women possessed uncommon beauty and talent. Inevitably, Martine and Philippa attract the attention of two sophisticated suitors—"lovers," to use Dinesen's exact appellation. The first suitor is a dashing but improvident cavalry officer named Lorens Loewenhielm. Lorens has a bad gambling problem, and so is sent by his unhappy father to his aunt's nearby country villa "to meditate and better his ways" (25). Out riding one day, he encounters Martine and falls deeply in love. In pursuit, he joins her father's prayer meeting, which both intensifies his desire and worsens his frustration. He soon leaves the village petulant and disillusioned, vowing to devote himself single-mindedly to his career.

The second suitor is a renowned French tenor named Achille Papin, who chances across a service at the village church while sightseeing on the Jutland coast. Philippa's angelic singing entrances Papin, who persuades her father to allow him to tutor her. Convinced that her talents promise to reinvigorate his own flagging career, he pleads with Philippa to return with him to Paris. Later, a romantic duet from Mozart's *Don Giovanni* ends with a stolen kiss, whereupon Philippa quits her lessons and asks her father to dismiss Papin, who departs for France empty-handed.

Babette makes her appearance fifteen years later, in the spring of 1871, long after the pastor has died. One rainy night she arrives at the sisters' door, drenched and distraught, carrying a letter of introduction from Papin. The letter explains that Babette has fled Paris after the execution of her husband and son in the Communard uprising of 1871. She has escaped arrest as a *pétroleuse* (a woman who sets fire to houses with petroleum), she is desperately seeking refuge, and she can cook. Although the sisters cannot afford to employ her, Babette convinces them to let her work without wages. Unknown to the sisters is Babette's former occupation: she is a renowned master chef, "a person known all over Paris as the greatest culinary genius of the age" (58), the proprietress of a famous Parisian restaurant called the Café Anglais.

After fourteen years, Babette has fully acclimated to life in the village. She cooks and cleans for Martine and Philippa; she charms the grocer and the fishmonger; she "miraculously" reduces household costs; she adds what native herbs she can to the sisters' parsimonious diet of ale-and-bread soup and split cod, much to the delight of the congregants. One day Babette learns that she has won ten thousand francs in a French lottery, her last thread of contact with Paris. This windfall promises to fund her return to France, and the sisters brace themselves for her departure. As a gesture of gratitude, Babette persuades Martine and Philippa to allow her to prepare a true French dinner on the occasion of the 100th birthday of their father.

Babette travels to Paris to arrange the shipment of ingredients and accoutrements for a magnificent dinner. She imports exotic foods (live quail, truffles, a sea turtle), exquisite wines, fine china, flatware, crystal, linens, and utensils—even ice. As the sisters and villagers watch this parade of unfamiliar culinary material, they grow anxious. In her nightmares Martine dreams that Babette poisons the villagers. As though to gird themselves against the witchcraft of Babette's cooking, the congregants vow not to talk at all about food during the meal. Meanwhile, Babette employs a young helper and sets to work in the sisters' small kitchen. The film settles into Babette's skilled preparation of each course, which she will send into the dining room accompanied by appropriate selections of wine.

The twelve guests arrive and take their seats, including the sisters and Lorens, now a distinguished general and member of the royal court, who has been invited as the escort of his octogenarian aunt, also a follower of the pastor. This is the dinner Babette has prepared for them:

> *Potage à la Tortue*
> *Turtle Soup*
> Amontillado Sherry
>
> *Blini Demidoff au Caviar*
> *Buckwheat cakes with caviar*
> Veuve Clicquot Champagne 1860
>
> *Caille en Sarcophage avec Sauce Perigourdine*
> *Quail in Puff Pastry Shell with Foie Gras and Truffle Sauce*
> Clos de Vougeot 1846
>
> *La Salade*
> Water
>
> *Les Fromages*
> *Cheese and Fruit Selection*
> Port
>
> *Baba au Rhum avec les Figues*
> *Rum Infused Yeast Cake with Dried Figs*
> Coffee[3]

As he begins to recognize the artistic depth of the meal, Lorens issues eager authentications of each dish and vintage, searching in vain for some eye at the table with whom he might share this unexpected pleasure. When the *plat principal* arrives, he pauses in astonishment. This could only be *Caille en sarcophage,* he declares! With earnest passion he tells the story of the Café Anglais and its renowned chef, a woman, celebrated for her artistry throughout Paris. Lorens had been taken to this restaurant as the guest of a French colleague, Colonel Galliffet, who declared of its gifted proprietress, "For no woman in all Paris . . . would I more willingly shed my blood!" *Caille en sarcophage,* he explains, was her signature dish. Galliffet claimed, Lorens continued, that she had the ability to transform a dinner into "a kind of love affair" (58).

As the meal progresses, smiles proliferate. Babette's cooking seems to alter the physiognomy of each guest, enabling contact, awakening long-forgotten and long-repressed affections. Old animosities and mistrust dissolve. Lorens, loosened by the world's noblest wine, rises to address his companions; and when he opens his mouth, he finds himself speaking "in a manner so new to himself and so strangely moving that after his first sentence he had to make a pause" (60).

One by one, transformed, the guests issue openhearted gestures of reconciliation and friendship. They retire to the parlor for coffee, awash in the emotional and physical glow of the evening: "[T]he rooms had been filled with a heavenly light, as if a number of small halos had blended into one glorious radiance. Taciturn old people received the gift of tongues; ears that for years had been almost deaf were opened to it. Time itself had merged into eternity. Long after midnight the windows of the house shone like gold, and golden song flowed out into the winter air" (61).

As Lorens prepares to leave, he confesses to Martine his lifelong love, admitting, "in this world anything is possible" (62). In Dinesen's text, the rest of the guests soon follow, spilling out of the house into freshly fallen snow. Dinesen animates this transformation of elderly bodies with bacchanalian verbs: they "wavered on their feet, staggered, sat down abruptly or fell forward on their knees and hands and were covered with snow . . . in [a] kind of celestial second childhood. . . . They stumbled and got up, walked on or stood still, bodily as well as spiritually hand in hand, at moments performing the great chain of a beatified *lanciers*" (63). In the film, holding hands, the guests dance in a ring around the village well.

Against this tender ending, we might contrast the opening scenes of the film, which adumbrate what Michael Shapiro identifies as the "antieconomy" of the village.[4] Under the title credits, Axel shows us a stark Jutland coastline set against the horizon of the sea. In a long 40-second take, the lens slowly retracts until the widened frame includes a small, gray village in the foreground. The film cuts to a close-up of flat fish, scored and salted, suspended by their tailfins on a simple birch-pole rack. Through this wooden frame, the camera pans vertically from a smoking chimney down a steep, thatched gable to the sparse village courtyard. Enter Martine and Philippa, busy on their morning rounds. As they deliver a breakfast of soup to their elderly wards, we learn from the female voice-over that the sisters "spend all their time and almost all their small income on good works." Next the film cuts to the villagers seated at the table in the sisters' house, joined in prayer and hymn. Here also for the first time we meet Babette.

This sequence sets the stage for a key moment in the flashback, when the sisters instruct Babette in the routine culinary practices of their household. Philippa pulls a fish off the rack and proceeds to show Babette how to fix it—"let it soak," she says, unceremoniously; next she breaks some bread into a bowl: let the bread soak, too. "They had distrusted Monsieur Papin's assertion that Babette could cook," Dinesen's narrator explains. "In France, they knew, people ate frogs. They showed Babette how to prepare a split-cod and an ale-and-bread soup; during the demonstration, the Frenchwoman's face became absolutely expressionless" (36).

> The idea of French luxury and extravagance . . . had alarmed and dismayed the [pastor's] daughters. The first day after Babette had entered their service they took her before them and explained to her that they were poor and that to them luxurious fare was sinful. Their own food must be as plain as possible; it was soup-pails and baskets for their poor that signified. Babette nodded her head; as a girl, she informed her ladies, she had been cook to an old priest who was a saint. Upon this the sisters resolved to surpass the French priest in asceticism. (36)

These two opposing systems of signs resemble the cultural polarity outlined by Adolf Loos in "Ornament and Crime" (1908):

> Ornament does not heighten my joy in life or the joy in the life of any cultivated person. If I want to eat of piece of gingerbread I choose one that is quite smooth and not a piece representing a heart or a baby or a rider, which is covered all over with ornaments. The man of the fifteenth century won't understand me. But all

DANIEL S. FRIEDMAN

modern people will. The advocate of ornament believes that my urge for sim-plicity is in the nature of mortification. No, respected professor at the school of applied art, I am not mortifying myself! The show dishes of past centuries, which display all kinds of ornaments to make the peacocks, pheasants and lobsters look more tasty, have exactly the opposite effect on me. I am horrified when I go through a cookery exhibition and think that I am meant to eat these stuffed carcasses. I eat roast beef.[5]

The proponents of plain beef and split cod disdain culinary superfluities. They prefer moral garnish. Luxury "can never shed its ties to its medieval past," Norman Bryson argues, or to "the battle of the soul against the deadly sins, *luxuria, superbia, vana-gloria, voluptas, cupiditas*."[6] Bryson notes that prior to industrialization it was impossible to separate the idea of luxury from ideas of prodigality and waste, a root sensibility not lost on Loos.

Loos's prohibition against ornament expands this moral code into a program for twentieth-century living, which rejects ornament on the same grounds that it rejects tattoos: both equally retard the evolution of modern culture. However, in Loos's universe, the crime of ornament registers most egregiously in its indifference to rational economics: "The twentieth century man can satisfy his needs with a far lower capital outlay and hence save money," he argues. "The vegetable he enjoys is simply boiled in water and has a little butter on it. The [eighteenth-century] man likes it equally well only when honey and nuts have been added to it and someone has spent hours cooking it. Ornamented plates are very expensive, whereas the white crockery from which the modern man likes to eat is cheap. The one accumulates savings, the other debts."[7]

Loos inveighs against wasted labor, devaluation, lost time, ruined material, and the exploitation of the artisan. "The ornamentor has to work twenty hours to achieve the income earned by a modern worker in eight," he argues. "Ornament generally increases the cost of an article; nevertheless it happens that an ornamented object whose raw material costs the same and which demonstrably took three times as long to make is offered at half the price of a smooth object." Loos renounces waste, not pleasure. "I tolerate ornaments on my own body when they constitute the joy of fellow men."[8] For Loos, the manifest joy of modern civilization, as Joseph Rykwert notes, is the pleasure of reason, which delights in useful objects unencumbered by wasteful decoration, pretense, or fuss.[9] "We have grown finer, more subtle," Loos states. "Freedom from ornament is a sign of spiritual strength."[10]

Loos's position turns on his interpretation of modern necessity and surplus, and on evolving customs that change the modern understanding of useful and wasteful expenditure. "Surplus" means first of all "what remains over and above what has been taken or used"—"an amount remaining in excess . . . a superfluity, [or] superabundance."[11] The broad spectrum of possibilities that fills the gap between necessity and surplus is filled with ideological claims. As Bryson has observed, industrialization only complicated the difference. Modern aesthetic culture, he argues, "takes up the slack from ethical culture [and] resolves the problem of [industrial] overproduction by indicating general models for managing the superabundance of goods." He explains how Victorian and modern reformist designers adapted to the problem of overabundance in their reinvention of domestic space—in the former case, through "rooms crammed with objects . . . , a general *horror vacui* which copes with the problem of overproduction by absorbing it into the household"; in the latter, "by carving out from the general profusion a secluded emptiness that marks an escape from the teeming and seething pool of commodities."[12]

Babette's feast arises in the context of a conflict between cultural superabundance and moral parsimony. In the opening scenes of the film, within the first few minutes, the director Axel takes care to show us the staple protein of the village midway along its path from sea to table. The table establishes the center of community life, the site of common daily prayer, and the scene of frugal if not utterly bland repast. "Important also in this or any dining situation, although largely latent and acknowledged unreflectively," David Leatherbarrow writes, in contemplation of typical forms of domestic order,

> is the room in which the table sits; and together with this, the room's relationship
> to the other rooms in the house; the house to the front street and rear yard; both
> to the town . . . and, finally, to one's taken-for-granted sense of the coherence of
> the whole world. . . . This set of relationships constitutes a field *or* horizon *within
> which discrete situations have their place and receive their orientation with re-
> spect to one another and to those outside the building.*[13]

In the film, food serves as a moral vector that traverses the middle ground between two opposing ontological "horizons." The first horizon we encounter is the ocean, a symbol of the "vast, undifferentiated region" of the exterior world,[14] mysterious and infinite—the source of sustenance, to be sure, but also the orientation of the "Other," especially outsiders such as Papin and Babette, who arrive by sea. Against this limitless expanse Axel contrasts a second horizon, the table—local, familiar, interior. Dinesen articulates the polarity between these two horizons in her description of the sisters' house, just before the arrival of the guests. "This low room with its bare floors and scanty furnishings was dear to the Dean's disciples. Outside its windows lay the great world . . . [in] its winter-whiteness. . . . And in summer, when the windows were open, the great world had a softly moving frame of white curtains to it" (49).

According to Gottfried Semper, all walls began as curtains. In Semper's reconstruction of the primitive hut, suspended textile partitions condition and delimit the original domestic interior. They were used "as a means to make the 'home,'" argues Semper, to separate the inner life from the outer life.[15] In Semper's principle of *Bekleidung*, which influenced Loos, Le Corbusier, and later moderns, the essence of architecture is atectonic. It resides in the "covering layer," as Mark Wigley notes, a "clothing of space" that arises out of the ancient patterns of woven fabric, which in its primitive role as divider connects the ornamented surface with the "production of social space itself." Structure is subordinate to what we hang from it; the structural wall is "merely a supporting player, playing the role of support, supporting precisely because it does not play."[16]

When Babette unfurls the tablecloth and proceeds to press out its creases, table-as-structure recedes into a secondary status. The bare dining table is "contingent scaffolding" that operates within the horizontal plane of domestic activity, no less a carrier of intentions than its vertical correlate.[17] The tablecloth masks but does not misrepresent the table, hides it but does not disguise it, to use Wigley's criterion—it "dissimulates in the name of truth."[18] Extending this logic, it is the tablecloth and not the table that defines the virtual space of Babette's feast, within which she assiduously arranges china, silverware, crystal, and candelabra, which in turn delimit the complex visual and gustatory space of high cuisine.

In the film, Axel moves back and forth between the dining room and the kitchen, where Babette labors over the preparation and delivery of the dinner, assisted by her red-haired helper and by Loewenhielm's carriage driver. Intermittently, Axel shows her helpers enjoying their dinner, too, but the effect of Babette's cooking is not quite the same. In the next room, the obvious savor of identical dishes in their proper order and setting has significantly greater consequence. In the kitchen, food is served catch-as-catch-can; and under these informal and even indecorous circumstances, the effect is necessarily limited and incomplete. In the dining room, however, the setting and decoration of the table equips the table for proper feasting, just as the embroidered vestment equips the dean to lead his congregation in prayer; just as the postal cap transforms the grocer into the mailman, so he can deliver Babette's letter; just as Lorens's uniform with its decorations and golden epaulets equips him for leadership.[19] The absence of these accessories lessens the effectiveness of religious intercession, postal delivery, and military command. "*Ornamentum*," notes A. K. Coomaraswamy, "is primarily 'apparatus, accoutrement, equipment, trappings' and secondarily 'embellishment.'"[20]

In Axel's rendition of the story, when Babette's table setting registers in the incredulous eyes of the guests as they first enter the candlelit dining room, the mise-en-scène bears out Wigley's observation, after Semper, that "the truth of architecture is always located in its visible outside."[21] The table setting frames the meal.[22] "Whitewash is inserted into the gap between the bodies of structure and decoration in order to construct a space for architecture which is neither simply bodily or theoretical," Wigley argues.[23] Babette too inserts pressed linen into the gap between the structure of the table and its decoration in order to construct a proper space for cuisine—shifting now to Dinesen's text—"in which one no longer distinguishes between bodily and spiritual appetite or satiety" (58). The mediative significance of the tablecloth finds expression in half a dozen Renaissance paintings of the Last Supper, to which both the numerological and the thematic composition of Babette's feast refer—not least in the power of the occasion to engender the resurrection of the senses, in particular those associated with the human heart.[24]

"Babette's Feast" carves out empty and secluded visual space against which Dinesen and in turn Axel contrast three eruptions of "modern" superabundance that arrive from "the great world": first Lorens, early on as an impetuously romantic career officer with a gambling problem, later as a highly decorated general who "strutted and shone like an ornamental bird . . . in this sedate party of crows and jackdaws" (51);

second, the red-mouthed Papin, full of histrionic passion and professional vainglory, whom "nobody could long withstand . . . when he really set his heart on a matter" (30); and finally, Babette, with her ten-thousand-franc lottery prize, through which Dinesen apotheosizes abundance, and her subsequent "destruction" of all that wealth in the production of a "real French dinner." All three protagonists represent the outsider, the "Other." All three in their own way and time transgress the boundaries of local decorum, and yet the product of their encounter with village life yields a middle possibility, expressed variously in Papin's letter, which envisions hope in the sisters' piety; in the emotional and spiritual dividends that flow from Babette's decision not to return to Paris; and in Lorens's recognition, near the end of his career, that real love is inextinguishable, and that "in this world anything is possible." By her culinary production, Babette introduces an intermediate ethos midway between indulgence and self-denial, through what can only be called the decorum of ornament, which frames and sustains new feelings and insights about love, loss, memory, and forgiveness.

In the denouement of the film, after the last guests have departed, Martine and Philippa return to thank Babette, who sits slumped in the steaming kitchen surrounded by pots and pans. She confirms that she was indeed the head chef at the Café Anglais, and further, that she has spent all her winnings on the dinner. In Dinesen's text, Martine suddenly recalls a tale she heard from a friend of her father's about a missionary in Africa: "He had saved the life of an old chief's favorite wife, and to show his gratitude the chief treated him to a rich meal. Only long afterwards the missionary learned . . . that what he had partaken in was a small fat grandchild of the chief's, cooked in honor of the great Christian medicine man. She shuddered" (66).

The sisters are stunned; you will be poor, they worry. "A great artist is never poor," Babette replies. She tells them that there is no one left in Paris to whom she can return: "What will I do in Paris?" she asks. "They have all gone. I have lost them all, Mesdames" (65). Babette understates the magnitude of this void: among her elite Parisian patrons the man perhaps most capable of acknowledging her artistic talent, Colonel Galliffet, is the same man (we know from Papin's letter) whose hands are stained with the blood of her husband and son. Thus Babette's "killing of wealth"—her "potlatch" (which in its verb form means both to nourish and consume)—binds her art into the matrix of ambiguity that surrounds all gift exchange: spontaneous generosity versus insidious obligation; life-giving self-sacrifice versus wasteful expenditure; symbolic reciprocity versus unconditional, uncountered, and anonymous donation.[25]

Philippa puts her arms around Babette. In Dinesen's text, which is significantly darker around the edges than the film version, this embrace contains a foreboding sensation: "She felt the cook's body like a marble monument against her own, but she herself shook and trembled from head to foot" (68). Lacking a vocabulary to express her own upwelling emotion,[26] Philippa seizes on the words she read in Papin's letter: "'Yet this is not the end! . . . In paradise you will be the great artist that God meant you to be! Ah!' she added, the tears streaming down her cheeks. 'Ah, how you will enchant the angels'" (68).[27] Notwithstanding this consolation, the inextinguishable kernel of Babette's gift is a shadow surrounding the irremediable loneliness of loss and violence that tinges her history and culture, essentially tied to its arts, its economy, and its "proliferation of signs."[28]

The ring dance at the end of the film is the real conclusion to Babette's feast, its enduring ornamental remainder. The dance suggests Semper's primordial knot and its varied progeny: daisy chain, funereal wreath, woven carpet, "the legislative and playful instincts" that animate the principle of cladding and the great (and continuous) dressing of walls that proceeds from it.[29] This ring dance offers a useful corollary to the ethical compass of ornament inherent in Babette's feast. The dance embellishes the moment of departure, both in the social and ontological sense. Like a garland on the gravestone, it ornaments Babette's memorial meal,[30] which she prepares in commemoration not just of the founding pastor but also of her own lost life—husband, son, city, country, clientele.

Babette's feast brings the villagers to their senses. It surmounts the restricted linguistic economy of the village, and in the course of the meal it gives the village the "gift of tongues" (61).[31] Yet true to their vow, the villagers don't talk about the food; they don't see food in a new way, they see each other in a new way. "The nature of decoration," Gadamer writes, "consists in performing that two-sided mediation; namely to draw the attention of the viewer to itself, to satisfy his taste, and then to redirect it away from itself to the greater whole of the context of life which it accompanies."[32] Likewise, the ring dance signifies newly strengthened seams, renewed relationships, even new possibilities, as Lorens has indicated to Martine in his soulful farewell speech, notwithstanding the dwindling days of the villagers and the proxim-

DANIEL S. FRIEDMAN

ity of death. More important, like all ornament proper to its context, the dance mediates between the ritual singularity of the monumental meal and the quotidian rhythms of daily life. As Lewis Hyde reminds us, "gift property serves an upward force."[33] Babette's gift begins its circulation here, on the middle horizon, around the village well, in "the playing body, externalizing its harmonies into acts."[34]

NOTES

In memoriam Michael Brill, 1936–2002.

1. "[O]bserve that 'décor' as 'that which serves to decorate, ornamental disposition of accessories' (Webster) is the near relative of 'decorous' or 'decent,' meaning 'suitable to a character or time, place and occasion' and to 'decorum,' that is, 'what is befitting … propriety'" (A. K. Coomaraswamy, "Ornament," in *Traditional Art and Symbolism,* vol. 1 of *Selected Papers,* ed. Roger Lipsey, Bollingen Series 89 [Princeton: Princeton University Press, 1977], 251).

2. Although my essay treats primarily the film version of *Babette's Feast,* for emphasis I employ quotes from Dinesen's original text; all citations are from Isak Dinesen, "Babette's Feast," in *Anecdotes of Destiny* (New York: Random House, 1958), with page references given parenthetically in the text. Axel's film was released in 1988; among other modifications to the original story, Axel changed the setting from Berlevaag, a small seaside town located at the foot of the mountains of a Norwegian fjord, to Denmark and the windswept coast of Jutland.

3. Several websites offer reconstructions of Babette's menu, including Barry Snyder, "Special Events: Babette's Feast" <http://www.lapoule.com/babette.htm> (accessed January 2003), and "Babette's Feast Menu," 31 December 2002 <http://www.babettescafe.com/feast.html> (accessed January 2003), from which I have adapted this version. The short story contains no reference to baba au rhum.

4. Michael J. Shapiro, "Mimetic Desire in *Babette's Feast,*" in *Reading the Postmodern Polity: Political Theory as Textual Practice* (Minneapolis: University of Minnesota Press, 1992), 62. I am indebted to this essay, which offers exceptionally useful insights into the theory of the gift.

5. Adolf Loos, "Ornament and Crime," in Ulrich Conrads, *Programs and Manifestoes on Twentieth-Century Architecture,* trans. Michael Bullock (Cambridge, Mass.: MIT Press, 1970), 21.

6. Norman Bryson, *Looking at the Overlooked: Four Essays on Still Life Painting* (Cambridge, Mass.: Harvard University Press, 1990), 96–97.

7. Loos, "Ornament and Crime," 21–22.

8. Ibid., 22, 24.

9. See Joseph Rykwert, "Ornament Is No Crime," in *The Necessity of Artifice* (New York: Rizzoli, 1982), 93.

10. Loos, "Ornament and Crime," 24.

11. *Oxford English Dictionary,* 2nd ed., s.v. "surplus."

12. Bryson, *Looking at the Overlooked,* 97.

13. David Leatherbarrow, "Adjusting Architectural Premises," *Practices,* nos. 5/6 (1997): 179.

14. Gianni Vattimo, "Ornament and Monument," in *The End of Modernity: Nihilism and Hermeneutics in Postmodern Culture,* trans. Jon R. Snyder (Baltimore: Johns Hopkins University Press, 1988), 82–83.

15. Gottfried Semper, "Style: The Textile Arts," in *The Four Elements of Architecture and Other Writings,* trans. Harry F. Mallgrave and Wolfgang Herrmann (Cambridge: Cambridge University Press, 1989), 254; quoted in Mark Wigley, "Architecture after Philosophy: Le Corbusier and the Emperor's New Paint," in *Philosophy and Architecture,* ed. Andrew Benjamin, *Journal of Philosophy and the Visual Arts,* no. 1 (London: Academy Editions, 1990), 86.

16. Wigley, "Architecture after Philosophy," 86.

17. Rykwert, "The Necessity of Artifice," in *The Necessity of Artifice,* 58; also see Wigley, "Philosophy after Architecture," 86.

18. Wigley, "Philosophy after Architecture," 87.

19. "If, for example, the judge is only a judge in act when wearing his robes, if the mayor is empowered by his chain, and the king by his crown, if the pope is only infallible and verily pontiff when he speaks ex cathedra, 'from the throne,' none of these things is a mere ornament, but rather equipment by which the man himself is 'mored'" (Coomaraswamy, "Ornament," 245).

20. Ibid., 250.

21. Wigley, "Philosophy after Architecture," 90.

22. "Ornament should serve the ornament bearer as a bracelet should serve the arm it circles; or as a picture frame should serve the framed picture. There is indeed a profound relationship between ornament and frame. Both re-present. Not that either is an indispensable condition of aesthetic beholding. To some extent, everything that strikes us as beautiful dislocates us as it captures our attention by its presence" (Karsten Harries, "Representation and Re-presentation in Architecture," *Via* 9 [1988]: 24).

23. Wigley, "Philosophy after Architecture," 89.

24. See, for example, Dieric Bouts the Elder, *The Last Supper* (1464–1467); Domenico Ghirlandaio, *Last Supper* (1476–1486); Leonardo da Vinci, *The Last Supper* (1498); Cosimo Rosselli, *Scenes from the Life of Christ: The Last Supper* (1) (1439–1507); Jacopo Bassano, *Last Supper* (1542); and Sebastiano Ricci, *The Last Supper* (1730). An Internet search on "Babette's Feast" yields innumerable posts on the religious significance and imagery of the film.

25. Antonio Somaini, "Visibility and Invisibility of the Gift," in *The Gift: Generous Offerings, Threatening Hospitality,* ed. Gianfranco Maraniello, Sergio Risaliti, and Antonio Somaini (Milan: Edizioni Charta, 2001), 27. See also Jacques Derrida, *Given Time,* vol. 1, *Counterfeit Money,* trans. Peggy Kamuf (Chicago: University of Chicago Press, 1992). On the meaning of *potlatch,* see Lewis Hyde, *The Gift: Imagination and the Erotic Life of Poetry* (New York: Vintage, 1979), 8; also Marcel Mauss, *The Gift: The Form and Reason for Exchange in Archaic Societies,* trans. W. D. Halls (New York: W. W. Norton, 1990).

26. Shapiro, "Mimetic Desire in *Babette's Feast,*" 63.

27. "Possibly there is consolation in this, but consolation is not one of the goals of critical thought" (Louis Menand, "Faith, Hope, and Clarity: September 11th and the American Soul," *New Yorker,* September 16, 2002, 98).

28. Shapiro, "Mimetic Desire in *Babette's Feast,*" 66–67.

29. Joseph Rykwert, preface to Gottfried Semper, "London Lecture of November 11, 1853," edited with a commentary by Harry Francis Mallgrave, *Res* 6 (autumn 1983): 5.

> *The work of art, [Semper] says succinctly in the Prolegomena, is man's response to the world which is full of wonder and mysterious powers, whose laws man thinks he might understand but whose riddle he never resolves, so that he remains forever in satisfied tension. The unattained completeness he conjures with play—and by building a miniature universe for himself. In this the cosmic law can be observed within the smallest dimensions of a self-contained object. By inference, therefore, the pleasures of art are analogous to those of nature. "And yet," Semper observes, "primitive man takes more pleasures in the regularities of an oar stroke and the hand beat, of the wreath and the bead-necklace, than in the less differentiated ones which nature offers him directly." ("Semper and the Conception of Style," in* The Necessity of Artifice, *127)*

Also see Harry Francis Mallgrave, *Gottfried Semper: Architect of the Nineteenth Century* (New Haven: Yale University Press, 1996).

30.

> *We could uncover other meanings . . . concerning an "ornamental" and monumental notion of the work of art. . . . What needs to be stressed is that ornamental art, both as a backdrop to which no attention is paid and as a surplus which has no possible legitimation in an authentic foundation (that is, in what is "proper" to it), finds in Heideggerian ontology rather more than a marginal self-justification, for it becomes the central element of aesthetics and, in the last analysis, of ontological meditation itself. . . . What is lost in the foundation and ungrounding which is ornament is the heuristic and critical function of the distinction between decoration and surplus and what is "proper" to the thing and to the work. (Vattimo, "Ornament and Monument," 87–88).*

31. Shapiro, "Mimetic Desire in *Babette's Feast*," 66–67.
32. Hans-Georg Gadamer, *Truth and Method*, rev. ed., trans. Joel Weinsheimer and Donald Marshall (New York: Crossroad, 1988), 140.
33. Hyde, *The Gift*, 25.
34. Rykwert, preface to Semper, "London Lecture of November 11, 1853," 5.

8

GINGERBREAD HOUSES: ART, FOOD, AND THE POSTWAR ARCHITECTURE OF DOMESTIC SPACE

BARBARA L. MILLER

Although architecturally humble by comparison, gingerbread houses share many qualities with their upper-class counterparts. Like the ornate edible structures that in past centuries graced the tables of kings and affluent bourgeois, these candy-laced, often single-story constructions have enchanted and bewitched their admirers. But unlike their majestic relatives, the bewitching qualities of gingerbread structures always had less to do with the baker's architectural skills—though in more lavish renditions they admittedly play a role—than with the folklore associated with gingerbread itself.

During the Middle Ages, gingerbread was a carnival delicacy and many European festivals were known as "gingerbread fairs."[1] At some celebrations, fairgoers brought gingerbread gifts to give to family and friends. The various shapes of these gifts often symbolized the seasonal timing of the fair: buttons and flowers were available at Easter, and animals and birds were found at late summer festivities. At other fairs, revelers bought the favor because, within the local folklore, it had the power to bring its consumer's desires to life. At more than one village celebration, unmarried women nibbled away at gingerbread "husbands," consuming the cookies to increase their chances of meeting a spouse.[2] Likewise, fantasies of oral gratification resurface in the story of the gingerbread boy; a cookie or pancake comes to life and runs away from its maker while a series of animals and people try to catch and eat the animated edible. Unsurprisingly, the enchanted qualities of gingerbread also appear in the well-known children's fairy tale "Hansel and Gretel," a story that unites edible architecture, oral gratification, and the cannibalistic undertones of fairground folklore and stories of runaway food.

The bewitching qualities of gingerbread have never really gone away.[3] They merely resurface in a number of stories and contexts, at times crossing over into real-life architecture. For example, in the nineteenth century the sugar-lace construction inspired an actual style. Many Victorians decorated their eaves, verandas, and porches with gingerbread-like ornamentation. Although these houses demonstrate a desire to become entranced within in a gingerbread fantasy, the tale of "Hansel and Gretel" provides a more appropriate metaphor for the postwar American housing boom and consumer culture. In a Hansel-and-Gretel-like fashion, working-class families bought single-story cookie-cutter bungalows and stuffed them with newly designed appliances and grocery-store-bought food. As in "Hansel and Gretel," the promise of a life of leisure and plentitude seduced families into suburbia. And, as in the fairy tale—or, as the brothers Grimm called them, household tales, thereby emphasizing their domestic origins—the kitchen played a dominant role, for it became the site of a plot reversal. In "Hansel and Gretel," as Allen Weiss astutely points out, oral gratification turns into an "eating disorder" and the fear of being eaten.[4] The very home and kitchen that was to provide freedom for working-class families and to furnish a life of luxury for the postwar bride—at least in the fantasies promoted in the media of the day—had by the end of the 1950s undergone a dramatic reversal and an "eating disorder" threatened the integrity of the domestic sphere.

In the opening of "Hansel and Gretel," a famine has beset the countryside in which a woodcutter and his family live. Fearing that they all will starve, Hansel and Gretel's father and stepmother decide to save themselves by abandoning their children deep in the woods. After three days of wandering, the children, now ravenously hungry, stumble upon a "miraculous gingerbread house in the middle of the forest, ornamented with cakes and tarts and windows formed of barleysugar."[5] Amazed at

BARBARA L. MILLER

their good fortune, Hansel and Gretel tear off pieces of the house. Just as they begin to bite into their architectural treats, they hear an old woman cry: "Nibble, nibble, I hear a mouse . . . Who's that nibbling at my house?"[6] The children, lost in gastronomic bliss, ignore her shrill voice and continue to feast on the house. Instead of scolding the young pair, the old woman invites them into her kitchen. Overwhelmed, they readily accept her invitation, and once inside are even more bewitched. The old woman treats them to a meal of "milk and pancakes with sugar and apples and nuts."[7] Now that they are fully within her trap, the old woman begins to force-feed the children. Once they are fattened up, she plans to roast them in her oversized oven and afterward enjoy a hearty meal of tender young prey.

In "Hansel and Gretel," oral gratification drives the plot as it shifts from abandonment to rescue. But oral gratification is an unstable concept that easily reverses into oral sadism. As they enter the kitchen, the very device that produced the gingerbread house—the oversized oven—foretells their destiny. The oven signifies "an ever greater and more primal fear" than that of starvation: the fear of being devoured.[8]

The story line in "Hansel and Gretel" uncannily resembles the events that animated 1950s postwar consumer culture. Like the fairy tale, the desire to live a life of leisure and plentitude drove the housing market in the 1950s when a large segment of the population, mostly white working-class families, bought low-cost, modest, ranch or bungalow-style structures.[9] Admittedly, these structures did not exhibit a clearly defined architectural gingerbread style, beyond their being mostly single-story homes with walls, windows, and kitchen cabinets often decorated by their owners with gingerbread-like trim. But the hunger for them was real: the unveiling of a new home in either the Long Island or Pennsylvania Levittowns could produce, as Thomas Hine points out, "mile-long lines of would-be buyers, snaking through the muddy remains of farmer's fields."[10] As many waited to walk through the cordoned-off newspaper-lined aisles that threaded through the interior of the model home, they experienced a sense of salivary anticipation and gastronomic excitement. Manufactured houses were more than just protection from the elements. They were a means to satisfy a decade-long feeling of deprivation.

After having endured the hardships of the Depression and World War II, many working-class families began to catch up. The postwar era was, as Hine states, "one of history's great shopping sprees" during which the American public went on "baroque benders" to fill their freshly acquired mass-produced houses with newly designed furniture and appliances.[11] Working-class bungalows, complete with appliances, were symbols of desire, reflections of identity, and showcases of consumer fantasy.[12] As such, they drew homeowners further into the woods.

As extolled in the media of the day, the architectural centerpiece of these fantastic homes was the kitchen or, more precisely, the "Kitchen of Tomorrow."[13] And while the kitchen of tomorrow was a dominant fantasy that appeared in a number of advertisements and in several women's magazine editorials, its most vivid incarnation appeared in the often-cited short film "Design for Dreaming"—a precursor of today's infomercial. In the 1956 M.P.O. production, a brisk wind magically carries an invitation through the night air. Landing on a bed, it awakens a "sleeping beauty" who discovers that she is invited to a Motorama. As the young woman excitedly twirls around the room, her pink pajamas melt into a satin evening grown. Now appropriately dressed, she glides through the air and lands inside New York's Waldorf Hotel. Suddenly, in the midst of the festivities, she sprouts a black-and-white striped apron. Aghast, she swoons into the arms of a masked man. He whisks her away, only to abandon her in a kitchen. Alone and forlorn, she sings: "Just like a man, you give him a break and you wind up in the kitchen baking a cake." No sooner are the words out of her mouth than the homemaker realizes that this kitchen is like no other that she has seen. "There's no need for the bride to feel tragic," she gleefully bellows, "the rest is push-button magic . . . You don't have to be chained to the stove all day. Just set the timer and you're on your way." With the push of a button, the oven bakes a cake—taking care of every step, from batter to candles—and she is free "to have fun around the clock."

In the 1950s, many advertisements depicted "model brides"—dressed in evening gowns, at times wearing gloves and tiaras—manipulating controlled appliances with multibutton controls. Advertisers used push-button gadgets to signify the fantasy of a carefree and leisure-filled life. This fantasy was meant to entice women to leave their wartime jobs and return to the kitchen.[14] Once inside, it was not the oven that became the homemaker's destiny, but "push-button magic." Inside the kitchen of tomorrow, a retrofitted site worthy of Dr. Strangelove, the push-button foretold her fate.

During the war, companies such as Raytheon, General Electric, Westinghouse, Goodyear, Motorola, and Chrysler were major contractors of defense weapons for the U.S. military. Afterward, these companies returned to the domestic appliance market.[15]

　　BARBARA L. MILLER

Many scrambled to meet consumer demands, expanding home versions of their commercial product lines. In addition, contractors used their wartime expertise to retrofit household appliances. To entice homemakers into replacing their old-fashioned appliances, companies added push-buttons to washers and stoves, and designed streamlined toasters and vacuum cleaners.[16] In this way, American domestic consumer culture incorporated the nation's wartime technology and economic policies. And the process of bringing the arms race into the domestic sphere transformed the consumer market into the strongest the world had yet known, breaking down the distinctions between domestic consumer culture and external cold war policies, between washing machines and rockets.

The most widely quoted moment in which the extent of this collapse becomes crystal clear was the "Kitchen Debate"—an informal conversation between two world leaders attending an international exhibition. In 1959, then Vice President Richard Nixon attended the American Exhibition in Moscow. The exhibition was part of a cultural exchange program between the Soviet Union and the United States. Earlier that year, the Russians had mounted a display in New York, exhibiting Sputniks, space capsules, furs, dishes, and refrigerators. While the technology was well received, critics poked fun at what they saw as outdated women's fashions and outmoded household appliance designs. Later that year, the United States responded with a similar display in Moscow. In his opening speech, Nixon capitalized on the perceived weakness of Russian domestic culture, promising its host a glimpse of "an extraordinary high standard of living" enjoyed by Americans. After his speech, the vice president and Premier Nikita Sergeyevich Khrushchev toured the U.S. exhibition together, briefly stopping at the kitchen display. Standing beside Khrushchev, Nixon exclaimed: "We hope to show our diversity and our right to choose. . . . Would it not be better to compete in the merits of washing machines than the relative strengths of rockets?"[17]

Nixon's comments are not simply glib. They demonstrate the degree to which the strength of consumer culture had become the new measure of national superiority. As Elaine Tyler May points out, American consumer culture "had tremendous propaganda value, for it was those affluent homes, complete with breadwinner and homemaker, that provided evidence of the superiority of the American way of life. Since much of the cold war was waged in propaganda battles, this vision of domesticity was a powerful weapon."[18] Within cold war propaganda battles, the image of American affluence was undeniably a powerful weapon that gave the United States an edge over the Soviet Union. However, this use of American domestic prosperity in international policies had profound ramifications at home.

In the late 1950s, the threat of nuclear disaster crossed the minds of most consumers. In a 1959 Gallup poll, as Hine notes, the majority of people believed that life would continue to improve year by year, but they also believed that nuclear war was likely.[19] In this context, "push-button magic" could mean turning on a wash cycle or dropping a bomb; it could mean living the good life or not living at all. The collapse between the kitchen and battlefield fostered an additional architectural alteration. In the late 1950s, the kitchen of tomorrow was itself an object of retrofitting. The kitchen became a veneer that hid—if not in reality, at least in the media fantasies then circulating—an underground bunker.

In the late 1950s and early 1960s, many began to discuss the necessity of underground bunkers. Some advertisers began to exploit this debate and again targeted the "honeymoon couple." One of the most whimsical instances is captured in a 1959 *Life* magazine article. Here, a two-page pictorial article depicts a newlywed couple who spent their honeymoon in a bomb shelter. The accompanying photographs show the newlyweds surrounded by canned foods, plastic plates, and portable furniture.[20] Even though the romantic sojourn turned out to be a builder's publicity stunt, bomb shelters were serious business. In 1961 President Kennedy addressed the American public with a letter published in the September issue of *Life* magazine, warning that nuclear weapons and "the possibility of nuclear war are facts of life we cannot ignore today."[21] Kennedy urged readers to study carefully the accompanying article that showed how to construct and stock a bomb shelter.

Although most families did not build a bomb shelter, American families internalized, at least on a fantasy level, a bunker or stockpiling aesthetic. As Karal Ann Marling points out, corporations, propaganda agencies, and news magazines alike promoted a bunkerlike hoarding mentality and encouraged families to overstock their kitchen shelves and to accumulate appliances. Consumers

delighted in pictures showing American families surrounded by all the groceries they would consume in an average year. Like the endless shots taken in well-stocked supermarkets, such photos celebrated abundance, insisted on its reality,

and served to ward off whatever threatened America's kitchens of tomorrow, crammed with instant mashed potatoes and ready-to-heat-'n-eat, homestyle, frozen Salisbury steaks.[22]

Egged on by these images, housewives became, as May puts it, "unwitting soldiers" who marched off to "the nation's shopping centers to equip their new homes," stock-piling food in kitchens, basement pantries, freezers, and refrigerators. In this way, housewives joined "the ranks of American cold warriors" and patriotically helped build a strong postwar economy.[23] In the process, however, they lowered their expectations.

Rather than holding out for a computerized kitchen—where machines cooked cakes from scratch while housewives played tennis—American homemakers bought dehydrated cake ingredients, packaged in smartly designed boxes decorated with enticing graphic illustrations.[24] By the late fifties, the fairy-tale home that had initially spurred fantastic shopping sprees—in which consumers expressed their desires and identities—became "America's symbolic first line of defense against the bombs [feared to be] concealed in Russian satellites."[25] Postwar policies effectively trans-formed pleasure in consumption into oral sadism *and* the fear of destruction into a marketing ploy.

Advertisers were not the only segment of the culture to capitalize on this rever-sal: the logic of consumer culture was not lost on pop artists. Many used images of food in their work to address the marketing ploy that had redesigned the very fabric of postwar consumer culture.

In *I Love You with My Ford* (1961; figure 8.1), James Rosenquist constructs a type of triple-decker sandwich. On the top layer, he depicts the front grill section of a 1950s Ford. Beneath the Ford, he portrays a black-and-white truncated image that, on closer examination, turns out to be the ear and the lips of a couple caught in an embrace. Beneath the lovers, the artist depicts the grotesquely enlarged contents of a can of Chef Boyardee spaghetti. In stacking the different layers, Rosenquist seems to sug-gest that the Ford, a popular make-out site for teenagers in the 1960s, was ultimately a type of meat grinder that transformed its occupants into "soupy" pasta. To "love" with one's Ford, Rosenquist suggests, is to become its casualty.

In works such as *F-111* (1965), the artist expands his critique of American con-sumer culture. In this piece, Rosenquist paints a life-size image of a U.S. bomber, an

BARBARA L. MILLER

F-111. He then uses a string of images, gleaned from magazines and newspapers, to camouflage sections of the plane. As in *I Love You with My Ford,* pasta plays a dominant metaphoric role. It is the backdrop that Rosenquist paints behind the nose cone. The enlarged red and yellow mass of noodles plays off the mushroom cloud of a detonated atomic bomb and the air bubbles of an underwater diver. In *F-111,* Rosenquist uses Chef Boyardee spaghetti to signify neither freedom nor, as Nixon had it, "our right to choose" from a variety of postwar products. Instead, he employs it to suggest that consumer choice oscillates between oral pleasure and self or mass destruction.

The reversible logic of consumer culture is also evident in Andy Warhol's work, from his early series of hand-painted ads to his later photo-silkscreens. In pieces such as *Icebox* (1960) and *Peach Halves* (1960; figure 8.2), Warhol replicates images from kitchen appliance and food ads. Rather than exactly copying these items, which he undoubtedly had the skill to do (he had been a successful commercial artist), the artist allows single drops of paint to drip down the canvas. While these drips playfully evoke abstract expressionism, they also hint at some type of internal breakdown or brewing catastrophe. The idea of an internal deterioration is expressed even more overtly in works such as *Tunafish Disaster* (1963; figure 8.3). Here, Warhol lifts the story of two housewives directly from newspapers: Mrs. Brown and Mrs. McCarthy shared a sandwich made from tainted store-bought tuna and died of food poisoning. Their death made headlines across the country. The A&P tin of tuna that, along with countless other industrially manufactured foods, was to liberate homemakers had suddenly turned into its opposite, linked to the fear of destruction.

Even though pop artists visualized the reversible logic of consumer culture, they rarely depicted the figure most central to the domestic space, the homemaker—save for some of Tom Wesselmann's domestic interiors and of course his "Great American Nude" series. The artist who most often visualizes the postwar homemaker, showing how the architecture of postwar culture transformed that figure's role in the domestic sphere, is Laurie Simmons. In "The Lady Vanishes: A Conversation between Laurie Simmons and Cindy Sherman," Simmons states that in her work she tries to show how the postwar homemaker disappeared into the domestic space and exists "only as some kind of stereotype."[26]

In works such as *New Kitchen/New View* (1978), Simmons returns to her memories of growing up in the postwar era and designs a miniature scene that mimics

8.2

Andy Warhol, *Peach Halves*, 1960.

8.3

Andy Warhol, *Tunafish Disaster*, 1963.

BARBARA L. MILLER

1950s kitchen advertisements. Like the creators of the ads, Simmons poses a figurine—seduced into buying appliances and lured into shopping for partially prepared food—next to an overstocked tabletop. But unlike the women pictured in the ads, Simmons's homemaker is unable to strike a stylish pose and show off her new appliances. The forlorn, shell-shocked miniature stands with her arms firmly pinned to her sides. Unable to display her push-button know-how and powerless to demonstrate her finely tuned stockpiling skills, she fades into her environment.[27]

In this series, Simmons suggests that the reversible logic of consumer culture turns on a fantasy of destruction that is most strongly associated with oral incorporation. As Margaret Morse argues, oral incorporation deviates from dominant identificatory fantasies, which are based on similarity: typically, we identify with those whom we resemble or aspire to become. In contrast, identification in oral incorporation is based on closeness and proximity. Here, according to Morse, an "oral-sadistic" or "cannibalistic" fantasy occurs in which "the introjected object . . . is occluded and destroyed, only in order to be assimilated and to transform its host." Distinctions between subjects and objects thus become unclear. The "fusion of oral incorporation is a more-than-closeness: it involves introjecting or surrounding the other (or being introjected or surrounded) and ultimately, the mixing of two 'bodies' in a dialectic of inside and outside that can involve a massive difference in scale."[28]

In her domestic interiors, Simmons rejects any nostalgic return to a "kinder," more domesticated prewar figure. Instead, she speaks to a postwar fantasy that by the end of the 1950s had gobbled up and incorporated the homemaker into the domestic interior. That result is far from being a fantasy dreamed up by the artist; Simmons merely exaggerates the furniture designs and domestic product ads of the era.

Designers of the 1950s refashioned objects from Coke bottles to kitchen chairs so that they took on a feminine or hourglass-shaped form. Even cars with rocket-inspired tail fins had breast-shaped bullets attached to their bumpers. They were, as Marling puts it, "a chorus girl coming, a fighter plane going."[29] The product ads of the day only furthered the synecdochic relationship between the female body and consumer culture. For instance, in a 1946 Proctor Silex advertisement, a shiny new toaster sits in the lower left portion of the image. The toaster partially obscures a bride dressed in a stylish off-the-shoulder satin gown. Like a genie in a bottle, she magically pops out of the toaster and dutifully takes on her role as housewife. Similarly, in a

1950s "Softasilk" Betty Crocker cake mix ad, a pink-frosted cake topped with fresh strawberries partially obscures a miniature image of Betty herself. Because her red top matches the berries, the figurehead seems to grow out of the icing. In many of these postwar ads, the female figure becomes an object among the consumables, and the authority of the product—either the appliance or the product name—usurps the importance of the female figure's role in the domestic sphere. She is consumed by the very fast food that the ads had promised would bring her a life of domestic freedom.

Likewise, in *New Kitchen/New View,* Simmons illustrates a synecdochic relationship between the female figure and her surroundings. In the piece, the female figurine's plastic dress picks up the red hues repeated in the decorative items on the kitchen counters and the fabric on the chair seats. In addition, the size of her torso almost matches the jar of "pure milk" that sits on the table. The plastic homemaker becomes an object among the objects.

Oral incorporation is a theme that pervades Simmons's work. In "Color Coordinated Interiors" (her next series of photographs), Simmons's homemakers fade more thoroughly into their environments. In her "Walking Object" series, she takes her analogy one step further: works such as *Walking Birthday Cake* (1989) suggest that the homemaker becomes a walking gastronomic favor herself.

The reversible oral logic of consumer culture also resurfaces in a host of second- and third-generation artists' work. Unlike their predecessors of the 1960s, who traded on the fear of destruction, many contemporary artists often use it to explore the limitations of postwar domestic propaganda and gender stereotypes. Some return to the kitchen to make their point; others use consumer items to highlight cannibalistic fantasies and interpersonal relationships.

For example, in *Grind, Sift, and Serve* (1998; figure 8.4), the multimedia artist Carol Prusa draws on her homemaking skills. In the piece, she transforms a simple act of consumption and collection into an artistic activity: for six years, she saved the eggshells from her family's daily meals. She then ground the shells into fine pieces with a mortar and pestle, poured them into a flour sifter, and carefully dispersed them onto unfired clay plates. Unlike the witch of "Hansel and Gretel," Prusa shoved plates instead of children into the hot oven. During the firing, the eggshells, like tiny seeds, adhered to the surface of the plates. In the public installation of this work, Prusa uses the fired mixed-bodied ceramic plates as building pieces. Rather than constructing a

gingerbread house reminiscent of those depicted on holiday magazine covers in the 1950s, the artist arranges them on top of a bed of broken eggshells. Although the shells point to the emptiness of the domestic sphere and the evacuation of the domestic act, the plates serve as new surfaces capable of sustaining new life. In her accompanying performances, Prusa paints individual images—ranging from yolk patterns to religious icons—onto the surface of each plate. Prusa develops the Virgin Mary as an alter ego, signifying a good and bad mother who both devours and regurgitates art forms.

Like Prusa, Janine Antoni also uses domestic materials, such as soap, lard, chocolate, and hair dye, and converts the most basic forms of personal activities—eating, bathing, mopping, and primping—into art. Through the use of these media, Antoni transforms such artistic practices as sculpture and drawing into intimate processes. "I imitate," states Antoni, "basic fine art rituals such as chiseling (with my teeth), painting (with my hair and eyelashes), modeling and molding (with my own body)." She describes biting as an evocative practice, "both intimate and destructive; it sort of sums up my relationship to art history. I feel attached to my artistic heritage and I want to destroy it: it defines me as an artist and it excludes me as a woman, all at the same time."[30]

In her best-known works, *Chocolate Gnaw* (1992) and *Lard Gnaw* (1992), Antoni fabricated two large cubes. While their shapes evoke Donald Judd's early minimalist sculptures, her choice of building materials takes the work in a different direction. Instead of masonry and steel that need to be formed in a factory, Antoni worked with more malleable substances—chocolate and lard. Antoni hauled these materials not to a factory but into her kitchen, where she carefully melted the chocolate and the lard into a viscous and motile matter. Layer by layer, she poured the hot liquids into separate molds. *Chocolate Gnaw* and *Lard Gnaw* are each 600-pound, 2-foot by 2-foot cubes, the building blocks of a would-be gingerbread house that both attracts and repels its viewer.

Antoni claims to have selected these materials because while they are both high in fat they elicit contrary responses: chocolate usually summons up oral pleasure, at times to the point of an erotic response, whereas lard often evokes oral revulsion. During the final fabrication of the pieces, Antoni played with ideas of seduction and repulsion. Over the course of several weeks, Antoni bit into each material. Rather than swallowing, she spit out the chewed chocolate and lard, collecting the spew in receptacles. The collected expectorations became raw material, used in the secondary stage of her production.

Antoni took the chocolate slurry and molded it into heart-shaped brown "plastic" trays. And she combined the lard spew with pigment and beeswax and transformed it into colorful red lipstick. In doing so, she destabilizes the boundaries between inside and outside. What was once inside now holds items meant to be ingested, and what once evoked oral repulsion is now worn as an outer adornment on the very orifice whence it came. In both cases, the connection to spit-out food adds a psychological dimension.

While Antoni was aware that many would associate her act of gnawing and spitting with bulimia, she was surprised that the piece, in her words, "would become a kind of illustration of the whole idea of eating disorders!" Antoni counters with the observation that bulimia is more than an individual eating disorder; it can also be seen as a "metaphor for a society that ferociously gobbles everything up, and rather than digesting it, they spit it up."[31] Additionally, she argues that it is not the psychological eating disorder that informs her work, but the notion that oral incorporation can become an intersubjective cultural exchange.

Biting and spitting in her work are concerned less with a specific gender relationship to food than with a desire for closeness. Antoni states that her act of biting in her artwork "has to do with the question of knowing an object or experiencing it." It has to do with being able to be close to her audience: "Have you ever," she asks, "had the experience of being on the subway and sitting on a seat that is still warm from the person who sat there before? I want to give the viewer that experience. That is *my* way of accounting for the viewer. I want to get a little too close."[32] Through embracing a strategy of oral incorporation, Antoni mixes two bodies in a way that involves not a massive difference in scale but a tremendous collapse of distance between the artist and the viewer.

Felix Gonzalez-Torres similarly alludes to a desire to be close to his audience. In the early 1990s, he did a series of candy spills that featured large quantities of colorful wrapped candies. In the installation, the artist either heaped the spills into piles in corners of galleries or spread them out into rectangular shapes in centers of museum floors. In a piece called *Untitled (Placebo)* (1991) Gonzalez-Torres constructed a shiny gold carpet of candy that covered a 6-foot-by-12-foot section of the gallery floor. In each installation of the piece, hundreds of foil wrapped candies would seduce gallery-goers into walking up and sampling some of the display. In the process, the samplers became involved in a highly charged activity that oscillates between the political and the private.

The parenthetical word in the title, *placebo*, refers to the controversial blind tests of AZT. In the late 1980s and early 1990s, in programs to determine the effectiveness of the drug in fighting AIDS, hospitals gave some patients AZT and others sugar pills. There was no shortage of voluntary participants, for many HIV-positive men had no health insurance and nowhere else to go. The total weight of the candies in the spill represents the combined weight of the artist and his lover, Ross, who in 1991 died of an AIDS-related illness.[33] In taking a candy, gallery-goers simultaneously entered into a desperate social contract and participated in the sense of personal loss acutely experienced by the artist. Gonzalez-Torres states that the idea to produce pieces in which gallery-goers helped themselves to an endless supply of candy was "an attempt on my part to rehearse my fears of having Ross disappear day by day in front of my eyes."[34] The candy spill series opened up a space in which gallery-goers, as the art critic Robert Storr notes, can comfortably (or uncomfortably) enter "into a conversation about art, and death, and public policy."[35] Ultimately, though the spills are about being generous, "giving back to the viewer, to the public," the simple act of giving away candy brings the artist closer to his audience.[36]

The metaphor of the "Hansel and Gretel" fairy tale elucidates the shifts within the postwar domestic space. Through the promise of oral pleasure, the homemaker and her wage-earning partner, like Hansel and Gretel, fell prey to a blurring of boundaries between inside and out, satiation and destruction. In 1950s consumer culture, push-button magic was applied simultaneously to household items and military defense systems. Moreover, oral incorporation was far from remaining underground; as artists from Rosenquist to Antoni demonstrate, it informed and continues to inform many artists' individual critical practices. Rather than merely repeating the threat, as did pop artists, more recent artists use the idea of oral incorporation to comment on cultural stereotypes, explore public policy, and demonstrate a desire for closeness. As we look back at some of the actions of visitors to the 1959 American Exhibition in Moscow, perhaps Nixon and Khrushchev had it wrong. On entering the grocery store section,

BARBARA L. MILLER

fairgoers mistook the display for samples and, like viewers of Gonzalez-Torres's candy spills, readily helped themselves to consumable items on the shelves. Rather than emphasizing strength through washing machines and rockets, perhaps new lines of communication could have been established, leading to new policies of closeness.

NOTES

1. A number of websites discuss the history of gingerbread: e.g., see Tarla Fallgatter, "A Taste of Cyberspace: The History of Gingerbread," January 1996 <http://www.wwwiz.com/issue04/wiz_d04.html> (accessed January 2003), and "Classroom Connections," on Jim Aylesworth, *The Gingerbread Man*, 2000 <http://www.ayles.com/gingerbread2.html> (accessed January 2003).

2. Roger Pelcher, "The History of Gingerbread" <http://www.worldrecordgingerbreadhouse.com/history.html> (accessed January 2003).

3. See Lyle Rexer, "Fairy Tales Move to a Darker, Wilder Part of the Forest," *New York Times*, April 7, 2002.

4. Allen S. Weiss, "Edible Architecture, Cannibal Architecture," in *Eating Culture*, ed. Ron Scapp and Brian Seitz (Albany: State University of New York Press, 1998), 161–168.

5. Ibid., 161. While the brothers Grimm do not explicitly describe the house as made of gingerbread, most other versions do.

6. *The Complete Fairy Tales of the Brothers Grimm*, trans. Jack Zipes (New York: Bantam, 1987), 61.

7. Ibid., 62.

8. Weiss, "Edible Architecture," 161.

9. When the first Levittown opened in 1952, houses were only sold to white families. By 1957, some black families had purchased homes, but often the community did not accept them. See Nicholas Wapshott, "In New York" (column), *Times* (London), June 28, 2002.

10. Thomas Hine, *Populuxe* (New York: Alfred A. Knopf, 1987), 10.

11. Ibid., 3. Also see Elaine Tyler May, *Homeward Bound: American Families in the Cold War Era* (New York: Basic Books, 1988), 165.

12. The family home was the site where the male wage earner "could display his success through the accumulation of consumer goods. Women, in turn, would reap rewards for domesticity by surrounding themselves with commodities" (May, *Homeward Bound*, 164).

13. The workshop—the analogous "male-"centered room in the house—ran a close second to the kitchen.

14. The infomercial, the retrofitted appliances, and the Hollywood melodrama did not invent the message, but all promoted it. At the end of the war, government and social campaigns sought to persuade women, most particularly married women, to give up their jobs to make room for returning veterans.

15. The connection between appliances and weapons was not hidden from postwar consumers. As Christin Mamiya points out, "Ads for Westinghouse defense hardware were often sandwiched in between ads for Westinghouse refrigerators or light bulbs, and in each case the slogan was the same: 'You can be sure if it's Westinghouse'" (Mamiya, *Pop Art and Consumer Culture: American Super Market* [Austin: University of Texas Press, 1992], 30).

16. Washing machines, refrigerators, and vacuums came into common use in the early twentieth century, and electric toasters and percolators were developed in the 1920s.

17. Nixon, quoted in "Special International Report," *Newsweek,* August 3, 1959, 17. On October 4, 1957, the Russians demonstrated their technological superiority by launching Sputnik I into orbit around the earth. Although the device was a harmless transmitter, its invasion of American airspace caused much concern. In 1959 Nixon could afford to make light of the Soviet breakthrough. On January 31, 1958, the United States finally put a satellite into orbit, Explorer I. See Michael Wright, "Here Comes Sputnik!" March 16, 2002 <http://www.batnet.com/mfwright/sputnik.html> (accessed February 2003).

18. May, *Homeward Bound,* 167.

19. Hine, *Populuxe,* 39.

20. Mr. and Mrs. Melvin Mininson spent fourteen days in a fallout shelter. The shelter was a 22-ton, steel-and-concrete 8-foot by 14-foot structure, 12 feet underground. After emerging, the couple threw a party at a Miami beach hotel and then went on to spend two weeks in Mexico, paid for by the "grateful" builder of the shelter. See "Their Sheltered Honeymoon," *Life,* August 10, 1959, 51–52.

21. "Fallout Shelters," *Life,* September 15, 1961, 95.

22. Karal Ann Marling, *As Seen on TV: The Visual Culture of Everyday Life in the 1950s* (Cambridge, Mass.: Harvard University Press, 1994), 251.

23. May, *Homeward Bound,* 168.

24. Admittedly, in the late 1950s computerized kitchens were probably not feasible. Only now, with new technologies—computers, the Internet and wireless connections (also legacies of World War II policies)—are we moving toward state-of-the-art homes, not just kitchens. While technologically enhanced kitchens may still never materialize, the 1950s fantasy of the kitchen of tomorrow fell by the wayside, not just because the technology was not there but also because cultural and economic policies shifted. It is more profitable to sell a multitude of partially prepared foods and a number of devices needed to prepare them than to promote a kitchen filled with single-purchase timesaving gadgets that make food from scratch.

25. Marling, *As Seen on TV,* 251.

26. Simmons, quoted in Cindy Sherman, "The Lady Vanishes: A Conversation between Laurie Simmons and Cindy Sherman," in *Cindy Sherman* (Tokyo: Parco, 1987), 12.

27. Here Simmons seems to address an overlooked theme in "Hansel and Gretel." Although the fairy tale is peopled with women—a mother, a stepmother, and an evil witch—these women are expendable. Meanwhile, the father, who goes along with his wife's plan to get rid of his children, is readily forgiven.

28. Margaret Morse, "What Do Cyborgs Eat? Oral Logic in an Information Society," in *Culture on the Brink: Ideologies of Technology,* ed. Gretchen Bender and Timothy Druckrey (Seattle: Bay Press, 1994), 160.

29. Marling, *As Seen on TV,* 141.

30. Antoni, quoted in Laura Cottingham, "Janine Antoni: Biting Sums Up My Relationship to Art History," *Flash Art,* no. 171 (summer 1993): 104–105.

31. Antoni, quoted in Laura Trippi, "'Untitled Artists' Projects by Janine Antoni, Ben Kinmont, Rirkrit Tiravanija," in Scapp and Seitz, eds., *Eating Culture,* 144.

32. Ibid., 144, 152.

33. Sadly, in 1996 Gonzalez-Torres also died of AIDS-related illnesses.

34. Gonzalez-Torres, quoted in Andrea Rosen, "Untitled (The Neverending Portrait)," in *Felix Gonzalez-Torres* (Ostfildern: Cantz, 1997), 44. While at a show at the Walker Art Museum, I asked about the management of the spills. Officials there told me that once the candies go down to a specified level, galleries are contractually obligated to restock the spill.

35. Robert Storr, "Setting Traps for the Mind and Heart," *Art in America,* January 1996, 71.

36. "Felix Gonzales-Torres," interview by Tim Rollins in *Between Artists: Twelve Contemporary American Artists Interview Twelve Contemporary American Artists,* ed. Lucinda Barnes, Miyoshi Barosh, William S. Bartman, and Rodney Sappington (Los Angeles: A.R.T. Press, 1996), 48. Gonzalez-Torres also did a series of poster stacks. In these pieces, visitors to the gallery take away not candies but individually designed posters.

9

SCIENCE DESIGNED AND DIGESTED:
BETWEEN VICTORIAN AND
MODERNIST FOOD REGIMES

MARK HAMIN

Secrets of Torture of Volunteers Students, Seeking Funds for College Expenses . . . Patients Are Strapped in Air-Tight Coffins, Mouths Sealed and Tubes Inserted in Nostrils . . . Students are fed strange diets to see what their stomachs will stand and what it will refuse . . . Human Subjects Work Like Mad Men on Empty Stomachs . . . Man Worked to Breaking Point on Machine Quits Job; One Athlete Collapsed . . . Weird Ordeals.[1]

One might well be forgiven for not discerning in these macabre 1912 newspaper headlines the popular representation of an emerging "modernist" science of calorimetry able to evaluate food economy, metabolic fitness, experimental control, or even the overall vitality of urban-industrial civilization. Despite the gulf between serious scientific discourse and sensational lay idioms, each conveyed a sense that comprehending how foods, bodies, and spaces were related was critical for the proper design of urban-industrial workplaces. How is it that we currently discern so little connection?

For late-nineteenth- and early-twentieth-century investigators, such associations were not merely an intellectual convenience or contrivance but also indicated significant institutional and instrumental conjunctures. Many fin de siècle scientists focused practically as well as figuratively on the nexus between ingested foodstuffs, internal organic functions, interior laboratory facilities, and exterior urban-industrial factors. While models that view the human body as an engineered construction (architectural form, built environment, or system of utilities), and vice versa, have a long intellectual pedigree, they were arguably far more commonplace by the late nineteenth century than they had been previously. How, then, might one characterize these fin de siècle transitions in conceptual preference?[2]

My essay examines the displacement of "Victorian" by "modernist" views of food science, focusing especially on the models informing scientists' theories and practices. From the mid-nineteenth to the mid-twentieth century, the conceptual emphasis of chemists and physiologists shifted from architectural "elements" to infrastructural "environments" in articulating models of *food composition, body constitution, laboratory configuration,* and *urban-industrial construction.* Architectural principles complemented the analyses of discrete elemental combinations, proportions, and stages characteristic of Victorian chemistry and physiology.[3] Much as with Victorian design styles (e.g., replicating organic texture or ornament in steel structures, electrogilding, synthetic substitutes), Victorian scientific methods comprised an eclectic repertory of materials, media, and modes, more typically rehabilitating than rejecting traditional forms through technical innovation.[4]

By contrast, infrastructural principles complemented fluid-dynamic formulation of alimentary forces and systems in "modernist" fields—for example, calorimetry or biochemistry.[5] Modernist principles of engineering and design, which called for technological "revolution" and systematization, served modernist research ideals of purity and efficiency.[6] Calorimetry in particular relied on a wide variety of mechanical devices and practices, among them bomb (combustion) calorimeters for physical-chemical study of heat properties and fuel economies; direct (chamber) calorimeters for physiological study of metabolic intake and output; indirect (respiration) calorimeters, with open or closed circuitry, for biochemical study of gaseous exchange; and partitional (modular) calorimeters for hygienic study of metabolism in various environments. Calorimetricians formulated uniform standards to calibrate the appara-

MARK HAMIN

tuses and to correlate the data produced by them, in the service of a comprehensive paradigm of energy efficiency.

During this reorientation from Victorian "elements" (i.e., individual chemical, organic, or spatial structures) to modernist "environments" (i.e., integrated metabolic or technical systems), experimental physiologists played a pivotal role; they articulated how new food composition models made possible reformulated standards of proper diet to promote fitness in body constitution, studied by means of standardized laboratory configuration to simulate and thus to assess novel urban-industrial construction. While typically dramatic and fundamental in principle (or in proclamation), such transitions were more equivocal, uneven, and incomplete in practice.[7] In what ways and to what extent do these Victorian and modernist views still inhabit current foodways? By way of conclusion, I will hazard a brief, rough sketch of twenty-first-century public ambivalence about new "designer" foods and spaces: that is, postmodernity in specialized market research, segmented mass consumption, and "neotraditional" modes of habitation.

FOOD COMPOSITION

Victorian chemists and physiologists tended to pursue basic analyses of chemical composition and proportion: that is, they examined proteins, carbohydrates, fats, and minerals as "building blocks" of diet. Some extended the vernacular of elementary structure further, invoking metaphors from architecture and literature to illustrate the value of nutrient analysis for public audiences. As the physiological chemist Russell H. Chittenden (Victorian by training, modernist in his later career) argued in a popular address:

> In the construction of a house the builder must know not only the materials to be employed, but also the due proportions of them. . . . [Likewise, one] should know not merely that protein, fat, carbohydrate, water, etc., are absolutely required, but that they are demanded in certain definite proportions. The nails and bolts that are put into a house, beyond what is needed for binding the structure together, are not merely a waste of material in themselves, but may become a detriment to the building. Similarly, the want of proper proportion among elements of food . . . [is] both a waste and damage.[8]

In this instance, the critical role of nutrients, their material and formal properties, was oddly likened to joining hardware rather than to basic structural materials and forms (e.g., wood, metal, stone). Analysis of protein composition in terms of constituent amino acids, though, revived models of elemental building blocks. In another essay, Chittenden cited a colleague's protein analyses, affirming their architectural and literary metaphors:

> We see that . . . out of these amino acids or building stones the body cells can select the appropriate groups to build up their own particular units of the union of which larger structures may be planned according to a determined plan or architectural idea. We have learned that . . . the multiplicity of the proteins is determined through differences in the nature of the constituent building stones or amino-acids and through differences in the manner of their arrangement.[9]

By the early 1900s, however, a greater emphasis on energy functions and dynamic factors in food, such as vitamins, had shifted focus from discrete architectural elements to general infrastructural flows or forces. The nineteenth-century studies of Benjamin Thompson, Count Rumford, on design criteria for fuel-efficient devices influenced Victorian views on the optimal uses of energy.[10] From Rumford's eclectic work on heat production, stove construction, facility planning, and dietary hygiene to early-twentieth-century interdisciplinary programs of home economists, advocates of rational domestic management increasingly accustomed their audiences to criteria focused on energy efficiency, extending them to caloric value, culinary technique, and consumer habit in formulating a "modernizing" synthesis.[11]

The modernist calorimetrician Francis Gano Benedict fully rationalized such energy models. Even as he likened food to fuel, Benedict acknowledged that people ordinarily entertained more complex views: "When we say that the chief use of food for the adult body is for fuel, this sounds like a distinctly commercial and mechanical statement. . . . We are more accustomed to think of these things as a source of pleasure, and of satisfaction to the body as a whole."[12]

Such models derived from modernist views of energy as resource and commodity, which took its physical, chemical, and biological forms to be wholly commensurate and interconvertible. These models promoted integration in facilities for generating power and for producing food, but ironically raised expectations and anxieties concerning the optimum use of food's energy potential. Similar shifts in focus took place with models of the consuming body.

BODY CONSTITUTION

For his 1929 Dunham Lectures at Harvard University, later published as *Features in the Architecture of Physiological Function,* Joseph Barcroft of Cambridge University struck an ambivalent note in his retrospective survey of early-twentieth-century experimental physiology, which followed the Victorian assumptions of the nineteenth-century physiologist Claude Bernard. Barcroft's review included a candid admission that "at the outset [ca. 1900] I had regarded the body as a noble building on the principles which it exhibits as unconnected features of its architecture. It became clear [later, however,] that the features were far from being independent." Describing Bernard's notion of the *milieu intérieur,* Barcroft noted that "the principle . . . , if dressed up in modern language, seems to me just a little grotesque." He thus called for modernist physiologists to reform their field's Victorian eclecticism and to reduce consideration of variable external factors (habitation, technology, geography) in relation to the regulatory "internal environment."[13]

Victorian physiological studies represented digestion in terms of separate organs and specific functions (e.g., production of chyme in the stomach or of chyle in the small intestine). In modernist accounts of alimentation as a continuous process, by contrast, liquefaction of food through mechanical reduction and chemical solution resulted in a uniform slurry in the alimentary canal. Along with this transition from a discrete-stage material conversion model to a continuous-process force mechanics model, physiological study shifted from reliance on the "Institutes of Medicine," which codified the foundational elements of physiological structure or function, to reliance on instrumental measurement of general physiological processes.[14] A collection of medical school dissertations at the University of Pennsylvania from ca.1850 to 1890 illustrates a pedagogic shift from Victorian Institutes of Medicine to modernist instrumentation.[15]

In earlier dissertations, there was remarkable uniformity in the definition of digestive stages: prehension (ingestion), mastication/ensalivation (chewing), deglutition (swallowing), gastric action, small and large intestinal action, and excretion. Concerning the beginning or end of this elementary sequence, however, earlier medical graduates offered divergent views, more natural-historical than experimental. Some noted that temperature, topography, and technique were factors as important as those of internal constitution. P. G. Skillern included climate and season; migration, inhabitation, work, and leisure; and modes of food production and preparation under his broad rubric of prehension.[16] In these early, taxonomic Victorian essays, alimentation represented a translation or transaction between exterior and interior spaces; in later essays, anticipating modernist experimental methods, alimentation represented a completely internal dynamic of motility and integration.

Moreover, earlier essays explicitly invoked architectural metaphors, likening the body's internal anatomy to a building's domestic interior; for example, they described the "office" of each organ as a "chamber" housing a discrete stage of digestion, with monitored corridors or secured doors communicating between compartments. Austin Armitage, for instance, (somewhat delicately) portrayed the ileo-cloacal valve to the intestinal tract as a set of folding doors separating two rooms of a dwelling.[17] By the 1880s, though, "systematic" infrastructural models had become more common than "elemental" architectural models. Students increasingly compared the body's organ systems to topographic areas traversed by canals, ducts, valves, and vessels. The configuration of organic tissue assumed greater significance, with later essays invoking funnels and tubes (i.e., designs for the efficient transmission of fluids or forces).

By the early twentieth century, along with using the metaphor of food as fuel, popularizers of modernist physiology compared metabolism to engineering or manufacturing operations. In a 1915 lecture, Benedict discussed the body's maintenance surplus of energy:

> *For example, in a factory, fuel must be used not only to keep the building warm, but for the warming up of the boilers, engines, and steam pipes so that they will be ready for instant use. Even on Sundays, holidays, and the modern so-called "heatless" days, a large amount of fuel must be burned or property will suffer much damage and nothing will be in readiness for the next work-day.*[18]

One newspaper account underscored this comparison of metabolic bodies with factories, noting that "Benedict is making experiments on men similar to the experiments made by mechanical engineers on . . . power plants, to determine their physical properties and efficiencies."[19] As Chittenden likewise noted:

> [W]hile man is ever ready to take advantage of the teaching of applied science in industry, ever ready to follow up any suggestion that promises increased efficiency or greater economy in the running of his industrial plant, that will prolong the life of his machinery, he is slow to give heed to . . . [the] teachings of science that bear directly on the welfare of his own bodily machinery and that of his children.[20]

In these instances, the conception of the body's "internal environment" coincided with changes in the "internal environment" of the physiological laboratory and the urban-industrial workplace: that is, systematic instrumentation and standardized infrastructure.

LABORATORY CONFIGURATION

For much of the nineteenth century, Victorian chemists and physiologists worked within spaces and with apparatus that often limited their research capabilities. In a retrospective tribute to Chittenden's Yale colleague Lafayette B. Mendel, the calorimetrician Graham Lusk called the (ca. 1880s) Sheffield Scientific School under Chittenden and Mendel a "miserable building utterly devoid of the trappings found in our stately modern laboratories." He found their instruments similarly lacking, averring that the "mechanical toys which are our present day [1920s] delight were not the meat on which this our Caesar [Mendel] fed."[21]

Late-Victorian scientists often relied on project-specific, temporary research sites rather than building anew or moving. They typically aimed to simulate "normal" living and feeding conditions, albeit with some modernist standards regarding space and equipment. The Johns Hopkins organic chemist Ira Remsen described to Chittenden "experimental table" facilities for a long-term feeding trial:

> Place of Serving Meals. *A well equipped club house can be used[;] . . . room[s] should be modern in all respects, including a thoroughly well equipped, spacious kitchen, a neat, well furnished, and well arranged dining room, a convenient, large, well furnished club and reading room, a specially planned and commodious toilet room, and pleasant, neat rooms for . . . [subjects] to use as much as desired for study, rest, etc.*[22]

Criteria for efficient design received even stricter consideration in modernist calorimetry. Benedict's lifelong interest in architecture influenced his design criteria for experimental facilities. In the mid-1930s, he recounted architectural highlights of his international travels (ca. 1910–1920s) to the architect Benjamin Hubbell, pointing out that he had "always been interested in architecture."[23] Two years later, he wrote to William Shimer, editor of *The American Scholar:* "As one who has been thrilled by the succession of modern efforts, I can safely claim sympathy with modernism. . . . [The] needs of the present day for housing, commerce and industry . . . [preclude] adherence to the old schools."[24]

His taste in laboratory design, like that in public sites, showed a modernist sensibility. Benedict favored modernist design principles because he regarded them as essential to the proper construction of a fully controlled artificial laboratory environment. In listing critical specifications for his proposed facility, he commented that "much would depend on the location and time of year of building, the style of architecture, and the size of building," which he wanted to be "built of the simplest, plainest style of architecture." Further underscoring this point, he insisted that "no expense be put upon the exterior of the building but all available funds used in the equipment."[25]

Benedict's various facility plans and designs indicated the degree to which he regarded instrumental, architectural, and environmental criteria as interconnected aspects of experimental design. Indeed, Benedict drafted a number of requests for support of his facility needs, which included accessible, affordable space for housing equipment and staff, as well as dependable utilities for improved experimental control and efficiency over long intervals. Although chamber calorimeters often remained custom-built, much like their Victorian antecedents, laboratory infrastructure had become increasingly "modernized."[26]

But there were limits to this ideal of experimental standardization. Against calls for efficiency in expanding research output within routinized, "industrial" laboratory spaces, Chittenden (despite calls for "industrial efficiency" in diet) stressed that patrons "must recognize the fact that the business of research cannot be run as an ordinary manufacturing concern, where output is calculated on the basis of the number of machines in operation and where any falling off in production calls for immediate scrutiny . . . [and] research workers must not be judged or their efficiency estimated on the basis of their daily production."[27] Graham Lusk's colleague E. F. Du Bois agreed; training Russell Sage Institute of Pathology (RSIP) "associate[s] to master the technique of the calorimeter and metabolism ward," he insisted that "it is more important to train one good research worker than grind out papers on metabolism at a uniform rate of six per year."[28]

Even the arch-modernist Benedict accepted limits. Primarily oriented to achieving optimal experimental conditions, he also realized that accommodating the physiological and psychological needs of subjects was critical to the success of his studies, even if it conflicted with total experimental control. Benedict described a calorimeter design that balanced subject confinement and comfort. A "hermetically sealed window admits ample light for reading and writing and a telephone gives communication with the world outside. . . . Receptacles for food, drink and other objects are removed or introduced through an aperture provided for the purpose."[29] In key respects, chamber calorimetry incorporated elements of late-Victorian domestic space within modernist laboratory infrastructure.

Despite such concessions, state-of-the-art utilities remained a major consideration in planning calorimetric facilities. Benedict took great interest in nearly every design and construction decision for his laboratory. He queried officials at Harvard's Medical School: "Is steam heat on night and day so nutrition laboratory could be heated during the night experiments? . . . Is refrigerating plant run continuously . . . ? [Regarding the high] contract price per year for furnishing heat for a building of modern construction, [it is] . . . proposed to have some [additional heating and] cooling pipes installed."[30] All such remarks indicate the importance of electrical and heating, ventilation, and air-conditioning (HVAC) systems in refinement of experimental facilities, as well as the urban-industrial environmental transformations that precipitated physiological studies of artificially conditioned interiors.

URBAN-INDUSTRIAL CONSTRUCTION

Victorian concerns regarding the conservation of energy—that is, anxieties over its dissipation, waste, or unproductive expenditure—often became conflated with concerns about preservation of national vitality. Which cultural circumstances encouraged the use of scientific knowledge in some cases to supplant, in others to support, traditional forms of social order (e.g., religion, rank, race)? Cultural historians have traced the significant intersections between Victorian urban-industrial development, techno-logical innovation, social reform, and public discourse relative to nineteenth-century concepts of energy.[31]

The environmental consequences of urban demographic and technological growth concerned some Victorian engineers and hygienists, but not until the turn of the century did industrial and institutional conditions raise widespread concerns among modernist researchers calling for improvements in interior environmental qual-ity. These concerns initially had to do with industrial output as much as if not more than with health, comfort, and efficiency.[32] The concentration of workers, capital equip-ment, and prime movers had by then reached levels sufficient to introduce serious indoor environmental effects, such as hygroscopic and thermoscopic instability (i.e., tolerance effects of moisture and heat). At first, one historian notes, the "big push . . . was into industries where the immediate concern was products and processes, not personnel": for example, the increased costs from spoilage, "sweating," or irregular tensile properties of materials in food-processing and -service operations.[33]

Nevertheless, physiological modernists had already begun to study environmen-tal conditions relative to human metabolism, formulating metrical and technical stan-dards of HVAC. Mechanical engineers designed and installed high-comfort HVAC systems using such "rational" standards.[34] Between calorimetricians assessing meta-bolic performance and engineers assessing environmental performance, an interme-diate cohort of hygienists emerged to assess the effects of interior air quality on fitness, efficiency, and comfort.[35]

Benedict recognized air-conditioning implications in his instrumental design, remarking in one lecture that his chamber calorimeter

> is thus, you see, of refrigerator construction. . . . In the winter time, we heat our
> houses with hot water passing through pipes, and I hope before long it will be
> customary for us to cool our houses in the summer time by passing cold water
> through pipes. We have . . . cooled this little house or little chamber by means of
> a current of cold water passing through a series of pipes which are not unlike the
> hot water radiator in a house.[36]

A 1909 newspaper story on the Nutrition Laboratory also noted the resemblance, adding that Benedict's apparatus would record "valuable data for the discussion of the problems of ventilation and hygene [*sic*]."[37] Benedict confirmed HVAC as a key focus: "The ease with which the ventilation of the chamber of the respiration calorimeter can be regulated . . . make[s] it especially advantageous for studies in this field."[38]

Hygienic considerations also became more central to the calorimetric studies of the Lusk–Du Bois group. The RSIP, Lusk wrote to the Russell Sage Foundation officer John Glenn, "already conducted important experiments and studies in the fields of housing and industrial conditions and has issued publications dealing with sanitation, fatigue, and efficiency," though rational diet remained its most important focus.[39] The balance had shifted considerably when the institute relocated in 1932; by then it had planned "to transfer the chief emphasis to a study of heat radiation, surface temperature of the body and a fundamental study . . . on the problems of ventilation, heating and clothing."[40]

Many physiological modernists addressed problems of environmental quality in order to improve human "fitness," articulated in terms of physical performance, labor productivity, military preparation, or national (racial) progress.[41] From perceived crises in manufacturing and service workforces to anxieties regarding urban stresses and strains, the professional middle classes in late-nineteenth-century America evinced an acute concern with the social risks and costs of fatigue and waste. Industrial hygienists advocated rational reorganization of work as a solution to industrial problems.

By the start of the twentieth century, cultural perspectives regarding rational control of power sources began significantly to influence public opinion, official policy, and reform advocacy. Industrial hygienists aimed to reorganize work, not only to make labor power more efficient but also to make the power of organized labor less effective. Benedict, for example, wrote of what he deemed the actual (i.e., scientific) rather than overstated (i.e., customary) value of a laborer's work pace, breaks, and vacations. He thus gave a physiological rationale for Taylorist principles. Indeed, Benedict expressed admiration for advocates of scientific management, to whose time-and-motion studies he considered his metabolism studies an underappreciated complement. He lamented that "while undue emphasis may not be laid upon the Taylor system and the Gilbreth studies, . . . [a] correlation between the motion studies and metabolism, the efficiency of the organism as a machine, has thus far been [almost] entirely neglected" by urban-industrial designers.[42]

In one essay, Benedict noted a Middletown, Connecticut, construction site where

the contractor used a large number of laborers to carry bricks and mortar up ladders in this building. At that time it was a new thing to have a strike, and these men were apparently dissatisfied with their conditions and decided to strike. The contractor was a man of considerable resource [and determination:] . . . instead of putting the fuel into the bodies of 25 or 30 Italian laborers, [he] put the fuel under the boiler of a steam engine connected to an elevator.[43]

Such public attempts to balance scientific purity and laboratory autonomy against wider urban-industrial applications risked compromising both the professional reputation and the practical relevance of metabolic models in modernist chemistry and physiology. The designers of modern experimental laboratories might be charged with ivory-tower detachment and esoteric insulation from real-world controversies—as a newspaper report on the Nutrition Laboratory's calorimeter illustrates. The "[m]ain purpose of the machine," the reporter wrote, "is to get exact tabulation upon those organs and members of the body that, because of their interior location, . . . shroud themselves with mystery." More crisply, however, he noted a similar mystery in his own investigation of the Nutrition Laboratory, especially in his thwarted "efforts to pass from the main hall into the laboratory interior."[44] Such popular impressions of shrouded mystery or expert elitism, whether connected to the internal workings of foods and bodies, to instruments used to study their workings, or to facilities designed to house instruments and bodies, vexed physiological modernists.

CONCLUSION: POSTMODERN (NEO-VICTORIAN?) REFLUX

What relevance might the foregoing historical discussion have for understanding current (postmodern?) perspectives on architectural or infrastructural metaphors in food investigation? While certainly more complex, flexible, and microscaled than Victorian and modernist regimes, twenty-first-century approaches to food composition, body constitution, laboratory configuration, and urban-industrial construction remain in basic respects much like those a century ago. Specifically, the continued dominance of infrastructural, fluid-dynamic perspectives on food science and technology echoes modernist models, but now with partial, ambivalent "remodeling" based on traditional artisanal and architectural elements. Some scholars, for example, have charted recent relations between dietary subcultures or countercultures and the dominant regimes from which they diverge, often in the name of cultural renewal or revival.[45] Likewise, cultural theorists of mass consumer practices and commercial enterprises often point to the spread of places oriented to popular leisure and consumption as a major watershed in late-twentieth-century American society.[46]

With regard to *food composition,* the "elemental" repertoire (e.g., proteins, fats, carbohydrates, vitamins, minerals), however great the expansion and differentiation of its membership, has long been encoded into food products and dietary supplements. What is perhaps novel (or retrograde?) is a retreat from the general dynamics of energy and growth to the specific virtues of nutrients for individuals according to sex, age, race, and lifestyle. Another change is more iconic: basic guides of food group "equivalences" (e.g., a circular pie chart or four-square grid plan) have been replaced with the current food guide pyramid, also schematic, though with an architecture of inverted hierarchy (healthy foods at the base or foundation, junk foods at the apex) and idealized proportion among its elements.[47]

As for *body constitution,* models of infrastructural systems and flows still tend to dominate popular and intellectual conceptions of issues such as risk, contamination, and immunity. However, the countercultural revival of traditional health habits has rehabilitated the image of the body as a spiritual temple or a natural place, not simply a factory or a laboratory. In this area, as in food composition, recent market diversification has encouraged a greater interest in custom design and self-fashioning of fitness regimens, in response to (perceived) mass-produced standardization and social homogenization. Over the past decade, historians, sociologists, and cultural theorists have produced a vast literature on body constitution, examining the meanings ascribed to particular aspects of bodies (e.g., gender, race, age, disability).[48] In some instances, art criticism or theory has eclipsed other approaches; nevertheless, interdisciplinary accounts have pointed to important areas of dissonance or resistance when expert and lay perspectives on the "nature" of bodies collide.[49]

In terms of *laboratory configuration,* "post-Fordist" scientific workplaces derive many features from early-twentieth-century antecedents, though new forms of infrastructure (e.g., electronic and informatic) allow for both greater dispersal of and also access to work, and for more multifaceted projects. This greater instrumental standardization and modularity has potentially amplified research opportunities with more portable, flexible equipment.[50] Technical diffusion has integrated networks for exchanging, correlating, and reproducing instrumental capabilities. Techniques are modified to specific workplace conditions, but uniformity and replicability neverthe- less remain key aims, if only as ideals.[51]

Finally, the *urban-industrial construction* of present-day food economies, still dominated by large, functionally integrated corporations and food-service chains, has in recent years involved adaptation and diversification into new markets: designer products (e.g., analog food, "nutriceuticals"), traditional principles (e.g., ethnic, reli- gious, holistic), and "environmental" practices. Elsewhere, local or community-based associations have emerged to serve such smaller-scale constituencies.[52] Recent analy- ses of biotechnology, for example, have assessed its implications for the global polit- ical economy and for ecological and cultural diversity.[53] All these areas of uncertainty mirror the cultural contradictions of spaces primarily designed to accommodate mass- consumer tastes and means, but also increasingly retooled in an effort to exploit new (and old) "frontiers" in consumption.[54]

So to return to our opening question: How is it that we currently discern so few connections between the "architecture/infrastructure" of foods, bodies, laboratories, and urban-industrial spaces? My conjecture is that growing disciplinary hyperspecial- ization, organizational and technological complexity, and interest in subcultures of tra- ditional or alternative "lifestyle" have undermined modernist ambitions to formulate comprehensive metabolic syntheses. Still, some recent authors have begun to stake out areas for further research, or to identify possible linkages between physiographic sprawl (autoburbs) and physiological sprawl (obesity). Like Victorians, we cannot con- coct a systematic structural theory connecting what we eat and where we live or work, though, like modernists, we find that those "elements" still tend to intermingle and congeal, albeit where we might least expect them.[55]

NOTES

1. "Scientific Starving in Roxbury 'House of Mystery' Revealed," *Boston American*, May 19, 1912; in Francis Gano Benedict Papers, Countway Library and Archives, Harvard Medical School, Collection MC62 (hereafter FGB), box 4, Clippings.
2. Focusing on cultural mentalities, interdisciplinary studies of environmental worldviews have traced changing perspectives on cultural spaces. They have characterized spatial identification discursively

or used material-cultural and architectural evidence to examine distinctions between natural and social environments; see Michael Bennett and David W. Teague, eds., *The Nature of Cities: Ecocriticism and Urban Environments* (Tucson: University of Arizona Press, 1999); Richard Sennett, *Flesh and Stone: The Body and the City in Western Civilization* (New York: W. W. Norton, 1994), chap. 10. Literary and cultural scholars have identified avenues by which "modernist" standards of efficient design achieved wider popular currency; see Martha Banta, *Taylored Lives: Narrative Productions in the Age of Taylor, Veblen, and Ford* (Chicago: University of Chicago Press, 1993); Cecelia Tichi, *Shifting Gears: Technology, Literature, and Culture in Modernist America* (Chapel Hill: University of North Carolina Press, 1987). Some intellectual and cultural historians have noted the significance of engineering imagery in public views of science and technology, especially the displacements of "everyday life" within expert-rationalized environments; see Tim Armstrong, *Modernism, Technology, and the Body: A Cultural Study* (Cambridge: Cambridge University Press, 1998); Terry Smith, *Making the Modern: Industry, Art, and Design in America* (Chicago: University of Chicago Press, 1993).

3. See Frank M. Turner, *Contesting Cultural Authority: Essays in Victorian Intellectual Life* (Cambridge: Cambridge University Press, 1993). For primary sources, see George Basalla et al., eds., *Victorian Science: A Self-Portrait from the Presidential Addresses of the BAAS* (New York: Doubleday, 1970).

4. See Tom F. Peters, *Building the Nineteenth Century* (Cambridge, Mass.: MIT Press, 1996); Julie Wosk, *Breaking Frame: Technology and the Visual Arts in the Nineteenth Century* (New Brunswick, N.J.: Rutgers University Press, 1992).

5. See Ronald G. Walters, ed., *Scientific Authority and Twentieth-Century America* (Baltimore: Johns Hopkins University Press, 1997); Dorothy Ross, ed., *Modernist Impulses in the Human Sciences, 1870–1930* (Baltimore: Johns Hopkins University Press, 1995).

6. See Gail Cooper, *Air-conditioning America: Engineers and the Controlled Environment, 1900–1960* (Baltimore: Johns Hopkins University Press, 1998); Mikuláš Teich and Roy Porter, eds., *Fin de Siècle and Its Legacy* (Cambridge: Cambridge University Press, 1990).

7. At the risk of schematic periodization, my account will assume that Victorian modes were hegemonic (ca. 1850–1890), followed first by a late-Victorian, early modernist transition (ca. 1890–1910), and then by a modernist dominance between the world wars.

8. Russell H. Chittenden Papers, Sterling Memorial Library Archives, Yale University, Collection 611 (hereafter RHC), box 3, folder 51, Chittenden, "Family Diet," n.d., 2.

9. RHC, box 2, folder 31, Chittenden, "Research in Chemistry," ca. 1922, 11–11a.

10. Sanborn Connor Brown, *Benjamin Thompson, Count Rumford* (Cambridge, Mass.: MIT Press, 1979). See also Edward Livingston Youmans, *The Handbook of Household Science: A Popular Account of Heat, Light, Air, Aliment, and Cleansing . . .* (New York: D. Appleton, 1872).

11. See Mark H. Rose, *Cities of Light and Heat: Domesticating Gas and Electricity in Urban America* (University Park: Pennsylvania State University Press, 1995); Dolores Hayden, *The Grand Domestic Revolution: A History of Feminist Designs for Homes, Neighborhoods, and Cities* (Cambridge, Mass.: MIT Press, 1981).

12. FGB, box 1, MSS 1906– , Benedict, "Food as Fuel [?]," 2.

13. Joseph Barcroft, *Features in the Architecture of Physiological Function* (Cambridge: University Press, 1938), ix, 1–2. See also F. L. Holmes, "Joseph Barcroft and the Fixity of the Internal Environment," *Journal of the History of Biology* 21, no. 1 (1988): 89–122.

14. See A. Lockhart Gillespie, *The Natural History of Digestion* (New York: Scribner's, 1898), and George E. Day, *Chemistry in Its Relations to Physiology and Medicine* (London: Balliere, 1860), for late-Victorian formulation of the Institutes of Medicine regarding digestion.

15. In the Rare Book Collection, Van Pelt Library, University of Pennsylvania (hereafter VP Rare), Collection 378.748 POM. Specifically, there are 36 dissertations on digestion; 36 on dyspepsia; 10 on indigestion; 10 on alimentation; 10 on food and disease; 8 on nutrition; and smaller numbers on animal heat, diet, absorption, and alimentary function—more than over 130 altogether.

16. P. G. Skillern, "The Process of Digestion," (VP Rare 1877.7), 1877; see also Alexander Crawford, "Digestion" (VP Rare 1871.4 Pt. 2), 1871, 1–3, 15–16.

17. Austin W. Armitage, "Digestion" (VP Rare 1869.5), 1869, 2 (uvula as "barrier" and epiglottis as "sentinel"); William. J. Ashenfelter, "Digestion" (VP Rare 1870.2), 1870, 7 (mouth as "ante-chamber").

18. FGB, box 1, MSS 1906–, Benedict, "Food for Muscular Work," 2–3.

19. FGB, box 4, Clippings, "Machine-Made Health," *Baltimore American,* January 11, 1908.

20. RHC, box 2, folder 31, Chittenden, "Research in Chemistry," ca. 1922, 12.

21. Graham Lusk Papers, Cornell Medical College and New York Hospital Archives, Collection 99E (hereafter GL), box 1, folder 2, American Institute of Chemists Meeting, May 11, 1927.

22. RHC, box 1, folder 3, Ira Remsen to Chittenden, December 1, 1913.

23. FGB, box 1, Art and Architecture, Benedict to Benj. S. Hubbell, February 21, 1935.

24. FGB, box 1, Art and Architecture, Benedict to William Shimer, December 25, 1937.

25. FGB, box 1, Carnegie Nutrition Laboratory, "Memorandum to accompany estimates of costs."

26. See Francis G. Benedict and Thorne M. Carpenter, *Respiration Calorimeters for Study of the Respiratory Exchange and Energy Transformations of Man,* Publication no. 123 (Washington, D.C.: Carnegie Institution of Washington, 1910).

27. RHC, box 2, folder 31, Chittenden, "Research in Chemistry," ca. 1922, 15. Contrast with Chittenden's remarks in the same essay, quoted above (see p. 157 and note 20).

28. Department of Medicine, New York Hospital, Collection 76B (hereafter DM), box 1, folder 5, E. F. Du Bois, "The First Metabolism Ward of the RSIP," 3.

29. FGB, box 4, Clippings, "Apparatus That Reveals Dieting Fallacies," *Boston Sunday Herald,* January 31, 1909.

30. FGB, GA7 B2, CNL: Correspondence with Walter B. Cannon 1905–7, "Points to be raised . . . ," January 23, 1906.

31. See Bruce Clarke, "Allegories of Victorian Thermodynamics." *Configurations* 1 (1996): 67–90; Greg Myers, "Nineteenth-Century Popularizations of Thermodynamics and the Rhetoric of Social Prophecy," in *Energy and Entropy: Science and Culture in Victorian Britain,* ed. Patrick Brantlinger (Bloomington: Indiana University Press, 1988), 307–338. See Edward Livingston Youmans, ed., *Correlation and Conservation of Forces . . .* (New York: D. Appleton, 1868), for primary sources.

32. For a late-Victorian treatise antedating modernist metabolic studies, see J. S. Billings, *The Principles of Ventilation and Heating and Their Practical Application,* 2nd ed. (New York: Engineering and Building Record, 1889).

33. Margaret Ingels, *Willis Haviland Carrier: Father of Air Conditioning* (Garden City, N.Y.: Country Life Press, 1952), 14–15, 40. See also Cooper, *Air-conditioning America.*

34. Barry Donaldson and Bernard Nagengast, *Heat and Cold: Mastering the Great Indoors* (Atlanta: ASHRAE, 1994), chaps. 7, 9, 10, 11.

35. Lindy Biggs, *The Rational Factory: Architecture, Technology, and Work in America's Age of Mass Production* (Baltimore: Johns Hopkins University Press, 1996), chap 3. See, e.g., C.-E. A. Winslow, "Health and Efficiency in Industry," in *Linking Science and Industry,* ed. Henry C. Metcalf (Baltimore: Williams and Wilkins, 1925), 103–110.

36. FGB, box 1, MSS 1906– , "Food as Fuel [?]," 14.

37. FGB, box 4, Clippings, "Apparatus That Reveals Dieting Fallacies," *Boston Sunday Herald*, January 31, 1909.

38. FGB, box 1, Carnegie Nutrition Laboratory: Memos and Reports 1903–1910, "Questions for Study by Use of the Respiration Calorimeter," 5.

39. DM, box 1, folder 5, Graham Lusk to John M. Glenn, June 8, 1926.

40. DM, box 1, folder 5, "History of the RSIP," 3.

41. See Michael Anton Budd, *The Sculpture Machine: Physical Culture and Body Politics in the Age of Empire* (New York: New York University Press, 1997); Anson Rabinbach, *The Human Motor: Energy, Fatigue, and the Origins of Modernity* (New York: Basic Books, 1990).

42. FGB, box 1, MSS 1906– , "Basic Research Plan," April 14, 1924, 14.

43. FGB, box 1, MSS 1906– , "Food as Fuel [?]," 10–12.

44. FGB, box 4, Clippings, "Machine-Made Health," *Baltimore American*, January 11, 1908.

45. See Alison James, "Eating Green(s): Discourses of Organic Foods," in *Environmentalism: The View from Anthropology*, ed. Kay Milton (New York: Routledge, 1993), 205–218; Warren Belasco, *Appetite for Change: How the Counterculture Took on the Food Industry, 1966–1988* (New York: Pantheon, 1989).

46. See Ron Scapp and Brian Seitz, eds., *Eating Culture* (Albany: State University of New York Press, 1998); Michelle Stacey, *Consumed: Why Americans Love, Hate, and Fear Food* (New York: Simon and Schuster, 1994).

47. Susan Welsh, Carole Davis, and Anne Shaw, "A Brief History of Food Guides in the United States" and "The Development of the Food Guide Pyramid," *Nutrition Today* 27, no. 6 (November–December): 6–11, 12–23.

48. See e.g., Sarah Nettleton and Jonathan Watson, eds., *The Body in Everyday Life* (New York: Routledge, 1998); Simon J. Williams and Gillian Bendelow, *The Lived Body: Sociological Themes, Embodied Issues* (New York: Routledge, 1998); Donna J. Haraway, *Simians, Cyborgs, and Women: The Reinvention of Nature* (New York: Routledge, 1991).

49. Barry Smart, "Digesting the Modern Diet: Gastro-porn, Fast Food, and Panic Eating," in *The Flâneur,* ed. Keith Tester (London: Routledge, 1994), 158–180; Jonathan Crary and Sanford Kwinter, eds., *Incorporations,* Zone 6 (New York: Zone, 1992).

50. See Peter Galison and Emily Thompson, eds., *The Architecture of Science* (Cambridge, Mass.: MIT Press, 1999); David J. Hess, *Science and Technology in a Multicultural World: The Cultural Politics of Facts and Artifacts* (New York: Columbia University Press, 1995), chap. 4.

51. See Adele E. Clarke and Joan H. Fujimora, eds., *The Right Tools for the Job: At Work in Twentieth-Century Life Sciences* (Princeton: Princeton University Press, 1992); Everett Mendelsohn, "The Social Locus of Scientific Instruments," in *Invisible Connections: Instruments, Institutions, and Science*, ed. Robert Bud and Susan Cozzens (Bellingham, Wash.: SPIE Optical Engineering Press, 1992), 5–22.

52. See Andrew Ross, "The Lonely Hour of Scarcity," in *Real Love: In Pursuit of Cultural Justice* (New York: New York University Press, 1998), 163–188; David Goodman and Michael Redclift, *Refashioning Nature: Food, Ecology and Culture* (New York: Routledge, 1991), conclusion.

53. See Bill Lambrecht, *Dinner at the New Gene Café: How Genetic Engineering Is Changing What We Eat, How We Live, and the Global Politics of Food* (New York: Thomas Dunne Books, 2001); Lawrence Busch et al., *Making Nature, Shaping Culture: Plant Biodiversity in Global Context* (Lincoln: University of Nebraska Press, 1995).

54. For "postmodern" design more generally, see Akira Asada and Arata Isozaki, "From Molar Metabolism to Molecular Metabolism," in *Anyhow*, ed. Cynthia Davidson (New York: Anyone Corporation, 1998); 65–73; Susan Yelavich, ed., *The Edge of the Millennium: An International Critique of Architecture, Urban Planning, Product and Communication Design* (New York: Whitney Library of Design, 1993).

55. For a comprehensive review, see Josef Konvitz, "Gastronomy and Urbanization," *South Atlantic Quarterly* 86 (winter 1986): 44–56. More recent accounts include Eric Schlosser, *Fast Food Nation: The Dark Side of the All-American Meal* (Boston: Houghton Mifflin, 2001).

10

THE MISSING GUEST: THE TWISTED TOPOLOGY OF HOSPITALITY

DONALD KUNZE

"There was a time," says a myth of the Chilouk people, "when no one yet knew fire. People used to heat their food in the sun, and the men ate the upper part of the food, cooked in this way, while the women ate the underneath which was still uncooked." The myth is not male chauvinism, but a kind of allegory of the sexual symbolism of fire.

—MAGUELONNE TOUSSAINT-SAMAT, *A History of Food*

Both cuisine and architecture wrap tightly around the details of our day-to-day life. As soon as we look at one, we find the other, but the connections linking the two have not always been simple or obvious. It is not enough to describe the spaces where dining takes place, the conditions of modern cities that gives rise to habits of consumption, or the crisscrosses between food and style. We have to go to the heart and essence of the matter—how the bounding of space and nourishment are related.

Architecture's relation to cuisine is nowhere more evident than in the evolution of hospitality. Hospitality involves specialized spaces as well as elaborate food customs. Its sophisticated attitude toward strangers is a comparatively late development of culture. The earliest stages of human life have been called "cyclopean" because of their resemblance to the race of unfriendly one-eyed giants described by Homer in the *Odyssey*. Early societies, like the Cyclopes, regarded strangers as a threat. Trade had to take place "silently," without face-to-face contact. Each group governed itself through the laws of family and clan. Military alliances, city-states, and the consolidation of nations took place only after cyclopean cultures could be united around common needs, customs, and religions. Hospitality developed in parallel with these new political institutions, requiring the social customs and physical supports of cities.

Was the evolution of hospitality a matter of isolated cyclopean cultures losing out to trade-oriented ones? Were "hospitable" peoples such as the Phoenicians or Greeks simply more successful in dominating other cultures? Darwinian explanations are true in part, but they're not the whole picture. Is it also possible that there might exist, within human culture at its most basic, some constant cyclopeanism-hospitality ratio, a kind of atom or fractal capable of supporting adjustments in either direction as occasion demands?

That atom would be evident in the parallels between the evolution of domestic space and that of civic space. We would see it in attitudes toward the dead, toward the visuality of living spaces, toward the new role accorded to the stranger. Houses, cities, and fields would reveal a topography that exemplified the French saying of *plus ça change*. Pursuing this cyclopeanism-hospitality fractal calls for a hopscotch methodology that allows jumping between cultures, periods of history, and types of evidence. Because food and architecture are superficially very different but really closely connected, the method that explores connections has to cover a broad and discontinuous ground.

We begin with relations of the living and the dead that were materialized around the domestic hearth, formalized by tombs and monuments, and eventually collectivized by the city's public spaces. The dead require nourishment, and their "places" have specific rules of location and visibility. This is the beginning of a theory of the architecture of cuisine.

DONALD KUNZE

WHO IS MISSING FROM THE TABLE?

Shall we start with the dinner table? Someone's missing—that's the key. The guest who couldn't make it, the departed loved one, the companion away in some foreign land. Through toasts, prayers, feasts for the dead, empty place settings, we refer to their absence. No matter who's there, someone is *always* missing. The hearth is the reference point of this absence.

In the city, the table becomes a tableau, a scene made to be seen. Someone's missing, a collective someone. We see things acting as placeholders for the missing: the statues, remindful obelisks, plaques, and flags. No matter who's there, someone is always missing, fallen, and recast as a hero who establishes our ownership of the place. *These dead shall not have died in vain.* . . . The civic altar and, later, monuments mark the spot of this absence, the place where in ancient times sacrifices were required, sacrifices of someone strange, a stranger.

In fields are tombs, where again someone is missing, a bunch of *no-bodies* who were somebodies, as we can read on the stone that marks the spot of their absence. Despite their lack of corporality, none have relinquished their appetite. All need to be fed honey, oil, and wine, and their hunger correlates to precise relationships imposed on the spaces of the household, city, and field by the conditions of absence. House, city, tomb—from the history of their images we might deduce an inside-out logic that starts with two terms, a topology that flips on behalf of our *desire to enclose ourselves* but identifies itself through an absence based on that desire, δ.[1] We dedicate and delay that desire with the invention of a substitute, a double, a representative; a ghost, a guest, a cipher; a stranger, a nobody, who can *come and go, appear and disappear,* created from and sustained by imagination, φ.[2]

"Location! Location! Location!"—the real estate agent's mantra—has a deep meaning for us. This inside-out fractal, based on a very simple principle of a reflexive self-transformation ("recursion"), manages to produce complex, often surprising outcomes. While one branch necessarily involves imagining what is not immediately present to the senses, the other branch has to do with location of this missing part. The absent one, this nobody, always has a *place,* and that place is, by direction of desire's small δ, connected to the empty existential center, an inside from which absence will erupt to reframe the house from the inside out (figure 10.1). In many if not most cultures, this inside is materialized as the hearth's relationship to the ancestral dead. The

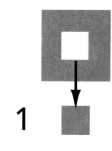

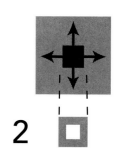

10.1
The missing guest/ghost/*Geist* who returns through the "inside frame" of the hearth. Drawing by author.

10.2
Marriage and the hearth fire.
Detail from Vincenzo Scamozzi,
L'idea della architettura universale
(Venice, 1615). Photo by Heather
Solimini, courtesy of Special
Collections, Paterno Library,
Pennsylvania State University.

hearth is thus a primordial center, a center no matter where it is geometrically posed. Like the *templum* whose location was determined through the intersection of *cardo* and *decumanus*, the hearth is an intersection, a crossing, a point of transaction.

Not only were the dead originally remembered in detail as permanent family members; they counted for more than their living descendants. They were, in fact, demigods.[3] Ancient Greeks and Romans believed that the fire, a collective spirit of the family *genius*, retained its procreative powers. The fire that reduced the corpse to bone transformed the soul, the *psuchē*, into a god. The cult of Hestia, goddess of the hearth, made the family's wife and daughters into the priestesses of the cult of the family, the *manes*, in Hades ("the invisible"). In a sense, the woman who tended the fire was *married* to the flame (figure 10.2). When the fire collectivized the spiritual *genii* of a whole city, it was essential that its caretakers, like the Vestals at Rome, be virginal and kept from public contact. Fustel de Coulanges reports that the family hearth, like the civic Vestals, was shielded from the view of visitors.[4] The belief that a look could contaminate is ancient and widespread. In some cultures, it was forbidden to look directly at the king, holy objects, or certain ceremonies. Even in contemporary societies, wealth, beauty, and pride attract the "evil eye," the leveler of uneven distributions of fortune.[5]

How was the sexuality of the fire of the *manes* connected to the need to protect the hearth from the view of strangers? The relationship is complex. It is impossible to decide whether such practices were intended to block the view of strangers or the view of the hearth. In the case of marriage, in fact, it seems that the *manes* had to be blinded to the marriage rite that transferred a daughter from her father's hearth to her husband's.[6] The bride was to avoid any signs of cooperating. In some cultures, the bride's family stages a mock fight to prevent the husband from taking his bride. The custom of carrying the bride over the threshold of the husband's house survives in popular culture. The forgotten meaning of this portage is that it originally indicated the bride's unwillingness or inability. The household hearth was, to borrow from film criticism, an element of *suture*[7]—a means of connecting outside to an inmost interior. Anything that affected it had perforce to employ the same inside-out logic: blindness for invisibility, hostility for hospitality, resistance for cooperation. Thus was the issue of location annealed to that of . . . what? Something both visual and antivisual; hence, something phallic, ϕ; something involving disguise.

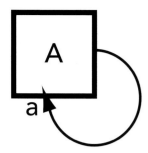

10.3
The inside-out fractal, a "recursion box" where self-reference exits and reenters at the center.

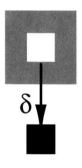

10.4
Cipher for the missing guest.

If we draw the simplest form of the inside-out machine, it is a box with an arrow going out and coming back in at the center, in a recursive motion (figure 10.3). We use the word *topology* to describe the situation if only because this device resembles the Möbius band, the toy known by every child that has "really" only one side and only one edge but, in our projective vision, appears to have a twist for its trick. If we try to create a projective map or picture of the Möbius band, we see a twist because a fixed eye is not allowed to follow the single surface without interruption. In topographical terms, the twist does not exist. Topology permits only techniques of touch that *duplicate* the structure by *following* it. It may sound unlikely, but this tricky twist is all we need to generate the complex situations surrounding cuisine, celebrations, festivals that punctuate calendars, songs to the dead and the voices of the dead given in return, houses that are homes, and houses with some- and no-bodies in them. Because the ways of getting in and out of a house or a city belong to a nearly universal language of doors, which is borrowed from the idea of the horizon, entries (where hospitality is intensified) and hearths (where it is prohibited) are co-conditioning. Their "logic" borrows from the language of the labyrinth, the imagined portal between the Olympian sky and the chthonian underworld.[8]

Let's keep things straight the Egyptian way, by using hieroglyphs. The "starter relationship," the missing guest, can be the hole in a square (figure 10.4). We can designate that guest/ghost, the surplus or lack of cuisine, with the Greek letter δ, and show the extra/missing part below it, in some "elsewhere" region inaccessible through established symbolic networks. "The unsymbolizable" has always figured prominently in the life of cultures, as an Elsewhere that, like a blank check, can be materialized in a variety of forms: Hades, the future, the unknown. This is the stuff about which Parmenides advised us not to speak and about which Sartre did speak with such unforgettable wit that Pierre, who did not show up for his café date, will forever be inscribed in our photo-album with four empty adhesive corners and a slight shadow on the page.[9] The thing to remember about this non-place defined by the thin distance δ is the rule of conflation: those things about which we know little or nothing are almost always presumed to have common cause and common rule. Thus, just because dreams and death were equally inaccessible, many cultures have regarded dreams as death-in-miniature, a glimpse forward or backward, exempt from the rule of normal time.

DONALD KUNZE

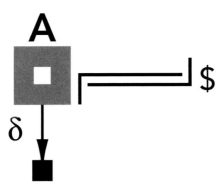

10.5
Evolution of the inside-out
fractal within symbolic
(subject-and-Other) and
nonsymbolizable space
(imagination and desire/fear).

This escape from time's one-thing-after-another is not an escape from time; it's more an escape *into* time. Our starter-fractal is thus primarily temporal. It's an "again," a "return"; the *wieder* and *zurück* that structure Mozart's *Die Zauberflöte*.[10] It's the doubles, rebirths, reborn souls, hierophanies, déjà-vus, and other devices of religion and comedy that, through disguises and mirrors, bring us back to the beginning. To wit: one of the first uses of the starter-fractal, the table with someone missing, has been divination: the science of augury. That's not a table, that's an altar! But, of course, there is the fire, there is the water (the substances of boundary). Later, the wine and bread, the substances of sacrifice, return. "As it was in the beginning, it now and ever shall be, world without end"—one of the verbal approximations of the fractal.

Back to the theme of Location Trismegistus: Out of this little table with its extra/missing guest/ghost δ, we need a space for the socioreligious effects of divination (figure 10.5). It's best to write this in a space other than that required by δ, so that we can see the difference between the *un*symbolizable desire δ and the symbolizable realm of the everyday (A ⇄ \$). In symbolizable space, the barred subject, the Lacanian "\$," finds itself constrained by orders of various kinds ("Other," symbolized by "A" for *Autre*), beginning with the advice of divination—the authorities, laws, and customs that shape the subject into an outward-facing superego. From the hearth-table-altar comes the voice that becomes the law that binds the subject.[11] The fixed location of this voice is what caused the first humans to stop wandering, to stay near the first altars set up in clearings in the forest to gauge the signs of the sky (according to Vico), to regard soil as the place of residence of those-who-are-missing from the family tables and civic tableaux, to invent the ruse of carrying soil from the old city to the new one, so that the *manes* would not detect this abandonment of place.

Location! location! location! and divination thus come in on the human scene at the same time. Authority's fixed locations would be sole centers of the subject's life were it not for an imaginary double through which the subject $ finds (with help from *fantasy*, ɸ) an ally, a hero, a representative, *f*, who has access to the unsymbolizable space of desire, δ. In Euripides' *Alcestis*, this is Admetus's guest Heracles, the hero who, as such, can visit and return alive from the Underworld. The prize he brings back with him is a veiled bride, δ, really Admetus's self-sacrificed wife, Alcestis ($), who returns to the center of Admetus's household.[12] The structural resemblance of *Alcestis* to David Lynch's *Mulholland Drive* is not accidental. The double Betty/Diane retrieves her own sacrificed bride, Camilla Rhodes (Rita), in a remarkable ascent from the murder scene to a banquet at a house on the hill above. Instead of nice Apollo, a seamy collection of mystery men (a dwarf, "the Cowboy," the Castiglione brothers) occupies the celestial/infernal control box.

This fractal, this little box with its flip side showing, this again-machine, has, rather than two faces, a "two-in-one face." Hence, it finds an early form in the god *Janus, Ianus,* or *Dianus*—the son of Cardea, goddess of hinges. It is interesting to find that during solar holidays marking seasonal change—celebrated with banquets, special foods, and symbolic sacrifices—the role of a "fool" was as central as the motif of twisted space. Again, the "time out" of such events calls for an inside-out device. Janusian masters of the boundary (May fools, boy bishops, fake kings-for-a-day) show how this is done. In popular culture we see displaced remainders of this fractal: plots with infants switched at birth, twins, doubles, mistaken identities—in other words, dramatic elaborations of the theme of *anamorphosis* ("anamorphy," or ω for short).

There is one tradition that holds that anamorphy is a mostly visual phenomenon.[13] This seems to be too limited, if only because we use "seeing" as a synonym for "knowing." The way we can "see double" in anamorphy presumes a cognitive correlation that can be played out in a variety of ways. For example, a pun is an acoustic anamorph planting two meanings within the same sound; and twins are dramatic anamorphs, planting two people within the same appearance. A joke is a structure built around the idea of quickly shifting the point of view to see something that was "in front of one's eyes" but formerly missed. A nickname, usually a substitution of an attribute for an individual (*antinomasia:* "Shorty"), can be reversed. A quality can be defined by the person who ideally exemplified it (reversed *antinomasia:* "You're no

Bobby Kennedy!"). In Alfred Hitchcock's *The 39 Steps,* "Mr. Memory," the music hall performer who opens the show, turns out to be the key to the mystery and, at the end, ties up all the loose ends, exemplifying the universalizing form of nicknaming.[14] When the hero returns to the music hall, we know that a cycle has been completed but not closed off; the anamorph ω has been "capitalized" (Ω) as an almost-closed circle that allows entry into the interior, the inside frame.

Anamorphy, ω, occupies the space of symbolic relations, but it creates a stain, hole, or blot that acts as a gateway to the nonsymbolizable, the realm of elsewhere out of which strangers appear and prophecies are uttered. Because the gateway appears *within* some otherwise ordinary image or sound, the meaning creates a "criss-cross" situation. Such is literally the case with what is perhaps the most famous case of visual anamorphy, Hans Holbein's portrait *The Ambassadors* (1533). John North notes that a line drawn from the small crucifix in the upper left-hand corner intersects the horizon at 27 degrees, the same angle required to view the anamorphic skull, a part of the assembly of "Golgotha," appropriate to the date of 1533 (3 × 500 + 33, Christ's age at the time of crucifixion), widely thought to be the time of the Apocalypse (figure 10.6).[15] This was also the angle of the sun at 4 P.M. at London on Good Friday,

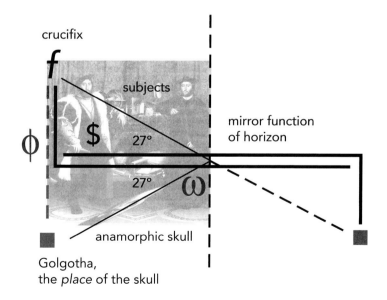

crucifix

subjects

mirror function
of horizon

27°

27°

anamorphic skull

Golgotha,
the *place* of the skull

(note: diagram direction is reversed)

10.6
Diagram of Hans Holbein's *The Ambassadors,* showing the thesis of John North. Lines drawn from the crucifix in the upper-left-hand corner and the skull intersect the horizon at 27 degrees, the precise angle of the sun at London at 4 P.M. on Good Friday 1533, a time widely believed to be the apocalypse. The fractal diagram is reversed to align with Holbein's portrait.

1533. This crisscross creates an open-ended interpretation, an "undecidability" factor, a *real Golgotha*—the anticipated end of the world—rather than a representation of Golgotha.[16]

John North demonstrates, if anything, the degree to which the fractal logic of anamorphy can, through overdetermination, support not only the layering of significance but different *modes* of encountering this significance. The barely visible crucifix becomes the basis for a Golgotha experience directly rather than symbolically. It is topography rather than projection that brings this about. The ω leads to Ω, an entry into the "gallery of pictures" Hegel described at the end of *The Phenomenology of Spirit*. Anamorphy demonstrates the rather Freudian principle that the unconscious (for us, the "unsymbolizable") has but one way to make its mark on the network of stable symbolic relationships that determine the social and visible world—that is, in the negative. The stain, blur, surplus, or lack becomes not just a marker but an entryway.

This somewhat surprisingly sheds light on the "problem" of the symbolism of cities, how the center can also be a "gateway." A possible answer begins by noting that anamorphic images and their counterparts in other media lie at the "heart" of the medium they interrupt. Yet anamorphy demands a displaced viewer, occupying a viewpoint at some oblique angle that brings the pied image into corrected focus. Is the viewer blind or invisible? The interchangeability of the two suggests that the popular use of disguises at festivals integrates anamorphy into the heart of civic ritual. The stranger is both invisible (we don't recognize him) and blind (he can't look at the city or household hearths). The rule that ω leads to Ω, blindness/recognition to passage, also ties Hermes, the god of boundaries and commerce (which originally took place at the edges of settlements), to Hestia, the goddess directing the collective worship of the ancestors amalgamated from the *manes* of separate families. As commerce was integrated into civic life, the *agora* moved from periphery to town center. The center could be radicalized because the hearth was *already a place of crossing*, a gateway to the liminal space of Hades. So it is that we continue to mark the centers of our towns with monuments to the dead, those whose identities establish a history of the place. This structural necessity of anamorphy makes the town a place for strangers and commerce.

Again, we find a central connection between space and cuisine. The "manic" insulation of the wall and tomb preserved the integrity of the *manes*; but, to secure the

DONALD KUNZE

prophecies of the *manes,* it was necessary to feed them. Tombs provided stone bowls with drains that carried wine, oil, and honey underground. Families celebrated holidays at the family tomb, arranging picnics that metaphorically included the ancestors. Mexico's famous Day of the Dead does as much at the usual family dinner table. The city collectivized this family practice with official festivals. Defending the city as well as the private space of the family required not just inviolable boundaries but also ritualized meals and special dishes.[17] Many modern civic celebrations contain remnants of this connection. Parades enact a virtual defensive labyrinth, "blessing" each crucial point and refurrowing the imaginary lines between them. Civic and private banquets—with foods and recipes special to the occasion—broker the ancient connections between cuisine, the spaces of hospitality, and the dead.

CYCLOPEAN MEALS

The negative function of anamorphy permits us to return to the central object of our concern: the evolution of hospitality. "*From* what *to* what?" might be the question in the minds of most readers. For the present, the question will have to be answered schematically: *from* the "cyclopean" (which can indicate a historical period or even any contemporary condition in which authority dominates desire and imagination) *to* the duplicitous and folded "spaces" of hospitality. The reason for focusing on this relationship is clear. Without hospitality, food is simply nourishment, a satisfaction of a bodily hunger. With hospitality, even on a microscale, preparing and eating food becomes the most intensive and direct of any significative medium. As Claude Lévi-Strauss stressed in *The Raw and the Cooked,* food is good not because it is good to eat but because it is "good to think."

Part of the transition from cyclopean privacy to hospitality involves the role of the stranger. Historical cyclopean societies forbade contact with strangers. The institution of silent trade—exchanges of goods at crossroads between parties that never meet—was established around this prohibition, and its widespread popularity and historic endurance is a testimony to the cyclopean sentiments behind it.[18] Strangers were at once volatile and attractive. This ambiguity was reflected in the seemingly opposite terms surrounding relations with strangers: *hostes,* meaning both host and enemy; *ghostis,* with roots in words suggesting both enemy and guest.[19] As the customs of hospitality spread with trade and exploration in the preclassical Mediterranean world, political alliances were extended by the exchange of gifts and intermarriage. But hospitality was ever in conflict with the cyclopean norm. Such was the subject of the Homeric tale of Odysseus's visit to the cave of the Cyclops, one of a race of giants famous for their lack of hospitality. This story is layered with cultural meanings. The Cyclopes mirrored the custom of family worship, where each extended family-clan maintained independent, severe laws based on the religion of the family gods, the *manes*. Auspices taken from the hearth were absolute; strangers were not tolerated. The legend of the Cyclops's "single eye" likely referred to the designation of clearings made in forests for the purposes of taking auspices as "eyes." To say the Cyclops had a single eye was to say that he worshiped family gods from a single and permanent altar.[20]

Homer's Cyclops, the giant Polyphemus, was made to fit the fabular tradition of traveler tales. The cave where Polyphemus lived alone with his flock of sheep in several senses followed the paradigm of the meander popularly scratched on walls and stones throughout the Mediterranean—the "Thesean labyrinth." This was a set of two identical structures connected by a twist. The pattern, used in games, dances, and rituals, was itself two parts connected by a twist—a sequence of counterclockwise, then clockwise, then counterclockwise circular motions. The connection is likely because the story itself involves two parts connected by a twist repeated at various scales. The labyrinth in this case extends the idea of anamorphy by formalizing the elements of the double image as fractal, such as that of Holbein's *Ambassadors,* as elements of the story. It thus is a model as well as an example of the transition from cyclopean to hospitable society.

The story is well known. Odysseus knows of the Cyclopes' infamous treatment of strangers, but he wants to test their custom, to see if he, a golden-tongued Greek, can charm Polyphemus into giving him the gifts traditionally accorded to strangers in much of the Mediterranean world. The optative mood in the verb translated as he "would give" supports the idea that we are witnessing an experiment.[21] The experiment turns out wrong. Polyphemus reveals that he is a practitioner of another cyclopean custom, cannibalism. The imprisoned Greeks slow the pace of anthropophagy by blinding the giant while he dozes in a drunken stupor, but they are still imprisoned within the labyrinthine cave. Their escape comes only when Odysseus devises a two-staged trick. He tells Polyphemus that his name is "Nohbdy" (*Oudeis*). At first, the audience is unaware of this device or its function. Odysseus is thinking ahead to the run

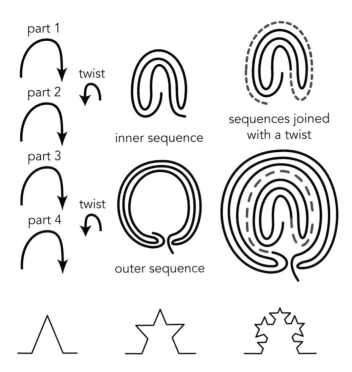

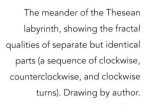

10.7
The meander of the Thesean labyrinth, showing the fractal qualities of separate but identical parts (a sequence of clockwise, counterclockwise, and clockwise turns). Drawing by author.

from the cave to the boats. Without a means of diverting the neighboring Cyclopes, the Greeks are done for. When the crew manages to slip out beneath the sheep (another case of anamorphy), Polyphemus tries to alert his neighbors, but they hear the name "Nohbdy" as a pronoun, not a name. "Nohbdy has blinded me" comes across as inane as the Abbott-and-Costello prattle "Hu's on first." It's not the name itself but the "idiotic symmetry" created by the double function of the name both as a name (reversed antinomasia) and a descriptive term (straight antinomasia).

The value of this story to the history of hospitality lies in its multiple use of the single "fractal" embodied in the labyrinth (figure 10.7). The story itself is divided into two parts: one that takes place before Polyphemus is blinded, a second that comes afterward. The "twist" here is the heroic act of sharpening an olive post to blind the giant. The second part of the story, another out-in-out sequence, also uses a twist, this time Odysseus's prudent invention of the double-edged fake name. Like the use of "Mr. Memory" in Hitchcock's *The 39 Steps*, the name comes in as a nickname and goes out as a universal. Odysseus *really is a nobody* who manages, by virtue of that negative existence, to escape the enfilade of giants.

We can follow the progress of the story using the "topographical" fractal with its Möbius-band logic—two sides connected by a twist (figure 10.8). The Cyclopean cave demonstrates the fractal qualities of the story and resembles, in plan, the digestive tract. Location! Location! Location! Inside the cave, $A \rightleftarrows \$$, subjects are bound to the authority of the Cyclops, truly "barred" in the strict Lacanian sense. The key to half of the escape is found in the hearth. Tempering the olive stake to an adamantine hardness enables the weapon to strike at the heart of the eye: $\delta \rightarrow A$. Odysseus, f, the hero of the moment, is able to execute this phallic act because he lulls the giant into a drunken sleep with his banter. Blind, like the *manes* at the wedding ceremony, the Cyclops will not see the Greeks escape his cave; but the logic of the story now moves from sight to touch, from metaphor to metonymy. This is the other "stem" of the formula that began with the absolute localization of the labyrinth (the mandate of cyclopean society). Metonymy is what gets the bride away from the father's hearth; it is Odysseus's guarantee of success. Knowing he will touch *only one side* of the sheep, the Greeks cling beneath. Knowing that Polyphemus will hear only the particular "side"

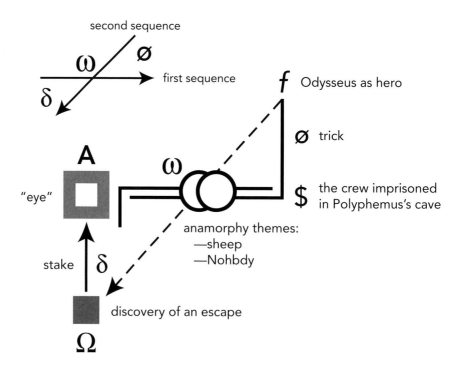

DONALD KUNZE

of the name, Nohbdy, Odysseus clings beneath, to the reversed part of antinomasia, the name as universal nobody. "If you think I'm Nohbdy, I am!"—the Missing Guest, that is.[22] The two parts of the story, the two parts of the sheep, and the two parts of the name use the labyrinth's logic: two parts connected by a twist. This fractalization of the Möbius-band structure is chiastic. It convenes through a "catastrophe" made inevitable by the symmetry/opposition of its internal mirror-structure. It is self-reference in the uncanny guise of the heroic epic.

ORIGIN OR CENTER?

Odysseus seems to have intended his encounter with the Cyclops as an experiment to test the relationship between cyclopean devotion to *manes,* the fathers, and the new principles of hospitality. The same provocative margin testing can be found in Euripides' play *Alcestis,* where King Admetus is blind to the trick played by his guest, Heracles. Could this be simply a historical conflict, present from the point at which the increasing cultural reliance on exogamy required the family to fool the *manes* into thinking that the daughter was not abandoning the hearth voluntarily? The historical appearance of the city-state supported by commerce suggests that hospitality was one of the traditions that contributed to the growth of democracy and the civic importance of the *agora. Alcestis* shows that there was at least enough social awareness of the conflict by the fifth century B.C.E. to provide plenty of comic material for the sophisticated audiences. It was no longer possible to be as cavalier as was Admetus about the wife's "ambiguous" position in the household without drawing public contempt.

On the other hand, there is a real possibility that the conflict between cyclopean devotion to the hearth and practices of hospitality was not just an event of remote history but an internal horizon present from the beginning in cooking and eating, with the same proportional divisions in every age. The captions vary, but the ratio remains the same. What for the ancients was played out in the domestic space of the house and the civic space of the *agora* is today played out in the decision whether to satisfy hunger in a "functionalist" manner or to make use of food's layered significations in some cultural or personal way, as in fasting and feasting. With hospitality comes escape, mobility, polity among strangers, the real life of cities—then and now. Hermetic boundary crossing and the role of the stranger open up cuisine to sophistication, theatricality, a relation to an audience. The fractal relationships that guided this historical development continue as a latent, renewable potential, fleshed out in new form whenever political and cultural conditions allow.

This continuity is suggested by the early use of the hearth for the worship of ancestors and the control of auspices. *From the beginning*, the hearth was protected from the gaze of strangers, the virulent "evil eye." The exchange of invisibility for blindness in the case of marriage customs makes use of the topographical peculiarity that "twists" cyclopean visuality into the hyperspace of hospitality, just as Odysseus twisted together the two parts of his escape plan following the labyrinth's fractal design. The vulnerability of the hearth shows precisely *where* hospitality must fit, and also shows hospitality/cuisine in perennial contention with a "cyclopean" point of view. It is not an issue we can resolve ideologically or intellectually, but rather a monad that couples two opposites in permanent contention. Thus, the stable topography that structured the ancient Greek and Roman household and cities is not just an artifact of bygone days but a pan-cultural and perennial quality of human life. The cyclopean/hospitable distinction is located precisely in the middle of contemporary situations. Why? How?

The answer lies in the "chiastic" nature of human thought, the coupling of "ideal" and "material" elements in every symbolic expression. This ancient rhetorical figure of *chiasmus*, crossing (χ), included verbal formulae for praising the departed at a funeral with an encomium that preserved the boundary between the dead and the living through double-edged praise. But it's clear that chiasmus is the figure proper to the ω of anamorphy. From cyclopean order (an inside) to the open invitation of hospitality, chiasmus is the crossed building (tomb, temple, labyrinth), the crossed inside-out space of the *agora*, and the focal space of the hearth, where the *manes* issue forth ambiguous prophecies.

What sustains these magic and effective spaces? The symbolic networks that bind the subject to the Other in various ways (⇄) are ironic, bipolar and self-sustaining. They are sustained by a circularity that creates an irrefutable interior logic. As Pascal pointed out, the king's power is sustained by the belief of the subjects that he is a king. Without this belief the king is powerless, so in effect the king is ruled by those he rules. A literary example of this idiotic symmetry occurs in Goethe's *Elective Affinities*. A husband and wife making love each imagine their partner to be their illicit lover. The husband imagines Ottilie, the wife Hauptmann. Through the pairing of the two acts of imaginary adultery, the couple can remain faithful—but the child conceived turns out to have the face and hair of Ottilie and the eyes of Hauptmann. Combining reality with the Real of the imagination in a crisscross (both χ and ω) means that there were four people involved: a couple bound legitimately and the "fantasmic" couple Ottilie and Hauptmann, two "Nohbdies."

SIMONIDES

A story that ties together the themes of cuisine, *encomia*, architecture, ancestral religion, and chiasmus is, curiously, the anecdote cited by nearly every Latin author as the origin of the "method of memory places."[23] The reader can by now pick out the clues and relate them to the curiously parallel story of the Cyclops. Simonides, poet and hence *parasite*,[24] or marginal person, was hired by a nobleman of Ceos, Scopas, to celebrate his recent victory in the wrestling ring. At the banquet, Simonides sang a poem divided into two parts to save his host from potential retribution from the evil eye; this part was devoted, in turn, to the *twin* gods, the Dioscuri. Scopas was not pleased with this piety and paid the poet only half his fee, telling him to "go to the gods" (i.e., to Hell) to collect the rest. Before Simonides could finish his dinner, a servant informed him that two strangers were waiting outside to speak with him; but when he got outside, there was no one to be seen. Just as he started to go back inside the banquet hall, the building collapsed, crushing all of the guests. Those who came to claim their relatives' bodies were alarmed to find that none were identifiable; but Simonides, who had practiced the art of memory places (attaching the guest's name to his place at the table to remember it more easily), could recall the name of each victim because of the crushed body's location, location, location. The relatives, relieved to be able to bury their kinsmen and thus avoid haunting by unsettled souls, generously rewarded Simonides with more than his missing half-fee.

The story grounds a memory method that is chiastic (place + name) but is also itself chiastic. The banquet hall stands and collapses; the guests are living, then dead. The poem is divided in two, with half of it about twins, the other half about a wrestler, one of a pair. Scopas's curse is exchanged for a "placement" that permits his proper burial. The χ assures us that the story's parts, like butterfly wings, will fold together perfectly.

DONALD KUNZE

The place at the table thus implies both cuisine and location within a precise geometry of Elsewhere, mediated by food. The place in the city presumes festivals and markers, a silent language of civic form. The place in the tomb is a point of nourishment, at least in ancient times when tubes would be used to pour oil, wine, and honey directly into the ground; but in ancient times at least, we know that the *termini* that defined this location were protected on pain of death.[25] So, cuisine is and always has been a matter of who's missing. Who *is* missing? Nohbdy.

NOTES

1. A quick explanation is afforded by connecting this desire to enclose with the filmic phenomenon of *suture,* mentioned later in the text. Suture is the emergence, from the center of a bounded space or group, of precisely the element bounding was intended to exclude. The best-known example for American readers appears in Edgar Allan Poe's "The Masque of the Red Death" (1842).

2. It's helpful at this point to mention the broader meaning of the phallic given by Jacques Lacan. Briefly, the phallic is anything that can appear and disappear, giving new meaning to the role of the horizon in perception and thought. The φ simultaneously stands for the imagination, particular fantasies, and the phallic aspect of the subject's escape from networks of symbolic relationships.

3. Richard Broxton Onians, *The Origins of European Thought about the Body, the Mind, the Soul, the World, and Fate* (Cambridge: Cambridge University Press, 1951), 263.

4. Numa Denis Fustel de Coulanges, *The Ancient City: A Study on the Religion, Laws, and Institutions of Greece and Rome* (Baltimore: Johns Hopkins University Press, 1980), 29.

5. See Alan Dundes, ed., *The Evil Eye: A Casebook* (1981; reprint, Madison: University of Wisconsin Press, 1992).

6. Fustel de Coulanges, *The Ancient City,* 37.

7. For a review of the expanded idea of this film term, see Slavoj Žižek, "The Short Circuit," chap. 3 of *The Fright of Real Tears: Krzysztof Kieslowski between Theory and Post-Theory* (London: British Film Institute, 2001), 55–70.

8. There is too much literature on the labyrinth for citations to be helpful. For the purposes of this essay, a very limited idea of the labyrinth is the most informative: the "Cretan" or "Thesean" labyrinth, a design of two sets of recursive turns connected by a twist (ABA:B:ABA).

9. See Jean-Paul Sartre, *Being and Nothingness: An Essay on Phenomenological Ontology,* trans. Hazel E. Barnes (New York: Philosophical Library, 1956), 278.

10. See Angus Fletcher, "On Two Words in the Libretto of *The Magic Flute,*" *Georgia Review* 29, no. 1 (spring 1975): 128–153.

11. The frontispiece of Giambattista Vico's *The New Science* shows as much. From the interpretations derived from divination, the first peoples derived laws that were initially severe but later led to humanizing social institutions *(res publica).* See Giambattista Vico, *The New Science of Giambattista Vico,* trans. Thomas Goddard Bergin and Max Harold Fish (Ithaca: Cornell University Press, 1968); Donald Kunze, *Thought and Place: The Architecture of Eternal Places in the Philosophy of Giam-*

battista Vico, Emory Vico Studies, vol. 2 (New York: Peter Lang, 1987), 169–206. See also Michel Ragon, *The Space of Death: A Study of Funerary Architecture, Decoration, and Urbanism,* trans. Alan Sheridan (Charlottesville: University Press of Virginia, 1983).

12. The backstory of Alcestis provides much of the necessary explanation for why this play, long regarded as a tragedy, is really a comic farce. Apollo had granted Admetus an extended life if only he could find someone to die in his place. This favor was in exchange for the kindness Admetus had shown Apollo when he was sentenced to be a servant in the king's household, penance for killing the Cyclopes in revenge for Zeus's destruction of his son Asclepius, the magic physician who, with blood from Medusa, could kill or resurrect the dead. See Donald Kunze, "Alcestis Backstory," *Potential Architecture Journal,* August 2001 <http://www.waac.vt.edu/paj/> accessed January 2003).

13. This tradition was begun, perhaps, by the monumental work of Jurgis Baltrušaitis, *Anamorphic Art,* trans. W. J. Strachan (New York: Harry N. Abrams, 1977). More recent studies continue the visual emphasis, such as Alberto Pérez-Gómez and Louise Pelletier's *Anamorphosis: An Annotated Bibliography with Special Reference to Architectural Representation* (Montreal: McGill University Libraries, 1995).

14. Reversed antinomasia is treated by Vico scholars as the basis of imaginative universality. See Andrea Battistini, *La degnità della retorica: Studi su G. B. Vico* (Pisa: Pacini, 1975). The idea is curiously close to Lacan's notion of the "quilting" of "sliding signifiers." On this, see Slavoj Žižek, *The Sublime Object of Ideology* (New York: Verso, 1989), 95–100.

15. I have summarized the thesis of John North, professor emeritus, working in Groningen, the Netherlands. See Tom Robbins, "Is This the Coded Secret of the Ambassadors?" *Sunday Times* (London), January 13, 2002.

16. The condition of undecidability created by boundaries has been analyzed in detail by Victor Stoichita, *The Self-Aware Image: An Insight into Early Modern Meta-Painting,* trans. Anne-Marie Glasheen (Cambridge: Cambridge University Press, 1997). Stoichita considers an extremely well defined period of painting, from 1522 to 1675, where the motif of the painting-within-a-painting was extensively exploited by (mainly) western European painters. The general principle behind this use of literal frames is, however, considerably broader and certainly not restricted to painting.

17. For an interesting compendium of Italian festivals and their special foods, see Carol Field, *Celebrating Italy: The Tastes and Traditions of Italy as Revealed through Its Feasts, Festivals, and Sumptuous Food* (New York: Harper Collins, 1990).

18. In relation to Hermes as god of boundaries and Hestia as a companion goddess of the hearth, Norman O. Brown has detailed a remarkable sequence of cultural mediations involving trade, theft, and the transformation of cities. See his *Hermes the Thief: The Evolution of a Myth* (Great Barrington, Mass.: Lindisfarne Press, 1990), 32–45.

19. See Walter W. Skeat, *Etymological Dictionary of the English Language,* new ed., rev. and enl. (1909; reprint, Oxford: Clarendon Press, 1968), 278.

20. See Vico, *New Science,* §503.

21. Henry W. Johnstone, Jr., "Odysseus as a Traveler," in *Categories: A Colloquium,* ed. Henry W. Johnstone, Jr. (University Park: Department of Philosophy, Pennyslvania State University, 1978), 108. For the optative verb, see *Odyssey* 9.268.

22. In *Duck Soup,* Groucho Marx defends an inept spy: "Gentlemen, Chicolini here may talk like an idiot and look like an idiot, but don't let that fool you. He really is an idiot."

23. Strange to say, the structure or significance of chiasmus is not noted in the most often cited re-counting of this tale, by Frances A. Yates, in *The Art of Memory* (Chicago: University of Chicago Press, 1966), 1–2. Two other famous versions are found in the *Ad Herennium* attributed to Cicero and in Quintilian's *Institutio oratoria*.

24. The term *parasite*, which means both "noise" and "parasite" in French, is complex. It was originally linked to the professional poets who crashed banquets to earn tips for extemporaneous performances. The sense of a space outside of the ordinary informs the idea of both poetry and noise. See Michel Serres, *The Parasite*, trans. Lawrence R. Schehr (Baltimore: Johns Hopkins University Press, 1982).

25. Fustel de Coulanges reports that Romans originally placed the tomb in an agricultural field, pro-tected from trespass by severe laws. *Termini*, or upright boundary stones, were set up at the margins and fed offerings of wine, oil, and fat. Strangers were forbidden to even touch a *terminus*, and tilting it out of position was a capital crime. The offender was ritually sacrificed and his own house and fields were destroyed (*The Ancient City*, 58–62).

11

SEMIOTICA AB EDENDO,
TASTE IN ARCHITECTURE

MARCO FRASCARI

Contemporary architecture is almost entirely tasteless. Architectural taste has been ruled out by the moral standards of the modern movement. This has, I think, resulted in a meaningless architecture. As a reaction to the buildings presented under the functional ethics of the International Style architectural expression, the postmodern condition presents an approach grounded in the generation of a new "morality" for architecture. This "morality" stresses the visual components of signification. This tendency results, paradoxically, from the nefarious puritan ideology of the modern movement, which evolved into the visually dominated manipulation of meanings proposed by the postmodern condition of architecture. Both the style and the condition strip away from architecture any pleasure to be had in either its use or conception. Such architectural products are rich in voluptuous processes of signification, but are completely bereft of tactile pleasures (the tactile means of signification), that is, "taste." And taste and tactility, as will be shown below, are closely related.

Characteristic of any theoretical work is the confrontation with the use and abuse of terms, i.e., language games. The results of such play of terms can lead to pleasant discoveries. Phenomenological language games do not necessarily reflect linguistic or geographical boundaries, but rather enrich the taste for knowledge. The key terms under scrutiny in the specific game joined here are "taste" and its related intellectual "pleasure." The latter begins in the tactile origin of taste and culminates in the interwoven ramifications of the architectural and culinary realms of knowledge.[1] The rigorous design morality imposed by the form-function polarity of the modern movement has reduced architecture to its untouchable structural and functional bones. For example, a completely different sensation is evoked when one rubs the naked hand across a marble column as opposed to rubbing it across a Miesian I beam. The ethical stance of both the modern and the postmodern theories aims to produce buildings that "look good" over a predetermined life span. In this sense, their built products are similar to another set of products generated under the spell of modern times: the edibles produced by fast-food chains. These look like the real thing, but they have been designed to be gulped down. They are a feast for the eyes but there is no possibility, no reason, to take the time and pleasure to taste them. In other words, the limited temporality of contemporary architectural production, a visual architecture produced *sub specie utilitatis*, has obviated the search for tactile pleasure in architecture, thereby halting the production of a tangible architecture *sub specie aeternitatis*.

Like every other subject or object of interpretation, architecture may be studied from two different points of view. One may describe it either by comparing the means of sign production and classification used in an ideologically dominant discipline without any reference to the origin of both, or one may regard it from an analogical point of view by tracing the causes of the origin of the analogy, thereby creating a new productive understanding. This is an important part of the language game as it is "played" below.

In the tradition of Western culture, sight and hearing have been given predominant consideration. Taste is considered the lowest of the senses in the cognitive process, a sense without moral value, an inferior sense. In the *Nicomachean Ethics* Aristotle points out that taste is the lowest among the human senses, the one which relates us back to animals. In his lectures on aesthetics Hegel opposes taste, a practical and consumptive approach to objects, to the visual and acoustic senses which rule our conception of the theoretical frameworks. However, in Greek and Latin, "taste" (*gustus, sapor*) is a term related etymologically and semantically with the act of gen-

MARCO FRASCARI

erating knowledge. The highest form of knowledge, *sapienza*, i.e., wisdom, is related to taste (*sapor*) as is clearly shown in an etymology written by Isidore of Seville:

> The word sapiens (a wise man) is said to be derived from the word sapor (taste) for just as the sense of taste is able to discern the flavors of different foods, so too is the wise man able to discern objects and their causes since he recognizes each one as distinct and is able to judge them with an instinct for truth.[2]

Tommaso Campanella recognized the importance of the tactile dimension of taste in a passage in his *Theologia* of 1613–1624, where he compares *tactus* and *gustus*. In this passage, the taste metaphor is used to indicate a peculiar form of immediate knowledge.

> It is not by deliberation that man judges whether a spirit is a devil or an angel. . . .
> It is rather by sensitivity and an intuitive understanding that he is persuaded . . .
> just as we immediately recognize the taste of bread and wine with our tongue.[3]

In the preface to his *Metaphisica* of 1638, Campanella contrasted knowledge based on reasoning with a form of knowledge based on immediate perception. The former works like "an arrow which strikes a faraway target without getting a real 'taste' of it (*absque gustu*)," whereas the latter is a form of knowledge "per tactum intrinsecum in magna suavitate" (through its inner touch in great gentleness).

In discussing the "visual versus the tactile" approach in architecture, Kenneth Frampton points to the large number of processes of interpretation involved in the appreciation of the built environment. Those processes are based on signs registered by "the labile body." They are

> the intensity of light, darkness, heat and cold, the feeling of humidity, the aroma of material; the almost palpable presence of masonry as the body senses its own confinement; the momentum of an induced gait, and the relative inertia of the body as it traverses the floor; the echoing resonance of our own footfall.[4]

In one of his *Fragments* (1797), Novalis states: "a body is to space as the visible is to light." The tactile "measure," the body's understanding of the signs in space, is the basis for taste and is the dimension which enables us to see whether there is a tasteful correspondence of general relations of signification among the "architectural facts" producing a nontrivial architecture. Furthermore, taste implies creative inferences—a productive approach. This inferential act is an interpretive process which singles out the appropriate solution from the existing architectural facts. The processes of interpretation, the result of architectural expression, are the summation of the acts of dwelling. Architecture as totality is the representation of the expression of dwelling. Resorting again to the etymological visions of Isidore of Seville, one can clearly articulate the tasteful and tactile origin of architecture:

> The ancients used the word aedes (i.e., dwelling) in reference to any edifice. Some think that this word was derived from a form of the term for "eating," edendo, citing by way of example a line from Plautus: "If I had invited you home (in aedum) for lunch." Hence we also have the word "edifice" because originally a building was made for eating (ad edendum factum).[5]

Isidore's interpretation is probably incorrect—edibles and edifices are not the same, etymologically speaking—but its value is in the identification of a dominant ideology, to which the gastronomical analogy adds the understanding of the acts of signification involved in the architectural construing.

Focusing on the concept of taste, one is able, through this theoretical analogy, to indicate a new direction for architectural production. Taste, a tactile procedure of sign production and interpretation, is the common factor existing between architecture and gastronomy in generating a well-established—but usually regarded as fanciful—analogy. The arrival on the architectural scene of the first moderns in the seventeenth century (see Joseph Rykwert's The First Moderns for a discussion of the emergence of modernism in this era)[6] began the alienation of "taste" from its tactile dimension, giving it a negative connotation. Ever since then, "taste" has been invalidated as a possible rule for architectural production. Understanding the denotative and connotative dimensions of taste in architectural design, however, can lead to a reevaluation of its role within the design process. The analogy between gastronomy and architecture is not only Isidore's fanciful etymological interpretation, but has been used many times. Ben Jonson, an English playwright who disliked architects, used the framework of the analogy in one of his masques to criticize subtly Inigo Jones and Jones's belief in the cultural predominance of the architect. Jonson's masque portrays the master builder as a preposterous master cook.

MARCO FRASCARI

In discussing the evolution from the deductive procedure of judgment to the inferential procedure of taste, Robert Klein[7] traces the changes in the understanding of the idea of taste and singles out the seventeenth-century Venetian notion of productive judgment—productive taste—an inductive procedure based on pleasure. Productive taste is a form of knowledge which results form the chiasmatic relationship between knowledge which takes pleasure and pleasure which knows.

In the eighteenth century, discussions of taste attempted to define the relationship between the perceiver and the work of art, thus generating a theoretical framework for the production of artistic texts in a contextual situation. Francesco Milizia, an architectural theoretician with "first modern" rigorist attitudes,[8] shows the process of removing taste from the tactile realm in one of his definitions:

> *Taste . . . this name is given to that understanding which feels and judges of natural and artificial works. In the beginning, taste was for judging the goodness of food, then for judging the goodness of books, statues, paintings, buildings, furniture, garments, carriages, and also all the unnecessary things, the bizarre caprices devised by luxury and fashion and quite often by the corrupted taste.*[9]

To understand the problem posed by this theoretical framework, one might usefully list some of the definitions given to "taste" and single out the different questions raised within each era. During the Enlightenment, "taste" was defined as "a judgment based on strict rules," or as "a feeling completely relative to the person who expresses it. It is not standard," or as "a faculty of the understanding in judging works of art. It is based on a standard." Sometimes "taste" was defined as "an extemporaneous judgment without attending to rules or reason," and again as "an impulsive tendency of the souls toward the true good." Taste is a faculty which presents "sensibility, but not reason" or "quick intellectual discernment plus delicacy of feelings."[10] Removed from its tactile roots, taste becomes a confusing, unnecessary, and meaningless tool. Taste complicated the solution of design problems. The only sphere of influence left to taste was the realm of gastronomical artifacts, where a negation of the tactile dimension of aesthetic enjoyment was quite impossible. Limiting taste to the process and the place of eating renewed its position in architecture; again, the dining room becomes the phenomenological origin of architecture.

11. 1

Cake tins resembling buildings. From M.-A. Carême, *Le patissier royal parisien, ou Traité élémentaire et pratique de la pâtisserie ancienne et moderne*, 3d ed. (London: W. Jetts, 1841), vol. 1, plate 9. Courtesy Parks Library Special Collections, Iowa State University.

The wonders of cuisine and its physical expressions in the dining room were the tasteful remains of Marie-Antoine (or Antonin) Carême, the first and in many ways the most important of all French chefs. Carême has been labeled the architect of French cuisine. This label is not only a metaphorical usage pointing out Carême's predominant role in the rise of French gastronomy, but indicates also his search for the relationship existing between the two disciplines. Carême, the sixth child of an impoverished stonemason, was abandoned in the street at the age of eleven. He found his way to the back door of a public eating house, where he began his career to become one of the most important *chefs de cuisine*. In this position he could afford to turn down a permanent job offer from Czar Alexander of Russia, for whom he had catered a series of feasts. Carême, however, did prepare a book of designs for landmarks he thought necessary for improving the architectural environment of St. Petersburg (figures 11.1, 11.2, and 11.3). Architecture was one of Carême's main interests. He carefully studied the architectural monuments of the past and designed elaborate table decorations called *pièces montées* (mounted pieces) as an outlet for his architectural passion. Those pieces were rotundas, temples, columns, and arches, constructed with sugar,

MARCO FRASCARI

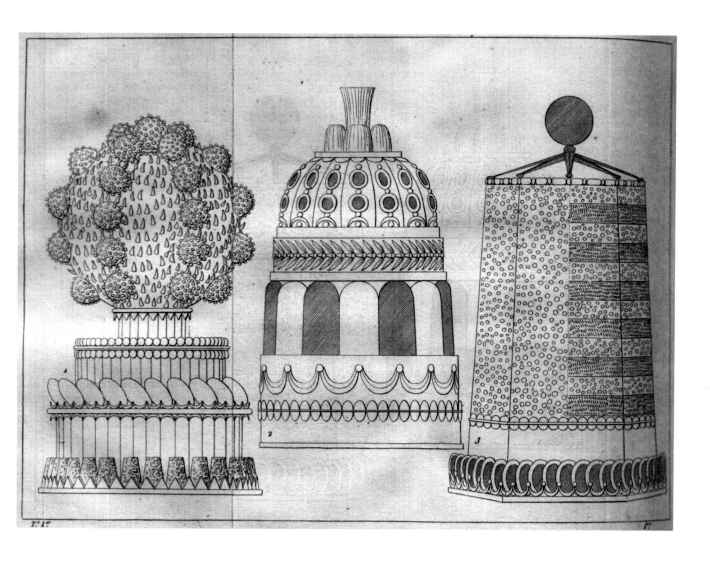

11.2

M.-A. Carême, architectural
confections: *grosse meringue
à la parisienne, croquante enpâté
d'amandes à l'ancienne, gateau
mille-feuilles à la moderne.*
From Carême, *Le patissier royal
parisien,* vol. 1, plate 10. Courtesy
Parks Library Special Collections,
Iowa State University.

11.3

M.-A. Carême, pastry in the form of specific architectural types: Chinese hermitage, Gothic tower, Indian pavilion. From Carême, *Le patissier royal parisien*, vol. 2, plate 21. Courtesy Parks Library Special Collections, Iowa State University.

MARCO FRASCARI

icing, and pastry dough. Each of these pieces was carefully designed with an architect's eye, for Carême considered confectionery to be "architecture's main branch."

At the beginning of the nineteenth century, in his fifteenth aphorism of the twenty written as preamble to his discussion of *The Physiology of Taste,* Jean Anthelme Brillat-Savarin states: "On devient cuisinier, mais on naît rôtisseur" (One can learn to become a cook, but one must be born knowing how to roast). A century later Auguste Perret rephrased this sentence and used it as his own first aphorism in *Contribution à une théorie de l'architecture,* stating: "On devient ingénieur, mais on naît architecte" (One can learn to become an engineer, but one must be born an architect). The concept embodied in both aphorisms singles out the conjectural nature of architecture and gastronomy. The cook and the engineer can learn their formulas and procedures, whereas the architect and the *rôtisseur* rely on symptoms, clues, and surprising facts to perform their own tasks using interpretive procedures. They deal with processes of design which cannot be methodologically explained; that is, they cannot be reduced to quantifiable recipes or formulas.

Architecture and gastronomy employ similar procedures of production. As James Fergusson pointed out, the process by which a hut built to house a holy image is refined into a temple, or a covered market transformed into a basilica, is the same as that by which a boiled neck of mutton is refined into *cotelettes à l'impériale* or a grilled fowl made into *poulet à la Marengo.*[11] In both disciplines taste, an interpretive procedure, is at the base of sign production. In their doing and making, both disciplines face ill-defined problems and solve them using conjectural procedures. Judging by the signs, both disciplines apply the "rule" of taste to solve their ill-defined problems in a nontrivial manner. Taste is defined by Jacques-François Blondel, an eighteenth-century French architectural theoretician, as the "fruit of reasoning," a sequence of appreciation and fast judgment by which one achieves a nontrivial result. It is the same procedure by which a *gourmet,* a person of taste, goes about food preparation. Taste is thus a reasoning which suggests what something may be: it is a knowledge which does not know, as opposed to a knowledge which knows.

The surrealists were not particularly interested in architectural expression, but Salvador Dalí is one of the rare exceptions. Inspired by the architecture of the art nouveau, Dalí pointed out the importance of edible edifices for creating a new poetic dimension of architecture. Dalí relates the origin of pleasure in architecture to childhood narcissism. This is a stage in human development when objects are interpreted only from the viewpoint of oral satisfaction. The tactile dimension of taste expresses a desire to learn through a cannibalism; that is, to incorporate the outside world into oneself. This productive inference is based on instinct, just as the incessant oral tasting of childhood is an instinctive part of cognitive appropriation. In surrealistic architecture, Dalí points out that

> *Art Nouveau . . . incarnates the most tangible and delirious aspiration of hyper-materialism. An illustration of the apparent paradox is to be found in the comparison made between an Art-Nouveau house assimilated into a cake and a pastry-cook's ornamental tart. . . . A noneuphemistic allusion is achieved to the nutritious, edible character of these houses which are nothing less than the first edible houses and the first and only heterogenetic buildings whose existence verifies the most urgent and necessary "function" which is so important to the amorous imagination; namely, the ability, in as real a way as possible, to eat the object of one's desire.*[12]

The surrealistic approach implies a creative inference, a productive approach based on surprise and wonder, in an attempt to generate new ideas. Wonder is at the basis of any childhood edible discovery.

Generating a new concept of image, this idea of wonder and surprising facts was a permanent concern of the surrealists. Pierre Reverdy, Apollinaire's friend, wrote in *Nord-Sud* (1918):

> *The image is pure creation of spirit. It cannot be born of a comparison but of the bringing together of two realities which are more or less remote. The more distant and just the relationship of these conjoined realities, the stronger the image—the more emotive power and poetic reality it will have.*[13]

In working out his semiotic doctrine Charles S. Peirce, the American pragmatist philosopher, deals with the inferential and iconic creation of images, an act which brings together realities which are more or less remote. Peirce's classification of inferential reasoning differs from most taxonomies of modes of reasoning. He adds a novel type of inference, "abduction," to the traditional typology of induction and deduction. Abduction is concerned with the reasoning necessary for adopting hypotheses or new ideas. It refers to "all the operations by which theories and concepts are en-gendered."[14] The structure of this process of reasoning is

The surprising fact "C" is observed. But if "A" were true, "C" would be a matter of course.

Hence there is reason to suspect that "A" is true.[15]

Deductive reasoning is based on the application of a general rule (B is C) to a partic-ular case (A is B) to obtain a result (A is C). Inductive reasoning is the inference of a general rule (B is A) from the specific cases (A's are B's) and results (A's are B's). Abductive reasoning is the inference of a case (A*n* is B*n*) from a rule and a result (A is C). From this point of view, abduction is a highly productive procedure. New under-standings are continually generated. A *rôtisseur* understands when a piece of meat is perfectly cooked (a case) by inference from rule and results. That is practice.

Peirce describes abduction as "the spontaneous conjecture of instinctive rea-son."[16] Reviving a Renaissance terminology, Peirce named this capacity the *lume na-turale* (natural light).[17] He selected this name to indicate that humanity has the possibility of looking into the laws of nature without going through the painstaking procedures of the traditional inference. Abduction "tries what *il lume naturale* can do."[18] It is a power concerned with the reality of external objects and not with the ideal picture. This power operates on the similarities with respect to form, figure, location, and function. Abduction is a productive inference and an instinctive activity. Peirce recognizes obtaining food as a productive and instinctive activity. He sees two kinds of instinct ruling human life: One is selfish, the other social. The social leads to the de-velopment of reason, whereas the selfish leads to the development of useful arts such as gastronomy and architecture.[19] Abduction is based on the selfish instinct and is a cognitive process of a known activity.[20]

The relationship between the premises and the hypothetical conclusion is iconic in nature, since the facts observed in the beginning are in the final artifact. The chief contribution of the *lume naturale* is economic in nature; its task is to formulate hy-potheses based on the tangible dimension of facts, things which can also be the basis for the semiotic shaping of them into artifacts. In a process of "transformation" the tactile icon of the fact is embodied in the artifact, such as the enjoyment of eating a successful gourmet dish, or dwelling in a successful building. The task of abduction is to initiate this process of transformation. Deductive and inductive inferences—that is, visual inferences—do not help if they are not guided by abduction, a tactically generated inference. Deduction and induction aid in theorization. Abduction helps to produce within practice, since it is an inference based on the sign interpreted by the "labile body" in search of taste (*sapor*), or pleasure in discerning, that is *sapienza*. A poetic statement on architectural practice by Louis Kahn (the italics are mine) encapsulates this relationship between touch and the tangible dimensions of architecture and the wonder of abductive inference.

> *Form comes from Wonder. Wonder stems from our "in touchness" with how we were made. One senses that nature records the process of how it was made. "In touch" with this record we are in Wonder. This wonder gives rise to knowledge. But knowledge is related to her knowledge and this relation gives a sense of order, a sense of how they inter-relate in a harmony that makes all things exist. From knowledge to sense of order we then wink to Wonder and say "How am I doing, Wonder?"*[21]

NOTES

Reprinted from *Journal of Architectural Education* 40, no. 2 (fall 1986): 3–7. A shorter and less surrealistic version of this article was presented at the Ninth Annual Semiotic Society of America Meeting in Bloomington, Indiana, in October 1984.

1. *The Oxford Dictionary of English Etymology*, ed. C. T. Onions (Oxford: Clarendon Press, 1966), 905, gives the following etymology of taste, from *teist*, which is "examining by touch, try, test . . . experience or try the flavour of . . . have a particular flavour . . . OF *taster* (mod. Fr. *tater*, It. *tastare* . . . a blend of L. *tangere* touch (cf. TACT) and *gustare* taste (cf. GUSTO)."

2. This passage is a translation of "Sapiens dictus a sapore; quia sicut gustus aptus est ad discretionem saporis ciborum, sic sapiens ad dinoscentiam rerum atque causarum; quod unumquodque dinoscat, atque sensu veritatis discernat" (Isidore of Seville, *Isidori Hispalensis Episcopi Etymologiarum sive Originum Libri XX*, ed. W. M. Lindsay [seventh century; Oxford: Clarendon Press, 1911], book 10, p. 240).

3. This passage is a translation of "Non enim discurrendo cognoscit vir spiritualis utrum daemon si an angelus . . . sibi suadet . . . aliquid; sed quondam quasi tactu et gustu et intuitiva notitia . . . quemadmodum lingua statim discernimus saporem vini et panis" (Tommaso Campanella, *Theologicum liber XIV*, in *Magia e grazia*, ed. Romano Amerio [Rome: Linceii, 1958], 147–158).

4. Kenneth Frampton, "Towards a Critical Regionalism," in *The Anti-Aesthetic*, ed. Hal Foster (Port Townsend, Wash.: Bay Press, 1983), 28.

5. This passage is a translation of "Omne aedificium antiqui aedem appellaverunt. Alii aedem ab edendo quiddam sumpsissee nomen existimant, dantes exemplum de Plauto: si vocassem vos in aedem ad prandium. Hinc et aedificium, eo quod fuerit prius ad edendum factum" (Isidore of Seville, *Etymologiarum sive Originum Libri XX,* book 15, p. 32).

6. Joseph Rykwert, *The First Moderns* (Cambridge, Mass.: MIT Press, 1979).

7. Robert Klein, "Judgment and Taste in Cinquecento Art Theory," in *Form and Meaning* (New York: Viking Press, 1979), 161–169.

8. Rykwert, *The First Moderns,* 305ff., discusses the relationship between rigorism and architectural matters in the eighteenth century.

9. This passage is a translation of "Gusto . . . si è imprestato questo nome all'intendimento che sente e giudica del merito di opere naturali ed artificiali. Da principio non si ebbe gusto che per giudicare delle bontà del cibo: si ebbe poi gusto per giudicare della bontà dei libri, delle statue, dei quadri, degli edifici, dei mobili, delle vesti, delle carrozze, e anche tutte le inutilità, delle bizzarie fantasticate dal lusso e dalla moda e speso dal gusto depravato" (Francesco Milizia, *Principij di architettura civile* [1780; reprint, Milan: Majocchi, 1847], 76).

10. Francesco Binni, *Gusto e invenzione nel settecento inglese* (Urbino: Argalia, 1970), 75.

11. See Peter Collins, *Changing Ideals in Modern Architecture* (Montreal: McGill University Press, 1967), 167.

12. Salvador Dalí, "De la beauté terrifiante et comestible de l'architecture modern style," *Minotaure,* nos. 3–4 (December 1933); English translation, "Art Nouveau Architecture's Terrifying and Edible Beauty," in *Architectural Design,* nos. 2–3 (1978): 139–140.

13. See Patrick Waldberg, *Surrealism* (London: Thames and Hudson, 1966), 22.

14. Charles S. Peirce, *Collected Papers of Charles Sanders Peirce,* ed. Charles Hartshorne and Paul Weiss (Cambridge, Mass.: Harvard University Press, 1960–1965), 5:590.

15. Ibid., 189.

16. Ibid., 6:475.

17. Peirce is referring to the fifteenth- and sixteenth-century theories of *fantasia* ("fantasy" derives from the Greek *phos,* "light").

18. Peirce, *Collected Papers,* 1:630.

19. Ibid., 7:378.

20. See Maryann Ayim, "Retroduction: The Rational Instinct," *Transactions of the Charles S. Peirce Society* 10, no. 1 (winter 1974): 34–43.

21. Louis I. Kahn, *Notebooks and Drawings,* ed. Richard Saul Wurman and Eugene Feldman (Philadelphia: Falcon Press, 1962), 91.

MORNING AND MELANCHOLIA

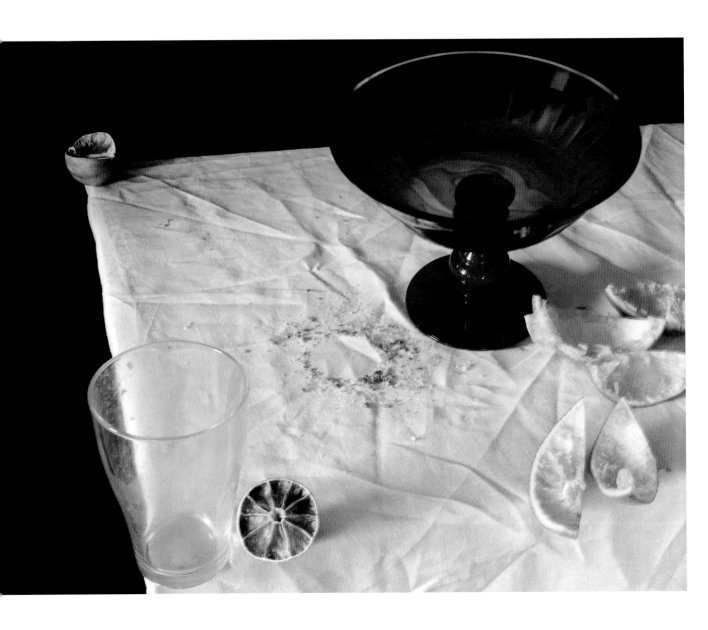

12.2
Laura Letinsky, Untitled #10,
New Haven, 1999. Courtesy of
Edwynn Houk Gallery, New York.

12.3
Laura Letinsky, Untitled #13, New
Haven, 1999/2000. Courtesy of
Edwynn Houk Gallery, New York.

12.4
Laura Letinsky, Untitled #21,
Chicago, 1998. Courtesy of
Edwynn Houk Gallery, New York.

12.5
Laura Letinsky, Untitled #33,
Rome, 2001. Courtesy of Edwynn
Houk Gallery, New York.

12.7
Laura Letinsky, Untitled #39,
Rome, 2001. Courtesy of Edwynn
Houk Gallery, New York.

12.8
Laura Letinsky, Untitled #40,
Rome, 2001. Courtesy of Edwynn
Houk Gallery, New York.

TABLE RULES

12

MORNING, AND MELANCHOLIA

LAURA LETINSKY

"Morning, and Melancholia" pictures dirty dishes and messy countertops, abandoned arrangements, stranded tidbits and crumbs: unexpectedly alluring tableaux of things and spaces that we touch, alter, devour, and discard. The pictures are still lifes, yet they don't aim for the traditional allure of bountiful meals that either await or attest to an unseen viewer's consumption. What I look for is all that remains "after the fact," what lingers and persists, as well as by inference what is already gone. Photographing these various scenes of remains, I discover formal relationships between ripeness and decay, delicacy and awkwardness, control and chaos, waste and plentitude, pleasure and sustenance. My still lifes reveal and revel in what Norman Bryson calls "creaturality": "No one can escape the conditions of creaturality, of eating and drinking and domestic life with which still-life is concerned. . . . Whether to see it as trivial, base and unworthy of serious attention, or to see it otherwise, is very much a matter of history and ideology."[1]

This project is part of my ongoing photographic exploration of domestic intimacy—both its homeliness and its beauty. The still lifes began as an attempt to make sense of my space, in particular the emotional aspirations and appetites that I invest in buying, preparing, serving, and eating food. In each of the photographs, a complex pictorial space confronts the viewer for a split second with the inability to recognize "one's place," and thus awakens a more reflective need to find one's balance—physically and psychologically. But the pictures' formal awkwardness is combined with discrete moments of prettiness, evoking that mixture of friction and affection that constitutes domestic everydayness. This pictorial composition allows seemingly random details of one's particular palate, personal habits, and preferred household implements momentarily to appear as evidence, indeed as inanimate witnesses to their own post-utopian possibility.

Modern painting, especially in works by artists such as Cézanne and Morandi, has made us familiar with what is called pictorial plasticity: the way space itself is molded and shaped on the picture's surface. Yet in photography the expectation of a more straightforward realistic space still predominates, despite our understanding that the photograph isn't real. My photographs, though, resist realistic space, insisting instead on their provisional status as spatial constructions. I want to force the viewer to take notice of the space in the photograph as not entirely natural, as being as much a hybrid as the rest of the spaces we inhabit.

The photographic moment is specifically a moment *after;* it always arrives, if you will, the *morning* after. Photographs, by their nature, are acts of holding on to something that exists elsewhere and at another time, or no longer exists—or maybe never existed at all except in the picture. My title alludes to an essay, "Mourning and Melancholia," in which Freud investigates two different reactions to traumatic loss: mourning, a process of working through and letting go after the loss of a beloved person or object; and melancholy, actually another means of holding on to the lost object in which one internalizes one's loss as a personal deficit or failure. In my title I substitute the word *morning*, not just a reference to the breakfast dishes found in some of the earliest pictures in the series but also a suggestion of the "morning after"—after the story is over, when a different less desiring mood intervenes. While this postnarrative implies a retrospective sense of an end or a loss, it is also just as much a chance simply for a kind of aesthetic attention that aspires to momentary dumbness. Indeed, I want my pictures to be dumb—not in the sense of ignorant or dull, but rather blithely for-

LAURA LETINSKY

getful of the way spaces and objects, actions and their meanings adhere. My pictures try to look at, and hold on to, this sensation.

My photographs strive to enact a spatial-psychological tension, standing in for the objects that were in front of the lens while at the same time holding on to the objects it pictures. The 4 × 5 inch negative literally holds on to more information, enabling one's attention to linger on the moment. The photographs refuse to let go of what has been. "I . . . decompose, I enlarge, and so to speak, I retard in order to have time to know at last," writes Roland Barthes in *Camera Lucida*.[2] In my pictures I wish to make manifest the play between the photograph as a kind of letting go and as a kind of obsessive holding on. The objects I photograph are food remains and accoutrements whose appearance wavers between precious and "icky." By intensifying both their repulsive and attractive aspects I mean to reaffirm the still life as a genre and an activity, devoted to what is still left over in the act of looking—by looking at leftovers.

NOTES

See the color plates following page 204. Special thanks to Jamie Horwitz, who sees what I am trying to show in these images, and to Eric and Clyde for their help in fomenting these photographs.

1. Norman Bryson, *Looking at the Overlooked: Four Essays on Still Life Painting* (Cambridge, Mass.: Harvard University Press, 1990), 13.
2. Roland Barthes, *Camera Lucida: Reflections on Photography,* trans. Richard Howard (New York: Hill and Wang, 1981), 99.

13

TABLE TALK

DAVID LEATHERBARROW

I magine returning to a restaurant in which you had just finished a meal—perhaps you went back for your keys. Before leaving a second time, take a minute to notice the way the table looks after everyone has gone.

Inscribed onto the table's surfaces are traces of what just occurred, in all its particularity. Like the clothes of a laborer at the end of the day, this cloth, china, and cutlery fully attest to the ways they were used. *Service* is a term we sometimes use to name tableware. It denotes two things: the physical premises of a meal and their readiness to assist whoever wants to eat. Surface stains result from the table's voluntary subjection because the contents of each receptacle—hardly ever dry—leave telltale marks. But to notice only these traces is to neglect a different way the elements that make up the table perform and present themselves.

Before the meal occurred, the table and its more permanent preparations displayed themselves as just the sort of setting we were looking for, as if by some miracle of foresight they had known this all the time. "Presaturated" with indications of possibilities, the setting proposed a possible meal because it had been prescribed for typical practices. Though the tabletop is particular once we have finished, it was general (generally OK) before we began. To describe a table—or for that matter a room, sidewalk, or garden—as a trace or chronicle is to recognize that it also served once as a prescription. Thus, a symmetry: inscription after the meal, prescription before it; the reply the table gave to our "orders" was written on the back of its invitation.

But that is not all the setting had to say, or to imply. The enjoyment of a meal hardly requires steady attention to the chairs, glasses, and napkins that allow it to take place. The "service" they perform involves not only subjection and anticipation but a particular kind of recession, a retreat or withdrawal from perceptual prominence. That they allow themselves to be overlooked during the meal is not a fault of their "form"; actually it demonstrates the reverse, its relative perfection. During a meal, the serving not the setting sustains one's interest. Good service tends to be quiet, good tables tacit. At the center of meal experience is thus a blind spot with respect to its instruments, as is true for furnishings and equipment of all sorts. Elements in service forgo conspicuousness once they commit themselves to sustaining events. Although quiet, they are not inarticulate.

Before, after, and during the meal, then, the table gives itself in different ways: as a trace once eating is over, as a type before one sits down, and tacitly while the meal is occurring. Though architects often concern themselves with the first two of these modes of articulation, trace and type, the third, the tacit voice, is equally important in what I would like to describe as "table talk."[1]

Familiar in experience but often neglected in architectural study, the everyday meal is a particularly instructive example of how spatial settings make sense in different ways. The meal's diversity of articulation probably results from each being one among many that, over time and through memory, accrue a history endowed with richly stratified meanings. Prosaic habits are not rituals, for they lack the latter's mythical substrate; but when meals are the practice under consideration the first may transcend their origins and become the second. Each serving spreads itself out over memories of anteceding practices whose historical accumulation saturates the situation with content that can be called symbolic, for its foundation or presumed origin is believed to be "right." Christianity has a sacramental history because a particular Passover meal was preceded by an emphatically prospective injunction: "do this in remembrance of me," demanding of each follower a performative mimesis. Compa-

DAVID LEATHERBARROW

rable commands exist in other traditions, often involving sharing and sacrifice. But often the meal is understood prosaically. Shorter than sleep and longer than a shower, most servings are similarly matter-of-fact. Whether seen as a reenactment or repetition, each lunch or supper both recalls and prompts others. The meal's extended temporality complements its levels of disclosure, from tacit to outspoken.

We tend to think of architectural settings as essentially spatial configurations, but in what follows I would like to use the meal to consider the temporal character of architectural settings in order to describe the ways in which spaces not only accommodate the patterns of our lives but also provoke reflection on their implications. My argument unfolds in three stages. The first, "Time Tables," describes the ways that settings—meals—enable one to remember and anticipate similar performances. Next, "Tables and Terraces" shows that these settings adhere to and crystallize latent characteristics of their surroundings, making the meal situation *topographical*. Finally, under the heading "Table Talk," I consider the levels of articulation in the setting, from those that are understated to those that give rise to thought.

TIME TABLES

As a site the dining table provides the many positionings and repositionings that occur across its surface with relative stability. From meals eaten on the run to lunch on a park bench, hors d'oeuvres at a party, or a full-course meal at a wedding banquet, there is generally some horizontal surface on which its stages succeed one another. Such a surface may be as immediate as the palm of your hand, as expedient as a molded plastic tray, or as refined as bone china on black lacquer. The stages that follow one another on these surfaces are not necessarily the meal's courses, ranging from soup to sweets. A meal's steps also can result from practical requirements, each with its own priority and timing. First comes the clearing and cleaning, then the "setting" of the surface. After this follows the sharing of the several courses, which are variously interwoven with periods of rest and talk for those around the table, giving rhythm and amplitude to the meal's social dimension. Finally comes a second round of clearing and cleaning. Not only the table's surface but its outer edge and interior space center and organize these stages and their configuration. Anthropological studies such as Mary Douglas's "Deciphering a Meal" map this geometry, describing the moral and religious injunctions that govern it. Manuals of domestic protocol—such as Mrs.

Beeton's *Book of Household Management* or the *Better Homes and Gardens New Cookbook*—provide rule and pattern for this layout and its sequences (figure 13.1).[2] In no two cultures are these positions and protocols precisely the same, but in each certain routines are taken to be correct and are taught to children at an early age.

Through the meal's several courses, some things or objects—such as the centerpiece—hold their position, as if permanent; others—such as the basket of bread, bottle of wine, salt and pepper—migrate. The elements of a "place setting" may not be anchored to a specific spot, but the relationships between them are relatively stable. This is true no matter what instruments are used; each item has its proper distance from others. But permanence of place is not permanence in time, for some things appear at different stages and then remain throughout; others disappear; while still others, such as the tablecloth, remain ever present, whether it has been spread out on a small table in the kitchen or on the ground during a picnic. These comings and goings are governed by relationships between the several elements of the situation. Some elements belong to "sets," others remain singularly present. Furthermore, some are shared, others not, for the dining table also configures public and private spaces. The steps that pace the meal's schedule exemplify a kind of change in which elements assumed to be long-standing play against those that are not.

Yet the stability of the situation is not guaranteed by objects alone, for the most durable aspects of the layout are the (implied) positions of things that answer to the reach and habits of the bodies around the table, as they variously but systematically follow and diverge from traditional protocols. These positions include plan locations with objects located at the right and left, center and margin; they also relate to sectional strata. Some items may occupy the horizon of the tabletop, which is stratified according to surfaces that are variously clean and polished. Some may occupy the horizon of conversation (normally eye-level), organizing glances, pictures on the walls, mirrors, and so on. And still other items occupy even higher or lower levels in the room: horizons below integrate the darkest and most recessive elements of the setting, those above gather together the lightest and most encompassing of elements. Objects (food, people, utensils) may occupy these positions in section and in plan but not one of them is more enduring than the horizon itself, for it antecedes and follows the arrival of each object, serving as the (ideal) place in which objects will have been positioned—an a priori of dining. If one can say that such a framework for positioning

DAVID LEATHERBARROW

13.1
Four table settings from *Better
Homes and Gardens*, 1975.

TABLE TALK   **215**

13.2

Nicole La Rossa, *Three @ Kisso*, 2001.

13.3.

Ariane Sphikas, *Meal Time*, 2001.

is "there," it is so as a result of the meal's typicality, "sedimented" in embodiments that range from stains on the table to the habits of the body to memories. Somewhat paradoxically, this means that the meal's uniqueness is conditioned on the frequency with which others like it pass. Put categorically: the particularity of an instance presupposes a history of repetitive performances.

A pair of drawings that explore this delicate choreography of a meal in time can be used to illustrate these observations.[3] In the first (figure 13.2), Nicole La Rossa superimposes a number of perimeter frames, recalling the table's ambient conditions, through which people find their bearings. A horizontal band runs through the drawing and the meal, guiding and tracing the arrival and departure of items to and from the surface. The waiter begins and ends this series of movements. As the meal unfolds (from right to left in this drawing), objects come into sharper focus, while ambient conditions recede. They come back into view when the plates are cleared—thus the vertical break in the drawing and the reorientation (reconnection) to the perimeter. The lateral drift of elements continues beyond this line or break, departing from the table at the left. This edge at the "end" of the lateral transit, like that at the "beginning," is black, which is to say capable of absorbing into its darkness all objectlike definition. But this absorption and disappearance of objects is temporary or provisional, for the blacks and whites at the edges are also the means by which the meal finds its place and attains its definition. The singularity of the event repeats others that have been occasioned by these premises, just as it anticipates those that will follow.

Time marked by transits across a surface is also what appears in a second meal drawing, by Ariane Sphikas (figure 13.3). The argument here, however, is that once the setting—the table setting—is taken up for specific purposes, the notion one has of its permanence or fixity is replaced by a more accurate idea of change or shifting positions. On the lower part of the drawing a filmlike band charts the progressive disappearance of the elements that make up the meal, steadily dissolving the integrity of the "set." The elements and objects one handles in the meal are scheduled by this band (contained within the drawing's verticals), variously apparent on the table, but not offering themselves to one's attention for very long. This movement into prominence and retreat begins when the food arrives—shown in this drawing by the strong vertical that edges the drawing's left quarter, which distinguishes the table set before the meal (in dark tones) from the table appropriated for use (lighter tones and disconnected figures). With this sequence of movements, this chronology of positions in mind, it would seem possible to call the surface of the table a clock; but the comparison is inexact because the intervals derived from the lateral drift of objects are also the means by which they lose their definition—into a set at the meal's beginning and into the background at its end. The time of the meal is no more regular than its ambient context is uniformly apparent, which is almost never the case, given the shifting interests that characterize this (and any other) situation.

TABLES AND TERRACES

When I sit down to order a meal—in the bar restaurant of a hotel, for example—the chalkboard menu on the wall interests me greatly, my table just a little, and the wall behind the menu or the light above it barely at all. I am not alone in this regard; everyone in the restaurant who wants to eat looks at the menu as I do, for a while, assuming the quiet suitability of the furniture and the room. But prominence, in each of its degrees, is never permanent; the freedom internal to perception allows for reversals in the figure-background structure. A shadow on the wall, next to the menu, may divert my attention, as may someone passing on the street. This suggests that "withdrawal" is as possible for an element as prominence. When I pick up a book its text immediately stands out; yet as soon as I begin to read through its lines, paragraphs, and pages, they begin to efface themselves so that the sense of the text can fully occupy my attention. Once I'm engrossed in or absorbed into the book, the print and pages are not not there, but their manner of being there has changed. Maurice Merleau-Ponty has observed in his essay on the experience of expression that the perfection of language lies in its capacity to pass unnoticed: "one of the effects of language is to efface itself to the extent that its expression comes across."[4] What is true for the experience of facial and textual expression is also true for a kind of articulation that occurs in architecture: its forms and figures efface themselves as they accomplish their practical purposes, their service.

The reversal of figures and grounds assumes a *field* or *horizon* structure of elements within a setting. Before any figure emerges as the object of thematic attention, it is pregiven as part of a wide context of interdependent elements, each materially and practically relevant to the others. With the table come not only the chairs but also the bar, the menu on the wall, the window sill, the garden terrace, and much more, each potentially conspicuous but all "tending toward" the others, somewhat horizontal because "horizonal." When I am eating (not thinking of architecture), the "near" and "far" elements of the setting release themselves from the places they had been assigned in perspective space and commingle with one another in a way that is "impossibly" congruent. Their "service" is to wait in that milieu until targeted by practical interests and their associated perceptual structures. Traditional discourse, and the design techniques it sustains, has nothing to say about this thicker space; in fact, it conceals it. The light and shadows on the dining table are as much a part (a property) of the linen cloth as they are of the window onto the café at the front and the trees in the garden at the rear, for without the cloth, the glass, and the leaves the play of shadows would never appear. Considering food, the meal's dependence on the remote landscape is recalled by flowers at the table's center, testifying to the interdependence of sun and soil, grasses, grain, and grazing. The table—much like a building site or even a city—concentrates (incorporates) the field in relationships that bear on the person having the meal: once I saw someone take a little bite out of a flower taken from his lover's place setting, as though appetite were desire. Downcast eyes and a blush answered the advance. Now, what is true of flower and friend, terrace and table—anterior continuity and implied consubstantiality—holds for all of the setting's elements and platforms; each reciprocates the others until some local interest (yours or mine) rewrites the agreements they had established among themselves. All together and latent they constitute something like an atmosphere, a disposition, or mood that is not easy to describe but is never unclear. This "character" is often what is memorable about settings.

Let me try to elaborate this atmosphere in view of a specific setting. A man and a woman face one another over a table at the edge of a restaurant interior painted by Edward Hopper in 1930 (figure 13.4). Neither the pair in conversation nor any of the others in the interior is distinctly prominent in the painting. In part, the painting's diagonal composition causes this effect, with the line of lemons on display accelerating to the right and the run of tabletops drifting to the left. In this weave, no figure proposes itself as primary; the wine at the center of the table talk—if wine is what the carafe holds—is no more important than the instruments of its supply and cost, the women in white and black, the kitchen and the cash register.

DAVID LEATHERBARROW

Although unobtrusive, each of these figures is distinct. The woman in the foreground has the features of a Veronese contessa, but adopts the posture of a Tintoretto saint. As an emblem she indicates abundance, much like the meal suggested by the produce spread before her. But she also expresses hygiene—hence her unblemished apron, white like a tablecloth; the tidy row of produce she organizes; and so on. Her attention has two vectors, however; with her hands toward the window display, her gaze beyond it, it joins kitchen and street, as if the dining room were not there. The waitress at the register is similarly specific. Her body trails behind her eyes like the tail of a comet. Flat black from the shoulders down, half hidden, she is entirely absorbed in counting. Although focused, she is not alone in her work; her stance and glance align three kinds of reckoning (counting, pricing, and timing) and their instruments (her gaze, the register, and the clock). This stance is also the most fixed point in the interior; the containers she oversees hold the cash and trinkets on display. While the first figure is an emblem of supply, the second embodies definition or restraint: white and black, giving and taking, substance and measure. The two of them, and their "performances," stand between the street and the table talk that is sheltered in the depth of the room.

If all of this seems beyond the border of the meal, that is because we tend to think of eating as a tabletop occurrence only. This painting shows us something different, that the simplest of meals depends on highly differentiated, even discordant, ambient conditions, on *topography*.[5] By this term I mean terrain that is endowed with implications of practice that extend beyond the edges of discrete objects and events. Such a structure integrates a vicinity, in this case an urban location. Lloyd Goodrich writes of Hopper's urban images: "In many of his urban subjects, individual men and women do appear, but as parts of the whole scene rather than in leading roles. The woman undressing for bed, the diners in a restaurant, the bored couple seen through their apartment window, the solitary passerby in the street at night, are integral elements in his version of the city; but their environment is as important as they are."[6] The compression of a figure (back) into its field proposes a unity that is not only pictorial or optical but also practical; thus it takes in the positions of the figures and items at the room's center or perimeter, their role in support of the event, and so on. Although the "serviceable" elements that structure such a field are recessive, the topography is expressive, for it traces practices we know but normally neglect.

TABLE TALK

Writing in *L'Esprit Nouveau*, Le Corbusier once compared architectural settings to servants: both are best when unnoticed in the performance of their several tasks. He seems to have preferred interiors and arrangements of "equipment" that are discreet and self-effacing. Thus settings and servants are best when taken for granted, much like the human body at work in the world, because all—bodies, servants, settings— are "limb objects." Operation, what something does, is important here, but even more important is recessiveness. Commenting on an exhibition of interiors and their furnishings, he criticized "chairs that are charming, intelligent, but perhaps too talkative. . . . If chairs and armchairs extinguish Picasso, Léger, Derain, Utrillo, Lipchitz, then chairs and armchairs are insolent . . . are extremely loud. One thinks: To live here one must be damned distinguished—and without respite. Good manners are commendable and they embellish life—but only when one is least aware of them."[7] Hence his statement of principle in *Precisions:* "The human-limb object [the chair or table] is a docile servant. A good servant is discreet and self-effacing, in order to leave his master free."[8] Does this silence the table's voice, or is there a kind of articulation that communicates implicitly? And what is the relationship between (self-effacing) furniture and (self-expressive) walls and windows, particularly when the former are conceived as "part of" the latter, built-in or not?

Le Corbusier was not the only twentieth-century architect to make this point about limb objects effacing themselves. Louis I. Kahn elaborated a similar concept of "servant" spaces. Before that, when Le Corbusier was still developing his arguments, Eileen Gray offered a comparable observation, without the analogy to servitude: "One must build for the human being, that he might rediscover in the architectural construction the joys of self-fulfillment in a whole that extends and completes him. Even the furnishings should lose their individuality by blending in with the architectural ensemble."[9] I take it that this loss of individuality allows the individual item to recede from one's awareness insofar as absorption into an ensemble means retreat into a context that "serves" as a background for "the joys of self-fulfillment."

Unobtrusiveness was also an aim of the architecture of Adolf Loos. His complaint against artistic furnishings in "Poor Little Rich Man" argues for this quality. So does his call for "discreet" architecture: "The house should be discreet on the outside; its entire richness should be disclosed on the inside." He made this point more fully a bit

DAVID LEATHERBARROW

later in the same essay: "In a few day's time, one of the last of the old Hietzing houses will be demolished. . . . What culture was in these houses, what refinement! How Viennese, how Austrian, how human! . . . It is well known that such houses do not have a facade, and this is not liked [by the planning council]. It is preferred that one does the same as the other newcomers, the one is to outshout the other."[10] The contrary stance, the one that Loos himself adopted, holds that the building, like its furnishings, should not proclaim prominence but should express its standing and history noise-lessly, like a silent witness, not commanding attention but—here is the difficulty—rewarding it when it is given.

One of Loos's students, Rudolph Schindler, also was concerned with architecture's inconspicuous standing, as his somewhat unusual application of the term *transparency* demonstrates. This use/practice/method invoked the customary sense of the word, the quality of some materials being penetrable by light or air, allowing one to partially or completely "see through" it; but transparency also characterizes things that are habitually used. Transparent figures were those that were unseen because unobtrusively present in a setting. One is reminded of Loos's quip about the best-dressed man being the one least noticed in public. Schindler's interpretation, however, was developed as he considered metal furniture: "The few places [in a house] which are necessarily moveable (chairs, etc.), become so in an accentuated degree. Moving, they are unfit to define the space conception and must therefore be elimi-nated architecturally for the sake of clarity. They are either folded up and stored away or made transparent to become inconspicuous. This is the real meaning of the metal chair. Its essence is its transparency[.]"[11] This quality distinguished all deployable items from those that were built-in or immovable, the permanent furniture used to "define" the "space conception." One of the most celebrated aspects of the Schindler-Chace house is its use of exterior fireplaces as sites for the preparation of meals. The house's floor slabs constitute one level of a beautifully elaborated site sec-tion (figure 13.5). The use of the slabs inside the house is obvious, but they are not confined to its limits, to the thermal barrier. As if to serve as the basic premises of an "encampment," the slabs extend into the garden court and serve as the surface on which open-air fires could be ignited. Otherwise, cooking, Schindler said, was to be done "right on the table, making it more a social 'campfire' affair, than the disagree-able burden to one member of the family."[12] In fact, there was a central kitchen or

13.5
R. M. Schindler, Schindler-Chace
House, Kings Road, West
Hollywood, 1921–1922, plan.

13.6
R. M. Schindler, Schindler-Chace
House, view from inside to
outdoor fires. Photo by Grant
Mudford.

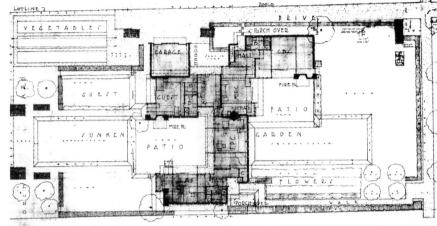

DAVID LEATHERBARROW

"utility" room. Meals prepared in the kitchen seem to have been served on trays. In the absence of a dining room or of functionally specific rooms of just about any sort, the stratification of platforms remained dominant, whether concrete or grass, canvas or timber. Seating for meals seems to have migrated across these surfaces; sometimes "interior" furniture was brought to surround an outdoor fire.

Viewed in plan, the topography can be read as a mosaic of dwelling platforms, each providing no more than a pretext or premise for some practical purpose and preferred posture. Frequently they are not in typical locations. This is to say not that outdoor dining was atypical but that meals were "set up" in different locations, thereby instituting a peripatetic practice of dining, as if the Schindler and Chace families envisaged eating as a sort of grazing, or cooking as a nomadic practice that resulted from hunting and gathering (figure 13.6). The accent here is on the primitive, which in California at that time might well have been described as the natural or authentic. One need not subscribe to this anthropology, nor to this version of the modern world, to recognize the expressive, even symbolic, aspirations of such outdoor dining. Obviously, this shift in domestic dining decorum has practical and material "premises," but it is also indicative of more than that, for it reveals what Schindler took to be new ways of living in a house and, more broadly, saw as modern existence. In this instance, the setup or topographical instruments of a specific situation give rise to thought about their wider implications: that modern life would usher in a new primitivism, that freedom from precedent would lead to a freedom for creativity, or that the traditional discord between art and life could in this way be overcome.

Just as tables talk in different ways, so settings articulate their sense variously. They can remain tacit while endowing experience with its instruments, its "limb objects," and they can give it characteristic expression, narrating its history or symbolizing its foundation. The topography of the meal invites us to consider how settings have different ways of voicing their contents, sometimes by speaking and sometimes by keeping quiet.

NOTES

1. *Table Talk* is one way to translate the title given by Leon Battista Alberti to his *Intercenales,* a collection of moral tales or parables that were typical of Renaissance dinner conversation; see Leon

Battista Alberti, *Dinner Pieces,* trans. David Marsh (Binghamton, N.Y.: Medieval and Renaissance Texts and Studies, 1987). Talk is what fills the gaps or pauses in the meal: what comes *inter cenales.* Alberti's stories are rhetorical, not philosophical; many take the form of dialogue. "Table Talks" is how Mark Jarzombek translates the title in *On Leon Baptista Alberti: His Literary and Aesthetic Theories* (Cambridge, Mass.: MIT Press, 1989), 20ff. While a few of the stories refer to architecture, the dining table itself does not come into focus. In this sense, Alberti's "table talk" exemplifies the architectural "oversight" I want to describe.

2. Mary Douglas, "Deciphering a Meal," in *Implicit Meanings* (London: Routledge and Kegan Paul, 1975), 249–275. The section in the *Better Homes and Gardens New Cookbook* (New York: Meredith Press, 1968) titled "Table Settings and Entertaining" is devoted to this topic. Particularly interesting are the instructions listed under "More Table Talk—type of service and seating guests" (369). *The Book of Household Management,* by Isabella Beeton, was first published in 1861.

3. These drawings were completed by Nicole La Rossa and Ariane Sphikas, students in my first-year design studio in the masters of architecture program at the University of Pennsylvania, in spring 2000. They were part of the preliminary work in the studio. I asked students to share a meal together and during its course "survey" its "premises" (material, metric, and spatial), paying particular attention to its development over time. The approach in the studio was analogical; the meal survey was followed by the development of an architectural plan that was similarly sensitive to spatial and temporal conditions.

4. Maurice Merleau-Ponty, "Science and the Experience of Expression," in *The Prose of the World,* ed. Claude Lefort, trans. John O'Neill (London: Heinemann, 1974), 9.

5. This topic is central in my book *Uncommon Ground: Architecture, Technology, and Topography* (Cambridge Mass.: MIT Press, 2000).

6. Lloyd Goodrich, *Edward Hopper* (New York: Abrandale Press, 1983), 69.

7. Paul Boulard [pseud. of Le Corbusier], "Le Salon de l'art décoratif au Grand Palais," *L'Esprit Nouveau,* no. 24 (June 1924); quoted in Caroline Constant, *Eileen Gray* (New York: Phaidon, 2001), 63.

8. Le Corbusier, *Precisions on the Present State of Architecture and City Planning,* trans. Edith Schreiber Aujame (Cambridge, Mass: MIT Press, 1991), 67, 79.

9. Eileen Gray and Jean Badovici, "From Eclecticism to Doubt," trans. in Constant, *Eileen Gray,* 238–240; quotation, 239–240 (first published in *L'Architecture Vivante,* winter 1929). For Kahn, see "Spaces Order and Architecture," in *Louis J. Kahn: Writings, Lectures, Interviews,* ed. Alessandra Latour (New York: Rizzoli, 1991), 75–80.

10. Adolf Loos, "Vernacular Art," in *The Architecture of Adolf Loos* (London: Arts Council of Great Britain, 1985), 112–113 (translation modified).

11. R. M. Schindler, "Furniture and the Modern House: A Theory of Interior Design," in *The Furniture of R. M. Schindler,* ed. Marla C. Berns (Santa Barbara: University Art Museum, University of California, 1996), 49–56; quotation, 49.

12. R. M. Schindler, letter to Mr. and Mrs. Edmund J. Gibling, November 26, 1921, in Kathryn Smith, *Schindler House* (New York: Harry N. Abrams, 2001), 80.

14.1
Drive-In Restaurant in Los
Angeles, 1949, by Loomis Dean.
From Maryann Kornely and
Jenny Hirschfeld, eds., *Moving:
Il viaggio e il movimento nelle
fotografie di LIFE* (Rome:
Contrasto, 1999).

FOOD TO GO: THE
INDUSTRIALIZATION OF THE PICNIC

MIKESCH MUECKE

FROM PICNIC TO DRIVE-IN

*Among the mobile cognoscenti, it was acknowledged that eating in your car with
the top down was the preferable way to dine.*
— MICHAEL KARL WITZEL, *Drive-In Deluxe*

Since the earliest times the picnic has depended on a triad of mobile bodies,
food, and utensils. Beginning in the late 1600s, any outdoor feast called for
a *nécessaire du voyage,* the equipment required for the transport and consumption of the food. Most important for the ubiquitous picnic basket, these artistic
tool sets would include a set of knives, forks, and spoons; a spice box for salt and pepper; a corkscrew; a toothpick; and an apple corer. This culinary toolbox foreshadows
the increasing dependence of the picnic on external equipment and service. While in
times before automobiles pedestrians would invade the landscape, "limited only by
roads and their own energy, . . . swarm[ing] into the country [on bicycles] and pic-
nick[ing] where they wanted on what they wanted,"[1] more recent picnic patterns exhibit a shift toward a fully mechanized dining behavior (figure 14.1). Contemporary

vehicle interiors now come factory equipped with an abundance of cup holders for the temporary storage of beverages and snacks, and some SUV interiors offer even refrigerators and built-in tables.

The idea of packing a lunch has existed as long as workers have toiled in the fields and worked in cities, depending on meals sold by hawkers in the streets. C. Anne Wilson traces early records of outdoor eating back to the second century B.C.E., when Posidonius described Celts eating meat with their fingers—while seated on straw mats spread on the ground—"in a cleanly but leonine fashion, raising up whole limbs in both hands and biting off the meat," and cites a court record from 1710 that mentions people "with wheelbarrows wherein they carry oysters, oranges, decayed cheese, apples, nuts, gingerbread and other wares to sell."[2] And yet eating out as a planned event was almost unheard-of until the eighteenth century. Venues such as alehouses, inns, and taverns offered food to travelers, but few patrons would think of taking a meal in these unhomely places. The outdoors, however, provided a powerful lure. In seventeenth-century France, a *cadeau* was the term used for a private outdoor feast arranged by a "young nobleman wishing to curry favor with some beautiful lady."[3] The sensual intersection of bodies and food converge in the prototype of the picnic, the hunting breakfast, a subject frequently depicted by seventeenth-century European painters.[4] However, fundamental changes of food consumption occurred at the intersection of architecture and motorized vehicles in the early part of the twentieth century with the invention of the drive-up drugstore, the development of the drive-in, and finally the appearance of the drive-through in the late 1940s. Today, bracketed between the two conventional modes of eating, dining in and dining out, a third mode of culinary consumption—dining on the go—has established itself firmly in contemporary culture. Eating while driving is the norm, with the attendant development of a new, mobile domesticity, which has transformed vehicles virtually into rolling residences that offer the creature comforts of home without taking on the form of a traditional house (figure 14.2). The picnic as the essential food-to-go may serve as a device for reading these transformations in eating habits and spaces.

Helen Stevens Fisher describes a picnic as a "party which takes itself outdoors," and Nancy Fair McIntyre writes that "a good picnic is a respite from the ordinary, an escape from routine, a time for adventurous feasting."[5] If the picnic is thus a staged event, an outdoor celebration that invokes an alternative to the everyday, perhaps

MIKESCH MUECKE

14.2

Interior of early house car, redrawn by the author from Roger Byron White, *Home on the Road: The Motor Home in America* (Washington, D.C.: Smithsonian Institution Press, 2000).

Claude Monet's impressionist painting of a picnic, *Déjeuner sur l'herbe* (1865–1866), approaches in its representational technique this alternate state created by an outdoor feast. And yet, in the painting the difference between the projection of the event and its execution is palpable in the apparent discomfort of the picnickers in their stiff but fashionable dresses. This discrepancy between projection and perceived reality may be explored in the theoretical underpinnings of picnics, which shuttle between occupying an ideal space of pastoral bliss and the exigencies of consuming food in often antagonistic surroundings. Unlike conventional meals, picnics rely on a fundamental temporal and spatial separation of food preparation and consumption. This distance between the everyday and the special event closely parallels a temporary utopia, a fleeting moment of a perfect world, an idyll that can exist only in the realm of the ephemeral.[6] One significant difference between utopia and idyll dwells in the temporal presence of loss attached to the latter that serves as a permanent condition of nostalgia, a looking backward rather than constructing anew. When placed in this context of utopian visions and Epicurean dreams, the picnic offers a site where it is possible to sensually ingest the exterior surroundings, thereby creating a corporeal interior world, a bodily universe where the space of an ideal landscape dwells within rather than without.

The borders of a tablecloth or blanket spread out in a forest clearing or a meadow create a temporary, rational, and minimalist territory for outdoor dining, a domestic space differentiated from the wilderness—or perhaps the idea of paradise—that surrounds it. If the picnic tablecloth functions as a memory of the conventional dining table inscribed in the landscape, in the 1940s this tablecloth grew to the size of a parking lot surrounding the now ubiquitous drive-ins. As a lure away from the highway, their flashy architecture invites both driver and passengers to rest from their motion, to replenish the body without leaving the protective cocoon of the car for too long. The motorized picnic has thus transferred al fresco dining from a bucolic outdoor setting in the clearing of a forest into a sheltered metal bubble that sits in the clearing of a parking lot, where diners participate in a form of urban and suburban voyeurism that is much more attuned to their contemporary sensibilities than to watching birds in a forest. These diners, nibbling on burgers and fries while sitting in their cars next to fast-food joints and watching the traffic roll by on the adjacent road, have become a common sight along America's business strips—recalling in their isolation perhaps Georges Seurat's *Un dimanche après-midi à l'île de la Grande Jatte* (1884–1886), which brings into relief the isolation of the human body through geometric depiction. T. J. Clark argues that Seurat "wished to show the nature of class distinction in a place given over to pleasure, but also the various things that made distinctions hard to grasp. It was important that his people looked alike, and yet were sharply discriminated from each other in detail."[7]

The origins of diners sitting transfixed in their automobiles can be traced back to the early part of the twentieth century, when driving was still an arduous task. Early drive-ins were drive-ups, carriers of both convenience and embarrassment. Not pampered by cushy suspension systems or fully enclosed vehicles, drivers and their dusty, grease-stained companions resisted in these early times of motorized mobility having to enter a conventional establishment for a quick repast. As a remedy, budding entrepreneurs sent out "runners" to the drivers and passengers to take food orders and then return with the prepared fare to the car waiting curbside. The convenience of being served while remaining seated in the vehicle quickly developed into a new culinary model that linked food production and consumption in a temporal loop of drugstore and automobile. Tray tables clipped onto the car door quickly began to bridge the edge between interior and exterior, connecting the tentative space between proper and automotive architecture.

MIKESCH MUECKE

Tradition, which has heretofore influenced styles, is a lateral movement. . . . Modernism, on the other hand, is better understood as a vertical movement, and to see what comprises it, you cut it down as you do a layer cake.

—RICHARDSON WRIGHT, "House and Garden Designs Its Own
Modernist House" (1930)

The lure of eating in the car was so pervasive that even the Apollo of modern architecture, Mies van der Rohe, fell under its spell in 1946, when he designed a sleek glass box topped by an exoskeleton supporting a hovering roof slab. I am not referring to Mies's modernist classic of that year, the Farnsworth House, but rather to his singular contribution to culinary mobility: the Cantor drive-in for Indianapolis (figure 14.3).[8] The unrealized building represents a formal and structural twin to the mother ship of Mies's midwestern designs, Crown Hall, which houses the Illinois Institute of Technology's (IIT) School of Architecture in Chicago. The similarity is no accident. Modernism's propensity for visual consumption, idealized in IIT's Crown Hall, finds its earthy counterpoint in the Cantor drive-in.

David Spaeth describes the Cantor as the first of Mies's "large-scale universal spaces,"[9] which consist of large, uninterrupted glass-enclosed volumes. Because of this shared characteristic, Spaeth suggests that the Cantor, the Farnsworth House, and Crown Hall belong to a typology of clear-span buildings. I would argue that the clear-span type is to architecture what the long-distance drive is to mobility. It is an uninterrupted event located between two points. Spaeth has argued that the Cantor borrows from industrial architecture, and here specifically from railroad and highway bridge designs.[10] In other words, the Cantor drive-in represents the archetype of the intersection between the industrialization of food-to-go and the industrialization of the infrastructure that facilitates culinary mobility.

What might surprise architectural purists is that the Cantor functions not only as a literal bridge between food and cars but also as a conceptual bridge between the Farnsworth House (1946) and Crown Hall (1950–1956). In all three designs, Mies suspends the roof from long, deep trusses or beams that rest on slender steel columns. In each case, suspending the roof from an external structural frame enabled Mies to create a floating overhead surface that hovers like a lid on the spaces below. But only

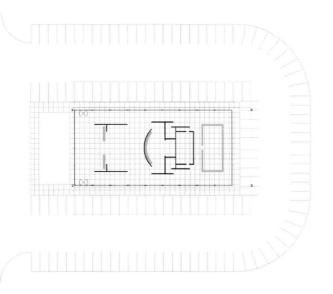

14.3
Floor plan of Cantor drive-in, project by Mies van der Rohe, 1946. Redrawn by the author based on a plan from David Spaeth, *Mies van der Rohe* (New York: Rizzoli, 1985).

14.4
Parking lot view of Cantor drive-in, project by Mies van der Rohe, 1946. Digitally modeled and rendered by the author based on a photograph from Peter Carter, *Mies van der Rohe at Work* (London: Phaidon Press, 1999).

MIKESCH MUECKE

in the Cantor does Mies reduce the enclosing "walls" to an absolute minimum with a continuous glass surface uninterrupted by supports.[11] It is remarkable how he developed this apparently simple edge condition into an intertwining space between car and food. A photograph that shows a model of the Cantor viewed from the street articulates how the cars can enter this arcadelike space between glass wall and roof edge to park and wait for food delivery (figure 14.4).[12] As a hybrid form, this columnless arcade creates an overlapping room of indoor and outdoor space that reflects its temporal occupation by cars and passengers. The intertwining arcade space links food, architecture, and mobility in a dynamic relationship, recalling perhaps the idealized region of Arcadia in ancient Greece where outdoor feasts were still celebrated without the assistance of machines; and recalling perhaps that universal space of the original picnic that is most convincing when it remains a utopia, just as the Cantor drive-in remains an unrealized project.

If, as Peter Carter argues, Mies believed that "architecture at its most valuable can be nothing more than a reflection of the driving and sustaining forces of an epoch"—Mies himself said, "I have tried to make an architecture for a technological society"[13]—then the drive-in project of the Cantor perhaps represents the intersection of technology, industrialization, and domesticity more clearly than any other building designed by Mies.

PICNIC IN THE CAR

"The sun is mirrored even in a coffee spoon," wrote the architectural scholar Sigfried Giedion in *Mechanization Takes Command*,[14] where he explored how mechanization has influenced the most intimate areas of human existence that were previously linked to nature. In the first part of the twentieth century, mechanization captured and controlled not only machine motion but also the human body.[15] Giedion observed, "Taylorism demands of the mass of workers not initiative but automation. Human movements become levers in the machine"[16]—tightly controlled, repeated, and therefore predictable motions of the human body in relation to and dependence on the machine.

Underlying the machine-assisted practice of eating-on-the-go is a theory of efficiency, a kind of culinary Taylorism; and it is none other than Henry Ford who raised Taylorism to a new level when he realized that mass production, in the words of David

Harvey, "meant mass consumption, a new system of the reproduction of labor power, a new politics of labor control and management, a new aesthetics and psychology, in short, a new kind of rationalized, modernist, and populist democratic society."[17] And yet Ford's assembly line simultaneously imprisoned the worker as it democratized the general population by bringing automobiles and mobility to the masses. In an ironic twist, the company's creation of means of widespread mobility depends for its production directly on the inverse of the mobile, as partial products are fed to stationary workers via the assembly line.

The eating machine in Charlie Chaplin's 1936 (mostly) silent movie *Modern Times* puts into relief the workers' static position by intersecting the relentless movement of the assembly line with a forced distribution of food (figure 14.5). The machine holds the worker in a fixed position during the feeding cycle, and the protagonist becomes quite literally a part of the machine when, in a form of technological cannibalism, the malfunctioning machine attempts to force-feed him its own mechanical parts.[18] However, the unstoppable advance of mass production and mass consumption would foil any attempts to return to a premachine state. Cafeterias, the culinary equivalent of the industrial assembly line, would soon dominate the eating environment in large institutions and factories. And contemporary cafeterias are nothing but a more sophisticated version of Chaplin's eating machine: the diner supplies the motive power to the assembly line, which consists of trays to be pushed along a stainless steel countertop, as he or she picks preassembled salads, dishes, and desserts out of racks of shelves, and thereby constructs a customized body-food hybrid.

This interdependence between body and machine extends also into the domestic realm of the kitchen. In 1955 the American industrial designer Henry Dreyfuss—responsible for projects ranging from vacuum cleaners to the interior of the advanced Super-G Constellation airplane—realized that the transformation of the modern kitchen was initiated by two things that had "nothing to do with cooking a meal . . . the automobile and the airplane."[19] However, it was the German designer Margarete Schütte-Lihotzky who had recognized thirty years earlier that she could transform the kitchen into a new space of production by applying industrial control processes. Schütte-Lihotzky's interest was in the streamlining of food production to make the *Hausfrau* into the kitchen/machine operator. When she designed the Frankfurt kitchen in the mid-1920s, she called it the "realization of the kitchen as machine,"[20] and her idealized space of food production represented a domestic version of Taylorism imported from the factory floor.

What Henry Ford had achieved in 1913 with the industrialization of motor vehicle production,[21] Richard and Maurice McDonald applied to fast food in 1940. In their quest to streamline the production and distribution process of food-to-go, the McDonalds eliminated car hop service and required their customers to step out of their vehicles and order burger-only meals at walk-up windows. By limiting the choices to one meal option only—the culinary equivalent to Ford's Model T, with its "choice" of one color—the McDonald brothers eliminated single-handedly the "surplus" of regional and local food differences. When Ray Kroc took the idea nationwide by opening the first McDonald's franchise in Des Plaines, Illinois, he applied Ford's insight that mass production requires mass consumption by couching culinary mechanization in convenience, which became the hallmark of the McDonald's product line.

This culinary convenience transferred well into the mechanical design of the early 1950s automobiles when Detroit introduced a new vehicle as a mobile accompaniment to the static drive-ins. Until that time, cars had been a spatial extension to the

14.5
Movie still showing Charlie Chaplin shackled to the Eating Machine, from *Modern Times* (dir. Charlie Chaplin, 1936).

round form of the drive-in, which consisted of not more than a central kitchen space (production) surrounded by a perforated wall (transfer) and a vast parking lot (consumption). With the introduction of the station wagon into the American streetscape, the mobilized picnic found its most appropriate expression. By extending the upper body of the car to the rear bumper, automotive designers created a tailgate that became the perfect table for the choreography of a machine-assisted picnic.[22] The station wagon became the suburban vehicle of choice, and its increased cargo capacity for the long drive to stores gave new emphasis to automotive mobility; it combined the transgressiveness of a picnic with the comforts of home, liberating its passengers from the vicissitudes of nature. The tailgate registered the intersection of indoor comfort and outdoor mobility by rotating out into the landscape, transforming a wall into a platform for cooking and dining.[23] Rather than gather around the table in a dwelling or lay out the feast on a blanket spread on the ground, driver and passengers found in the station wagon's tailgate a new gathering place as well, an improvised yet improved mobile hearth.

In some automobiles the tailgate migrated forward in the car, tracing a shift from the outdoors to the indoors. Barthes wrote in 1957 about the futuristic Citroën DS that its "dashboard looks more like the working surface of a modern kitchen than the control-room of a factory."[24] And the mid-1980s dashboard of a Cadillac Eldorado morphed into a large, tablelike slab that can easily accommodate the dinner settings for two people (figure 14.6). These more recent developments demonstrate how the automobile has replaced the kitchen/hearth at the center of the house with a new mobile domesticity. In 1939 the architectural firm Adams and Prentice designed a demonstration house for the New York World's Fair and called it the *Motor Home for the Town of Tomorrow* (figure 14.7). This radical design consisted of a rectangular box with a large two-car garage. Spatially the garage pushes into the core of the house, and the only pedestrian access to the house is through a conventional entry door framed by the two garage doors. The owner/visitor has to pass through the garage to reach the living room, dining room, and kitchen. The garage's small mullioned windows and shutters belie the radical idea of the design, as they dissimulate the importance of the automobile, now an integral part of the future American household, behind a pastiche of old-world domesticity. The interior of this prototype represents a functionalist's realized utopia, where the centrally located, domestically incorporated automobile

MIKESCH MUECKE

14.6
Dashboard dining table sitting
on dashboard of 1985 Cadillac
Eldorado. Photo by author.

14.7
The Town of Tomorrow
Demonstration Home No. 21.
From *High Styles: Twentieth-
Century American Design* (New
York: Summit Books, 1985).

has taken over the formerly central space of the kitchen; according to Ivan Margolius, it is "idolized and worshipped rather than regarded simply as an instrument for work or leisure."[25] Adams and Prentice's motor home represents the stable precedent to the mobile copies that Winnebago would begin to build ten years later.

Even earlier the car had begun to take on the domestic qualities of home. In 1909, fifteen years before Walter Gropius designed reclining seats for his Adler convertible, an automobile manufacturer from Los Angeles, William J. Burt, modified a standard touring car so that the front seat back could be detached and laid flat to form a table, allowing the passengers to dine while seated in the rear seat. A small gas stove for onboard cooking complemented the formal comforts of home: Roger White itemizes "a set of dishes, table linen, silverware, glasses, bottles, aluminum cookware, and other utensils."[26] The same adaptive sensibility exhibited in these hybrid constructions can be discerned in the development of the automobile itself. In the early parts of the previous century, cars were mostly used for pleasure trips and adventurous cross-country travel. Increasingly, though, cars became the prime mode of transportation to and from the workplace. By now the number of vehicles on the nation's highways has grown proportionately to the expansion of cities into the surrounding land, and the automobile has become a hybrid space of domesticity to the point that current commuters and travelers have re-created a technologically advanced mirror image of early hunter-and-gatherer societies. The hunting instinct is expressed in road rage, the gatherer instinct in the trip to the supermarket or, for more immediate satisfaction, the drive-through window.

The early adaptation of grafting a house body onto a truck or bus chassis continues unabated, and today's motor homes represent nothing less than ranch houses on wheels. They come equipped, White notes, with "aluminum siding and picture windows, . . . contemporary furniture, modern kitchens with built-in appliances, and forced-air furnaces."[27] With the invention of these houses on wheels, the outdoors picnic has been completely usurped by the domestic comfort of the interior. In 1953 Arthur Drexler declared that the "interiors of American cars are often designed to duplicate in domestic comfort the living room of the driver's home,"[28] and today's separation of food preparation from food consumption signifies a transfer of the domestic into the mobile where neither cooking nor eating is any longer strictly associated with being at home.

MIKESCH MUECKE

By the mid-1960s many drive-ins had been transformed to drive-throughs or drive-bys,[29] suggesting a transition from a stable picnic in a parked car to mobile eating while driving, or to a takeout, the contemporary version of a picnic. The fast-food restaurant had changed from a terminal destination to no more than a tangential node along a driving route. The space between kitchen and car increased over time, too. In the few drive-ins remaining today, most offer amplified two-way communication systems for ordering a meal. Names such as Ordaphone, Fon-A-Chef, Serv-us-Fone, Teletray, Dine-A-Mike, Auto-Dine, and Electro-Hop are applied to these disembodied servants in the form of an audio speaker and microphone. While the space of cooking has been relegated in these establishments to the ever more distant kitchen, the space of informal dining has migrated into the increasingly domesticated automobiles, which one architect points out as "a perfect little exercise in interior design, [provide] a controlled environment more perfect than most homes."[30]

TEMPORAL DWELLING

In *Bauen, Wohnen, Denken*, Martin Heidegger asks what it means to inhabit, to dwell: "Was ist das Wohnen?" And to what degree is building a part of inhabitation: "Inwieweit gehört das Bauen in das Wohnen?" Through the German etymologies of *bauen* (build) and *wohnen* (to inhabit, to dwell), Heidegger concludes that both building and inhabiting/dwelling mean "to stay" or "to remain"; and he argues that our contemporary society has lost the original meaning of building as inhabiting. Furthermore, *bauen* (to build) and its related words *buan, bhu*, and *beo* give us the word to be *(sein)*. "I am" means for Heidegger "I inhabit," "I dwell."[31]

This dyad of temporal being and inhabitation converges in the architecture of the drive-in, which marks the midpoint transition of the picnic from the outdoors to the indoors, from the garden into the machine. Mobile picnicking, then, represents a temporal form of dwelling, a lingering in motion. In a 1984 essay, J. B. Jackson articulates this temporal quality in relation to mobile homes. He argues that the verb *to dwell* originally meant to hesitate, to linger, to delay, implying that "we will eventually move on," and that this "usage suggests a certain detachment from the dwelling." Without solidity or permanence, the mobile home's inexpensive convenience charms us with a "kind of freedom we often undervalue: the freedom from burdensome emotional ties with the environment, freedom from communal responsibilities, freedom

14.8

Advertisement for Honda
Odyssey minivan. From *Road &
Track Magazine* (December 1998).

from the tyranny of the traditional home and its possessions; the freedom from belonging to a tight-knit social order; and above all, the freedom to move on to somewhere else."[32]

However, that freedom, when transferred to automobiles and their domestic function as places to eat, comes at a cost. In his analysis of the multipurpose modes of vehicular inhabitation, the sociologist John Urry lists "speed, home, safety, sexual desire, career success, freedom, family" as the sign-values that correspond with the car. As Urry points out, these values operate through "the car's technical and social inter-linkages with other industries, including car parts and accessories; petrol refining and distribution; road-building and maintenance; hotels, roadside service areas and motels; car sales and repair workshops; suburban house building; new retailing and leisure complexes; advertising and marketing."[33]

While the domestic attributes of cars are manifest across the history of their design, Urry frames the pros and cons of an automotive architecture in arguing that the automobile is both "immensely flexible and wholly coercive," offering the freedom to drive almost everywhere while simultaneously dividing workplaces from homes, entrapping their occupants in long, congested commutes, and encapsulating people in a "privatized, cocooned, moving environment." As a result, contemporary drivers, "strapped into a comfortable armchair and surrounded by micro-electronic informational sources, controls, and sources of pleasure," experience both the isolation and comfort of a domestic dwelling—including the consumption and sometimes even the cooking of food—while parked or moving at high rates of speed[34] (figure 14.8).

Our cars have become second living rooms. And yet this convenience has a price. As Eric Schlosser argues in *Fast Food Nation,* "The United States now has the highest obesity rate of any industrialized nation in the world. More than half of all American adults and about one-quarter of all American children are now obese or overweight[, and obesity] is now second only to smoking as a cause of mortality in the United States."[35] There are other risk factors as well. The car insurance company Hagerty Classic has published a list of dangerous foods that, if eaten while driving, are likely to increase accidents because of driver distraction. In a news release the company refers to a recent analysis of more than 30,000 drivers nationwide, in which the National Highway Traffic Safety Administration concluded that "eating was a bigger distraction than using a hand-held cell phone."[36]

MIKESCH MUECKE

The new benchmarks for mobile food are that it can be eaten with one hand and that it fits in a cup holder. Campbell introduced a new soup in September 2002 that consumers can sip on the run. It is called Soup at Hand and consists of a container with a wide lid that can double as a bowl. And in the summer of 2002, Nabisco started to sell plastic cups called Go-Paks that contain mini Oreos, Ritz Bits, and other cookies and crackers.[37] Marketers call this new phenomenon *dashboard dining*.[38] Hagerty Classic Insurance used the following criteria for evaluating mobile food: the degree of distraction (which depends on the messiness of the food), the degree of difficulty in eating with only one hand on the wheel, and the food's popularity. The list of the top ten most dangerous foods to eat while driving, from bad to worse, is chocolate, soft drinks, jelly and cream-filled donuts, any barbecued food, juicy hamburgers, chili, tacos, hot soups, and finally coffee.[39]

There are, however, also signs of a countermovement. Acknowledging the pervasiveness of vehicular dining, the online journal InteliHealth published a list of dos and don'ts for eating in the car: avoid fast food, pack your own breakfast, keep healthy nonperishables in the car, don't eat toaster pastries or donuts, and bring along a small cooler lunch bag for healthy perishables.[40] There exist alternatives to factory food even on the fast-food circuit. In-N-Out fast-food restaurants, for example, beat the trend by offering high-quality, low-cost food, paying the highest wages of any fast-food chain, providing medical benefit packages, and cooking their food fresh without the use of microwaves, freezers, or heat lamps.[41] On the other end of the spectrum is the slow food movement, which originated in Rome as a result of McDonald's opening a restaurant at the foot of the Spanish Steps; Schlosser praises it for "stand[ing] in direct opposition to everything that a fast-food meal represents: blandness, uniformity, conformity, the blind worship of science and technology."[42] And yet, slow food and mobile picnics do not exclude each other. While its members call for the food to be prepared in the company of family and friends, it may still be taken on the road and consumed in the car. Perhaps slow food and eating in your car represent just the two end points of a line that connects the preindustrialized picnic, the house car, and the drive-through.

I would like to thank the editors, Jamie Horwitz and Paulette Singley, for their invaluable contributions to this essay.

1. Michael L. Berger, *The Devil Wagon in God's Country: The Automobile and Social Change in Rural America, 1893–1929* (Hamden, Conn.: Archon Books, 1979), 23; quoted in Roger Byron White, *Home on the Road: The Motor Home in America* (Washington, D.C.: Smithsonian Institution Press, 2000), 3.

2. Posidonius is quoted by Athenaeus and Diodorus, and the court record is quoted in Peter Earle, *A City Full of People: Men and Women of London, 1650–1750* (London: Methuen, 1994), 223; both are quoted in C. Anne Wilson, "The Great Outdoors," in *Eat, Drink, and Be Merry: The British at Table, 1600–2000,* ed. Ivan Day (London: Philip Wilson, 2000), 131, 133.

3. Jean Latham, *The Pleasure of Your Company: A History of Manners and Meals* (London: Adam and Charles Black, 1972), 149.

4. The word *picnic,* from the French *pique-nique,* meant originally a shared indoor meal to which each person contributed a dish from a prearranged menu.

5. Helen Stevens Fisher, *A Good Time at Your Picnic* (New York: M. S. Mills, 1942), 11; Nancy Fair McIntyre, *It's a Picnic!* (New York: Viking, 1969), x.

6. See Jens Tismar's theory of the idyll in Tismar, *Gestörte Idyllen: Eine Studie zur Problematik der idyllischen Wunschvorstellungen am Beispiel Jean Paul, Adalbert Stifter, Robert Walser und Thomas Bernhard* (Munich: Hanser, 1973), 7.

7. T. J. Clark, *The Painting of Modern Life: Paris in the Art of Manet and His Followers* (Princeton: Princeton University Press, 1984), 263.

8. The Cantor drive-in has not received appropriate press, even though it probably represents one of least compromised versions of Mies's clear-span designs. Werner Blaser, for example, mentions the Cantor briefly as a precedent to Crown Hall but does not elaborate on the importance of the design; see Blaser, *After Mies: Mies van der Rohe, Teaching and Principles* (New York: Van Nostrand Reinhold, 1977), 156. Liane Lefaivre, in contrast, argues that the Cantor is the birthplace of Mies's universal space; see Lefaivre, "Burgers, Fries, and a Side Order of Mies," *Architecture* 89, no. 7 (July 2000): 67–71.

9. David Spaeth, *Mies van der Rohe* (New York: Rizzoli, 1985), 148.

10. Ibid., 152.

11. In both the Farnsworth House and (even more obviously) in Crown Hall, the steel columns stepping around the periphery of the building take away from the floating character of the roof.

12. In fact, the Cantor and the Farnsworth House are Mies's only midcentury designs that cantilever the roof out over the surrounding landscape. And here the Cantor wins the contest scale-wise over the Farnsworth residence, as Mies extends the roof 30 feet out over the sidewalk and the parked cars.

13. Peter Carter and Mies quoted by Carter, *Mies van der Rohe at Work* (London: Phaidon Press, 1999), 7.

14. Sigfried Giedion, *Mechanization Takes Command: A Contribution to Anonymous History* (1948; reprint, New York: W. W. Norton, 1975), 3.

15. For Giedion, mechanization represented the cause of the division between thought and feeling, a division he had identified in his other seminal analysis of modernism: *Space, Time and Architecture: The Growth of a New Tradition* (Cambridge, Mass.: Harvard University Press, 1941). See also the introduction of Sigfried Giedion, *Building in France, Building in Iron, Building in Ferro-concrete,* trans. J. Duncan Berry (Santa Monica, Calif.: Getty Center for the History of Art and the Humanities,

1995), and also Stanislaus von Moos's essay on Giedion, "Dank an S. Giedion," *Hommage à Giedion: Profile seiner Persönlichkeit,* ed. Ulrich Stucky (Basel: Birkhäuser Verlag, 1971), 148.

16. Giedion, *Mechanization Takes Command,* 99.

17. David Harvey, *The Condition of Postmodernity: An Enquiry into the Origins of Cultural Exchange* (Oxford: Blackwell, 1990), 126.

18. See also Giedion, *Mechanization Takes Command,* 124–126. Chaplin's apparent goal, a revolt against human domination by machines, leads at the end of the movie to a clichéd escape into unmechanized nature, when Chaplin and his sweetheart leave the industrial town and walk hand in hand down a deserted road, into the sunset.

19. Henry Dreyfuss, *Designing for People* (New York: Simon and Schuster, 1955), 80; quoted by Adrian Forty, *Objects of Desire: Design and Society since 1750* (1986; reprint, London: Thames and Hudson, 1995), 199.

20. Schütte-Lihotzky, quoted in Susan R. Henderson, "A Revolution in the Woman's Sphere: Grete Lihotzky and the Frankfurt Kitchen," in *Architecture and Feminism,* ed. Elizabeth Danze, Debra Coleman, and Carol Henderson (New York: Princeton Architectural Press, 1996), 235.

21. Giedion locates the nonmechanized version of mass production—that is, the assembly line prototype—as early as 1800, in the manufacture of biscuits for the British navy, and in the 1830s in the systematic teamwork of killing and dressing hogs in Cincinnati (*Mechanization Takes Command,* 77).

22. With funding from Ford, Buckminster Fuller's students at MIT designed a sliding kitchen cabinet for station wagons (see White, *Home on the Road,* 97). The 1958 Ford Pushbutton Camper, designed by William Moss, featured a slide-out tailgate kitchen unit. It was shown at Ford's station wagon advertising campaigns in the late 1950s and early 1960s.

23. White writes that "the tailgate served as a convenient cooking surface or dining table" (ibid., 96).

24. Roland Barthes, "The New Citroën," in *Mythologies,* trans. Annette Lavers (New York: Hill and Wang, 1972), 89.

25. Ivan Margolius, *Automobiles by Architects* (Chichester: Wiley-Academy, 2000), 135.

26. White, *Home on the Road,* 15. White also writes that in 1903 a vehicle called Le Bourlinguette, built by a rich gentleman from Bordeaux, France, "was patterned after private railroad cars but was referred to as a 'motor caravan' or 'automobile house car'" (19).

27. Ibid., 142.

28. Arthur Drexler, *Ten Automobiles* (New York: Museum of Modern Art, 1953), 3; quoted in Margolius, *Automobiles by Architects,* 7.

29. Harry Snyder and Esther Snyder opened the first In-N-Out drive-through hamburger stand on the road between Los Angeles and Palm Springs in 1948. See Eric Schlosser, *Fast Food Nation: The Dark Side of the All-American Meal* (Boston: Houghton Mifflin, 2001), 259.

30. Stephen Bayley, "Grace, Pace, Space," *Architectural Review* 176 (November 1984): 77; quoted in Margolius, *Automobiles by Architects,* 7.

31. "Das alte Wort bauen, zu dem das 'bin' gehört, antwortet: 'ich bin', 'du bist' besagt: ich wohne, du wohnst"; Martin Heidegger, "Bauen, Wohnen, Denken" (1951), in *Vorträge und Aufsätze,* vol. 7 of *Gesamtausgabe* (Frankfurt am Main: Vittorio Klostermann, 2000), 148, 149.

32. John Brinckerhoff Jackson, *Landscape in Sight: Looking at America,* ed. Helen Lefkowitz Horowitz (New Haven: Yale University Press, 1997), 211, 222, 223.

33. John Urry, *Sociology beyond Societies: Mobilities for the Twenty-First Century* (London: Routledge, 2000), 57–58.

34. Ibid., 59, 60, 63. On the mobile cooking of food, see Chris Maynard and Bill Scheller's book *Manifold Destiny: The One! The Only Guide to Cooking on Your Car Engine!*, rev. ed. (New York: Villard, 1998).

35. Schlosser, *Fast Food Nation*, 240, 241.

36. Hagerty Classic Insurance, "'Drivers Beware': The Ten Most Dangerous Foods to Eat While Driving," *News Room*, April 29, 2002 <http://www.hagerty.com/about_news_article.asp?PR=04/29/2002> (accessed January 2003).

37. Ameet Sachdev, "In a Cup, in the Car: Sips, Snacks, Now Soup," Philly.com, September 4, 2002 <http://www.philly.com/mld/philly/living/food/3998411.htm?template=contentModules/printstory.jsp> (accessed January 2003).

38. The origins of the term are not clear. Dr. Pamela Peeke refers to eating in the car as "dashboard dining" in her book *Fight Fat after Forty: The Revolutionary Three-Pronged Approach That Will Break Your Stress-Fat Cycle and Make You Healthy, Fit, and Trim for Life* (New York: Viking, 2000).

39. Hagerty Insurance Company, "Drivers Beware."

40. See "On the Road to Breakfast," *InteliHealth Content*, July 18, 2001 <http://www.intelihealth.com/IH/ihtPrint/WSIHWOOD/325/22006.html?hide=t&k=basePrint> (accessed January 2003).

41. Schlosser, *Fast Food Nation*, 259, 260.

42. Schlosser, quoted by Chef Boy Ari in a "Flash in the Pan" column, "Getting in the Slow Food State of Mind," *Missoula Independent*, January 16, 2002 <http://www.missoulanews.com/AE/News.asp?no=2609> (accessed January 2003).

15

TABLE SETTINGS: THE PLEASURES OF WELL-SITUATED EATING

ALEX T. ANDERSON

The encompassing pleasure of a good meal depends on its setting.

This statement seems at first to warrant little comment. Chefs, restaurant critics, and no doubt many restaurant-goers often regard it as dogma. Nevertheless, one could counter it by citing the pleasure of eating just about anywhere on an empty stomach, or the delights of take-out food, which can hardly boast an "appropriate" setting. Of course, food can provide pleasure—to a hungry person—in virtually any context. The enjoyment associated with assuaged hunger is an unavoidable fact of our physiology, and it lies behind much of the satisfaction that dining provides. Epicurus regarded it as the basis for human artistry, contending that "the beginning and the root of all good is the pleasure of the stomach."[1]

However, the pleasure of eating differs greatly from the pleasure of dining. Early in the nineteenth century, Jean Anthelme Brillat-Savarin constructed the "science" of gastronomy on this presumption, declaring that "the pleasure of eating is one we share with animals. . . . The pleasures of the table are known only to the human race."[2]

The act of dining aspires to satisfy far more than the feral cravings of the belly. And it requires more than hunger. Perhaps Brillat-Savarin said it well enough: "The truth is that at the end of a well-savored meal both soul and body enjoy an especial well-being." This complex, obscure, and often elusive sensation results from the propitious combination of many factors. Brillat-Savarin explained that it depends "on careful preparations for the serving of the meal, on the choice of place, and on the thoughtful assembling of the guests."[3] Contemporary chef-restaurateurs pay very close attention to these elements.[4] And the designers of places for dining must work, using similar presumptions, to complement the production of their chefs. For the diner's part, the well-being made possible by a good and well-situated meal demands attentive ingestion of the food—and its setting—which requires a good appetite.

This essay demonstrates the extent to which the setting for a meal is involved in bringing about the sense of well-being that accompanies the act of dining. Through a series of increasingly complex examples drawn from literary sources, it shows that the pleasure of dining radiates outward from the alimentary tract to encompass impressions of the food, table, room, and the larger context. These examples, drawn from fiction, show with particular intensity and clarity that cuisine and place conspire to intensify sensual experience, to consolidate and to elicit memories, to satisfy curiosity. Working on presumptions extracted from these sources, I argue that gastronomic knowledge should contribute more fully to historical and theoretical discussions of architecture. I seek, in brief, to support a stronger alliance of disciplines whose products so pleasurably intertwine in everyday practice.

SITUATED EATING

One of the twentieth century's great eaters, the *New Yorker's* long-time food writer A. J. Liebling, once said, "A good appetite gives an eater room to turn around in."[5] Although he was speaking figuratively—indicating that a person who cheerfully maintains a substantial capacity to eat avails him- or herself of all the pleasure that food and a given situation might offer—the spatial image his assertion conveys is fitting. A good appetite expands to fill out not just the body but the place surrounding it. The very human experience of dining incorporates the meal and its context. When a meal and its setting fit particularly well, when they resonate and thereby stir the senses and sentiments, the results can be especially memorable. Often, however, this pleasure,

ALEX T. ANDERSON

built on the serendipitous combination of many factors, remains elusive or fleeting. Liebling therefore calls for "good appetite" as a kind of safeguard. A good appetite improves the chances of capturing and extending moments of gustatorial pleasure. It not only gives hearty eaters room to turn around in; it also situates them well for good eating.

Sometimes the food and its setting correlate so well that the diner need do little more than participate in the spectacle presented, following where the designers of the meal lead. The Argentine storytellers Jorge Luis Borges and Adolfo Bioy Casares describe just such a trajectory in their fictional tale "An Abstract Art." In this story they recount the invented evolution of "culinary cooking" and fabricate its obscure architectural counterpart, the *tenebrarium*.

The aim of culinary cooking, as they describe it, is to develop "a cuisine owing nothing to the plastic arts or to the object of nourishment."[6] It seeks to satisfy only the sensation of taste. Its presumptive origins lie with the scientific discovery, in 1891, of the five fundamental tastes: sour, salty, bitter, sweet, and (their addition) insipid. Acting on this discovery, the astute Parisian chef of Les Cinq Saveurs treats gastronomic cognoscenti to "taste" in its most pristine state: "identical pyramids, each an inch high and each affording the palate one of the now celebrated five tastes" (71). They describe later and more sophisticated iterations of this cuisine that allow for the revival of "the age-old ancestral tastes," but only after all visual and tactile characteristics have been removed from the dishes that incorporate them. "Vivid colors, elegant serving platters, and what common prejudice calls a well-presented dish—all these were banned" (73).

But it is not until an audacious moment in 1932, when an ingenious chef also excludes the very dining room from view, that their fanciful history comes to its fitting conclusion: "[In] a restaurant like all others, serving dishes in no way different from those of the past[,] . . . [he] carried out the simple act destined to place him forever at the top-most point of the pinnacle in the entire annals of cookery. He snapped out the lights. There, in that instant, the first *tenebrarium* was launched" (73).

Although the meal and its setting in this story are not concerned with a sense of well-being so much as with the satisfaction of an isolated sense of taste, Borges and Bioy Casares demonstrate powerfully that the pleasures of dining, whatever they might be, do not result solely from the isolated act of eating. The diner needs the place as much as the food to experience a meal properly. In this case, the absurdly reductive—or refined—"culinary cooking" and the darkened room in which one experiences it complement and require each other. Only in their fastidiously coordinated association does the anticipated pleasure unfold for the diner.

Sometimes, by contrast, a diner might discover an expansive, unexpected pleasure that unfurls itself with slight provocation from unremarkable food taken in just the right setting. Through a strange alchemy unleashed by their combination, a sense of well-being expands in the imagination, even as the specific flavors and atmosphere that precipitated it fade.

Marcel Proust recounts such an event, in a well-known passage of *Remembrance of Things Past,* when on a cheerless afternoon in Combray his mother offers him tea and a *petite madeleine:*

> And soon, mechanically, dispirited after a dreary day with the prospect of a depressing morrow, I raised to my lips a spoonful of the tea in which I had soaked a morsel of the cake. No sooner had the warm liquid mixed with the crumbs touched my palate than a shudder ran through me and I stopped, intent upon the extraordinary thing that was happening to me. An exquisite pleasure had invaded my senses, something isolated, detached, with no suggestion of its origin.[7]

Seeking to prolong this pleasure and to find its source, Proust takes a second and a third mouthful, but begins to lose the sensation. To force it back to consciousness, he says, "I shut out every obstacle, every extraneous idea, I stop my ears and inhibit all attention against the sounds from the next room. . . . I clear an empty space in front of it." And at last winning back the sensation of pleasure again, Proust finds that far from existing in an empty space, it has attached itself to a place that takes shape and grows in his consciousness: "And as soon as I had recognised the taste of the piece of madeleine soaked in her decoction of lime-blossom which my aunt used to give me . . . the old grey house upon the street, where her room was, rose up like a stage set . . . and with the house the town, . . . the streets along which I used to run errands, the country roads we took when it was fine."[8] It is not the immediate sensation of taste or of satiated hunger that interests Proust in these experiences, but the rich, pleasurable evocation that the aroma and flavor of tea and the madeleine bring about. From them he raises up the room, the house, and the village with all of their characteristic odors, colors, textures.

Liebling lamented that "in the light of what Proust wrote with so mild a stimulus, it is the world's loss that he did not have a heartier appetite."[9] What he might have conjured one can hardly imagine. Nevertheless, the frugality of the event serves to demonstrate how manifold and expansive the relationship between food and its setting can become.

A good appetite helps one capture and make sense of far more complex experiences, but it also has limits. Gourmands, even those with the most impressive capacities, have deplored the constraints of appetite since before the fabled days of Roman *vomitoria*—ever since, according to Brillat-Savarin, "poets long ago began to complain that the throat, being too short, limited the length of the pleasure of tasting."[10] To advance beyond the narrowly circumscribed pleasure of taste, beyond the confines of the alimentary passages, and into the dining room, gastronomy enlisted the help of other arts. For the most sumptuous meals the ancients contributed music and entertainments of all sorts. They filled the air with perfumes and placed ornaments on anything that could support them. The French maîtres d'hôtel of the generations preceding Brillat-Savarin far surpassed these efforts. These masters of fantastic baroque feasts, with which the courts of Louis XIV and XV indulged themselves, added elaborate artificial dinner "sets" arranged in monumentally reconfigured gardens and surmounted by profusions of fountains and pompous displays of fireworks.[11] Such "artificial embellishments," as Brillat-Savarin called them, aim to arouse every sense.[12] The attention of ears, nose, hands, and eyes is drawn outward toward these, even as the mouth and stomach ingest a great succession of lavish dishes.

Just as satisfaction of the alimentary system does not fully characterize gastronomic pleasure, however, neither does the more comprehensive physical pleasure augmented by architectural embellishments. Gastronomic pleasure also involves the intellect. A good meal piques the imagination, conjures memories, conveys ideas. Often, it does so through surprising combinations, placing flavors in resonance with each other and with their settings to provoke the complacent and astonish the alert diner. To discover this kind of pleasure demands not only appetite but also attention.

Adventurous diners often seek such pleasure in the variety that a change of venue provides—by going to many different restaurants, for example, or by traveling to "exotic" places. Italo Calvino vividly demonstrates the benefits of the latter in "Under the Jaguar Sun," a fictional essay on taste.[13] Its Italian protagonists, a married couple approaching middle age, undertake a gustatorial journey in Mexico, far from home. Through a series of shared encounters with the artifacts of the culture, intensified by its characteristic and idiosyncratic cuisine, they discover fascinating shades of a Mexico that would otherwise have remained obscure to them. They take exquisite, mutual pleasure in the food; however, a dawning awareness of the places that surround them outshines this pleasure. A deeply satisfying comprehension of their surroundings—and its sometimes sordid past—suffuses and dominates their gustatory experiences.

In one instance, as they savor piquant dishes under the orange trees of an old convent, they sense the latent passions of aristocratic nuns subdued long ago in the dark rooms that surround them. In their quiet confinement, these nuns had created a "bold cuisine bent on making the flavors' highest notes vibrate, juxtaposing them in modulations, in chords, and especially in dissonances that would assert themselves as an incomparable experience—a point of no return, an absolute possession exercised on the receptivity of all the senses" (5). These nuns, the protagonists discover, did not create dishes merely to exercise their considerable culinary abilities, nor solely "to satisfy the venial whims of gluttony." Their recipes also expressed the ardor of more consequential fantasies, carnal fantasies: "the fantasies, after all, of sophisticated women . . . whose reading told of ecstasies and transfigurations, martyrs and tortures" (6). As they taste these exquisite dishes, the protagonists recognize the same clandestine passions they had earlier discovered enfolded into the ornate baroque churches of Oaxaca:

> Architecture . . . the background to the lives of those religious; it, too, was impelled by the same drive toward the extreme that led to the exacerbation of flavors amplified by the blaze of the most spicy chiles. Just as colonial baroque set no limits on the profusion of ornament and display, in which God's presence was identified in a closely calculated delirium of brimming, excessive sensations, so the curing of the hundred or more native varieties of hot peppers carefully selected for each dish opened vistas of flaming ecstasy. (6–7)

Thus, the apparently unremarkable scene that Calvino places before the reader—of a tourist couple enjoying a meal together in a cloister garden—becomes a passionate exploration of an unfamiliar place. Its subtleties reveal themselves only as flavors resonate with the intricacies of its buildings and landscapes—the somber, cracked plaster walls, the incomprehensible scrollwork and gilded ceilings, the shimmering sunlight, the aroma of orange blossoms.

Later, the protagonists chance upon a banquet in the chapel of the convent (converted some time ago into the lobby of a hotel). They are now attuned to the startling associations possible in the place, which they probe, alert both to their heightened imaginations and to a deepening curiosity about what such an event might tell them about Mexico:

> We were struck by a sound like a cascade of water flowing and splashing and gurgling in a thousand rivulets and eddies and jets. . . . From the doorway (the room was a few steps lower than the corridor), we saw an expanse of little spring hats on the heads of ladies seated around tea tables. . . . Under the broad, empty vaulted ceiling, three hundred Mexican ladies were conversing all at once; the spectacular acoustical event that had immediately subdued us was produced by their voices mingled with the tinkling of cups and spoons and of knives cutting slices of cake. (16–17)

Although seemingly innocuous, this gathering of the society women of Oaxaca invites strangely sinister associations. The event intertwines itself in their imaginations with the ancient religious feasts of Monte Albán, where earlier in the day the tourists had examined the settings for details of Mexican history far more sordid than the carnal fantasies of cloistered nuns. At Monte Albán the priests had devoured the flesh of sacrificial victims.

That, at least, is the presumption of their friend Salustiano, a guest of honor at the tea party and an "impassioned connoisseur" of Mexican history. In conspiratorial tones, partly obscured by the discord of the banquet, he recounts the horrifying details: "*Sangre . . . obsidiana . . . divinidad solar*" (Blood . . . obsidian . . . solar divination; 18, Calvino's ellipses). He speculates on the mysterious preparation of the sacrificial flesh and its flavor—"A strange flavor, they say." He holds forth on the sacred and atavistic origins of this esoteric cuisine, explaining that it celebrated "the harmony of the elements achieved through sacrifice—a terrible harmony, flaming, incandescent" (20). And thus he leaves the protagonists with the curious thought that in such feasts, flavor (of cake or flesh) bears an almost insignificant relationship to the spectacular events and the almost overwhelming architectural settings in which they take place. Although they might be characterized as the "backdrop" to tea and cake, the bare, resonant vault, the high plastered walls, and the hard expanse of floor in the convent chapel—like the endless stone stairs, exposed platforms, and vehement relief sculptures of Monte Albán—capture the imagination so thoroughly that the roles of hunger and taste are almost inconsequential.

In both of these examples Calvino reveals another important aspect of the pleasure derived from the settings for cuisine: it often reaches well beyond the dining room and into its regional context. Terrain, habits, and legend often manifest themselves in the cuisine of a place. They appear in the recipes that incorporate local ingredients, in the special tools and methods used for their preparation, and in the environments most suitable for their consumption. Accordingly, the cuisine of Oaxaca that Calvino describes developed characteristic "embellishments." Through them it accommodates and discloses available ingredients and sustains historical narratives that exemplify indigenous values. Similarly, the cuisines of the Dordogne in France, of Hunan in China, of northern California in the United States, and so on distinguish themselves largely through the unique appurtenances—architecture, furniture, tools, ingredients—with which they developed over time. A "foreign" visitor to such a place may even sense that the central idea behind a culinary event there is its regional identity.[14]

Attentive diners can uncover much about their territorial surroundings in the richly layered sensations provided by a well-prepared and situated meal. Calvino argues that to experience such an event out of its proper context, therefore, is to experience a shadow of its significance. Transplanted into another environment—into an "exotic" restaurant somewhere in an American city, or into a take-out box—the characteristic embellishments of a particular cuisine fall out of place.[15] In many cases, regional context is as essential to the experience of a good meal as the dining room, table, or plates set before the diner.

The examples drawn from "Under the Jaguar Sun" also hint at the role that architectural settings and their broader physical contexts play in framing shared experiences with food. Even when their meals differ, the setting for their shared experience is the subject that remains equally available to the heightened awareness of each participant.

GASTRONOMY AND ARCHITECTURE

This essay has so far shown that the compass of pleasurable experience in dining moves outward from the alimentary passages to include food, setting, and context. As the body takes in the meal, it also incorporates the table service, furniture, dining room, and their various embellishments. Extending still further, the pleasure of a good meal contains thematic resonance between the food and its contexts, contexts that include not just the diners' immediate surroundings but also the broader regional and cultural environments. While by no means refuting the assertion that eating can provide some pleasure in virtually any context, the examples above, drawn from great works of fiction, provide particularly vivid accounts of the complex relationships that develop between food and setting.

Given the ubiquity of these relationships in everyday life, and the value that people evidently ascribe to them, it is remarkable that architectural theory has so seldom engaged the subject of cuisine. Marco Frascari was the first to treat the relationship between taste and architecture, in a 1986 essay on the subject that still stands almost alone.[16] Likewise, public dining spaces play a surprisingly minor role in histories of architecture. For example, in the nearly 350 pages of his critical history of modern architecture, Kenneth Frampton mentions only five public dining spaces: the Willow Tea Rooms by Charles Rennie Mackintosh, the Café Museum and American Bar by Adolf Loos, the Midway Gardens by Frank Lloyd Wright, and the Café L'Aubette by Theo van Doesburg, Jean Arp, and Sophie Taeuber-Arp. Of these, only the last two are illustrated—out of 362 figures in the book.[17]

The relatively recent development of dedicated spaces for dining may account for some of this. After all, public dining spaces comparable to contemporary restaurants did not exist in Europe until the second half of the eighteenth century.[18] And rooms dedicated solely to dining did not appear in modern houses until the beginning of the nineteenth century.[19] Moreover, the strict division of disciplines that characterized academic endeavors after the Enlightenment may have helped to maintain strong distinctions between the culinary and visual arts.[20] But a more significant hindrance to examining the correlation between cuisine and architecture is the long-standing, although recently weakening, distrust in architectural theory for any appeal to sensuality or to intuitive judgment, both of which are highly characteristic of gastronomic knowledge.[21]

Frascari has argued, however, that the practitioners of gastronomy and architecture justify their creative endeavors in analogous ways, similarly employing the faculty of "taste" in judging their work. He maintains that chefs and architects both use "the 'rule' of taste to solve their ill-defined problems in a nontrivial manner." They "rely on symptoms, clues, and surprising facts to perform their own tasks using interpretive procedures. They deal with processes of design which cannot be methodologically explained."[22] Chefs depend heavily on this faculty not only in preparing particular dishes, whose parameters for "quality" they can only roughly define but also in assembling menus, setting out tables, and outfitting spaces for dining. Architects, confronting myriad issues related to user demands, site, context, material availability, and so on, must also rely on intuitive judgments to make buildings and rooms that seem "right."

In everyday life, as in literature, practitioners of these disciplines often cooperate to provide experiences that arouse the mind and satisfy the body. Their mutual effort brings about an encompassing pleasure that is complex, expansive, enigmatic, and peculiar to the act of dining. More comprehensive investigation of their joint endeavors, and the motivations that underlie them, promises even more room in which devotees of well-situated meals can turn around and exercise their good appetites.

NOTES

1. Epicurus, *Epicurus: The Extant Remains,* with short critical apparatus, translation, and notes by Cyril Bailey (Oxford: Clarendon Press, 1926), frag. 29.
2. Jean Anthelme Brillat-Savarin, *The Physiology of Taste,* trans. M. F. K. Fisher (San Francisco: North Point Press, 1986), 182.
3. Ibid., 183, 182.
4. A recently published manual for aspiring chef-restaurateurs in the United States asserts that this correlation underlies diners' perception of their efforts: "when a chef becomes a chef-restaurateur, his or her reputation rests not only on what is served on the plate, but on the very plate itself—not to mention the glasses, the flowers, the wait staff, the host, and every minute detail the customer, who

is a guest of the restaurant for a few hours, notices and discusses the next day with co-workers" (Andrew Dornenburg and Karen Page, *Becoming a Chef* [New York: Van Nostrand Reinhold, 1995], 170).

5. A. J. Liebling, *Between Meals* (1962; reprint, New York: Modern Library, 1995), 4.

6. Jorge Luis Borges and Adolfo Bioy Casares, "An Abstract Art," in *A Literary Feast: An Anthology,* ed. Lilly Gordon (New York: Atlantic Monthly Press, 1993), 73. This edition of the story is hereafter cited parenthetically in the text.

7. Marcel Proust, *Swann's Way,* in *Remembrance of Things Past,* trans. C. K. Scott Moncrieff and Terence Kilmartin (New York: Random House, 1981), 1:48.

8. Ibid., 49, 51.

9. Liebling, *Between Meals,* 4.

10. Brillat-Savarin, *The Physiology of Taste,* 183.

11. The legendary extravagance of a feast assembled by Vatel for Nicolas Fouquet enraged Louis XIV, who could not have matched the solid gold table setting, 1,200 fountains and cascades, games, aquatic tournaments, and a new comedy by Molière (Pneu Michelin, *Île-de-France: The Region around Paris* [Harrow: Michelin Tyre; Clermont-Ferrand: Michelin, 1989], 173).

12. Brillat-Savarin, *The Physiology of Taste,* 183.

13. Italo Calvino, "Under the Jaguar Sun," in *Under the Jaguar Sun,* trans. William Weaver (San Diego: Harcourt Brace Jovanovich, 1988), 1–29; this edition of the story is hereafter cited parenthetically in the text.

14. Of course, such expression of regional identity can closely match the intentions of a chef. Alice Waters, chef at Chez Panisse in San Francisco, asserts that its cuisine "began with our doing the very best we could do with French recipes and California ingredients, and has evolved into what I like to think of as a celebration of the very finest of our regional food products" (Waters, *Chez Panisse Menu Cookbook* [New York: Random House, 1982], x).

15. Recent developments in what might be called "pan-global" cuisines complicate this assertion. For example, Deborah Madison, proprietor of Greens at Fort Mason in San Francisco and a student of Alice Waters, asserts that in founding Greens "we drew upon a wide variety of traditions—the Mediterranean cooking of southern France and Italy, dishes from Mexico and the American Southwest, a few adaptations from the cuisines of Asia and others—but what pulled it all together was our reliance on the freshest vegetables, herbs and spices" (Madison and Edward Espe Brown, *The Greens Cook Book* [New York: Bantam, 1987], xvii). These of course must be acquired locally. In this case it might be argued that the breadth of influences on the menu merely reflects the cultural constitution of San Francisco, and the diversity of climates in northern California accommodates the great range of necessary ingredients. Similar restaurants in other cities often fail to demonstrate such connections.

16. Marco Frascari, "*Semiotica ab edendo,* Taste in Architecture," *Journal of Architectural Education* 40, no. 1 (1986): 2–7; reprinted in this volume.

17. The illustrations also include two private kitchens, one dining room, and a snapshot of Le Corbusier and Walter and Frau Gropius at a café in Paris. See Kenneth Frampton, *Modern Architecture: A Critical History,* 3rd ed. (New York: Thames and Hudson, 1992).

18. Stephen Mennell, *All Manners of Food: Eating and Taste in England and France from the Middle Ages to the Present* (Oxford: Basil Blackwell, 1985), 135–144; Rebecca Spang, *The Invention of the Restaurant: Paris and Modern Gastronomic Culture* (Cambridge, Mass.: Harvard University Press, 2000).

19. Catherine Arminjon, "The Art of Dining," in *L'Art de Vivre: Decorative Arts and Design in France, 1789–1989*, ed. Nancy Aaker (New York: Vendome Press, 1989), 143–170.

20. Mennell explains, for example, that prominent critics of the great eighteenth-century French chef Antonin Carême dismissed his elaborate "architectural" confections as inappropriate, arguing that "the cook's job was not to please the eye but the palate" (*All Manners of Food*, 145).

21. Frascari argues that the demise of taste as a legitimate theoretical analogy for architecture is traced to the great intellectual revolutions of the seventeenth and eighteenth centuries. At that time this component of human knowledge was demoted to "a faculty which presents 'sensibility, but not reason'" ("Semiotica ab edendo, Taste in Architecture," 195).

22. Ibid., 199.

16

EATING SPACE

JAMIE HORWITZ

T he table, Luce Giard tells us, is "social machinery" as complicated as it is effective.[1] By definition, a table is a piece of furniture, with a flat horizontal surface supported by legs. It is also the objects laid out for a meal set upon this surface, the food and drink served, and the company of people assembled around the furniture. Despite this thick etymological congruence, contemporary eating space is not defined exclusively by the table, the social life, or the settings that occur there.

This essay examines instances in the life of the table selected from the domestic, or private, realm; from the commercial and public space of transportation; and from the extreme environment of the International Space Station. In each case the spaces of eating shift from the sociality of a shared table into something more isolated, contained, and encapsulated. These transformations in eating space are read through an understanding theorized by Henri Lefebvre as encompassing the fabric and settings of everyday life as well as the activities "which connect and join together systems which might appear to be distinct."[2] The historian of the built environment Dell Upton has argued that since the English translation of Lefebvre's *The Production of Space* in

1991, "theories of everyday life have begun to infiltrate Architecture with a capital A—the realm of high design and theory," as an alternative to "a quarter century of the post-modern elevation of representation and language over space and materiality."[3]

Reading the narrower realm of design practice through a study of the more inclusive realm of material culture, Elizabeth Collins Cromley offers specific analytic insights to the study of food and Architecture through her investigation of nineteenth- and twentieth-century American domestic architecture.[4] Tracing the "historically unstable" position of cooking and dining from early-twentieth-century houses, in which the kitchen was segregated from other social spaces, to the midcentury "open-plan" houses in which food-related activities are integral to the "flow" of household activity, Cromley shows how such designs are not products of architectural thought. Rather, changes in food-related activity space are better understood as shifts in "a food axis," which Cromley defines as the "acceptable relationships between cooking, storing, serving, eating, disposing," and the tools and furnishings that make them possible.[5] Instances of table redesign can be located along the food axis as consequences of the everyday—where macroeconomic and political structures (such as mass consumer appliances and workforce participation) intersect with what the anthropologist Pierre Bourdieu refers to as *habitus:* the "habitual *and* improvisatory, the rote *and* novel."[6]

During the second half of the twentieth century, as the variability in the conventions of food preparation and consumption widened, manufactured products such as the frozen TV dinner might be read as a stark compression of the food axis. Light, thin, and easily stacked or stored for transport, or unbundled and converted—like a Murphy bed—into a plate of hot food, the TV dinner reorders the chaotic field of kitchen and table into a meal and entertainment grid. The TV dinner on its tray table set before a couch transposes the visual variety of the television into a checkered field of food offerings. With its pressed aluminum ridges between rectangles of yellow, brown, and red—a quilt for sampling without any prescribed sequence or pace—the TV dinner suggests a perimeter around the body. This meal is singular and precooked, predictable, and without hierarchy.

If the table is a field where the tension or order of a meal is inscribed by setting, and the arrangement of seating mirrors social power, then the TV dinner and the associated tray tables permit a departure from the accepted social and spatial conventions of the food axis. In this sense, the TV dinner functions as a liminal space, offering—as do the clearly bounded periods of carnival or festival—a temporary abandonment of social hierarchy, temporal order, and conventions of everyday life.[7] Of course, none of these interpretations were constructed "by design."

In 1954 Gerry Thomas, vice president of marketing for Swanson, conceived of the TV dinner product as a solution to a post-Thanksgiving inventory problem: a shortage of warehouse space that led to 520,000 pounds of unsold turkey being hauled coast to coast in refrigerated railroad boxcars. During a routine sales call to a distributor, Thomas noted the single-compartment metal trays that were being tested by an airline as a way to serve heated meals on international flights. Thomas recalls thinking that this was an interesting packaging idea; he introduced the concept at Swanson, where it was well received. That same year, the company pioneered the turkey dinner on an aluminum tray with four compartments for buttered peas, sweet potatoes, and cranberries. The individual frozen turkey dinner was highly attractive for Swanson, which could enjoy all the economies of scale from mass purchasing and manufacturing, and at the same time turn a higher profit by selling individual portions to retail consumers. The single-portion frozen meal that could be reheated by nearly anyone at any time was not a product of market research, though Thomas explains that the name "TV dinner" derives from the cultural context: "research suggested that this product was likely consumed by mom and the kids when dad wasn't home, and often in front of the television." Even though only 20 percent of U.S. households had television sets in the mid-1950s, Swanson wanted to associate the product with television because "the word TV meant you were cool and modern."[8]

Since the 1950s, as television has become an ever-present feature within U.S. households and outside them, the association of watching screens while eating a meal has grown nearly as common. In her study of the presence of television outside dwellings, Anna McCarthy finds a setting type she calls "television while you eat."[9] These TV-and-food combinations are usually accompanied by waiting in such places as transit stations, airports, and hospitals. The presence of television accompanies meals in sports bars and some theme restaurants, where video screens may be in ubiquitous public display or tucked inside booths to "help create miniature 'homes' that make the space seem like an oasis of privacy, an escape and retreat from the pace and crowd of city life."[10] In other words, in these commercial eating establishments

the TV reintroduces the world (as broadcast and transmitted by mainstream media) beyond one's self, albeit in a highly controlled and distanced visual frame.

•••

The sociospatial logic of perimeter containment and convertibility, such as that found in the TV dinner's tray, appears in fully spatialized translation in the freestanding chair with attached tray table. One of the earliest examples of the conversion of singular dwelling and eating can be found in the Circle Restaurant, designed by Skidmore, Owings & Merrill for the Charles A. Stevens Co. store in Chicago. Opened just after World War II, it was intended to appeal to the pent-up consumer demand of the middle-class shopper who spends her day in department stores and seeks an alternative to the lunch counters typically located on the first floor or in the basement of stores.[11] By providing "table service" without the table, the chair-tray-table combination gave shape to a new capsulated form of dining[12] (figure 16.2). Set equidistant, hinged together, and fixed in place—leading to an experience similar to eating on an airplane—the chair-tray-table offers an alternative to the lunch counter and the formal dining room by creating a space that encapsulates the customer who is lunching alone, together.

Table service without the table appears to have been an oddity in the history of restaurants. However, the chair-tray-table has become a fixture in commercial airlines and passenger trains that serve commuters, such as those on the east coast in the United States. While all passenger trains were once lavishly equipped with white tablecloths, galley kitchens, and freshly prepared foods, only those U.S. passenger trains that cater to long-distance and vacation travel have not replaced their dining cars with snack bars. Snack bars on the trains require less labor, less space, less food storage, and almost no food preparation. Along with the static table, snack bars also eliminate the whiff of romance lingering from memories of Alfred Hitchcock's 1959 film *North by Northwest* in which the spy, played by Eva Marie Saint, masquerades as an industrial designer who tips the waiter so that he will seat the man she is shadowing, played by Cary Grant, at her table in the dining car.

Profitability as well as convenience (for those passengers and commuters who wish to spend their travel time sleeping or working) may have led to the drop-down tray tables on trains and airplanes, but they are simply one design solution along a shifting food axis. In 1948, as Marshall Field and Company was trying to anticipate how the expanded mobility could shape postwar "consumer perception," it repositioned shopping within an eating space at the transit intersection of work and home.

Three years earlier, when the Chicago Airport (renamed Midway in 1949) was reported to be the busiest in the world, city officials and Houston McBain, the president of Marshall Field, began to negotiate the development of the company's first retail base in an airport. McBain told the press that he had always regarded airport restaurants as civic enterprises, and Marshall Field paid the city a percentage of its restaurant's gross profits in exchange for exclusive rights to all food service in the airport for a period of ten years.[13]

Although Marshall Field was well known for prepared foods, its tea room for ladies, and its Grill Room for men, McBain did not think he was extending the store's retail base into the hospitality industry by opening the Cloud Room (figure 16.3). The airport restaurant venture instead was perceived as part of "the store's long commitment to tourism, to attracting tourists."[14] This tradition dates back to the nineteenth century, when the company would dispatch horse and carriages to the train depots to bring passengers to and from the store. The first Marshall Field, the founder of the store, sat on the boards of numerous railroad companies. When a transcontinental train stopped in Chicago to refresh crews, Marshall Field made sure that its schedule allowed plenty of time to shop.[15]

Opening the only restaurant at the Chicago Airport situated Marshall Field and Co., once again, as the first and last thing that travelers saw when they came to Chicago. Cloud Room menus provided prime advertising space:

> *Are you a traveler with a time-shortage? Take a shopping shortcut. Call or visit our Tip to Toe Shop, the Shop that shops for you. Whether you are a man who'd like to send a lovely dress home to your wife. Or a woman with a craving for a new, complete costume—just give us a clue to your wants and whims and, without any further ado, our efficient staff of trained fashion counselors will take over. You may either inspect them at your convenience or use our mailing service, which extends to the far-flung corners of the globe.*[16]

The first department store to have foreign buying offices, Marshall Field operated within an early global market economy that it portrayed as bringing the world home to Chicagoans.

16.2
Table service without the table.
The Circle Restaurant, Charles A.
Stevens Co., Chicago. Skidmore,
Owings and Merrill, architect.

16.3
The Cloud Room interior, Chicago
Airport. Courtesy of the Marshall
Field and Co. Archive.

Perched on the second floor of the U-shaped terminal, the Cloud Room sported 75 feet of bay windows, clad in aluminum venetian blinds overlooking the airfield, and an interior of Chinese red leather upholstery offset by pale gray walls. The staircase was surrounded by boxwood hedges that provided a screen between diners and those standing in line to be seated or waiting for the preparation of box lunches to be taken on board the plane. Directly above the entrance stairway hung Chicago's first Alexander Calder sculpture, a mobile that Calder named *Brass in the Sky*, which had been commissioned by Alfred Shaw, the Cloud Room's architect.[17]

Modernist design and sculpture at the edge of airspace and the city made the Cloud Room a popular eating space for Chicagoans as well as visitors arriving at or departing from the airport. This extension of Marshall Field was never intended for an elite clientele traveling to Chicago for unhurried excursions of shopping and entertainment. Instead, Field's director of display, John Moss, engineered a space that would later be viewed as providing virtual shopping in the Cloud Room restaurant: he included "plugged-in telephone service at each of the 75 tables."[18] Moreover, the Cloud Room kitchen was designed to be in continuous operation. Just below the restaurant, on the runway level, was a coffee shop serving a modified menu to the thousands of passengers and airline personnel who passed through this airport all night and day. Delivering a telecommunications-based retail interface along with fine dining in 1948, the Cloud Room gave a foretaste of the premium on both luxury and convenience in contemporary consumer culture.

The French philosopher Michel Serres has written that in the emerging global information networks, the airport can be seen as a descendant of the medieval cathedral. Visitors to an airport, like those at a cathedral, see only that aspect that is on the ground. But the building is merely the visible foundation of a vast virtual architecture. In this case, it is an architecture of radio signals, electronic relays, and encoded information enveloping the thousands of passengers and crew who are aloft at any one moment: frescoed angels in the invisible cathedral's vaulted spire.[19] The Chicago Airport's Cloud Room operated for fourteen years until shortly after O'Hare International Airport opened 30 miles from the city, even further from the former restaurant's urban intensity and aesthetic where diners sat and ate together at the edge of a network society.

●●●

The coincidence of individuated meals and tableless dining—within a global environment of increased electronic and physical connectivity—problematizes the relationship between food and architecture. Both the connectivity and the compartmentalization create an increasingly common and comfortable eating space in the second half of the twentieth century in the United States. The reticulated form of communications networks, with its promise of nearly magical social connectivity, is the dominant representation of the interactions and transactions organizing the world.[20] Communications networks are, however, not the only means by which individuals know themselves and one another as part of society.

Precisely because railroads' dining car tables, originally fixed, were shared public spaces that brought strangers into intimate spatial contact—even more than did the spaces of lunch counters—those tables were instrumental in the struggle for social equity and civil rights in the United States. One strand of this broad history began in 1942 when Elmer Henderson, an African American field representative for Franklin D. Roosevelt's Commission on Fair Employment Practices, traveled south from Washington on business. As the Southern Railway passed through Virginia, he went to the dining car where two tables at the end were normally reserved for blacks, unless the "whites only" tables were full. On this day white patrons were occupying the black patrons' tables, filling every seat but one. When Henderson tried to take the empty seat, he was denied service; he later complained about this denial to the Interstate Commerce Commission (ICC), which decided that he had been mistreated. The Southern Railway issued new rules reserving two tables exclusively for blacks and separating them from other tables by a curtain. These rules satisfied the ICC and the federal courts but not Henderson, who appealed to the Supreme Court.[21]

The ICC's position had been defended by the Justice Department in the first trial; however, when the case headed for the Supreme Court, it was reviewed by the Solicitor General's Office, which handles government business before the tribunal. Philip Elman, a lawyer in that office, urged the solicitor general, Philip Perlman, to argue that the dining car segregation was indefensible. Perlman agreed and Elman wrote a brief attacking the separate-but-equal doctrine that then prevailed under the Supreme Court's *Plessy v. Ferguson* ruling of 1896. In 1950 the Supreme Court unanimously found that segregated dining cars violated the Interstate Commerce Act, though they did not rule on the constitutionality of the separate-but-equal doctrine for four more years—that is, not until the case of *Brown v. Board of Education* came before the Court in 1954 and Elman, who was again the principal author of the government briefs, argued that the racial segregation of public schools is unconstitutional. He used the language that he had developed in the case against segregated dining cars in what is considered to be the most important civil rights legislation of the twentieth century.[22]

Part macroeconomic structure and part serendipity, eating space does not escape the interests of the state, or fall outside the constitutional rights guaranteed by this democracy. By investigating the contexts in which eating space is configured and reconfigured, this essay traces the dynamic of everyday life, the *habitus* that Bourdieu defines as part habit and part improvisation, part continuity and part invention. It is a space where, Dell Upton reminds us, we can see a reuniting of "the ordinary and extraordinary" as "inseparable aspects of experience."[23]

● ● ●

Drawing spatial perimeters around the body creates a psychological distance; it protects individual consumers from the obligation of and the opportunity for both social and antisocial customs or inclinations. Eating from trays while facing screens or a seat back (such as is common in all classes of commercial airline service) eliminates much of the unpredictability of social encounter as well as much of the delight. There are other motivations, of course, for the increased singularity (and decreasing sociality) of contemporary eating space—from drop-down tray tables stored in seat pockets to the proliferation of single-serving meals that are easy to eat while working, walking, or orbiting, to "nonstop" menus and service—such as the practice of constantly working and the associated appeal of multitasking.[24] It needs to be noted as well that the notion of devoting eating space and time to social exchange does not appear to be deeply embedded in the *habitus* of American life. The following illustration of the redefinitions of eating space occurs in the rarified conditions of microgravity, thousands of miles from Earth and home.

In anticipation of designing a space station intended to be a laboratory for investigating daily living experiences over an extended period of time, NASA administrator Dr. George Mueller decided that a study was needed to reconsider the psychophysiological, safety, and efficiency issues of the capsule interior; in 1967 he hired Raymond Loewy of the industrial and interior design firm Loewy/Snaith (New York) to undertake this investigation.[25] Loewy was born in France and unschooled in design when he began working his way up after arriving in the United States as a young man. Loewy and his team immersed themselves in "extensive indoctrination of space matters" as the habitability consultants; they submitted numerous drawings and full-scale mock-ups of a variety of functional elements, which were also based, he said, "upon logic and educated intuition."[26] Loewy argued for three requirements of extraterrestrial habitation: a space to sleep that could double as a place to withdraw from others, a means of eating meals face-to-face, and a porthole to the outside. Of all of Loewy's designs, the face-to-face tray table was most closely replicated and also the shortest lived (figure 16.4).

To accommodate flights of long duration, NASA had redesigned the space food system as well as the interior. Engineers and nutritionists developed preselected menus of dehydrated, frozen, and thermostabilized bacon squares and strawberry cubes to be stored in onboard freezers, then set into individual magnetized warming trays. These were, in turn, plugged into the center table where the food would be injected with water and eaten with conventional cutlery at morning, noon, and evening. A version of Loewy's centripetal design proved to be a convergence of food storage, preparation, serving, and eating—nearly an entire food axis within close proximity— yet hardly a model of stable formality associated with face-to-face dining.

Despite the layering of wet and dry elements, the interlocking of components, and the Velcro-hinging of astronauts into correct positions, a science writer who studied flight recordings and interviewed astronauts describes eating in Skylab as "*Rabelaisian* from the point of view of squalor, if not abundance."[27] Henry Cooper, Jr., also reports that the breakfast food cans were smaller than the holes provided and when astronauts opened the tray lids the food floated off. They had no more success in rehydrating the solid food, as the process often caused the food to explode from its plastic-covered aluminum case and blast food particles all over the wardroom, splattering walls and windows, the grid flooring and ceilings. Water injected into the food contained air bubbles that in weightlessness could never float to the surface; they remained mixed in the water, giving astronauts gas and rupturing their food packs. What didn't explode was difficult to deliver to the mouth, astronauts reported to Cooper. One described spooning a bit of rehydrated egg and then stopping his hand to ask someone to pass the salt while the egg continued on its trajectory toward his face. At first, astronauts had to bring their mouths down very close to the food,

16.4

Eating in Skylab, the first international space station, at a tray table designed by Raymond Loewy. Courtesy of NASA.

16.5

Russian and U.S. crew gather at the ward table in the International Space Station, 2000. Courtesy of NASA.

JAMIE HORWITZ

hoping to shovel it in before the food flew off; with practice they learned to keep the spoon in continuous motion.

> They developed a smooth, arc-like motion tipping the spoon slowly as it went so that it would always be directly in back of whatever was on it. And they had to keep their mouths open and perfectly aligned with the spoon arc because there would be no way to stop the spoonful once it was on its way.[28]

The design of the next generations of Skylab food storage, preparation, and eating did not require astronauts to gather face-to-face at mealtimes and the foods no longer require hydration. Now that a standard wardroom table has replaced Loewy's tray tables designed for togetherness, meals appear to have become more improvisational. Astronauts are seen popping little carrots in their mouths while working at computers or staring out the window; only on special occasions, such as when docking with the space shuttle that rotates crew, delivers supplies, and removes waste, do the astronauts gather for a celebratory meal and commemorative photograph. On the occasion of docking with a supply ship, the Alpha crew log from December 9, 2000, reads:

> We take about 45 minutes out for dinner with the Endeavour crew. We have the first IMAX shot ready in the wardroom—trying to get a group shot with everyone around the table. . . . After chow, everyone back to their "post" and we continue to work the schedule.[29]

The NASA photo file shows Russian and US crew loosely gathered, more widely spaced, and differently seated than they would have been at Loewy's tray table design (figure 16.5). One person eats out of a can with a fork. The figures might be mistaken for hikers pausing to eat from their backpacks, if it were not for the fresh fruit tethered with Velcro straps to prevent it from floating away.

The cultural context of dining in space gains complexity with post-glasnost orbiting as Russian and U.S. crews bring provisions from their own country. The United States provides foods and snacks for dining alone or together. "Some American crew members are content to eat 'on the run' and by themselves," NASA nutritionists write, "whereas many European crew members prefer eating a complete meal as a group."[30] However, both "U.S. and Russian work schedules are structured to encourage common meals as much as possible," explains Marilyn Dudley-Rowe, a specialist in design for multinational crews in extreme-environment research stations. She adds: "Now, the big questions are: will there be common food stocks aboard ISS? Will there be common meals among all occupants?"[31]

> *Around lunchtime, we missed another Earth Orbs site, and we figure it could be for several reasons—Yuri's laptop is gaining a couple of minutes each day. . . . After lunch, Shep worked on the IMS database and bar code readers.*[32]

While the absence of food-related comments with regard to "lunch" points to the larger, well-documented subject of a disinterest in food during space travel, meals themselves still mark the sequence of a day's work and astronauts maintain the convention of suspending work at mid-day.[33]

● ● ●

Parallels to this tendency toward encapsulated eating (as displayed in the many previous examples) can be found at a very different scale in writings of urban theorists who have adopted the term "capsules and networks" as a trope for the dominant spatial structures emerging during the later half of the twentieth century. For example, Manuel Castells theorizes that in the organization of information capitalism there is a *space of flow* that is increasingly disconnected from a *space of place*. Thus, airports, shopping malls, big box stores, and fast-food franchises are disconnected from their immediate surroundings and simultaneously fed by, and dependent on, the expansive network of electronic, interurban, and intermodal connectivity. By hyperfocusing on the *space of flow,* Dutch urbanists suggest, it is difficult to see that we live not in networks, but in capsules and in a "capsular logic."[34]

Such apparent cellular or encapsulated realities, whether at the scale of suburban big box stores or the "TV while you eat" booth, operate in a less visible, yet equally dynamic, network of connections. Tables are evocative objects in this realm, prompting and positing, cueing and construing what is focal and peripheral. An intriguingly flexible table mediating the extremes of solely individuated and collective experience is given shape in a set of designs for use in microgravity by Ted Krueger and Jeff Shannon, professor and dean of architecture respectively at the University of Arkansas; their students developed a series of individual yet interlocking tables that allow astronauts to use a wearable table top alone or in groups.[35] In this case a table represents simultaneously a space of individuality and the shared space of collectivity.

 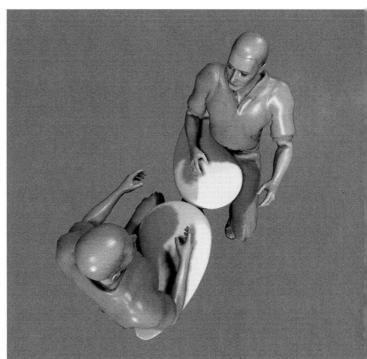

16.6, 16.7
"Wearable" tables serve individual needs and are designed so that they can be grouped. Design team: Gustavaus Ferguson, Nick Kozlowski, Brent Ruple, and Grant Smith. Faculty: Ted Krueger and Jerry Wall. NASA contact: David Fitts. Courtesy of the School of Architecture, University of Arkansas, and the designers.

1. Luce Giard, "Doing Cooking," in *The Practice of Everyday Life,* vol. 2, *Living and Cooking,* by Michel de Certeau, Luce Giard, and Pierre Mayol, ed. Luce Giard, trans. Timothy J. Yomasik, rev. ed. (Minneapolis: University of Minnesota Press, 1998), 197.

2. Henri Lefebvre, "The Everyday and Everydayness," in *Architecture of the Everyday,* ed. Steven Harris and Deborah Berke (New York: Princeton Architectural Press, 1997), 34.

3. Dell Upton, "Architecture in Everyday Life," *New Literary History* 33 (2002): 707–723. Upton notes this shift as well as its evidence in Mary McLeod's discussion of Lefebvre's influence on architectural discourse in "Henri Lefebvre's Critique of Everyday Life: An Introduction," in Harris and Berke, eds., *Architecture of the Everyday,* 9–29.

4. See Elizabeth Collins Cromley, *Alone Together: A History of New York's Early Apartments* (Ithaca: Cornell University Press, 1990), and "Transforming the Food Axis: Houses, Tools, Modes of Analysis," *Material History Review,* no. 44 (fall 1996): 8–20.

5. Cromley, "Transforming the Food Axis," 10.

6. Upton, "Architecture in Everyday Life," 720.

7. The idea that ritual festivals—or less ritualized periods of departure from the everyday, such as "Spring Break"—represent the clear boundaries of liminality was first enunciated in 1909 by Arnold van Gennep in *The Rites of Passage* (trans. Monika B. Vizedom and Gabrielle L. Caffee [Chicago: University of Chicago Press, 1960]), and developed through many studies by Victor Turner and Michael Bristol. An exploration of the political and aesthetic context of liminality can be found in Richard Schechner, *The Future of Ritual: Writings on Culture and Performance* (London: Routledge, 1993).

8. The quotations from Gerry Thomas and details about the development of the TV dinner were taken from an article on Vlasic's website, <http://www.vlasic.com/swanson/celebration.html> (accessed October 6, 2002).

9. Anna McCarthy, *Ambient Television: Visual Culture and Public Space* (Durham, N.C.: Duke University Press, 2001), 219.

10. Ibid., 222.

11. The spatial pattern of restaurants and lunch counters in department stores is diagrammed in the Architectural Record Book by Dr. Louis Parnes, *Designing Stores That Pay: Organic Design and Layout for Efficient Merchandising* (New York: American Institute of Architects, 1948).

12. Ibid., 82–83.

13. "Airport Café Diners to Have View of Field," *Chicago Daily News,* March 18, 1948.

14. Anthony Jahn, director of Marshall Field Archives, personal communication with the author, November 2000.

15. Ibid.

16. Example of menu advertisement; Cloud Room menus are kept in the Marshall Field Archives in their original building on State Street in Chicago.

17. Press releases, in the Marshall Field Archives.

18. Although none of the photographs show the phones, they were mentioned in conversations I had with former restaurant managers.

19. Michel Serres develops the analogy between the medieval cathedral and the modern airport in his book *La legende des anges* (Paris: Flammarion, 1993), in English as *Angels: A Modern Myth* (Paris: Flammarion, 1995). For a discussion of Serres's idea in an exhibition catalogue about the perception

of contemporary airports, see *Airport,* ed. Steven Bode and Jeremy Millar (London: Photographers' Gallery in association with Netherlands Foto Institut, Rotterdam, and Netherlands Design Institute, Amsterdam, 1997), particularly Bode's essay "Planespotting," pp. 130–132.

20. Marmand Mattelart, "Mapping Modernity: Utopia and Communications Networks," trans. Anne-Marie Glasheen, in *Mappings,* ed. Denis Cosgrove (London: Reaktion Books, 1999), 168–192.

21. This account of Elmer Henderson's suit against the Interstate Commerce Commission and the role it played in the history of civil rights and desegregation can be found in Henderson's obituary by David Stout, "Elmer Henderson, 88, Dies; Father of Major Rights Case," *New York Times,* July 19, 2001, A25.

22. Material in this paragraph is slightly paraphrased from ibid.

23. Upton, "Architecture in Everyday Life," 720.

24. See, for example, Jamie Horwitz, "Working Lunch," *Architectural Design* 72, no. 6 (November/December 2002): 38–43.

25. Rebecca Dalvesco, "Architecture in Motion: The Interior Design of Skylab," in *Building for Space Travel,* ed. John Zukowsky, exhib. cat. (New York: Harry N. Abrams, 2001), 162–167.

26. Raymond Loewy discusses his preparation for this project and in part reproduces "The Habitability Study Shuttle Orbiter" in Loewy, *Industrial Design* (Woodstock, N.Y.: Overlook Press, 1979), 205–217.

27. Harry S. F. Cooper, Jr., *A House in Space* (New York: Holt, Rinehart, and Winston, 1976), 41.

28. Ibid., 41, 47 (quotation).

29. "Expedition One December Crew Log," *NASA Human Space Flight,* December 28, 2000, <http://spaceflight.nasa.gov/station/crew/exp1/exp1shepdec.html> (accessed January 2003).

30. Helen W. Lane and Dale A. Schoeller, "Overview: History of Nutrition and Spaceflight," in *Nutrition in Spaceflight and Weightlessness Models,* ed. Lane and Schoeller (Boca Raton: CRC Press, 2000), 7, 8.

31. Marilyn Dudley-Rowe, e-mail communications with the author, September 20, 2001.

32. "Expedition One December Crew Log."

33. Rarely mentioned, "space sickness" that makes some crew nauseated and gives others vivid hallucinations in which the entire world is perceived to be upside down is discussed in Rebecca Dalvesco, *Dwell,* August 2001, 70–71.

34. These ideas appear in many permutations in the journal *OASE,* no. 54 (winter 2001), which contains papers delivered at a colloquium titled "The Generic City and the Old Metropolis" organized by the Research Group Urbanism and Architecture at the Catholic University in Leuven, Belgium, February 4–5, 2000. See especially in that issue Lieven De Cauter, "The Capsule and the Network: Some Notes toward a General Theory."

35. Ted Krueger, "The Architecture of Extreme Environments," in *Space Architecture,* a special issue of *Architectural Design* (70, no. 2 [March 2000]), guest ed. Rachel Armstrong (London: Wiley-Academic, 2000), 48–59.

EMBODIED TASTE

17

BUTCHER'S WHITE: WHERE THE ART MARKET MEETS THE MEAT MARKET IN NEW YORK CITY

DORITA HANNAH

PHOTOGRAPHS OF THE NEW YORK CITY
MEATPACKING DISTRICT, SUMMER 2002, BY SHULI SADÉ

Slaughterhouses, along with the Museum, make up a system in which the ambivalence defining the sacred nucleus is at work: the slaughterhouses are the negative pole, the generator of repulsion, the centrifuge. . . . Museums, the pole of attraction, are centripetal. But within the heart of one the other is hidden. At the heart of beauty lies a murder, a sacrifice, a killing (no beauty without blood).

—DENIS HOLLIER, *Against Architecture: The Writings of Georges Bataille*

"Flesh," both alive and dead, forms a significant presence within Manhattan's meatpacking district. Caught like a relic within the net of the metropolis, the area has long associations with the marketplace and, until recently, almost exclusively with the meat industry and transvestite prostitution. However, more upmarket trades have infiltrated the district with the conversion of abandoned processing plants into fashion houses, nightclubs, restaurants, and art galleries. Although the common explanation for this phenomenon is economic, "lower rents for larger spaces," there are also more profound and complicated reasons, which emerge through an investigation of the visible and invisible in the everyday life of the area.

In "Ghosts in the City," Michel de Certeau and Luce Giard see the urban environment as "a fascinating theatre" transformed, by unusual and fragmentary pasts, into "an immense memory where many poetics proliferate." Awakening the stories that sleep in the streets reveals "An Uncanniness of the 'Already There'" and creates a city to be imagined, dreamed, and lived in.[1] What follows is an attempt to stir the phantoms of the meatpacking district, through an investigation of both the existing area and butchery itself that reveals a fresher, fleshier way of approaching art gallery space and the city.

Rather than drawing on the discourse surrounding contemporary art and architecture, I approach the gallery via the slaughterhouse. Within five main sections a series of dualities is highlighted, particular to the district under investigation; the human body is doubled with the animal body, the temple with slaughterhouse and museum, the craft of butchery with carnage, and the cleansing of space with its contamination. The first section, "Flesh," establishes the materiality of the subject by setting the scene of the contemporary meatpacking district in Manhattan. From this thick description the uncanny manifests itself as the absent "Sacrifice," a discussion of which forms the second part of the essay. The third section, "Slaughter," establishes the history of meatpacking in New York and demonstrates its link to further doublings inherent in the horror of killing and mechanization. The taint of killing in the slaughterhouse leads to a desire for "Purification" in the art gallery with its clean white walls, investigated in the fourth section. However, the reuse of existing buildings also suggests an inherent corruption. The final main section therefore proposes the principle of "Putrification" as a potential strategy for the presentation of art and future development within the area.

FLESH (THE SITE)

In New York City the meat trade is currently focused in Hunts Point in the Bronx, with a smaller (and shrinking) market on the fringes of the West Village of Manhattan. The latter provides the site for this investigation, which, like flesh itself, is both visceral and vulnerable. Physical corruption, violence, and mortality haunt this highly sensory environment, which is currently undergoing a considerable transformation.

The district forms a curious triangle on the western side of Manhattan, where the named streets of Greenwich Village tangle with the numbered streets of Chelsea, and

DORITA HANNAH

17.1

17.2

17.3

DORITA HANNAH

is uniquely defined by a sensory onslaught that begins in the air as the odors of raw meat carry beyond its delineated boundaries. The distinctive stench of dismembered animals is unfamiliar in the contemporary city, constituting an estrangement for the city dwellers who tend to purchase their meat preportioned and plastic-wrapped from supermarkets and boutique butcher shops. Evidence of the raw also manifests itself underfoot, through the slippery substance of fat—constantly sluiced away with water, puddling in the gutters, and trickling between the cobblestones. Men in white rubber boots and blood-stained aprons chase the debris from chilly plasticated interiors with high-pressure hoses, saturating the sidewalks with a constant dampness. The cobblestone streets, patched with bitumen, testify to an area (until recently) considered unworthy of upkeep by the metropolitan authorities. They present an antique charm, the result of neglect rather than any nostalgia for the past.

The area, with its particular odor, materiality, and historical associations in the city, constitutes what de Certeau and Giard would call a "legendary object," an urban persona conjuring up other worlds:

> These wild objects, stemming from indecipherable pasts, are for us the equivalent of what the gods of antiquity were, the "spirits" of the place. Like their divine ancestors, these objects play the role of actors in the city, not because of what they do or say but because their strangeness is silent, as well as their existence concealed from actuality. Their withdrawal makes people speak—it generates narratives—and it allows action; through its ambiguity, it "authorizes" spaces of operations.[2]

A close look at the area reveals the characteristics of this wild object.

Decay signifies itself everywhere. Paint peels, steel rusts, mortar dissolves, cladding lifts, and pavements crack. Old fire escapes and balconies cling like burnt lace to the sides of buildings with bricked-up windows. They are redundant and dangerous as they flake, corrode, and threaten to fall in pieces to the sidewalk below. This is mirrored in microcosm by a shifting organic detritus on sidewalks, soiled cardboard boxes and plastic bags leaking indefinable matter. Organic waste oozes and stains at the boundary between the public zone and the private interiors of the processing plants. Puddles clogged with flotsam and jetsam lie still and fetid in the shadows.

These details serve to signal the area as one where death is prevalent and where matter, both built and biological, is prone to perish.

For almost twenty-four hours a day, there is dynamic activity behind the steel doors and plastic-strip screens of the meatpacking houses. Trucks deliver huge carcasses of flesh, which are hooked and hoisted into the cool interiors on rattling overhead rails. These are then transformed into smaller vacuum-sealed plastic portions, leaving the various establishments in cardboard boxes before dawn. Health and safety are a constant issue in these places presided over by the local office of the USDA (United States Department of Agriculture). This also forms a reminder that infection and disease are an imminent danger. Butchers work the meat with their sharp knives or stand at machines, which grind, slice, and seal the flesh. It is then parceled into orders for the various restaurants and collected by trucks for delivery. The color and texture of animal flesh seem rich and vibrant under the bright lights of these white interiors with their concrete floors, washable laminate walls, and stainless steel cladding. The floors, often awash with blood and fat, are constantly doused with water in this daily cycle of reduction and morcellation.

The meatpacking industry continues to serve Manhattan's restaurant industry: portioning, packing, and delivering orders for the city's chefs. But the district no longer deals exclusively in the raw material. A range of restaurants, diners, bars, and cafés, as well as specialist catering businesses, have opened up in the area. Clubs, design stores, and fashion boutiques are tucking themselves into the domain of refrigerator trucks and processing-plant cool rooms, characterized by low-lying nineteenth-century warehouses, with steel awnings, roller doors, and metal runners adorned with hooks. The local transvestites are now upstaged by models and actors who, surrounded by film crews and photographers, utilize the well-worn walls of industrial buildings as backdrops for the new mediatized "grunge" aesthetic of popular culture. Commodification of flesh is stepping up in the area, with its transformation well under way.

Amid this multilayered spectacle of flesh, art galleries are also opening up in the area, extending the Chelsea art market into the meat market. Within hushed white interiors, fine art is exhibited by new and established dealers who have converted abandoned meat coolers and warehouses into exhibition spaces. The industrial character of the area is being utilized within the built fabric of these renovated spaces, which continue to maintain the established white cube aesthetic associated with con-

DORITA HANNAH

temporary art galleries. Yet these spaces, as reinhabited processing plants, belie the classic modern chic of the traditional white cube galleries. As with the clubs, restaurants, and design stores, they are superimposing their specific spatial characteristics on a powerful typology: that of butchery, which has profound associations with death and sacrifice. This secret intrusion of terror disturbs the aesthetic dimension of such boutique venues, causing a spatial estrangement.

In the new millennium, New York's meatpacking district maintains its tenuous autonomy as the professions and industries within it shift and realign themselves. Binding them all, however, is this uncanny doubling of flesh, alive and dead. The dead flesh of the beast is dismembered and reduced to parceled portions, its residue filtering out onto the street. Within the same precinct it is also prepared, cooked, and devoured. Simultaneously, live human flesh is displayed, served, and surveyed in nightclubs, manufactured and controlled in the fashion industry, and negotiated over in the dark alleys. The body of the inhabitant doubles with the body of the beast. Flesh is doubled and redoubled. It is both visible and invisible. This is significant and unique for an area debating issues of change and the future. It also has implications for exhibiting, consuming, and trading art.

The original role of the meatpacking district was the wholesale business of buying and slaughtering live animals and then distributing their carcasses and portions thereof to retailers. Although the slaughtering is carried out off-site and the meat shipped in, at the core of the business remains the death of the beast; and at the origin of the slaying is a sacrifice. As a "legendary object," this area conjures up the ancient sacrifice of the beast and all that it implies. The doubling therefore is most evident in relation to the sacred and profane. De Certeau writes: "What interests the historian of everyday life is the invisible."[3] In the meatpacking district, the phantom of the sacrifice haunts the slaughterhouse without slaughter, and therefore the boutique refurbishments within.

SACRIFICE (THE ACT)

Sacrificial slaying is an act performed to establish or sustain a proper relationship with the divine, through an offering consecrated by its own destruction. This offering/victim acts as an intermediary between the sacred and the profane. Its existence allows for the two worlds to be present and interpenetrable while remaining distinct. As

Henri Hubert and Marcel Mauss point out in *Sacrifice: Its Nature and Function,* sacralization and desacralization are interdependent elements of the sacrifice.[4] The duality embedded in the act of sacrifice is pursued by Sigfried Giedion, who, examining "the animal and the sacred impulse," establishes the double meaning of the word *sacred,* which includes both the "holy" and the "unclean": "This ambivalence is merely another form of interlocking visible and invisible. . . . Animals are simultaneously objects of adoration, life giving food and humble quarry."[5] According to Giedion the double significance of the animal, as an object of worship and as a source of nourishment, is linked to the concept of sanctity. Such ambivalence and doubling allowed the animal to be considered simultaneously as an object of veneration and food, and therefore to be truly sacred.

Standing before the Polytechnic Association of the American Institute in June 1865, the New York butcher Thomas De Voe introduced his topic—abattoirs—as "uninteresting and unsuitable to 'ears polite.'" However, he soon stressed that although the slaughterhouse was a place for "converting animals into food," its origins lay in the sacrifice and that it was the office of priests to slay their victims as offerings for the gods and for food. "Thus we also learn that the first butchers were those that held the highest and most holy office, but at what period the killing became a separate trade or profession it may be difficult, if not impossible to determine."[6]

In Judeo-Christian traditions the slaying of the beast was associated with the altar, which only the purified could approach and upon, by, or beneath which the blood was poured. Sacrifice, linked to a cleansing through the shedding of blood, establishes the altar as the site for both slaughter and purification. This doubling between killing and worship concerned Georges Bataille, who saw the spectacle of sacrifice as creating a rupture in everyday life because it represented "the troubled feeling where a vertiginous horror and drunkenness come together, where the reality of death itself, of the sudden coming of death, holds a meaning heavier than life, heavier—and more glacial."[7] The confrontation of mortality is an inherent part of the sacrifice, which demands some form of surrender.

Sacrifice could be described as a creation by means of loss and destruction, which is inextricably linked to violence and death. René Girard, in *Violence and the Sacred,* claims that all violence can be described in terms of sacrifice.[8] He considers sacrifice and murder as reciprocal, with the former preventing the latter through the

DORITA HANNAH

17.4

17.5

DORITA HANNAH

act of collective substitution. Sacrifice therefore becomes a civilizing act, as it absorbs pent-up tensions within society. This conflation of sacrifice and murder presents a further uncanny doubling. The following investigation of butchery, and its complex connotations, reveals violence and destruction as ever-present in the act of slaughter.

SLAUGHTER (THE ART OF BUTCHERY)

Although the large-scale conversion of live animals into food, within Christian societies, loses a direct link with the sacrifice (a connection that persists in Jewish and Muslim cultures), a transformation still takes place. This transformation is reliant on the art of the butcher, no longer the high priest of sacred slaughter but still a skilled and specialized artisan. For Giedion, who documents the industrialization of the meat industry in *Mechanization Takes Command*, the nineteenth-century reduction of butcher's work to component operations changed the orientation of slaughter "from the miraculous to the utilitarian."[9] Yet the horrors of death and destruction cling to this profession through both act and association. The trajectory of the butcher and his art took him from sanctified priest to skilled artisan and finally industrial workman, linking him inextricably to the spectacle of death.

From the time New York was colonized, independent butchers purchased animals from drovers and brought them to slaughter in the city within buildings known as "shambles." Often located near residential neighborhoods, these poorly ventilated timber buildings became controversial and contaminated sites of waste, from which blood flowed onto the streets and unpleasant smells of live and dead animals hung in the air. The public could also hear the sounds of animals dying.[10] By 1656 the regulation of both the slaughterhouses and the profession of butchery was under way. "Slaughter farmers" were designated to oversee and control the killing of animals in the city, a change that gave rise to the erection of public abattoirs. But as the city grew and the value of residential land rose, the presence of these sites of carnage and killing became untenable. In 1720 the public petitioned for their removal "in oreder [sic] that more convenient and ornamental buildings may be erected there, and in that neighborhood, which is now retarded by occasion of said slaughterhouses."[11] The act of slaughter was no longer acceptable in areas undergoing social transformation.

Public protest and issues of health and hygiene are bound up within the history of meatpacking in New York. Slaughterhouses in the city were clearly unwanted and increasingly associated with disease. As the city became more cosmopolitan and residential areas were upgraded, the conspicuous presence of killing and death was considered repellent. This resulted in the constant relocation of the abattoirs, pushed to the margins of an ever-expanding metropolis.

Negative attitudes toward the industry are inherent within the English language itself. The words *slaughter* and *butchery* contain double meanings that collapse violence into a time-honored act and skill, conflating a trade with a crime. *Slaughter* is defined as the killing of animals for food as well as the brutal slaying of people and is associated with the savage, the carnal, and the excessive. A *butcher* is one who kills and deals in animal flesh, as well as an indiscriminate and brutal killer of people— "a man of blood."[12] *Butchery* is not only the business of a butcher and the place where animals are butchered but also a barbarous and cruel act of killing. It is "a place where blood is shed."[13] The blood of the beast becomes conflated with the blood of man. A *slaughterhouse* is the place where animals are butchered as well as a scene of massacre and carnage. This association was used to effect by Sergei Eisenstein in his 1924 film *Strike*. The scene titled "Carnage," which depicted the killing of 1,800 striking workers, was interspersed with the images of a bull being slain by a butcher. Eisenstein intended "to extract the maximum effect of bloody horror" through "a demonstration of the real horrors of the slaughterhouse where cattle are slaughtered and skinned."[14]

Girard would contend that such excessive violence manifests itself when there is a lack of sacrificial outlet. He maintains that sacrifice continues to have a real function in society because it protects the community from its own violence, restores harmony, reinforces the social fabric, and establishes order. Violence is a form of contagion to be kept in check. Lying at the "heart and secret soul of the sacred," violence is double in nature. This dual aspect enables it to occur both legitimately and illegitimately. As Girard writes, "Blood serves to illustrate the point that the same substance can stain or cleanse, contaminate or purify, drive men to fury and murder or appease their anger and restore them to life."[15] Butchery therefore presents itself as a spectacle of horror and a necessary violence as well as an established and skilled profession.

Although the artisanal craft of the butcher has evolved into a production-line activity, the hand of the butcher cannot be replaced by automation. This was noted by Giedion; in *Mechanization Takes Command*, he maintains that full mechanization in slaughterhouses was never possible because "the material to be handled . . . largely refuses to submit to the machine."[16] The animal's body still requires the particular qualities of the human body to supplement the process; "only the organic can adapt to the organic." The human body remains implicated and involved in the death and dismemberment of animals for food because the hand must still guide the instrument that performs the transition from life to death efficiently and humanely. The butcher is a required character in this *danse macabre,* which involves "the eternal terror of death. The horror resides in the sudden, incalculable destruction of an organic creature."[17]

Giedion was struck by the complete "neutrality" of the act of slaughter, which carried out this transition from life to death. Writing in 1947, he asks whether this neutrality toward mass killing has had a further effect on us, claiming it may be lodged deep in the roots of our time; "It did not bare itself on a large scale until the War, when whole populations, as defenseless as animals hooked head downwards on the traveling chain, were obliterated with trained neutrality."[18] Here is where the everyday life and anonymous history collide with epic history. The death of the beast confronts us not only with our own mortality but also with our own cruelty—an indifference in the face of death en masse.

The meatpacking industry in Manhattan may no longer be directly involved with the physical killing of animals, but the specter of mass death clings to the carcasses, viewed by the public, as they are transferred from trucks into interiors that are out of bounds to the general public. Though part of everyday life, they are also shrouded from the gaze. As with human death, we are removed from the spectacle of the animal corpse in everyday life. The work of the butcher, like that of the undertaker, becomes veiled and taboo.

Through the act-of-sacrifice and the art-of-slaughter, historic and cultural associations establish both the district and the meatpacking houses themselves as legendary objects. Links to the sacred and the profane, as well as to mass carnage, trigger complex reactions from the human bodies that brush up against them. We therefore emerge from the internal labyrinth of the slaughterhouse to purify ourselves in the art gallery/museum. However, because art galleries in the meatpacking district reinhabit processing plants, the purification takes place within the very buildings where the beast was dismembered. The washable white interiors of butchery are skinned, gutted, and relined with smooth white walls for the display of art. The spaces are transformed into places where, as Pierre Bourdieu and Alain Darbel suggest, "bareness and lack of ornamentation encourage the aesthetic which leads to the beatific vision."[19]

PURIFICATION (THE ART OF ARCHITECTURE)

For Georges Bataille, the sacred horror represented in the slaughter and dismemberment of the beast also confronted the "unseemliness" of the human condition, which in turn triggered a "pathological need for cleanliness."[20] Because the abattoir had lost its links with the sacrifice, and therefore the sacred, it became associated primarily with the profane. The public considered it an unclean place and consequently one to be avoided: "They exile themselves, by way of an antidote, in an amorphous world, where there is no longer anything terrible."[21] The museum consequently presented a location for the public to escape the unsightliness of butchery. Visiting the museum was seen by Bataille as a purification whereby the architecture filtered the crowds, who left the building "purified and fresh." Yet the museum remains a temple without a sacrifice because it lacks violence and loss.

The physical environment of the gallery serves to consecrate the artwork by isolating and concentrating it within an abstract atmosphere. This consecration bestows a power on the material object to transport the spectator to immaterial matters. Bourdieu and Darbel argue in *The Love of Art* that the gallery's white and silent environment "opposes itself to the world of everyday life, just as the sacred does to the profane."[22] Bataille would refer to it as a "sacred instant," as the work no longer exists in the reality of past or present but constitutes "its own reality."[23] Cultural works, produced within a field of restricted production, are therefore elevated and isolated as "pure," "abstract," and "esoteric."

Bourdieu and Bataille consider the pristine modern gallery an elaborate mise-en-scène constructing the idea of sacred space. This space increases the value of the artwork by removing it from the body of the artist and preserving it in a rarified environment, thereby suggesting longevity if not immortality. However, the persistence of slaughter, specific to the meatpacking plant, confounds this theory as the past architecture remains an inescapable palimpsest. The placement of art within a space where once butchers dissected meat collapses the work of the artisan/butcher on that of the artist/creator. It sets up an oscillation in which the work, hung like a carcass, is haunted by sacrifice and violence and the consecration of the work is linked to a certain economy of death.

Bataille's opposition of abattoir and museum, as one repels and the other attracts, creates a useful tension in which one cannot exist without the other. Denis Hollier points out that although the two institutions remain distinct, "museums have a strange way of following in the footsteps of the slaughterhouses."[24] He illustrates this observation by examining the abattoir of La Villette, established on the outskirts of Paris by Baron Haussmann in the mid-nineteenth century to replace the more central slaughterhouses he demolished as part of the logic of modernizing urban space. The smaller neighborhood butcheries were recycled into urban parks just as, a century later, La Villette itself was recycled into a park of science and industry. "Thanks to this conversion a nice, clean expenditure takes the place of a dirty one and the visitor takes over for the worker."[25] The contaminated site of slaughter is purified by the park or the museum. With Haussmann's Paris and Mitterrand's La Villette, the slaughterhouses were eradicated and replaced by more seemly public programs. This strategy of returning to a tabula rasa cannot help but leave traces, but the traces are faint and become principally inscribed into archives. In New York's meatpacking district, the white cube gallery is deliberately inserted into the existing built environment of the meat market.

Within the galleries that reoccupy disused meat-processing plants, the walls of modernity exhibit the quest for cleanliness through the simple gesture of the color white: white that blinds the eye and veils the surface, white as a freezer where the cold kills the microbes, the white of cleanliness where dirt cannot be concealed, the white of purity to sanctify. Butcher's white. Disused meatpacking plants hover between a lingering putrification of past use and what Bourdieu calls the art market's desire for "the purified sublimated pleasures demanded by the pure aesthetic."[26] As bare and skeletal structures they recall the stripped carcass of the butcher's beast. They are white cubes with a difference. But the persistence of white, coating the surface of these bleached spaces, proves to be the thinnest of membranes.

In *White Walls, Designer Dresses,* Mark Wigley examines white walls as a phenomenon of modern architecture, which sought to clean up the mess and fuss of nineteenth-century clutter, clearing excess away in favor of a sleek, smooth, clean surface. He asks: "What violence necessarily accompanies, and even constructs, the seemingly innocent look? What are its guilty secrets?"[27] In eliminating decoration, removing all distraction, and eradicating the superfluous, this new form of architecture posited a civilization in transition from the sensual to the intellectual, from the tactile to the visual. This "strategic blindness" appealed to the look of hygiene rather than to its reality. Whitewash, purifying the eye rather than the architecture, is like talcum powder or a clean white shirt on the unwashed body, or bandages concealing diseased flesh. "The white surfaces that traditionally mark cleanliness do just that, they mark rather than effect it."[28] In butchery "shrouding" or "clothing" gives a smooth, dense appearance to the fat. Cotton shrouds, veiling the flesh, absorb the blood and some of the bruise discoloration on the carcass. Analysts of the industry observe, "The main purpose of the shroud is to improve the appearance of the carcass for the potential buyer."[29]

We find ourselves implicated once more in flesh. The modern body may have attempted to represent itself as clean, smooth, and sleek through its hermetically sealed white interiors, but the postmodern body is proving more problematic. As Kim Levin writes: "This uneasy contemporary body is all too aware of its visceral innards, its mortality, its evanescence, its decrepitude."[30] The modernist notion of purification has become contaminated. The white space, which cannot stay forever fresh, is showing signs of wear and tear—leaks and discoloration, cracks and stains.

Unlike the ubiquitous white cube, the gallery space in the meatpacking district can never be a tabula rasa. Neither the preceding architecture nor its history can ever be completely wiped away to create a hermetically sealed white cube. It is haunted by dismembered flesh. The 1996 work of the English artist Damien Hirst, *Some Comfort Gained from the Acceptance in the Inherent Lies in Everything,* could serve as a visual representation of this phenomenon. The dissected bodies of cows, isolated in a number of vitrines filled with formaldehyde, create a spectral amalgam that draws our attention to the fragmentation of the beast and the space it now occupies. Hirst, who aims to "corrupt" the environment,[31] creates a tension between the glass cases, the space they occupy, and the suspended contents they hold at bay. These tanks reflect and disturb the calm control of the white cube. They represent the containers of natural history museums and their desire to arrest decay. The large glass vessels that maintain us at a scientific distance conserve flesh, which has lost its richness, color, and texture. We are confronted with a horror without blood or decay.

DORITA HANNAH

Whilst Hirst's *Cows* reflects a preserved, bleached, and sanitized gallery, Jana Sterbak's 1987 *Flesh Dress* exposes it as a more visceral and perishable space. *Vanitas: Flesh Dress for an Albino Anorectic* is sewn from 50 pounds of salted flank steak. This garment of beef is suspended fresh in the art gallery and then allowed to age and perish. At first it stretches under its own weight and drips blood. Then it shrinks, discolors, desiccates, and darkens.[32] This memento mori reminds us of the fallibility and mortality of our bodies and is more akin to the doubling of sacrifice and slaughter than the cool taxidermy of Hirst. The *Flesh Dress* recalls Elaine Scarry's claim that the act of creating can be represented as "the turning of the body inside out."[33] This notion of reversing the body linings is an attempt to disrupt the binary oppositions between the interior and exterior and project the "awareness of aliveness" out onto the object world.[34] Sterbak's *Flesh Dress* allows a transformation to occur. As it deteriorates it also corrupts space.

Flesh, either alive or dead, is destined to eventually perish. Meat, whether vacuum-packed, plastic-wrapped, freeze-dried, frozen, or cured, can never remain fresh. All art, like the body, is in a constant state of decay, unless science intervenes to arrest this decomposition. The museum with its conservators, vitrines, and controlled environments provides the science to convince the public that art and culture endures. This system, which purifies the public, also cryogenically suspends the art.

Whereas purification implodes the body, the museum, and the work of art, "putrification," as an organic phenomenon, provides a dynamic system of expansion. Spoilage, infestation, and decay allow for dead flesh to be acted on and therefore become re-active. The notion of art that rots calls into question the economy in which the value of an artwork, and its surrounding architecture, is dependent on their own stability, immutability, and longevity.

PUTRIFICATION (AGAINST MUSEUMIFICATION)

Putrification is associated with the meatpacking district, through the general decay in the built environment, evidence of organic waste, and its relationship to slaughter. As a "legendary object" it acknowledges the complex urban debris, surviving as a ruin within an unknown, strange city. It represents the remains of a waning past, surprising us and creating exotic effects, as well as bumps in the smoothness of the imagined homogeneity of the metropolis. Its persistence and its psychic charge suggest a resistance to gentrification.

"Gentrification" could be viewed as a form of purification, exorcising the phantasmagoria. Linked to ideas of "urban renewal," according to which areas threatened with decay are "cleaned up," it proposes rejuvenation and a making new. Debates over the future of the meatpacking industry in Manhattan, and whether the area should achieve landmark status, speculate on the directions that future development will take. The presence of fine art, haute couture, and haute cuisine has already signified a radical shift. Local meatpackers are aware that their days within this zone may be numbered, and many are relocating to Hunts Point in the Bronx. The perceived sense of evolution in the area portends dissolution for the meatpacking business.

Although the history of slaughterhouses in New York is a history of banishment in the name of purification and gentrification, a sea change has occurred. At the beginning of the twenty-first century, the area is suspended in a moment in which limousines negotiate meat trucks, transvestite prostitutes exhibit themselves next to fashion models, fashionistas share pavements with butchers, lean cuisine is served near frozen carcasses, and expensive perfumes compete with more pungent odors. The area's inherent grittiness has attracted consumer aristocrats to the area, pursuing the raw contrast. Ironically, those seeking the area because of its contamination may end up purifying and destroying it.

Tours of the meatpacking district, advertised in the *New York Times*, proclaim "The New Meat Market: Butchers, Bakers and Art Scene Makers."[35] The area is developing swiftly with the constant appearance of new galleries, restaurants, and clubs, slotting into growing numbers of abandoned buildings and raising the rents and property values. Investment companies are buying buildings in the area, hoping to cash in on its "emerging chic." The current drawbacks to large-scale developments in the area are lack of proximity to public transport and the absence of a local population base. This isolation and unhomeliness, characteristics of the legendary object, have attracted the recent inhabitants, visitors, and media attention. The area is now undergoing fundamental change.

De Certeau and Giard insist that "legendary objects" should not be pacified by renovation, but rather "returned to their existence wild, delinquent." They write of the danger of "museumifying the city" by removing objects from everyday use, preserv-

DORITA HANNAH

ing them as artifacts, and offering them up as curiosities. The restored object becomes a museum piece and the "question no longer involves the renovated objects, but the beneficiaries of the renovation."[36] This museumification is a form of purification, under the guise of the science of conservation. It is also a form of "subtraction." Without the existence of the processing plants in the meatpacking district, those businesses rein-habiting the abandoned spaces lose their potency. It is the juxtaposition between art and slaughter that throws both into sharp relief and confronts us with the uncanny. The doubling of flesh in the meatpacking district creates the imagined, dreamed, and lived-in city of de Certeau and Giard.

PU(T)RIFICATION

Autonomous upmarket businesses are actively inhabiting sites associated with slaughter in New York's meatpacking district. As they voraciously seek the uncanny qualities of the area, they are undoing these qualities and erasing the object. Gentri-fication, with its charge of the new economy, is capitalizing on the qualities of the meatpacking businesses tied to the old economy. Such a juxtaposition presents an interesting moment in time that lacks stability and a clear trajectory, though radical shifts toward hyperconsumerism in the area are already well under way.

This essay has attempted to recall the ghost of butchery, which haunts the every-day life of Manhattan and troubles the boundaries between the sacred and the pro-fane, art and mortality, life and death, pleasure and pain, interior and exterior. Unlike Bataille's museum-seeking public, who exiled themselves from the abattoir, New York-ers are in search of sites of slaughter within which to trade in fine art, music, food, and fashion. They are seeking a more visceral and haunted environment to inhabit, and in doing so are chasing the ghosts away.

In the meatpacking district, ever-present flesh is both implicated and denied. The presence of meat, with its dual associations with contamination and sacrificial cleans-ing, proposes an alternative to the white cube gallery as hermetically sealed environ-ment, which bears little relationship to the life of the city, the body of the inhabitant, or the work (i.e., labor) of the artist. Death and decay in the area suggest that art itself has its limits and challenge the assumption that it should be scientifically pre-served. This question of museumification extends to the city itself and confronts notions of gentrification.

The art galleries in the meatpacking district cannot escape the stench of mortality, which not only permeates from the outside but also phantasmatically remains within the built fabric. They have the potential to turn the body inside out to reveal its fleshiness, acknowledging the complexity of the area where men in blood-stained aprons smoke on corners as the haute-coutured sidestep puddles of fat on their way to brunch.

NOTES

1. Michel de Certeau and Luce Giard, "Ghosts in the City," in *The Practice of Everyday Life,* vol. 2, *Living and Cooking,* by Michel de Certeau, Luce Giard, and Pierre Mayol, ed. Luce Giard, trans. Timothy J. Tomasik, rev. ed. (Minneapolis: University of Minnesota, 1998), 141, 133.

2. Ibid., 135–136.

3. Michel de Certeau, "The Annals of Everyday Life," in de Certeau, Giard, and Mayol, *The Practice of Everyday Life,* vol. 2, *Living and Cooking,* 3.

4. Henri Hubert and Marcel Mauss, *Sacrifice: Its Nature and Function,* trans. W. D. Halls (Chicago: University of Chicago Press, 1964), 99.

5. Sigfried Giedion, *The Eternal Present: The Beginning of Art, a Contribution on Constancy and Change,* A. W. Mellon Lectures in the Fine Arts, 1957 (New York: Pantheon, 1962), 278.

6. Thomas F. de Voe, "Abattoirs: A Paper Read before the Polytechnic Branch of the American Institute," June 1865, in Archives of Mr. Thomas F. de Voe, New-York Historical Society.

7. Georges Bataille, *The Tears of Eros,* trans. Peter Connor (San Francisco: City Lights Books, 1989), 199.

8. René Girard, *Violence and the Sacred,* trans. Patrick Gregory (Baltimore: Johns Hopkins University Press, 1977).

9. Sigfried Giedion, *Mechanization Takes Command: A Contribution to Anonymous History* (New York: Oxford University Press, 1948), 34.

10. Edwin G. Burrows and Mike Wallace, *Gotham: A History of New York City* (New York: Oxford University Press, 1999), 475.

11. Quoted in de Voe, "Abattoirs."

12. *Oxford English Dictionary,* 2nd ed., s.v. "butcher."

13. *Webster's Third New International Dictionary,* s.v. "butcher."

14. Sergei Eisentein, "The Montage of Film Attractions" (1924), in *The Eisenstein Reader,* ed. Richard Taylor (London: British Film Institute, 1999), 38.

15. Girard, *Violence and the Sacred,* 37.

16. Giedion, *Mechanization Takes Command,* 93.

17. Ibid., 237, 243.

18. Ibid., 246.

19. Pierre Bourdieu and Alain Darbel, with Dominique Schnapper, *The Love of Art: European Art Museums and Their Public,* trans. Caroline Beattie and Nick Merriman (Stanford: Stanford University Press, 1990), 2.

20. Bataille, quoted in Dennis Hollier, *Against Architecture: The Writings of Georges Bataille,* trans. Betsy Wing (Cambridge, Mass.: MIT Press, 1998), xiii.

21. Ibid.

22. Bourdieu and Darbel, *The Love of Art,* 112.

23. Georges Bataille, *Visions of Excess: Selected Writings, 1927–1939,* trans. Allan Stoekl with Carl R. Lovitt and Donald M. Leslie, Jr. (Minneapolis: University of Minnesota Press, 1985), 241.

24. Hollier, *Against Architecture,* xi.

25. Ibid., xv.

26. Pierre Bourdieu, *Distinction: A Cultural Critique of the Judgement of Taste,* trans. Richard Nice (Cambridge, Mass.: Harvard University Press, 1984), 272.

27. Mark Wigley, *White Walls, Designer Dresses: The Fashioning of Modern Architecture* (Cambridge, Mass.: MIT Press, 1995), xxii.

28. Ibid.

29. John R. Romans and P. Thomas Ziegler, *The Meat We Eat,* 10th ed. (Danville, Ill.: Interstate Printers and Publishers, 1974), 134.

30. Kim Levin, "Blood Relations," in *Dui Seid—Artist's Estate / Aus dem Besitz des Künstlers,* ed. Michael Fehr (Hagen: Karl Ernst Osthaus-Museum, Neuer Folkwang-Verlag, 1997), 9 (available on-line at <http://www.keom.de/kuenstler/text/seid_levin_e.html> [accessed January 2003]).

31. Damien Hirst, "The Exploded View of the Artist," interview with Francesco Bonami, *Flash Art,* no. 189 (summer 1996): 112–116.

32. See Jana Sterbak, "Interview with Milena Kalinovska," in *Jana Sterbak: States of Being / Corps à Corps,* by Diana Nemiroff (Ottawa: National Gallery of Canada / Musée des beaux-arts du Canada, 1991).

33. Elaine Scarry, *The Body in Pain: The Making and Unmaking of the World* (New York: Oxford University Press, 1985), 185.

34. Ibid., 286.

35. See, e.g., "Guided Sightseeing Tours," *New York Times,* October 29, 2002.

36. De Certeau and Giard, "Ghosts in the City," 135, 138.

18

DELECTABLE DECORATION: TASTE AND SPECTACLE IN JEAN-FRANÇOIS DE BASTIDE'S *LA PETITE MAISON*

RODOLPHE EL-KHOURY

Si j'ai du goût ce n'est guère
Que pour la terre et les pierres.
　　—ARTHUR RIMBAUD, "Fête de la faim"

OPTIC TASTE/HAPTIC DESIRE

The first discussion at the Académie Royale de l'Architecture was launched in 1672 with the question "What is good taste?" For the next century, architectural theorists sought practical and theoretical answers to this problem. The Romantic movement eventually relegated the issue to the periphery of art, while it focused on invention and expression in the act of artistic creativity. The preoccupation with taste coincided initially with the pursuit of equilibrium and *justesse* in a culture of *honnêteté* and *bienséances* and was bound to become incompatible with the "great passions" of the Romantic era. In the eighteenth century, however, the emancipation of taste from a doctrinal classicism and its reorientation toward an aesthetic of subjectivity allowed for Dionysian modes of engagement with beauty and the sublime and encouraged the meeting of the aesthetic and the erotic.

Architectural criticism in the seventeenth century tended to confine the sphere of taste to an aesthetic of "rules" based on the objectivity of a potentially quantifiable and analyzable language. As a faculty of critical discernment, taste tended to merge with judgment and came to designate the apprehension of rules as much as their application.[1] In the eighteenth century, the mechanisms of taste were recast in psychological terms. Under the dominant influence of an English empiricist epistemology, the sensuous categories of knowledge were rehabilitated: the apprehension of art became strictly aesthetic—that is, sensuous—and its psychological mode was grounded in the "natural harmony" of the world.

Taste was not only identified with a natural faculty and, more or less literally, with a sensory organ for the apprehension of the beautiful—"le sens interne du beau": "It is this sixth sense within us, whose organs we cannot see."[2] The purpose of aesthetic apprehension was also assigned to taste, "which is nothing other than to discover quickly and keenly the degree of pleasure that each thing should afford us," and was realigned with pleasure.[3]

In *Traité du beau essentiel dans les arts* (1752), Charles-Etienne Briseux accordingly theorizes the analogy of human and natural organizations to account for the psychological mechanisms of aesthetic pleasure: "Since this universal mother [Nature] acts always with a single wisdom and in a uniform manner, we could rightfully conclude that the pleasures of seeing and hearing consist in the perception of harmonic relations as analogous to our constitution. This principle applies not only to music but to all the arts since the same cause could not have two different effects." The pleasure derived from the experience of the beautiful is thus due to a sympathetic rapport with the object of beauty. Furthermore, the intensity of the pleasure is calibrated to the resonance or intimacy of this sympathetic rapport: "If proportions in music make a greater impression on the soul than do those in other objects of sensation, it is because music is more in sympathy with it, being more alive, as it were. So pronounced is this sympathy that we are more touched by a human voice than by the sound of instruments"[4]

When the object of beauty comes to life in the intimacy of aesthetic rapports, the pleasures of taste can equal the pleasures of love and the theory of taste coincides

RODOLPHE EL-KHOURY

with the theory of love. The equation is most often noted in the case of gustatory sensation. Gastronomy and eroticism have overlapped ever since the tasting of the forbidden fruit, but the oral proclivities of eros were particularly pronounced in the eighteenth century, when the libertine was typically known to match sexual excess with gastronomic indulgence.

Despite its undeniable occularcentrism, the aesthetic discourse of the Enlightenment repeatedly appealed to the mouth in order to demonstrate the immediacy and perspicacity of aesthetic apprehension: "We taste the stew, and even without knowing the rules governing its composition, we can tell whether it is good. The same holds true for painting and other products of the intellect that are intended to please us by touching us."[5] Voltaire's article "Goût" in the *Encyclopédie* also hinges on a rhetorical (even aphoristic) comparison of "the ability to distinguish the tastes of our foods" and "a feeling for beauties and defects in all the arts." He thus writes that taste "is like that of the tongue and the palate: a ready and unreflective discernment, sensitive and sensual in appreciating the good, violent in rejecting the bad, often lost and uncertain, not even knowing if it should be pleased by what is presented to it, and sometimes forming only by dint of habit." Voltaire's comparative argument eventually abandons the rhetorical symmetry of the simile to collapse the two parallel notions into "a kind of touch": "Taste is not content with seeing, with knowing the beauty of a work; it has to feel it, to be touched by it."[6]

Such comparisons were commonplace and consistently converged on the tactility of taste.[7] The gustatory analogue stressed the immediacy of apprehension in taste, the direct sensory contact with matter.[8] It projected a virtual tactility onto a visual mode of apprehension that operated at a distance from the object of its assimilating faculty. This distance—spatial and conceptual—is momentarily abolished in the virtual tactility of a latent (i.e., ideological) carnality. Thus implying haptic sensation in optic discernment, taste could naturalize and describe its aesthetic assimilation in a kind of tactile vision, combining the immediacy of touch with the distance of sight.

ARCHITECTURE IN THE BEDROOM

The literature of the eighteenth century provides many instances in which the semantic polyvalence and epistemological (ideological) indeterminacy of taste has a structuring role in the narrative, and the device is most vividly illustrated in Jean-François de Bastide's *La petite maison* (first published in 1758). This novella narrates a plot of seduction involving a host, a guest, and a building. Trémicour, the host, is "an extraordinary man, a man of wit and taste." Mélite, the guest, "had yet to take a lover; time that other women squandered in love and deception, Mélite spent in instruction, acquiring true taste and knowledge." Trémicour challenges Mélite to visit his *petite maison* after she has frustrated his otherwise irresistible advances: "they called a wager and there she went."[9] The calculated procession through the house, alternating interior and exterior spaces of shifting illusions and delicious luxuries, structures the progress of the couple through the various stages of the seduction.

The most remarkable aspect of the house is the "proto-functionalist" adaptation of the decoration to the specific purpose of each room. This architectural feature is emphasized in the structure of the narrative: a series of episodes with highly differentiated and precisely described settings. Mélite savors their distinct "tastes" with increasing pleasure and abandon, propelling the plot with her incremental loss of inhibition.

The notion that architecture could inspire lustful designs is totally foreign today; the tendency is to trivialize this aspect of the work as a fanciful narrative twist that was concocted for the mere amusement of eighteenth-century readers, dismissing it as a literary device that has little pertinence in historical analysis. Anecdotal or rhetorical inflation is unmistakable in Mélite's infatuation with architecture; yet hyperbole is most effective when grounded—however tenuously—in reality. An investigation of the text in relation to eighteenth-century culture might thus reveal the extent to which this allegory is in tune with actual aesthetic attitudes, beliefs, and modes of reception.

The key to this investigation is the notion of taste, considered in its inherent ambiguities and historical vicissitudes. Bastide's use of the term *goût* often overlaps with *caractère*—a term shared with natural scientists such as Linnaeus, Buffon, and Adanson, whose taxonomical procedures relied on the identification of "general and particular characters." The words *goût, génie,* and *caractère* do tend to overlap and are often interchangeable in eighteenth-century texts. At the risk of oversimplification, one might distinguish their semantic spheres by situating them along the different stages of the cycle of production and consumption. Taste is accordingly a fundamental precondition of genius; character is the imprint or mark left by genius in the work; taste, again, is the receptive faculty that can discern character. Taste hence

RODOLPHE EL-KHOURY

encapsulates the system, as it is a condition of both production and reception. As a pivotal element in Bastide's text, it reconciles the quality of the object with the mode of its reception: the decoration in good taste is savored by people of good taste. It is instrumental to the intimacy that takes hold among the three protagonists, primarily in its tendency to oscillate between incarnate sensory perception and disembodied intellectual discernment—the capacity, in short, to blur the distinction between the beautiful, the desirable, and the edible.

In the climactic scene, Mélite, led by deception into a second boudoir, collapses into a *bergère*, to assume her designated role among the *marquises, duchesses,* and *otomanes*—other objects furnishing the boudoir: "The threat was terrible, the situation even more so. Mélite shuddered, faltered, sighed, and lost the wager" (110). The narrative thus concludes with the imminent execution of the deferred act while the last word cynically switches the tone of the climaxing narrative to the bare "economics" of the sexual transaction.

This second boudoir, the ultimate destination for the concluding seduction, is described as follows: "This new room, next to which lay a wardrobe, was stretched with thick green gourgouran. The most beautiful engravings by Cochin, Lebas, and Cars were hung symmetrically on the walls. The room was lit just enough to allow the masterpieces of these skillful masters to be seen" (106). In comparison to the gilded, mirrored, and lavishly decorated rooms of the house, the boudoir stands out for its sobriety. The author/architect has even taken the care to substitute the severe lines of presumably monochromatic engravings for the ethereal rococo paintings found elsewhere. Lighting is one of the few mentioned features; it is designed to favor the engraved contours. Everywhere else, lighting is spectacular: it is meant to enchant, dazzle, and deceive. The contrast is sharpest in the first boudoir, where light is cast in a characteristically theatrical mode:

> The walls of the boudoir were covered with mirrors whose joinery was concealed
> by carefully sculpted, leafy tree trunks. The trees, arranged to give the illusion of
> a quincunx, were heavy with flowers and laden with chandeliers. The light from
> their many candles receded into the opposite mirrors, which had been purposely
> veiled with hanging gauze. So magical was this optical effect that the boudoir
> could have been mistaken for a natural woods, lit with the help of art. (75–76)

None of the optical devices and illusions of the erotic theater are tolerated in the austere light of the museumlike boudoir, yet it is deliberately chosen as the setting for the denouement of the sexual battle. Indeed, Trémicour deviously led Mélite into the second boudoir and "stepped on her dress when she was at the threshold, so that in turning her head to disengage her dress, she would not see the place she was entering" (106). One wonders why he took this precaution. Why should he avert Mélite's gaze from seemingly inoffensive decor when her delicate sensibility had braved more sensually composed effects? And why should this sober room, and not any other, occupy the privileged position at the conclusion of an erotically charged itinerary?

No particular features could indeed characterize the room as a boudoir except for the furniture. Unlike other spaces in the house, where signs of sensuality are encrypted in the decoration, the erotic is here delivered literally—that is, in functional pieces of equipment. Without Trémicour's deceptive intervention, Mélite would certainly have avoided a distasteful room, distasteful in the explicit destination of its furnishings and especially in its blandness—that is, *in its lack of taste*. The second boudoir is most threatening to Mélite because it offers no objects to her taste. In the second boudoir, she is left alone with Trémicour and has no other channels for the sublimation of her libidinal appetite in aesthetic assimilation.

In the second boudoir, architecture provides a support, a functional decor for an action unfolding separately in the foreground; in the garden, in all the other rooms, and especially in the first boudoir, architecture participated in the action. Not only was it a catalyst that provided the optimal ambience and the necessary lubricant for the machinations of seduction, it also engaged the protagonists as the subject of a sublimated amorous rapport. We may say that architecture, in *La petite maison*, performs the role of a sexual partner—with the exception of the second boudoir, where Trémicour could more effectively deal his last card, in the absence of his rival and accomplice.

ARCHITECTURE IN THE DINING ROOM

Let us backtrack to another critical episode in the narrative: the scene in the dining room, where our protagonists are involved in a more literal mode of consumption. In a narrative organized around taste and vision—or, more precisely, around the *taste of vision*—the supper scene, the moment when taste literally switches to a haptic mode, should prove significant.

No mention of actual food is made in *La petite maison*'s culinary scene; we merely learn that Mélite "ate little and wanted to drink only water." During the brief meal where only tasteless water is specified, her attitude displays no signs of the alert and inquisitive concentration of the gourmet; she was rather "distracted." Her mood was introspective, detached: "she was more preoccupied with her anguish than with the things that had caused it" (97). As Mélite's body engages in a most tactile activity, her mind disconnects from the external objects of sensory assimilation to withdraw into an idealizing interiority. The sensuous experience of matter in eating does not interfere with the reflecting consciousness that remains indifferent to its taste. In *La petite maison*, food is indeed tasteful as long as it is assimilated into decoration and consumed as spectacle.

In the dining room, *"where a table was laid out with an elaborate meal"* (98), no servants are in sight and no service is mentioned. We are thus to assume that the meal in question is a *repas en ambigu*. In fashion since the late seventeenth century, this consists of a simultaneous presentation of more or less contrasting dishes in lieu of the usual consecutive courses. In *L'art de bien traiter* (1674)—a milestone in a growing culinary literature—L.S.R. defines the *ambigu*: "This manner of serving is, strictly speaking, the combination of a supper and a light meal and is generally served at day's end; and instead of dividing a meal into several courses, all is set out together from the start, but arranged and ordered in a highly specific way that is agreeable and pleasurable to the senses and that brings appetite even to the most disgusted."[10]

The *ambigu* is distinguished primarily by its spatial organization. It rivals a "souper" or a "collation," not necessarily in the constitution and taste of individual dishes but rather in the potential for elaborate formal compositions. Indeed, in instances of particular luxury the *ambigu* could transform the whole dining room into a culinary theater, "for aside from the ordinary meats that are set out on tables, sweets, wines and lights are everywhere visible in the banquet room, on cabinets, on fireplace mantles, and in other more convenient locations where they are so immaculately displayed that there is no image, painting, spectacle, or ornament, however rich and orderly, that might compare to them."[11]

In the *ambigu,* the temporal succession of multiple courses is thus eliminated in favor of the visual effect of a unified tableau. Such meals are composed as a spectacle for the eyes and do not necessarily involve an oral consumption of food: "the pleasure of seeing them is greater than that of touching them," states L.S.R.[12] They are modeled after painting, sculpture, and architecture and conform to those arts' "rules" of visual composition. Grimod would thus praise a Duffoy, "the most dexterous decorator in Paris in terms of the dessert *surtout,*" for the architectural orthodoxy of his culinary constructions: "We have admired the majestic scope of his temples and his palaces, wherein all the laws of architecture are perfectly observed; platters constructed with the highest elegance and in the most excellent taste."[13] The *surtout de table,* the central element of the *ambigu,* is often directly transposed from the stage set of the theater and is evidently not meant for oral consumption. One particularly elaborate model is described in Grimod's *Almanach des gourmands:*

> *This* surtout *or rather this reclining scape . . . was three feet long, twenty inches wide, and thirty high. It displayed the two principal stages of the* Opéra des Bardes; *behold the dream scene on one side and the recognition scene between Rosmala and her father on the other, and in the cavities of the rock that graced the center of the decoration were nestled several other scenes, among these that of the bridge.*[14]

Antonin Carême, celebrity cook and architect manqué, later took a particular interest in the architectural potentials of pastry and devoted many copiously illustrated volumes to this art. They demonstrated designs in different styles and with considerable attention to decoration and proportion. The *pâte fine* allowed for minute details and great precision in execution, while the traditional *pâte d'office* provided the primary building material for this edible architecture. Here is Carême's recipe:

> *Pâte d'Office (Office or Confectioner's Paste)*
> *This is of the utmost use in modern pastry. Sift one pound and a half of flour, make a hollow in it, and put in two eggs and three yolks, on a pound of pounded sugar, and a little salt; stir these for two minutes, that the sugar may be somewhat melted, then work in the flour, and if necessary, another yolk, so as to render it as firm as if for building a pie; "fraiser" it five or six times; it ought to be smooth and*

RODOLPHE EL-KHOURY

well blended, otherwise add another yolk or white of egg: afterwards cut the paste in pieces, mould and roll it for the thickness of an inch, to serve for the bottoms (or boards) of a "pièce montée"; put the paste on a baking sheet slightly buttered, and with the fingers press out the air between the paste and the sheet (without this precaution the heat would deform it, and from the heat not acting equally throughout, it would possess less solidity); when thus arranged, cut it with the point of a knife, as may be wished, and prick it to assist the escape of the air; wash the surface slightly, but not the sides, put it into a moderate oven, and if it blisters, pass the blade of a large knife under it (if done enough) turn it over to obtain a light brown color on both sides; when taken from the oven lay it on the most even part of the dresser, and place the baking-sheet upon it to remain until cold, when the paste will be perfectly level on both sides. All boards of "Pâte d'office" are thus made.[15]

In the scopic regime of this culinary *appareil*, the haptic character of food is entirely undermined: to *eat* an *ambigu*, to *taste* it, is to *consume a spectacle* modeled after painting, decoration, and architecture, laid out in a particular formal style and with *bon goût*. The *repas en ambigu* is thoroughly theatrical; "it is a one-act play," writes Philip Stewart, "it seeks the utmost impact in the first glance; it attempts to embrace the entire range of possibilities in a single scene."[16] L.S.R. provides specific staging instructions for this culinary ensemble in his treatise, and the glittering *appareil* of the baroque theater is no doubt the prime source of inspiration: "A confusion of lights should fill the room; use mirrored panels and other carefully imagined flourishes to form a glorious device that offers a pleasurable spectacle to the guests and unleashes joy by its charming diversity."[17]

In the blinding light of the *petite maison's* dining room, the baroque drama peaked when the theatrical machinery was set in motion, when the table flew down into the basement kitchen while another one rushed down from the upper floor to fill the gap left by the vanished meal.[18] This coup de théâtre, worthy of the new Salle des Machines at the Tuileries, pulled Mélite out of her momentary rêverie: "This feat, incredible to Mélite, roused her from self-absorption and invited her to consider anew the beauty and the ornamentation of the place that was offered for her admiration." The meal that Mélite barely touches thus participates in the decorative program of the dining room; it is designed to suggest an *avant-goût* of the ornamental delicacies on the wall depicting "the pleasures of the table and the pleasures of love" (100).

La petite maison's supper stages a scene of transubstantiation: stone comes alive for the cannibalizing gaze of an excited *goût*, while food is petrified into an architecture of "the highest elegance and in the best of taste" (100). In Bastide's dining room, food, the object of haptic assimilation, does not escape the tyranny of the scopic regime. Its haptic character is dissolved in a theatrical presentation that mobilizes the senses for a scenography of flying tables and blinding six-stemmed candelabra. Nonvisual modes of assimilation and other senses are of course involved in the experience of the *petite maison;* they conform to the logic of the spectacle, however, and do not challenge the supremacy of sight—the privileged perceptual apparatus in the projection of desire. In Trémicour's *petite maison,* the scents of violet, jasmine, and rose are wonderously perceived (they are released from the varnish of woodwork) and music is magically heard at a sign from the host (it is performed by musicians hidden behind a partition). In both cases, the cause or source of sensation is inaccessible and incomprehensible to the spectator. The senses are disoriented and the feeling is one of wonder and bewilderment: in *La petite maison,* the pleasures of scents and music are diffused and intoxicating; they belong to the total *éblouissement* of the spectacle.

Food is equally spectacular. After it has performed as an appetizing extra in the mise-en-scène of sublimated desires, it is promptly withdrawn from the scene so as not to interfere with the taste of the pièce de résistance. As an omnivorous gaze begins to savor the decoration, to lick and fondle its delicate carvings, to penetrate the perspectival cavities of its pictorial representations, the meal—material evidence and reminder of a genuinely haptic experience—is dramatically rushed down into the coulisses, with the help of the baroque machinery that might have snatched a Don Juan, through a trapdoor in the stage, from the *festin de pierre.*

NOTES

1. See Françoise Fichet, *La théorie architecturale à l'âge classique: Essai d'anthologie critique* (Brussels: P. Mardaga, 1979), 36.

2. Jean-Batiste Dubos, *Réflexions critiques sur la poësie et sur la peinture,* 7th ed. (1770; reprint, Geneva: Slatkin Reprints, 1967), 225 (1st ed. published in 1791).

3. Montesquieu, "Goût," in Denis Diderot and Jean Le Rond d'Alembert, *Encyclopédie, ou Diction-naire raisonné des sciences, des arts et des métiers, par une société des gens de lettres* (M. Neufchastel, 1751–1777), p. 762.

4. Charles-Etienne Briseux, *Traité du beau essentiel dans les arts* (Paris, 1752), 45, 47.

5. Dubos, *Réflexions critiques,* 225 (emphasis added).

6. François Marie Arouet de Voltaire, "Goût," in Diderot and d'Alembert, *Encyclopédie,* p. 761.

7. Etymologically, the tactility of *taste* is more evident than goût. It is related to the French *tâter* and features "touch, grope, feel, explore by touch, to have carnal knowledge of . . ." as immediate antecedents to "perceive by the sense of taste" (*Oxford English Dictionary,* 2nd ed., s.v. "taste").

8. "Taste is not content with seeing, with knowing the beauty of a work; it has to feel it, to be touched by it" (Voltaire, "Goût," 761).

9. Jean-François de Bastide, *The Little House: An Architectural Seduction,* trans. Rodolphe el-Khoury (New York: Princeton Architectural Press, 1996). This edition of the novella is hereafter cited parenthetically in the text. De Bastide (1724–1798), a prolific writer who had gained some notoriety in the eighteenth century (Madame de Pompadour was one of his readers), was mostly appreciated for novels and plays dealing with *l'amour galant: La trentaine de cythère, Les ressources de l'amour, Les graduations de l'amour,* etc.

10. L.S.R., *L'art de bien traiter* (Paris, 1674), pp. 359–360.

11. Ibid., 372–373.

12. Ibid.

13. A. B. L. Grimod de La Reynière, *Almanach des gourmands* (Paris: Maradan, 1808), 227.

14. Ibid., 71.

15. Marie-Antonin Carême, *French Cookery: Comprising L'art de la cuisine française, Le pâtissier royal, Le cuisinier parisien,* trans. by William Hall (London: J. Murray, 1836), 143.

16. Philip Stewart, *Literature et gastronomie,* 87. As Stewart notes, the relation between the *ambigu* and the theater extends beyond the analogy with spectacle. In the late seventeenth century, the *repas en ambigu* lends its name to a series of plays and, in 1769, to a theater specializing in the genre: L'Ambigu Comique on the boulevard du Temple. The title of Montfleury's play of 1673, *L'ambigu comique ou les amours de Didon et d'Énée, tragédie en 3 actes, mêlée de trois intermèdes comiques,* is particularly evocative in its culinary inspiration: "the play is much like a course that alternates flesh with sweets" (Stewart, p. 89).

17. L.S.R., *L'art de bien traiter,* 74.

18. *Tables volantes* (flying tables) or *tables machinées* were built by Guerin for royal residences such as Bellevue and Choisy. One was also projected by Loriot for the Petit Trianon but was never built. One of its many versions is described in the *Mercure de France:*

> This table is composed of a fixed frame and of four side platforms. The whole is lifted all at once by a machine in such a way that the surface of the table, the frame as well as its attachments, is composed by a section of the raised floor. . . . When the guests enter the dining room, there is not the least sign of a table; all that can be seen is a uniform floor that is adorned by a rose at its center. At the slightest nod, the leaves are retracted under the floor, and a table laden with food makes its sudden ascent, flanked by four servants emerging through the four openings. (Quoted in Grimod de La Reynière, *Écrits gastronomiques,* ed. Jean-Claude Bonnet [Paris: Union générale d'éditions, 1978], 64–65.)

19

DALÍ'S EDIBLE SPLITS: FACES, TASTES, AND SPACES IN DELIRIUM

JOHN C. WELCHMAN

THE PHILOSOPHY OF THE JAW

If only to bear witness to the uncanny scale and promiscuous metaphorical extension delivered to it by Salvador Dalí, I want to start closest to the mouth. At six, as he famously pronounced, Dalí wanted to be a cook, and in his early years he ate and drank around his native Catalan acres with the same delirious relish that drove his fascination for its fragrant, anthropomorphic landscape. From the beginning, Dalí's culinary dreams were lined with Gallic nostalgia—as in his reverie of French gourmands serving seasoned woodcock flamed in brandy, or his vision (as crisp as a Manet still life) of a glass of Pernod taken with a lump of sugar. But when his tongue found its groove, Dalí was a passionate advocate of the Catalan table. At Cadaqués, where his fastidiously middle-class family spent their summers, he mused on the epic quality of the regional delicacies—those "Homeric dishes," as he nicely termed them, such as *riz de langouste* (lobster rice), *dentos a la marinesca, rubellons a la llauna* (fresh mushrooms fried on thin sheets of metal), and beans with *butifarra*, the Catalan blood sausage, mixed to disturbingly brilliant effect with chocolate and laurel leaves. In the winter, he would take brief leave from a feverish stint at the easel to down three dozen sea urchins, or "five or six chops fried on a fire of vinestalks." For supper he recalls "a fish soup and cod with tomato, or else a good big fried sea-perch with fennel." At Port Lligat, where he established his own bayside summer house in the late 1920s, his truest friends were the fisherman sons of his surrogate mother, Lydia of Cadaqués, whose feasts of freshly fried sardines he and Gala sometimes shared when the locals returned from a nighttime trawl.[1]

In later life, as his manner of living, tastes of all kinds, and pecuniary instincts became more self-consciously flamboyant, Dalí aligned himself with the culinary internationalism of French haute cuisine. His cookbook, *Les dîners de Gala* (1973), is the final testament of this entente, combining the bombastic legacy of named dishes ("Salade composée selon Alexandre Dumas"), feasts, special galas and anniversaries (the menu for a "Dinner given by their Imperial Majesties, the Shah Aryamehr and the Empress of Iran in honor of their illustrious guests participating in the Celebration of the 2500th Anniversary of the Foundation of the Persian Empire by Cyrus the Great [Persepolis, October 14, 1971]" appears as a kind of frontispiece), gaudy 1970s color food photography, and promo opportunities for Maxim's and other pillars of the aristocratic table, with a thoroughgoing, would-be deviant neotraditionalism epitomized in the prefatory effusion: "From the *Positivist Matérialism* of the 'Physiology of taste of Brillat-Savarin' to the Spirito-Mystic-Monarchic, Catholic, Apostolic, Romanism of DALÍAN GASTRO ESTHETICS."[2]

By 1973, of course, Dalí's work and persona had long been caught up in the dandified endgame of surrealism. But traces of the radical disturbance he suggested some forty years earlier between the economies of consumption, construction, and representation still remain in *Les dîners de Gala*. This is most apparent in the first section, "les caprices pincés princiers," which begins with a meditation on the "sadomasochistic pleasure" of eating "'cooked and living beings'" (ascribed significantly to "the Neapolitan, of Catalan descent, Giambattista della Porta"). Here Dalí finds a gastronomic confirmation "of our Catholic, Apostolic and Roman Rumanian Religion, i.e; to swallow the living God as is done in the Sacrament of the Eucharist."[3] As we will see below, cannibalistic consumption, the ingestion of one's own kind, functions almost continuously for Dalí as the inevitable death-driven obverse to the notion of eating as healthy consumption. Alongside and in competition with the normative itinerary

19.1
Salvador Dalí's face painted onto
the door of El Barroco restaurant,
Cadaqués, Catalonia, Spain.
Photo by author.

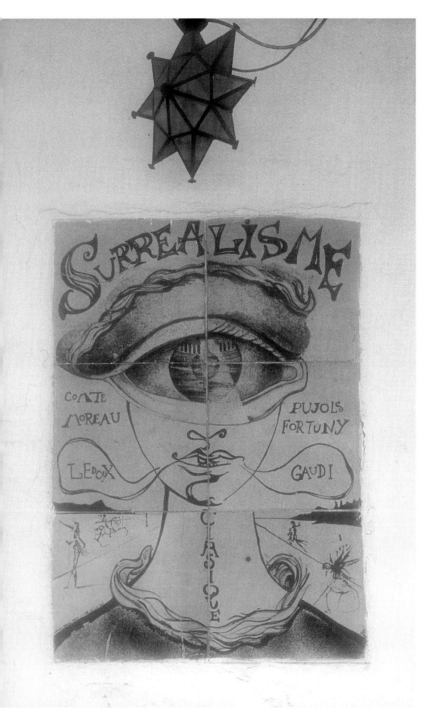

19.2
Salvador Dalí, *Surréalisme;*
ceramic copy on the wall outside
L'Hostel bar, Cadaqués, Catalonia,
Spain. Photo by author.

19.3
Detail of above. Photo by author.

JOHN C. WELCHMAN

of food—starting with natural display and confected culinary reordering (preparation, recipes, menus), and using the face as its entryway, the stomach as a locus of digestive incorporation, and the bowels as an exit for the precipitation of surplus—Dalí sets up a logic of putrefaction, cannibalism, and death. Even in a coffee-table cookbook.

Dalí was as scrupulous a connoisseur of drink as he was of food. His early temperance—"*half* a tiny glass of chartreuse," gingerly imbibed under his father's watchful eye at Sunday lunches in Cadaqués—gave way to the manic consumption of his student days and a number of alcoholic predilections that he never renounced. During his art school years in Madrid he took his first dry martini at the Palace Hotel; downed brown German beers, accompanied by dozens of minuscule boiled crabs; and caroused around sundry champagne bottles in most of the hostelries of note. As for the robust wines of Emporda, these for Dalí were so earthily vivid that he imagined in them "the sentimental prickling taste of tears."[4]

From the mouth to the palette is a brief journey of epic proportions, beginning in literal transfer and ending with a profound recalibration of edibility. Dalí was the most sensitive of all the surrealists to the number and nature of the transcriptions, reproductions, and allusions to food in the avant-garde art practice of the early twentieth century. A key passage in his essay on surrealist "objects" attends to the iconographic concentration of food-related elements in the paintings of Giorgio de Chirico:

> The persistent appearance of eatables in the first surrealist things painted by de Chirico—crescents, macaroons, and biscuits finding a place among complex constructions of T squares and other utensils not to be catalogued—is not more striking in this respect than the appearance in the public squares, which his pictures are, of certain pairs of artichokes or clusters of bananas which, thanks to the exceptional cooperation of circumstances, form on their own, and without any apparent modification, actual surrealist articles.[5]

De Chirico's work, then, announces the objectlike modality of isolated depictions of food that appear in, but are also constitutive of, the communal social space of the "public square." But Dalí bears witness to another representational register of food: "the predominance of eatables or things that can be ingested is disclosed to analysis in almost all the present surrealist articles (sugared almonds, tobacco, coarse salt in Breton's; medical tablets in Gala's; milk, bread, chocolate, excrement and fried eggs in mine; sausage in Man Ray's; light lager in Crevel's)."[6] The objectlike public presentation of food joins with its metaphorical annexation in surrealist writing, revealing that for Dalí comestibles were clearly not just for tasting, or painting; they were also key elements in his creative process, and an integral part of his vision of the nonedible world that spun around him. Dalí's Mediterranean nights were presided over by the "'dying silver' garlic-clove of the incipient crescent moon"; and in a delicious Dalían metaphor, he even likened the work of his imagination to frying up "the mushrooms, the chops and the sardines of my thought." "The jaw," he wrote elsewhere, "is our best tool to grasp philosophical knowledge."[7]

Formed at the conjunction of his experience as consumer, painter, object maker, and writer, Dalí by the early 1930s had worked up his own analytic relation among these functions, predicated on a "sudden consciousness of *a new hunger* we are suffering from."[8] The elevated status accorded by Dalí to edibility and ingestion is underlined by their association with the last of his four quasi-evolutionary stages in the development of the surrealist object. Succeeding objects that function "anthropomorphically," "dream-state articles," and "articles operating symbolically," the fourth and most interactive phase is one in which "the object tends to bring about our fusion with it and makes us pursue the formation of a unity with it (hunger for an article and edible articles)." Edibility becomes the cornerstone of an alternative aesthetic in which optical contemplation is supplanted by oral consumption: "As we think it over, we find suddenly that it does not seem enough to devour things with our eyes and our anxiety to join actively and effectively in their existence brings us to want to *eat them*."[9]

FACE, TASTE, SPACE

Throughout his writings in Catalan, Castilian, French, and English, but especially in the texts achieved in the decade beginning in 1929 with his remove from his native Figueras in northern Catalonia to Paris—and engagement with surrealism—to the start of World War II, Salvador Dalí offered an important and far-reaching, if typically unsustained, reallocation of the relations posed among the forms and consumption of food; a disorienting, centripetal theory of identity; and the production and inhabitation of architectural space. Food objects, facial signs, and space production are bound together in Dalí's vertiginously metaphoric dream-life and the Paranoid-Critical Activity that simultaneously constructed, invaded, and annotated it. Each of these

JOHN C. WELCHMAN

three clusters—food (raw or cooked), faces (real or projected), spaces (built or fanta-sized)—is mapped in a fractal system of unpredictable exchanges within which their forms and surfaces, interiors and exteriors, histories and fictions are split or com-pounded in a logic dependent only on Dalí's devouring interpretation.

Within Dalí's delirious repertoire of governing images and obsessions—excre-ment, putrefaction, masturbation, sadism, and what Yvonne Shafir calls their "infinite iconographical correlates (such as . . . the gastronomic system of olives, bread, sea-urchins, chocolate)"[10]—faces, foods, and spaces are imagined in a Larousse of para-noid projections. They are soft, hard, blank, minute, gigantic, horrific, decayed, and detachable. Each is apprehended in terms that rational discourse reserves for the oth-ers. Thus faces are conceived as places and objects, as well as subjects and others: they are sites of narcissistic self-reference—the deliquescent center of what Dalí termed his "Soft Self-Portrait"—the locus of ingestion, both screen and origin for the privileged act of looking, and the most exquisite and divisible of locations. Faces are constituted in an elaborate, concrete fantasy of apertures and bizarrely autonomous part-objects (noses, lips, hairs, eyes); and they function as originary sign or displaced signified in the split register of Dalí's "double" images.

The perverse capacity of Dalían signs to split into part-objects and nonchalantly realign themselves with other signifying domains emerges in the artist's thought in the later 1920s. In his three-part article "The New Limits of Painting," published between February and May 1928 (perhaps the most significant text he wrote before develop-ing his theory of Paranoid-Critical Activity), Dalí argues that the new tendencies in painting in the mid-1920s—notably the work of surrealists, including Joan Miró and André Masson, in Paris, and Picasso's post-cubist reorganization of the body—had ne-gotiated a relation of continuity and surplus with the dominant styles of the recent past, advancing the artist toward the double goal of the next avant-garde: hyperex-pression and self-referential plasticity.

In 1928, then, Dalí is already reaching for forms of radical dislocation that find a significant register in the matrix of exchanges and mutations often beginning—or ending up—with the face, but reaching across to food, furniture, and design. From a catalogue of examples, which include the relocation of birds in aquariums, the coun-tersyntactical dispersion of words, and the "crazy suffocation" of "the hands of a clock" by the addition of "bread crumbs," Dalí offers a pictorial vision in which facial parts are removed from the grid of face, and heads—and faces themselves—severed from the body:

> For us, a nose, far from being necessarily positioned on a face, seems more suitable on the edge of a sofa. Nor do we see anything inconvenient in the fact that the same nose is atop a little trace of smoke—far from it. . . .
>
> For us an eye no longer owes anything either to the face or to the static condition or to the idée fixe; it must no longer expect anything from the idea of continuity. Quite the contrary; we learnt several days ago that the eyes, just like grapes, have a proclivity for the craziest velocities and that both have a gift for launching themselves into the most contradictory pursuits.[11]

Here one particle of the face is reallocated to the edge of a sofa, an item of furniture that, as we will see below, Dalí obsessively redesigns elsewhere around another facial object, the lips. The nose is also posed "atop a little trace of smoke," a deliquescent location whose abstraction is emblematic of the conjuring tricks that animate the artist's associative reverie. While one face part is linked to furniture and combustion, a second, the eye, is also doubly defacialized: first by its formal analogization to a grape, and second by virtue of its propensity for speed, contradiction, and displacement—measured against the static conditions of facial precision.

Face parts, then, participate in something akin to "the poetic autonomy of words" ushered in as the era of contingent—or what André Breton called *mendicant*—signification comes to an end.[12] They are units of special expression and feeling picked out amid conditions that are "accidental," "fugitive," and "unstable," in a new art that would be probabilistic, absurd and popular. Picasso's wrenching of the figure epitomizes the daring disequilibrium cultivated by Dalí, who writes approvingly of "the curves of his profiles, of his poetic torsos (authentic monsters) [that] will risk anything, up to the most audacious forms of death and the will."[13] The face is relegated from its traditional primacy both in painting and in physiognomic premodernity. Its fractured parts, the nose, the eyes, become probes that couple with the domestic (the sofa) and the comestible (the grape), forming key new compounds in a promiscuously imaginative periodic table of delirious elements.

In his paintings, and more emphatically in his writings, Dalí subjects almost every part of the face to the counterintegral poetic autonomy he championed. The nose is

JOHN C. WELCHMAN

Dalí's preferred facial object, and it is fittingly drafted into service at the beginning of the history of hallucinatory reading by the "'sublime madman' of Antiquity, Aristophanes," who "in *The Clouds,* drew our attention for the first time to the fact that, as one contemplates the sky, one can see the shapes of clouds change—from the naked body of a woman into a leopard or an enormous nose."[14]

"At the very end" of a list of demonstrative affirmations in the "Anti-Artistic [or Yellow] Manifesto," written with Sebastià Gasch and Lluís Montanyà in Barcelona in 1928, Dalí directs us to a clinching image of "one motionless ear over a little puff of smoke," conjugating this body part, as he had the nose and would the olive, with a magiclike cloud of smoke that seems to conjure it up out of thin air.[15] Elsewhere, in the course of an associative reverie on a grape, Dalí elaborates its metamorphic relation to the eye ("a grape becomes their eyes").[16] He also crosses the eye with hairs, imagines one fabricated "by Max Ernst . . . from a piece of a chair suspended by a thread,"[17] and, in the famous image from *Un chien andalou* (1929), severs it with a razor, turning the violence of the face's dissection against the integrity of its individual attributes.

GORGING ON GAUDÍ

Four capital cities and their impressionable architectures orbited around Dalí's Mediterranean domain: Madrid, where he went to art school and perfected his dandyism; Paris, where he joined the great Spanish émigré artists Pablo Picasso and his fellow Catalan Joan Miró, cultivating the most extravagant surrealist persona of the moment; New York, to which, like Marcel Duchamp and Francis Picabia a decade or so earlier, he attempted to export his brand of magic realism and social mischief; and finally Barcelona, capital of Catalonia, scene of the miraculous urban modernism of Antoni Gaudí, and object of numerous Dalían architectural pilgrimages.

Gaudí's encyclopedia of dripping forms drove Dalí to distraction. Only the metal fronds and tendrils of the Paris Metro came anywhere close to provoking so strong a reaction. Gaudí epitomized the deliciously suffocating ornamentation of the art nouveau style. His passionate antagonism toward commonplace reality was the soulful foundation for buildings Dalí thought of as "true realizations of solidified desires."[18] Dalí was convinced that the swirls, patterns, and seething instability of Gaudí's designs were the closest material things to the imagined worlds he so ferociously cultivated in his paintings. Their mixtures and interlacings, splicing forms together then splitting

19.4
Antoni Gaudí, Parc Güell,
Barcelona, 1900–1914, columns
under the great esplanade.
Photo by author.

19.5
Antoni Gaudí, Casa Batlló,
1905–1907, Passeig de Gracia 43,
Barcelona. Photo by author.

them apart or vaporizing them into another dimension, offered a streetside replay of the faceted logic of dreams. Dalí's homage to Gaudí reached its peak in an essay titled "Of the Terrifying and Edible Beauty of Art Nouveau Architecture," in which he likened its shifting, melting, vertiginous surfaces to the "hard undulations of *sculpted water.*"[19] Gaudí was the genie in Dalí's architectural bottle, an antidote to the false purity of avant-garde modernism, a magician of form whose sensationally senseless masterpieces revolutionized Mediterranean design. Dali declared, "the last great genius of architecture was Gaudí whose name in Catalan means 'orgasm' just as Dalí means 'desire.' I explained that . . . orgasm and desire are the distinctive figures of Catholicism and the Mediterranean Gothic reinvented and carried to paroxysms by Gaudí" (355).

Nowhere in his writings does Dalí dwell in more detail on the expressive contingencies of the face than in the satirical opening to his essay on turn-of-the-century architecture. He castigates the whole regime of deceitful, ideologically blinkered facial expression that testifies to "the colossal and ravishing incomprehension" of what Dalí terms "the terrifying and edible beauty of art nouveau architecture" (a description that titles his text). The language deployed here is a tour de force of ironic equivocation, as Dalí simultaneously pillories and enacts an exaggerated form of physiognomic analysis. His point of departure is the facile contemporary reception (at the beginning of the 1930s) of the built environments of "1900," which he reveals as concrete and banal by imaging, then explaining, its physiognomic registers. His tirade tilts against the "'sentimental perspective'" and "'sordid-critical' humor" driven by a small-minded and impoverished "'superiority complex'" that fuels the reaction to art nouveau structures and their whimsical decoration. It finds its most sustained image in his elaborate description of "a particularly repugnant 'sort of smile'" supplied by "decent, appropriate facial contractions":

> These reflexive, treacherous, facial contractions of "defensive-repression" will make benevolent and understanding smiles—tainted, it is true, by the well-known and indispensable tear, corresponding to simulated "conventional memories"—alternate with the frank, explosive, irresistible, though not revelatory smiles of vulgarity, each time one of these violent and hallucinatory "anachronisms" appears. (198–199)

This accumulation of terms needs further explanation. The arch, self-righteous visages of Dalí's antagonists offer their faces as machines of tradition-bound looking, locked into the registration of primitive effects and dutiful misrecognition. Their faces are reflexive arenas of sentiment, superiority, and sordid, socially treacherous humor. But Dalí does not leave it at this. Identifying the controlling mechanism of their facial contractions as the product of "defensive-repression" (very much the passive, interiorizing, opposite of the Paranoid-Critical Activity), he pluralizes the scene of facial expressivity by crossing it with the tangibly "indispensable tear" released by the stimulation of conventional memory, then doubling it with more active ("frank, explosive") "smiles of vulgarity." Common to these physical reactions of the face is their nonrevelatory relation to the interior disposition of the smiler (if that could be determined). The physiognomies Dalí conjures are palpably false, even to their own self-understandings. In the end, these faked smiles of ignorant approbation cleverly emblematize the systematic disingenuity of physiognomic interpretation.

As Dalí's discussion moves away from the credulous parade of smiling faces, his disparagement of physiognomic interpretation becomes clearer still. Turning his attention to art nouveau itself, he refuses the possibility of determining either the "'manifest,'" "'latent,'" or more general "'phenomenological'" causes of the movement, referring its originality and impact to a "ferocious individualism," "violent eruption," and "'leaping'" revolution. The speed, heterogeneous clamor, and "hideous impurity" of art nouveau is comparable only to "immaculate purity of oneiric interlacing." As with the face, the shifting, melting, "vertiginous" aspect of this architecture defeats any attempt to explain its contents with reference to a score of interpretational constants (200). In the same way that face-parts are correlated with dissolving puffs of smoke, Dalí compares art nouveau to the "hard undulations of *sculpted water*," and later to "authentic *sculptures of the reflections of crepuscular clouds in water*" (201, 203). The face must not be mistaken for a mere instrument of consumption. Like architecture, it must be consumed itself, rendered sublimely edible and subject to the "new Surrealist age of 'the cannibalism of objects'" (204). If architecture's final design is a house for "'living madmen'" or "erotomaniacs" (204), then the face becomes a container for paranoid projection. Both face and structure can be known only through being experienced, or occupied, by dreams, erotic reveries, and delusions, replete with their characteristic condensations and displacements. Physiognomy, the science of external signs, is replaced by a Dalíesque version of psychoanalysis, conceived as the interactive co-production of psychic conditions. Dalí underlines the substitution

JOHN C. WELCHMAN

by rewarding his made-over methodology with a paradoxically inverted physiognomy when he describes psychoanalysis as "still very young in spite of a forehead wrinkled with the delicate traces of madness."[20]

Setting himself against the interpretive assumptions caught up in the tradition of contiguous expressive subjects, the face for Dalí is a zone of positive incompletion, dreamlike fragmentation, and paranoid intensity. Not only is the face dissected and its parts reallocated as wandering object-signs, but the very fabric of the head is turned inside out. The face is no longer a surface of signs radiating a menu of predetermined expressive meanings gathered up by the subjects of its social encounters. Instead Dalí seizes on the face—as on its sibling objects—as moments of paranoid fixation subject to the terrifying exteriority of the gaze that falls upon them. The face is no longer a screen displaying the legible signs of original passion or social disposition. It is, rather, a schizoid frame that releases its parts from their physiognomic orbits, reallocating their meanings as a function of the irrational fixations hurled against them. The face is smashed by the atomizations and capricious, burning intensity of the paranoid-critical gaze, a process that allows its parts and insides to compound in an irrational chemistry and superficially alogical syntax with other items in the fixated consciousness of the delusionally hyperactive looker who consumes them.

19.6
Fountain with lips sofa and Pirelli advertisement (detail) in the courtyard of the house of Dalí and Gala at Port Lligat. Photo by author.

19.7.

Salvador Dalí, *Face of Mae West
(Useable as a Surrealist Apart-
ment),* c. 1934. Art Institute of
Chicago, Gift of Mrs. Charles B.
Goodspeed, 1949.517.

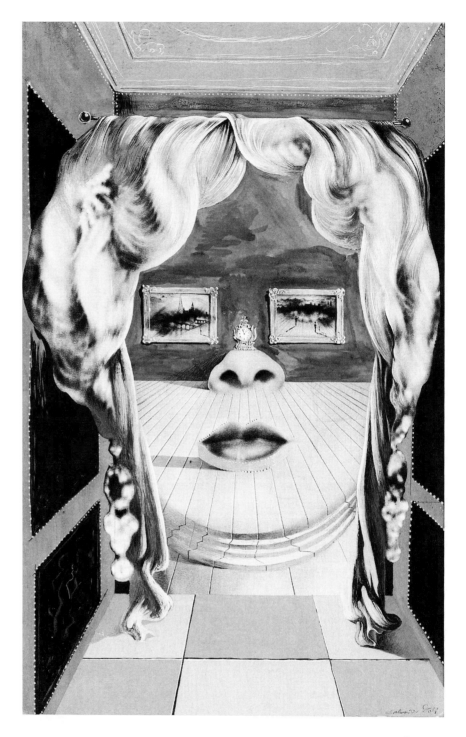

JOHN C. WELCHMAN

APARTMENT COMPLEX

Perhaps Dalí's most fetching image of the lips is found in an itemization of the contents of the wallet of a "boxer friend"—emptied for Dalí during what he terms a "documentary" offering at the Select American bar on the Champs-Élysées in Paris—whose first product is "a recut photo of lips."[21] But Dalí's fetishization of the lips would culminate, of course, in *Face of Mae West (Useable as a Surrealist Apartment)* (c. 1934), which gave rise, in turn, to the remarkable Mae West–lips sofa and finally to the Mae West Hall in the Dalí Theater-Museum in Figueras, the most elaborate of Salvador's face-to-space dreams-come-true. In the Mae West Hall the installation of a lip-shaped sofa, paired with giant nostrils and two retouched pointillist views of Paris, is resolved into a trompe l'oeil face only when the visitor ascends a flight of steps, stoops underneath a plastic dromedary appropriated from the Camel cigarette company, and gazes through a reductive lens.

As with most of his morphological fixations, the precise origins of Dalí's fetishization of Mae West and his transformation of her image into architecture and design are unclear. But the excavation of her iconic features into a dwelling and the swelling of her lips as a seat pose the actress's celebrity demeanor as the site for a kind of deviant domesticity that attaches the erotic bravado and irreverent sociality of her Hollywood manner to a surrealist vision of living. West's personae in the 1930s, both on- and off-screen, were quite at odds with the wholesome image cultivated by an emergent mainstream stardom, epitomized by Mary Pickford. Interestingly, Pickford's real-life and celluloid "normality" was also symbolized in a denominated structure, in this case the comforting high-society conservatism of a former hunting lodge set in 18 acres on Sunset Drive in Los Angeles, given as a wedding present to Mary by Douglas Fairbank. Named Pickfair after their union, the house came to emblematize the symbiotic closeness ("Dougandmary," as one account put it) of Tinsel Town's version of America's model couple.[22]

Against the normalized propriety of Pickfair's personified compound, Dalí offers an obsessive projected interior, puncturing habitable space into the chamberlike recesses of West's fantasized cranium. In addition to a common interest in sexual manipulation and display, several other concerns were shared by Dalí and West. West's prurience, like Dalí's early anti-clericalism, for example, aroused considerable antipathy from the Catholic Church, whose envoys and pressure groups used her as a negative example to advance the cause of moral "purity" in the movies.[23]

I want to dwell a little on the implications of Dalí's Mae West apartment, situating this version of the surrealist interior in relation to some of the wider concerns of the movement—and of modernism at large. First, the architectural subdivision of living space into small one-family or one-person compartments, and the advent of the cell-like construction of these units in mid- and then high-rise multiples, is carried out in a form of spatial fissuring and replication that clearly relates to modernist precepts of splitting, dividing, gridding, faceting, and collage. Second, the emphasis in surrealism on interiorization, secrecy, and experiential fragmentation led—as it also led Freud, though for somewhat different reasons—to an extensive reflection, both metaphoric and literal, on chambers, enclosures, boxes, and rooms, which were conceived not just as privileged locations, or as exemplary arenas of modern self-reflection and reverie, but also as incubators of surrealist style and method. Third, declarations such as Francis Picabia's in 1922 that "space is not a receptacle, space is in us"[24] offer a fusion between spatial and mental production whose legacy was explored, perhaps most radically, by Dalí himself.

Such concerns emerge in Marcel Duchamp's domestic iconography with the fastidious bourgeois bedroom of *Apolinère Enameled* (1916–1917), based on an advertisement for "Sapolin Paints"; his "ready-made" coat and hat racks; staircases; and the series of windows and apartment doors that commence with *Fresh Widow* (1920), a miniature French window whose eight panes are covered with black leather. This last group of works includes his *La Bagarre d'Austerlitz* (1921), another small window, this time surrounded by brickwork; the *Door, 11 Rue Larrey* (1927), fabricated by a carpenter to Duchamp's instructions for the apartment in Paris where he lived between 1927 and 1942 (the door was hinged between the doorways to Duchamp's bathroom and bedroom so that when one entrance was closed, the other was fully open); and the old Spanish door punctured with two peepholes that fronted Duchamp's *Etant Donnés* (1944–1946). Duchamp viewed these elements, the windows in particular, as media devices and stylistic signatures: "I used the idea of the window to take a point of departure, as . . . I used a brush, or I used a form, a specific form of expression, the way oil paint is, a very specific term, specific conception."[25] Troubling the window's status as an aperture or threshold by camouflaging its normal transparency,

Duchamp's architectural units are formats for the doubling of spatial boundaries with the dry enigma of his wordplays and puns.

Duchamp's structural linguistics is constitutionally different from the efforts of the visual surrealists to make fantasy and the everyday collide on the site of the domestic interior. Hans Arp, for example, recalls such childhood exercises as painting "on a part of his window-panes a blue sky under the house that I saw through the window," so that "the house seemed to hang in mid-air"; or sawing "a hole in the wall behind the frame, disclosing a charming landscape."[26] Arp thus continues (or anticipates) Duchamp's project of ironic interference with architectural elements, but detours it toward optical fantasy and trompe l'oeil. In his later sculptures (made after his remove from Paris to Meudon in 1926), especially his *Concretions* series, Arp, like Dalí, attempted to correlate bodies, faces, food, and forms. But he did so by appealing to what he termed "cosmic forms,"[27] as he sought to produce a system of abstract-universal equivalences whose weight, exteriority, and forced integrity were quite at odds with Dalí's concrete irrationality. From Max Ernst's offbeat collaged Victorian chambers and menacing claustrophobic spaces to the spooky, recessional vistas of half-open apartment doors in Dorothea Tanning's *Birthday* (1942), the quadruple doors of her *Interior* (1953), and the doors, passageways, and apartment interiors that feature in several other works (*Eine kleine Nachtmusik*, 1946; *Bon soir*, 1951; *Lumière du foyer*, 1952), we witness the transformation of domestic space into nightmare visions of organic proliferation, demonic possession, or spatial infinity.

In the work of Matta (Roberto Sebastián Antonio Matta Echaurren), who studied with Le Corbusier in Paris between 1934 and 1936, such interests reach a denouement as the artist returns spatial inquiry to the fracturing of language associated with Duchamp (by whom Matta was influenced when he arrived in New York in 1939). At the same time, beginning with his six-work series of *Psychological Morphologies* (1939), Matta explosively combines the site of painting with the interior architecture of the mind. The result is perhaps the only serious alternative among the surrealists to Dalí's negotiation with the excavation and building of psychic space.

In several of his writings, Matta interrogates the social centrality of the cubic regulation of space on which architectural modernism was apparently founded, suggesting the vertiginous dissolve of the cube in the surrealist tradition of countercubic biomorphism.[28] He claimed that his birth from the global cubic womb of modernity produced "one of those who came from the four corners of the earth to work for Le Corbusier."[29] The psychological morphologies of his signature works were predicated on the implosion of an external cubic logic and the demoralization of standard architecture in a newly spun network of "strange mucous webs."[30] Trapped early on by the "tyranny of right angles" and equal sides, Matta spat invective against the edges of his geometric cell and proclaimed the need for "walls like wet sheets which change their shape to match our psychological fears"[31]—a concern that remained central in his thought and paintings until the late 1950s and beyond (see, for example, *The Unthinkable* [1957], in which the four plain white sides of a cubic space are seemingly forced apart by a proliferation of tubular elements). Matta's white, wet, mutable sheets become shrouds for the ghost-like emanations of a psychological para-cubism. Embossed with thoughts and actions, they emblematize the spectral, folded machineries of a pataphysics at war with "the epidermis of people and things."[32]

Matta's 1938 article "Sensitive Mathematics—Architecture of Time," quoted above (see n. 31), was illustrated by a "project for an apartment" based on such countermodernist principles as inflatable materials, curved and pliable surfaces and the co-productivity of psychological occupancy.[33] Much of its imagery draws on a repertoire of objects and allusions seemingly based on such familiar Dalían obsessions as "a crumb of bread," "the desolation of smoke," and the "liquid bustle of life."[34] Most significantly, perhaps, Matta's largely alogical correlations of architectural, psychological, and somatic space are framed by three apparitions of the lips. Attendant to Matta's vision of "walls like wet sheets" is a confusion of light, forms, and colors that "awakens" "the very gums as sculptures for lips." A few lines later, his facial metaphors continue with an invocation of the liberatory potential of "objects for teeth." The essay concludes with a plea for a "waste"-oriented alternative temporality to "this dirty, hole-ridden time given us by the sun," which prompts a final question: "we shall ask our mothers to give birth to a warm-lipped piece of furniture."[35] Matta completes the surrealist journey of Dali's lips, aligning them with soft sculptural form, oracular furniture, and half-heated maternal elementalism as puckered double columns supporting the last surrealist apartment.

From his first moments in Paris, Dalí's prodigious imaginative capacities were likened to the excavation of interior para-worlds of fantasy and delirium. Interestingly, Breton's first essay on Dalí, written as a preface to his exhibition at the Goemans

JOHN C. WELCHMAN

Gallery in Paris in November 1929, uses the metaphor of cranial dwelling to signify the daring intellectual reach of the young Catalan artist: "With the coming of Dalí, it is perhaps for the first time that the mental windows have been opened really wide."[36] I want to suggest that it is the extreme apertures Breton points to here, those "really wide openings," that separate Dalí's architectural psychoses from the more instrumental reveries of surrealist spatial metaphor and iconography. The really wide openings double as the phantasmatic (philosophical) jaws that Dalí used to consume the built environment, and thereby digest it into his vision, and as the cannibalistic totality of Dalí's architectural embodiments. Dalí cannot conceive of architecture, spaces that actually or potentially contain us, without first consuming that which encloses. Likewise, furniture and items of design are not just softened or distorted; they are incorporated as structural amalgams with the body, and only then become surreal metaphors—as in *The City of Drawers* (1936), a Gradiva-like female figure propped up on one arm, her torso rendered as a "chest of drawers," and *The Ghost of Vermeer van Delft, Which Can Be Used as a Table* (1934).

Like buildings and bodies, the crutches and props that Dalí often used as scaffolding to support his melting forms are also interchangeable with anatomical elements. In *Soft Construction with Boiled Beans: Premonition of Civil War* (1936), bony feet and arms prop up a head and other soft body parts in an elaborate scaffold that pivots on a cubelike shack or crate, which in turn doubles as a enclosure of canvases. In this work, too, we glimpse another defining separation between Dalí's deep architectural metaphoricity and the similitudes of the surrealists: the delirious equation between molten corporeality, dismembered architectural form, and comestible items—here the beans, remaindered like so many engorged corpuscles in the foreground of the composition, and a steak (or possibly a liver) draped around a stumplike body part at the right lower edge of the painting. The sustaining delirium of this conjunction is made even more apparent in works such as *The Weaning of the Furniture Food* (1934), "in which," as Sarane Alexandrian points out, "he espies through an opening in the body of his nurse the piece of furniture containing the feeding bottle."[37]

One aspect of Dalí's critical paranoia, then, took the form of a spatial parasitism as the artist's surrogate projections took root and then dwelled in the any-object-whatever of Dalí's obsessive desire. Dalí's oneiric annexation of space was a project of psychological colonization carried out according to a consumptive logic as he digested, and reformulated, his split locations. It is in this sense that Dalí's mental apartments give pride of place to the dining room.

Unlike Dalí, the literary surrealists were interested less in the proliferating singularity of the psychological apartment than in the use of their own domestic interiors as platforms or incubators for automatic experiments and games, and in the cluster effect of plural apartments organized in an uncanny series and precipitated by a kind of literal citywide nomadism. "When the [surrealist] friends met [to play games such as 'The Game of the Analogical Portrait, the Truth Game, the When and If Games, and the Game of Exquisite Corpse'—'methods devised to extract marvels from everyday reality'] in each other's apartments," notes Alexandrian, "they felt the brotherhood of their imaginations."[38] In another reference to the surreal effects of urban reinterpretation produced by "walking" or "strolling" through the metropolis, Breton comments on how his Parisian wanderings with Louis Aragon gave rise to "intoxicating reveries on a kind of hidden life of the city": "I can still recall the extraordinary walking companion he was. The areas of Paris I visited with him, even the most nondescript, were enhanced several notches by a magic, romantic fantasizing that was never caught short for long, and that burst forth at a bend in the street or before a shop window." But for Breton the defining image of the "hidden life of the city" arrives not as a surprise encountered around a corner or in a shop vitrine. It is supplied, instead, by "the renowned fable of the 365 secretly connected apartments that supposedly exist in Paris."[39] Dalí's short circuit of parasitic indwelling is met here by what we can term a long circuit of the ultimate basement fantasy, a kind of buried high-rise—predicated not on the clarities of modernist functionalism, but on the covert assemblage of surrealist obscurity—made up of one apartment for each day in the year.

Dalí's consumptive defection from what we can tentatively describe as the "standard" surrealism propounded by André Breton is attested in several registers. Occasional exceptions notwithstanding—I'm thinking, for example, of the "Experimental Researches (On the Irrational Embellishment of a City)" (1933)[40]—neither Breton's creative nor critical writings attend in detail to the architectural or gustatory domains; and, on my reading, he nowhere explicitly imagines their conjunction. Indeed, from the later 1920s on, as he struggles to control his movement; initiates, defends, and then retreats from its political orientations; and bureaucratizes surrealism's administration with committees, questionnaires, blacklists, and expulsions, the matrix within

JOHN C. WELCHMAN

which Breton comes to terms with architecture becomes progressively conformist. The section of *The Immaculate Conception* (1930) titled "Force of Habit," for example, conjures a typical bourgeois interior space ("The table is placed in the dining room; the taps give out clear water . . .") set against a predictable provincial outside ("I suddenly thought there was no longer any street outside the window, but there it is just the same as ever. The druggist is even raising his metal shutters").[41] While Breton clearly sets out to trouble these signs of normality and everyday routine, the fantastic ("green ants"), metaphorical, and psychic (the anxieties of attendant love) disturbances he offers seem to lack the capacity of Dalí's deliriums to corrupt or creatively reconfigure the banalities of the typical. In any event, they seldom effect a compelling reciprocity with an environment that they occupy like furniture rather than compound, meld, or dismantle.

In a sense, Breton's perception of built space and the architectural environment shares with Freud's classicizing aesthetic a kind of perspectival traditionalism quite at odds with the effects of paranoia, duplicitous photographic realism, and oneiric doubling conjured by Dalí from a mimetic stylization that appears—at first sight—to be predicated on similar conventions. We are afforded a glimpse of Breton's spatial dispositions in a number of asides and occasional remarks. In a discussion of Philippe Soupault's automatic modernity, for example, the great bohemian playground of the Parisian café becomes a maternal space, where waiters provide umbilical assistance for the impromptu immediacies of poetic release: "in a café, for instance, in the time it took to ask the waiter for 'something to write with,' he [Soupault] could satisfy the request for a poem."[42] Consider also Breton's description of René Crevel following his suicide in 1935: "without [him] Surrealism would have lacked one of its most beautiful volutes."[43] This is one of the most direct of Breton's relatively infrequent architectural metaphors. But if we follow the logic of a more complex example, which also arises in the course of a personal characterization, we will see that the surrealist chief was quite uncertain, even inconsistent, about the relations he posed between buildings and the mind. Commenting on Tristan Tzara's "Dada Manifesto 1918," Breton says that it "seemed to throw the doors wide open, but you discovered that these doors led to a corridor that turned around in circles."[44]

Breton's relations to the street and the city are also quite different from those of Dalí, who never explicitly invested in the well-trodden avant-gardism of the flâneur and whose "penchant for wandering" was seldom as directed and self-conscious as Breton's explicitly romantic desiderata: "Our taste for adventure in every sphere had never died—I'm speaking of adventures in language as well as in the street or in dreams."[45] The one thing Breton couldn't do, however, was to look the city in the face and digest it. Witness his covertly formulated "preference" to avoid the architectural clamor of New York: "Instead of talking about New York itself, I believe you'd rather tell us about the countryside around New York," says his interlocutor, Charles Henri Ford, during an interview for *View* in 1941, thereby feeding Breton an excuse to recount his experiences at André Masson's house in the Connecticut woods during his wartime exile in the United States, and to discourse on the "mystery of American butterflies."[46] Breton's urbanistic evasion is the third side of a perceptual triangle, whose other dimensions, as Rem Koolhaas has suggestively described, are formed by Le Corbusier's desire to annihilate and reconstitute Manhattan and by Dalí's paranoid consumption of the city.[47]

How, finally, can we locate Dalí's apartment complex in relation to the precepts of architectural modernism? At first, of course, his ideas appear antithetical to the more extreme functionalism espoused, for example, at the Bauhaus, especially by Hannes Meyer, its director from 1928 to 1930. As opposed to Dalí's psychotic individuality, proliferation of stylized detail, and delirious nonrigidity, Meyer conceived of the building process as a form of "deliberate organization" guided by "the function diagram and economic programme" and carried out by collective endeavor.[48] Meyer wrote in the curriculum vitae accompanying his application to the Bauhaus in 1927 that "By 'ARCHITECTURE' I understand something which collectively and with the exclusion of everything personal meets all the needs of life, whose realization is subject to the law of least resistance and economy, whose aim must be to achieve an optimum of functionality."[49] Far from operating as the locus of projective imagination, the production of apartments, "hundreds of thousands of apartments for the people," was, for Meyer, a social necessity; and their design, like art, should be the exclusive function of an overriding "order" predicated on the determining experience of the landscape, the "destiny" of which he claimed it "fulfilled."[50]

Yet in the macrocosmic vision of Meyer we glimpse a meeting between the rhetoric of socialized functionalism and Dalí's projective delirium. While for Meyer, architecture was a product of the containing environment, for Dalí it was identified with a

JOHN C. WELCHMAN

landscape that consumed and reinvented it. It is the heady scope of Meyer's visionary pronouncements that supports the dissolution of their seemingly closed logic, for in addition to being a form of "social, technical, economic" organization, Meyer also ordained that building is an expression of "psychological" order.[51] Dalí might have concurred with this suggestion, though he would have reversed its terms. Yet the bizarre pseudo-conjunction between Dalíesque surrealism and Bauhaus totality is actually clinched when Meyer, in a famous equation, anchors "all forms of construction" in a formula for life based on "a striving for oxygen + carbohydrates + sugar + starch + protein."[52]

Meyer's bio-aesthetics locates building as a function of dietetically balanced constructive digestion; the gastro-aesthetics at the heart of Dalí's critical paranoia reconvenes it as an imaginatively excessive deconstructive cannibalism.

NOTES

1. These and other details of Dalí's food obsessions can be found in Salvador Dalí, *The Secret Life of Salvador Dalí*, trans. Haakon M. Chevalier (New York: Dover, 1993); see 132, 252, 267, 270, 304, 306, etc.

2. Salvador Dalí, *Les dîners de Gala*, trans. Captain J. Peter Moore (New York: Felicie, 1973), 10, 15.

3. Ibid., 31

4. Dalí, *The Secret Life of Salvador Dalí*, 200, 177–96, 17.

5. Salvador Dalí, "The Object as Revealed in Surrealist Experiment" (1932), trans. David Gascoyne in *Surrealists on Art*, ed. Lucy Lippard (Englewood Cliffs, N.J.: Prentice-Hall, 1970), 95. Outlining the several stages through which de Chirico's paintings passed—the "period of arcades and towers"; the "period of ghosts and omens"; the "mannequin period"; the disappearance of structures and their replacement by "inanimate objects related to the role [man] played (as a king, a general, a sailor, etc.)"—André Breton concludes with another observation about the presence of food in the artist's work: "Finally, these symbolic objects entered into the composition along with instruments of measurement—bearing no obvious relationship to human life except through the medium of dehydrated food, such as hardtack—and the great de Chirico cycle closed with the period of 'metaphysical interiors'" (Breton, "Genesis and Perspective of Surrealism in the Plastic Arts" in *What Is Surrealism? Selected Writings*, ed. Franklin Rosemont [London: Pluto Press, 1978], 221–222).

6. Dalí, "The Object as Revealed in Surrealist Experiment," 95.

7. Dalí, *The Secret Life of Salvador Dalí*, 243, 176; Dalí, *Les dîners de Gala*, 10.

8. Dalí, "The Object as Revealed in Surrealist Experiment," 95.

9. Ibid., 96, 95.

10. Yvonne Shafir, introduction to "Corpus Daliecti: A Translation of Salvador Dalí's Oui 1 and 2" (Ph.D. diss., Columbia University, 1995), x.

11. Salvador Dalí, "New Limits of Painting," in *Oui: The Paranoid-Critical Revolution, Writings, 1927–1933*, ed. Robert Descharnes, trans. Yvonne Shafir (Boston: Exact Change, 1998), 28, 37, 28–29.

12. Ibid., 29.

13. Ibid., 30, 36.

14. Salvador Dalí, "Dalí, Dalí," text for the catalogue of the Dalí exhibition at Julien-Levy Gallery, New York, March 1939; trans. in "Corpus Dalíecti," 276. Dalí also mentions Aristophanes' paternity of the "masters of illusion," and cites the same examples of cloud reading, in "Total Camouflage for Total War," *Esquire,* August 1942, 65–66.

15. Salvador Dalí, Sebastià Gasch, and Lluís Montanyà, "The Anti-Artistic Manifesto" or "The Yellow Manifesto," in *Oui,* 49.

16. Salvador Dalí, "Fish Pursued by a Grape," in ibid., 57 (originally published in *L'Amic de les Arts* [Sitges], no. 27 [August 31, 1928]).

17. Salvador Dalí, "Documentary—Paris 1929—IV," in ibid., 103.

18. Salvador Dalí, "The Rotting Donkey" (1930), in ibid., 118.

19. Salvador Dalí, "Of the Terrifying and Edible Beauty of Art Nouveau Architecture," in "Corpus Dalíecti," 201 (originally published in *Minotaure* [Paris], nos. 3–4 [1933]); this translation is hereafter cited parenthetically in the text. For another translation, by Haakon M. Chevalier, see Salvador Dalí, *Dalí on Modern Art: The Cuckolds of Antiquated Modern Art* (1957; reprint, New York: Dover, 1996), 31–45.

20. Dalí, "Dalí, Dalí," 277.

21. Salvador Dalí, "Documentary—Paris 1929—III," in *Oui,* 99.

22. See Eileen Whitfield, *Pickford: The Woman Who Made Hollywood* (Lexington: University Press of Kentucky, 1997), 206–207.

23. For details on the deployment of Mae West, see Kenneth Anger, *Hollywood Babylon* (San Francisco: Straight Arrow Books, 1975), 183–185.

24. Francis Picabia, "Cerebral Undulations," trans. Lucy R. Lippard in Lippard, ed., *Surrealists on Art,* 186.

25. Marcel Duchamp, unpublished interview with Harriet Janis; quoted in *Marcel Duchamp,* ed. Anne d'Harnoncourt and Kynaston McShine (New York: Museum of Modern Art, 1973), 295.

26. Hans Arp, "I Became More and More Removed from Aesthetics" (1948), in *Arp on Arp: Poems, Essays, Memories,* ed. Marcel Jean, trans. Joachim Neugroschel (New York: Viking, 1972), 237.

27. Hans Arp, "Forms" (1950), in ibid., 274.

28. For an account of the "cubic unconscious" of visual modernism, see John C. Welchman, "From the White Cube to the Rainbow Net," chap. 7 of *Art After Appropriation: Essays on Art in the 1990s* (Amsterdam: G+B Arts International, 2001), 215–244. Some of my remarks here are drawn from that essay.

29. Roberto Matta, "Place Blanche" (1966), in Matta, *Entretiens Morphologique (Notebook No. 1936–1944),* ed. Germana Ferrari (London: Sistan, 1987), 215; for a brief account of Matta's years with Le Corbusier in Paris, see 199.

30. Roberto Matta, "Organic Magnetic Field," in ibid., 217.

31. Roberto Matta, "Sensitive Mathematics—Architecture of Time" ("adapted by Georges Hugnet"), in ibid., 209, 208 (originally published in *Minotaure* [Paris], no. 11 [1938]).

32. Roberto Matta, "Inscape" (1938), in ibid., 219.

33. Lucy Lippard's headtext to her translation of Matta's "Sensitive Mathematics—Architecture of Time," in *Surrealists on Art,* 167, points to those details.

34. Matta, "Sensitive Mathematics—Architecture of Time," 208–209.

35. Ibid., 208, 210.

36. André Breton, preface to Dalí's exhibition at the Goemans Gallery, Paris, November 1929; trans. David Gascoyne, in *What Is Surrealism?*, 45.

37. Sarane Alexandrian, *Surrealist Art* (New York: Praeger, 1970), 104–105.

38. Ibid., 50–51.

39. André Breton, interview with André Parinaud (no. 3), in *Conversations: The Autobiography of Surrealism,* trans. Mark Polizzotti (New York: Marlowe, 1993), 27–28.

40. Responses to "research" questions in "On the Irrational Embellishment of a City" were published in the sixth edition of *Le surréalisme au service de la révolution* (May 1933); Breton's responses are reprinted in Breton, *What Is Surrealism?*, 95–96.

41. André Breton, "Force of Habit," from *The Immaculate Conception* (1930), in *What Is Surrealism?*, 56.

42. André Breton, discussion with André Parinaud (no. 3), 25–26.

43. André Breton, discussion with André Parinaud (no. 13), in *Conversations*, 139.

44. André Breton, discussion with André Parinaud (no. 4), in ibid., 46–47.

45. André Breton, discussion with André Parinaud (no. 10), in ibid., 106.

46. André Breton, interview with Charles Henri Ford, in ibid., 183 (originally published in *View,* August 1941).

47. See Rem Koolhaas, "Dalí and Le Corbusier: The Paranoid-Critical Method," *Architectural Design* 48, no. 3 (1978): 153–164.

48. Hannes Meyer, quoted in "The Primacy of Architecture," in *The Bauhaus: Masters and Students by Themselves,* ed. Frank Whitford (London: Conran Octopus, 1992), 261.

49. Meyer quoted in "Hannes Meyer and the New Department of Architecture," in ibid., 251.

50. Meyer, quoted in "Hannes Meyer as Director," in ibid., 257.

51. Meyer, quoted in "The Primacy of Architecture," 261.

52. Hannes Meyer, "My Ejection from the Bauhaus" (1930), excerpted in "Meyer's Dismissal," in Whitford, ed., *The Bauhaus,* 283; Mies van der Rohe was said to have remarked: "Try stirring all that together—it stinks" (quoted in ibid., 286).

HARD TO SWALLOW: MORTIFIED GEOMETRY AND ABJECT FORM

PAULETTE SINGLEY

The question is a matter of time and space: what is the relation between the paradigm or geometric diagram of the body, between this rational and intelligible extension, and the abysmal cavity, pit, and orifice of the living body?
    —LOUIS MARIN, *Food for Thought*

The Italian village of Colonnata, isolated in a steep cleft that slices through the marble quarries of Carrara, maintains the culinary distinction of being the only location in the world to produce authentic *lardo di Colonnata*. The name Colonnata, as one might expect, signifies a column or colonnade. The quarries date back at least as far as imperial Rome, and the recipe for *lardo di Colonnata*, too, may well date from that time period, with the local families handing down, from generation to generation, their unique method for preparing *lardo*. In order to properly nourish the quarrymen working long hours in a harsh climate—too harsh for grazing animals, and distant from markets—the inhabitants of Colonnata raised pigs that could feed on the local acorns. From this set of circumstances—the need to provide

20.1

Chocolate tools by Creative
Chocolates of Vermont.
Photograph by Paulette Singley.

lasting sustenance to men working high up in the quarries, the remote location of the village itself, and the difficulty of growing plants or grazing animals on the rocky sub-soil—a regional dish emerged that allows one to taste the very marble of Carrara itself.

The sense of taste, not really one sense after all but a concert of perceptions shared among all of the senses, resides primarily in the mouth and on the tongue, the same location where the faculty of speech dwells. Such a functional doubling marks the mouth as unique among the sensory organs insofar as one must decide to speak, to chew, or to talk with one's mouth full. Our teeth and their attached nerves, in fact, serve as more than mere cutting and shredding devices; they also convey the texture and density of materials. Imagine, if you will, chewing on sand or glass, biting a new wood pencil, or simply sampling a single piece of pasta to determine if it is sufficiently *al dente*. While it may be difficult to eat our words when we have erred in judgment, it also is hard to swallow while we are speaking. Such a near-seamless union of the mouth's vocal and masticating capacities renders objects in a certain oral hieroglyph-ics. We might envision, in this instance, translating these glyphs into the philosophi-cal products of Jonathan Swift's Academy of Lagado, whose members proposed replacing the wasteful activity of speech with sacks of iconic objects that one might pull out on demand in order to strike up a conversation.[1] What if these word-objects were edible? But, then again, they already are (figure 20.1). The foods we have tasted, chewed, or swallowed tell us how an object would feel sliding to the back of the tongue, down the throat, into the stomach, and so forth. As it relates to the duality of hard and soft, interior and exterior, empty and full, and buildable and unbuildable substances, architecture defines food's edibility and, conversely, food describes architecture's mutability.

We may acquire taste not only from repetition, hunger, or culture but also through blind experiment, through the courage required to shut our eyes, suspend all reasonable judgment, and swallow. Invariably the body can vehemently reject that which is too repugnant for cognitive incorporation. In specific response to the act of disgorging food, the art of eating introduces a critical form of contamination into those Kantian aesthetics that prohibit the eating of art. In this respect and with regard to mutability, abject form emerges from the mutual conspiracy of taste and bodily incorporation when objects are physically apprehended, thereby rendering pliable shapes into substances that resemble either something the body has emitted or something too repugnant to swallow. Mortified geometries operate in a similar morphological field of decayed or rotting lines on which we might draw other purer or more abstract forms of architecture. These abject and mortified geometries contaminate the progress of architectural form-making from still life painting or collage to the production of space. A false logic might do here in which the mortified remainders, captured within *nature morte,* by extension find their way into an architectural formalism derived from such compositional techniques. To put this another way: at the intersection of flesh and stone we find mortified geometry, while in the interstices of words and food we find the architecture of abjection.

FLESH-EATING STONE

The marbled taste of *lardo di Colonnata* is not a metaphor. The flavor of this cured pork fat—produced by "11 families making less than a ton a year"—relies on stone tubs, basements, and Colonnata's special mountain air.[2] While this recipe speaks of the intricate dialogue among the land, labor, and climate of a particular geography and its concomitant food production, my interest in *lardo* concerns instead the (disgusting) metonymy of glistening white marble and lard. In other words, the combined visual and spatial proximity of marble and fat offers the possibility of linguistic exchanges between stone and food.[3] Put in more literal terms, through language we have "veined" slabs of marble and "marbled" slabs of beef—blood pulsing through stone and stone striated meat.

Such metonymy prompts the question, when does food stand in for architecture and when does architecture make us think about eating? The ancient Egyptian tradition of burial and embalming offers a useful entry point toward understanding the composite relationships among architecture, cuisine, and stone. As repositories of goods to be used in the afterlife, tombs maintain records of the dietary patterns of this millennia-old culture and enable the canny archaeologist to reconstruct an ancient Egyptian menu of beer, bread, fish, figs, and cucumber. To *embalm* literally means "to place in balsam or resin," and embalming is a form of cookery that involves the careful cleansing and transformation of mortified flesh into a dried and enduring substance through the chemical assistance of herbs and natron (a combination of sodium carbonate and sodium bicarbonate), which cures a carcass into a mummy. Priests removed organs from the corpse—the intestines, the lungs, the liver, and the stomach—and placed them in canopic jars, while leaving the heart in the body and drawing the brain out with a straw inserted into the nasal cavity. The canopic jars, made either of clay or stone, gave form to the four sons of Horus: the falcon, the baboon, the human, and the jackal. The body of these vessels was traditionally rendered with animal and human torsos, but the canopic jars found in King Tutankhamen's tomb were carved in alabaster with heads resembling that of the young pharaoh (figure 20.2). As the mummy becomes an all-too-literal example of Gilles Deleuze and Félix Guattari's "body without organs," conversely, the displaced organs allegorically give life to these stone figures or houses.[4]

One of the more enduring and also mysterious monuments to the gastronomic arts—a structure that amalgamates eating, writing, and architecture—is the so-called Baker's Tomb (the Sepulchrum Eurysacis, or tomb of Eurysaces) at Rome's Porta Maggiore (figure 20.3). Scholars have interpreted the curious form of this *architecture parlante* as replicating the shape of a baker's oven—with the lower section of columnar shafts representing some kind of measuring instrument and the upper portion of circular voids standing in for the openings that lead to where the bread was baked. The ashes of Eurysaces' wife, Atistia, according to William MacDonald, would have "been placed in a marble bread-basket," while in the frieze above the grid/square of "ovens" the story of baking unfolds.[5] In a specific example of semantic doubling, this unique and haunting monument preserves the story of baking in its stone frieze while it simultaneously entombs the baker and his wife in its stone oven. More abstractly, the travertine ornaments and concrete structure distill into the tomb the presence of the absence of bread. The oven-tomb symbolizes both cremation and cooking. Georges Teyssot provides another tool with which to apprehend the latent and

PAULETTE SINGLEY

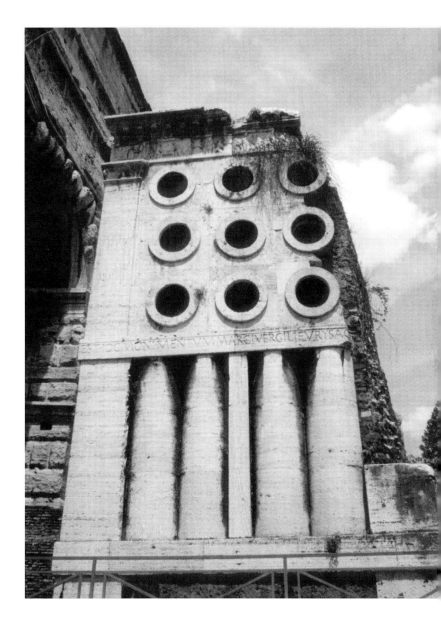

20.2
Canopic jars found in King
Tutankhamen's tomb.
Egyptian Museum, Cairo.

20.3
Sepulchrum Eurysacis, Rome.
Photograph by Jeffrey Balmer.

20.4
Sandy Skoglund, *Luncheon Meat on a Counter*, 1978.

20.5
Greek *asaraton*, or unswept floor, 2d century C.E., mosaic variant on a 2d-century B.C.E. painting by Sosos of Pergamon. Vatican Museums.

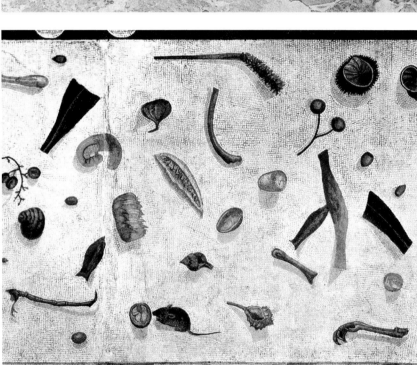

manifest culinary potential of stone, explaining that "the sarcophagic practice (from *sarkos*, 'flesh,' and *phagein*, 'to devour') is motivated by the wish to eat the flesh."[6] The flesh-eating stone of the sarcophagus emerged from the practice of placing corpses in sarcophagi made of limestone, a material known for its ability to rapidly dissolve flesh—thereby creating a buried world where architecture behaves as a carnivore and stone acts as an oven.

MORTIFIED GEOMETRY

In her 1978 photograph *Luncheon Meat on a Counter,* the artist Sandy Skoglund identifies a reciprocity between fleshy stone and stony cold cuts—such as salami, head cheese, or mortadella—that may be found in the face of stone veneer, marble blocks, or granite paving (figure 20.4). If, as previously suggested, carnivores favor marbled meat for its tenderness and architects seek veined marble for its beauty, then such reciprocal desire determines a specific arena of edibility in which stone approximates flesh. Marble that has been quarried and cut as the matching faces of a book may be installed as a revetment that looks like the mirrored fold of a Rorschach inkblot test, exacting monstrous responses to the hybrid forms of combined animal and vegetable pelvises, ribcages, or skulls that emerge from such veneer. Baroque confections like Johann Balthasar Neumann's Residenz at Würzburg, featuring columns glazed with polished marble aggregate and ceilings frosted with a pastel polychromy of rocaille stucco work, may evoke the imagery of confectionary edibility, but other baroque architectures, such as Rome's San Luigi dei Francesi, look more like butcher's than baker's shops, with unidentifiable carcasses of marble meat hanging off their stone walls.

In a less sanguine example of edible stone, carved marble fruit (the kind we might place in a basket on a table) also bears a disarming resemblance to the objects it simulates, insofar as the natural yet arbitrary veins and defects within the stone precisely mirror the similar imperfections and bruises found on peaches or apples—and the same applies to the sculptural depiction of human skin. The delight of such inedible centerpieces is the surface oscillation between living flesh and the translucent, living marble from which this fruit is carved. Because these objects look good enough to eat but cannot be chewed they render stone into an object of insatiable carnal desire. The technique of intarsia locates inlaid stones under our feet, on tabletops, or in cabinetry, making the luminescent pulp of pomegranate seeds, apricots, or grapes glow from within the polished depths of carnelian, amber, or lapis lazuli. Perhaps more important, the presence of such artwork on the floor evokes the tradition of the ancient Greek *asaraton*, or unswept floor, that depicts in mosaic tile the various debris of fish bones, cherry stems, figs, and more that have yet to be cleaned up after the preparation of a meal (figure 20.5). These culinary surfaces invite us to walk among the rotting and discarded remnants cast off from the preparation of a meal without actually stepping on filth. They also invite us to walk upon a work of art and momentarily defile it in a willful yet entirely abject act of pollution.

ABJECT FORM

When displaced from the building site to the cutting board, Ludwig Mies van der Rohe's architecture of skin and bones emerges as visceral space. Moreover, the displacement underscores the presence of the absence of flesh within this working metaphor for a building's enclosure and supporting frame. If it is possible to apprehend stone as an incarnate material, then Mies's use of marble at the German Pavilion in Barcelona offers a paradigmatic example of a fleshy substance that complements the curvaceous stone body of Kolbe's statue *Morning*, which stands in the reflecting pool. The reconstructed Barcelona Pavilion plays on the senses much as do those lurid, polychromatic reconstructions of the Parthenon—historically accurate but nonetheless disturbing to neoclassical sensibilities accustomed to the black-and-white version (figure 20.6). In his critical biography of Mies, Franz Schulze describes the single element dominating the central space of the pavilion as "a freestanding wall roughly ten feet high and eighteen feet wide made of a ravishing and rare marble called onyx dorée, golden with a venation that ranged from dark gold to white."[7] As the centerpiece to a sumptuous material palette of travertine veneer, chrome plating, bottle-green glass, Tinian marble, black carpet, and scarlet drapery, the freestanding, matchbook-faced marble wall—what Robin Evans refers to as the "grotesquely varicose orange onyx dorée"[8]—serves the same function as does the red square in Francis Bacon's 1980 painting titled *Carcass of Meat and Bird of Prey:* it abstracts material flesh into a mortified geometry (figure 20.7).

Distant from the gridded regime of Mies's geometric orthodoxy, but quite close in fact to his trajectory of material seduction and formal abstraction, the work of Bernard Cache invokes Francis Bacon as a model for his complex curvilinear forms, further

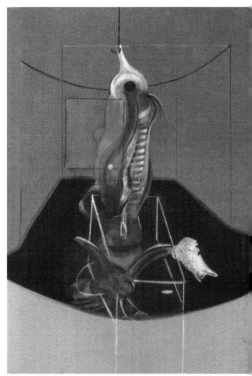

20.6
Onyx dorée wall in the
reconstructed Barcelona Pavilion
(after Ludwig Mies van der Rohe,
German Pavilion at Barcelona
International Exposition, 1932).

20.7
Francis Bacon, *Carcass of Meat
and Bird of Prey*, 1980.

cementing this particularly carnal appetite to mortified beginnings. In Cache's view,

> *Painting leads Bacon from an experience of the body to an experience of the earth. That is why we don't find the abstract sign of inflection in his work but in a very direct way, the surface of the variable curvature. It is a visible directness when it occurs in abstract landscapes, but it is equally direct when it is that invisible perspective that disfigures faces: the mirror of variable curvature. Landscapes with faces bend like velvety surfaces under the hold of the vector. Tendency is exposed to the bite. Perhaps because of the problem of giving colored expression to white skin.*[9]

Quite literally inviting one to "bite," Cache admits the fatty tissue of Bacon's painting into his ostensibly bony work of geologic morphology and variable curvature. He demonstrates that the inspiration of a carnal and even perverse appetite can inspire the calculated and quite mortified morphology of computer-assisted conception and fabrication systems (CFAO). From the lithic terrain of Cache's publication *Earth Moves* to the pliable tissues, alimentary allusions, and embryonic metamorphoses that find their way into Greg Lynn's animate forms, it is but one short step back into the canopic jars filled with organs, into the fatted tubs of marble from which this story of flesh and stone first emerged.

Form within form, curvilinear or gastric shapes, and fluid geometries are subject not only to bodily or excremental theorizing but also to the demands of appetite insofar as these shapes both attract and repel, both assault the conventions of taste and make them pliable. At least such excremental and bodily theories contaminate the quasi-scientific territory of pure abstraction and Deleuzian "folding" that Lynn has staked out for himself. The illustrations for the introduction to his publication *Animate Form* include the following: Duchamp's *Nude Descending a Staircase*, Borromini's San Carlino, spline surfaces, the morphology of a coffee cup from Stephen Barr's 1964 *Experiments in Topology*, Etienne Marey's motion studies, Hans Jenny's "sequence of flowable mass through a vibrational magnetic field," and even the "study of crustacean carapaces" deformed onto flexible grids. Though the coffee cup and the crustacean may be the closest Lynn gets to cooking, in an earlier essay he in fact references the culinary arts as an appropriate metaphor for his work:

If there is a single effect produced in architecture by folding, it will be the ability to integrate unrelated elements within a new continuous mixture. Culinary theory has developed both a practical and precise definition for at least three types of mixtures. The first involves the manipulation of homogeneous elements: beating, whisking, and whipping change the volume but not the nature of a liquid through agitation. . . . Folding, creaming and blending mix smoothly multiple ingredients: through repeated gentle overturning without stirring or beating. . . . Folding employs neither agitation nor evisceration but a supple layering.[10]

Aside from this analogy imbued with food, there is another, more corporeal, genealogy to his work: Georges Bataille's *informe*, Julia Kristeva's *abjection* and the space of *chora*, Dalí's soft paranoid-critical structures—those murkier, shakier, fattier, and far less firm ways of thinking about form that the idea of an animate (hence unstable) geometry necessarily implies.[11] The inflections of such distorted geometries can be read in many ways, leaning toward either the abstract or the all too corporeal— to flesh and sundry body parts. Lynn's deployment of Maya—born in Hollywood as a tool developed to create animation—incorporates from its foundational moment the presence of an unstable and hence mortified geometry (see the "Gallery of Recipes" in this book). The nickname "rubber-sheet geometry," given to the mathematical discipline of topology, might thus apply equally well to the analytical process as to the sense of contamination that at least one function of the rubber sheet tends to imply. The point, in short, is that we might look at the curvilinear and complex forms found in the work of figures such as Frank O. Gehry, Greg Lynn, and others as featuring mortified geometry.

Daniel Cottom's essay "Orifices Extended in Space" inspired my interest in the possibility of a mortified geometry. In his postmodern, postmortem act of ecphrasis, Cottom teases out the tensions between the repulsive gaping wound and the animal's geometrically attractive body in Jean-Baptiste-Siméon Chardin's 1728 painting *The Ray* (figure 20.8). He notes,

With the diamond and diagonals set against the rough-hewn rectangles of the stone wall and accompanied by the oval, circular, and spherical figures of the plate, mortar and pestle, pepperpot, oysters, and vessels, the rectangle of this canvas appears to be grounded on the lines, planes, and forms of geometry. It

20.8
Jean-Baptiste-Siméon Chardin,
The Ray, 1728. Louvre, Paris;
photo copyright Erich Lessing /
Art Resource, New York.

PAULETTE SINGLEY

might have been expressly designed to prepare us for Paul Cézanne's most fa-
mous remark: that the artist should get a handle on nature "by means of the cylin-
der, the sphere, the cone, everything brought into proper perspective."[12]

As with the red square floating in Bacon's wire-frame cube or the marbled wall of Mies's pavilion, the ray's trapezoidal body offers a specific geometric excuse for Chardin to explore those larger compositional interests that seem to anticipate Cézanne's cubic abstraction. At the same time, its morbid tissue contaminates the semantic purity of the trapezoid with layered allusions to death, orifices, violence, and vulnerability. According to Cottom, the ray presents us with a "non-Euclidean geometry of perception endlessly opening onto the desire of cultural organization." Cottom privileges orifice over surface (more specifically, the surface of the orifice) by positing a "symbolic equivalence" among "canvas-fish-face-food-form-object-ground"; in so doing, he identifies mortified geometry as forms eroded in a state of semidigestion, or boundary lines displaying signs of decay.[13] These are lines that open onto "heterogeneous surfaces," lines that twist from inside out and turn space upon itself; they force space to devour itself as a kind of Ouroboros, a snake eating its tail.

The ray's gaping wound invites closing with Jean-Paul Sartre's essay "The Hole," which contemplates the human drive to fill up empty spaces. While summarizing the patent psychosexual desires present in the hole's profound condition of absence, Sartre also muses on the condition of eating, commenting that "It is not a matter of indifference if we like oysters or clams, snails or shrimp, if only we know how to unravel the existential significance of these foods."[14] Eating Sartre's crustaceans and mollusks requires a strong stomach or at least an inquisitive palate, given that they may resemble certain bodily excretions and that we devour the entire creature, stomach and all. Rather than playing the safer game of *corps morcel*—the dismemberment into legs, thighs, breasts, nuggets, and so on that transforms the animal into an abstractly edible object—Sartre's menu requires one to eat all of the creature. When devouring a work of art or architecture, as Sartre observes with respect to food, we both chew it into pieces and swallow it whole:

To eat is to appropriate by destruction; it is at the same time to be filled up with
a certain being. And this being is given a synthesis of temperature, density, and

flavor proper. In a word this synthesis signifies a certain being; and when we eat, we do not limit ourselves to knowing certain qualities of this being through taste; by tasting them we appropriate them. Taste is assimilation; by the very act of biting the tooth reveals the destiny of a body which it is transforming into gastric contents. Thus the synthetic intuition of food is in itself an assimilative destruction. It reveals to me the being which I am going to make my flesh.[15]

Whether we plug the empty hole of unfulfilled desires with literal foodstuffs or with symbolic substitutions, the act of incorporation necessarily involves Sartre's critical mastication.

What concerns us here is less the condition of hunger than the actual shape of the opening, which Sartre describes as follows: "the ideal of the hole is then an excavation which can be carefully molded about my flesh in such a manner that by squeezing myself into it and fitting myself tightly inside it, I shall contribute to making a fullness of being exist in the world."[16] In this sense, to fill the hole not only is a bodily sacrifice but also a way of inflecting and deforming the aperture. It also describes the most fundamental kind of shelter. The filling of the hole requires Sartre's "sickly paste" or a cementitious material that is able to conform to all shapes and plug all leaks—a kind of polymorphic gel, a plastic extrusion of compound complex surfaces, marzipan, stuffing, poured-in-place concrete.

Robert Smithson similarly describes Frank Lloyd Wright's Guggenheim Museum in "Quasi-Infinities and the Waning of Space": "No building is more organic than this inverse digestive tract. The ambulatories are metaphorical intestines. It is a concrete stomach."[17] Smithson fosters an image of Wright's curvilinear ramps spilling into Central Park like the remains of an eviscerated giant. He calls for a visceral interpretation of art, arguing that "the biological metaphor is at the bottom of all 'formalist' criticism"; indeed, the work of Willem de Kooning or Jackson Pollock "in a formalist system is simply a critical mutation based on a misunderstanding of metaphor—namely, the biological extended into space." He illustrates this argument with, among other things, the labyrinth at Amiens Cathedral, an anatomical theater in Padua, a section of the crypt inside the pyramid of Meidum, Kepler's model of the universe, an unidentified project by Claude-Nicolas Ledoux, the Tower of Babel, and a photograph of the Guggenheim, "perhaps Frank Lloyd Wright's most visceral achievement."[18]

While Smithson extends biological form into space, Louis Marin answers the question posed in the epigraph of this essay by positing the extension of space into biological form. Marin explores "the intelligible, geometric space of logos" as inhabiting "the instantaneous, intense, and obscure sites of vibrant pulsation, the sites of *bios*."[19] In questioning the "relationship between body and utopia," he enters the curvilinear and liquid landscape of human anatomy through a Rabelaisian orifice in the Abbey of Thélème. He there discovers "an immense body that has been reduced to a mouth, to a tongue and teeth, a pharynx, a larynx, and a throat." It is "a deep, thick, and dark body-mouth, replete with slopes and inclines." Despite the slipperiness of these slopes and inclines, Marin substitutes this topological anatomy for "projective and metric space" where "the mouth is part of the world and the world is part of the mouth," where "the internal is external, the inside outside, and vice versa."[20] Marin's analysis of Rabelaisian architecture not only invokes the similar oscillation between the gigantic and the miniature in *Gulliver's Travels,* with its big and little comestibles, but also extracts a mortified geometry from the interior landscape of biology. This suggests that Marin's "projective and metric space" in fact describes, rather than substitutes for, the topology of the orifice.

HORS D'OEUVRES

Smithson's vision of an architectural digestive tract is not without philosophical pedigree. In a certain sense, Jacques Derrida inverts the body-building metaphor that Smithson finds in the Guggenheim; the museum with stomach emerges instead as a body with crypt. In his introduction to Nicolas Abraham and Maria Torok's *The Wolfman's Magic Word,* Derrida identifies the specifics of an introjection that resembles what Sartre had earlier described: "The mouth's empty cavity begins as a place for shouts, sobs, as 'deferred filling,' then it becomes a place for calling the mother, then, gradually, according to the progress of introjection or autoaffection, it tends toward phonic self-filling, through the linguo-palato-glossal exploration of its own void."[21] For Derrida the urge to fill oneself, to fill the body torn open by unrequited desires, becomes an oral moment in which words substitute for introjected objects and, more important, the eating of food comes to represent the introjection of loss that acknowledges the space of psychical absence within the body—the space of longing that remains empty no matter how much we may devour. Derrida lays out the spatial implication of the introject/incorporate pairing as establishing a precarious border between inside and outside where, once again, we swallow not in order to introject a psychic disturbance, but in order to "vomit" inside of ourselves (not projectile but internal abjection), thereby creating a space in which longing for the lost other may dwell.[22]

In terms of bodily cavities, the need to "fill," to satiate, forms both a psychological and a physical site of longing that may be requited with food but may also accept other substitutions, as we place our own bodies into the desiring and devouring mouth of architecture in order to be swallowed, like Jonah in the whale, by the edifice. The interior room where we hide psychic trauma—Derrida's crypt or vault—may find its exterior embodiment in architectural form. It is likewise possible—as Allen Weiss's title "Edible Architecture, Cannibal Architecture" suggests[23]—to think of psychological distress enacted as a kind of swallowing in which we both devour and are devoured by the edifice. This, at least, is how Roger Caillois interprets extreme schizophrenia, in which "space seems to be a devouring force." According to Caillois, space pursues, encircles, and even digests the schizophrenic's body to the degree that "he feels himself becoming space, *dark space where things cannot be put.*"[24]

Perhaps architecture might duplicate this space that is neither inside nor outside. And if so, what would it look like? Where would it be? Perhaps we might find it in Mies's stone veneers in Barcelona, where, as Evans claims, "it is appropriate that the walls of the pavilion ring hollow to the knuckles."[25] The space of *poché* might serve to replicate the phenomena of the bodily vault or crypt found in the space of mourning. Likewise, if we understand *poché* as the flesh or fatty tissue of architecture, it is perforce accompanied by a certain repugnance or *dégoutant* that the project of aesthetics necessarily abjects. The art of eating stands sharply against yet also within the art of architecture as Immanuel Kant discusses it in *The Critique of Judgment*. Mark Wigley summarizes Kant's position with regard to the state of bodily dissociation required when evaluating a work of art: "taste is that encounter with an object in which the object is not consumed, not mastered through appropriation, not made servile, not used as a means to some independent end. Aesthetic pleasure is attained through the suspension of all bodily desire and its 'gratification' in the 'mere enjoyments of sense found in eating and drinking.'"[26]

PAULETTE SINGLEY

If aesthetic pleasure requires a disinterested body, then by extension, according to Wigley, architecture too must remain disengaged from the mundane requirement of eating. Kant supports architecture's inedibility and in so doing privileges the mouth's vocal capacity. As Wigley puts it, Kant subordinates buildings to speech because they are bound to consumption. Thus, in philosophy, there is a structural affinity between appetite, eating, drinking, and building: an affinity that throws the utilitarian function of architecture out of the aesthetic economy. But edible architecture and mortified geometry challenge this economy, forcing a confrontation with disgust against which Kant's aesthetics defend.

ABJECT FORM

Disgust remains a primary condition within Julia Kristeva's portrait of abjection, a psychological affliction in which the subject may demonstrate extreme aversion or attraction to certain oral acts such as speaking or eating. Where Kant attempts to thwart architecture's edibility, Kristeva and Victor Burgin urge that the incarnate possibilities of space, geometry, and form are very much determined through the tyranny of the stomach as well as the desires of the mind. Theories of abjection, in this respect, problematize the happy story of corporeal detachment, telling us that even geometry bears the traces of some kind of physiological threshold. When it comes to the digestive dimension of this psychological condition, Kristeva observes that "food loathing is perhaps the most elementary and most archaic form of abjection." Operating at the intersections of several psychoanalytic terms, *abjection* does battle with the presence of the archaic mother; it disturbs identity, order, borders, and rules. Abjection is a "kind of *narcissistic crisis*," "the violence of mourning for an 'object' that has always already been lost."[27] Abjection may be found at the heart of the deep humiliation involved in swallowing one's pride or eating one's words.

As Kristeva's writings focus on abjection's relation to primary narcissism, the loss of the maternal object, language, writing, and speech, her theory constructs an opening in space as an unbearable and disturbing indistinction between inside and outside, through which Victor Burgin will enter. In his important essay "Geometry and Abjection," Burgin puts forward Kristeva's premise that abjection stands as a precondition of all geometry: "Insofar as geometry is a science of boundaries . . . we might say that the origin of geometry is in *abjection*."[28] But what does this mean—or, at least, what is Burgin trying to get at here by introducing this psychic condition of profound ambivalence into the production of space?

Ultimately he argues for the unique form of postmodern space as a geometry that implodes or folds upon itself through the vanishing point, or hole, of one-point linear perspective. Burgin develops this history of space from its classical origins as "a sphere with centre and circumference," through the medieval cosmology of "super-celestial and celestial spheres," and straight into the hole of the vanishing point of the panel that Filippo Brunelleschi constructed in order to demonstrate the mechanism of one-point perspective. In Burgin's brief history of space, quattrocento perspective may be understood as Euclid's conic section now sliced by a picture plane. He identifies the act of looking as an act of incorporation, a move that further enables him to draw a relation between abjection and perspective. He writes that "the subject first confronts an absence in the field of vision, but an absence disavowed: the vanishing point is not an integral part of the space of representation; situated on the horizon, it is perpetually pushed ahead as the subject expands its own boundary. The void remains abjected." He then himself pushes "the torus, the Möbius strip, the Klein bottle" into this abject void, "where the apparently opposing sides prove to be formed from a single continuous surface."[29]

Abjection offers a relation between food, cuisine, appetite, desire, hunger, and architecture that moves into the production of space itself, indeed into the pure abstraction of curvilinear form and computer-generated design. Burgin argues that "one of the phenomenological effects of the public applications of new electronic technologies is to cause space to be apprehended as 'folding back' upon itself." As proof, he points out that "spaces once conceived of as separated, segregated, now overlap: live pictures from *Voyager* 2 as it passes through the rings of Saturn may appear on television sandwiched between equally 'live' pictures of internal organs, transmitted by surgical probes, and footage from Soweto."[30] What is significant, for our purposes here, is that this "fold-over space" exemplifies geometrical abjection. The same terms that Lynn and others develop in the production of architecture through the "baroque fold" of geometric abstraction are equally implicated in theories of abjection; and, in turn, such theories uniquely impinge on the contents of our stomachs. Burgin's work leaves a wonderfully messy spot on the rubber mat of topology, contaminating and infiltrating all experiments in geometric abstraction with base materialism. He demon-

20.9

Diller + Scofidio, *Soft Sell*, a temporary video installation at the entrance to the Rialto (porno theater), 42nd Street, New York, 1993.

strates that the architects of folded planes and spline curves actually wear the mathematical frock coat of Bataille's *informe*.[31]

It is thus that the act of incorporation, both a psychical condition and a bodily phenomenon, provides a physical model for simultaneous inhabitation. Stuffed foods, chicken pot pie, goldfish swallowed live, buildings inside of buildings, the Temple of Dendra in New York's Metropolitan Museum, Frederick Kiesler's "Tooth House," Zaha Hadid's Moonsoon restaurant, the fossilized travertine cladding of Meier's Getty Center, Peter Cook's Kunsthaus Graz, Vito Acconci's boardroom table, Diller + Scofidio's *Soft Sell* (figure 20.9), the marble sugar cubes in Duchamp's *Why Not Sneeze Rose Sélavy?*, Dalí's *Soft Construction with Cooked Beans*, and Koolhaas's Paris library all imply edible geometries.[32] The entire spectrum of the aesthetics of incorporation dodges and skirts and wholeheartedly engages abjection. It concerns the surrounding, engulfing, and ensuing negotiation of having swallowed or apprehended an object of either desire or repulsion. It is the slippage between ellipses, eggs, eyes, testicles, and even the spherical white balls of buffalo mozzarella floating in a container of salted water. And it also is more than this.

The formal exchange value between eggs, eyes, and testicles interested Bataille, as did the Paris abattoir that was to become the site of Bernard Tschumi's Parc de la Villette.[33] Although Denis Hollier has rehearsed the special interest Tschumi shares in Bataille's oeuvre, this influence bears repeating in the context of abject form and mortified geometry. Tschumi's evocation of the "rot" of eROTicism, a specific example of architecture's transgressive potential, leads quite specifically from Bataille's mouth to the little bolus of spit the waiter deposited in your soup.[34]

The problem with this approach is that my explication of abjection through example limits it to the realm of the literal and thus reduces the potential of thinking between boundaries into a highly bounded stylistic game of internal organs or, to borrow from Benjamin Buchloh, "infantile celebrations of bodily fluids and excrement."[35] In a discussion about the intersections and differences between abjection and the *informe*, Hal Foster posits that any attempt to discuss these terms as presenting a dichotomy between the abstract and the material further hardens boundaries that should remain blurred. He finds himself "really interested in this horror of literalization."[36] Why, after all of the work that has been done in this area, does abstraction still dominate literalization to the point of horror and why do literal examples remain contaminants to be expelled from the larger theoretical project? This is the moment of abjection that the examples of gastronomic architecture seek to invoke, the literal and quite carnal display of theory at the base level of incorporating and introjecting space.

NOTES

1. I am grateful to Jesse Easley for directing me to Swift's *Gulliver's Travels*.
2. See Kyle Phillips, "Snippets from the Italian Scene: Lardo di Colonnata: Protecting Traditional Foods from EEU Regulators," *About Italian Cuisine* <http://italianfood.about.com/library/snip/blsip037.htm> (accessed January 2003).
3. The use I make of metonymy in this instance parallels Stephen Bann's use of the term when discussing ancient Greek paintings of grapes (Bann, *The True Vine: On Visual Representation and the Western Tradition* [Cambridge: Cambridge University Press, 1989], 8).
4. I am grateful to Stephen Knowles for pointing out to me Rachel Armstrong's essay "The Body as an Architectural Space—From Lip to Anus the Gastrointestinal Tract as a Site for Redesigning and Development," in *Integrating Architecture*, ed. Neil Spiller, *Architectural Design*, vol. 66, no. 9/10 (Lon-

don: Academy Group, 1996), 86–91. Offering a surrealist pedigree to Deleuze and Guattari's "body without organs," Armstrong writes: "Antonin Artaud dreamed of a body without organs. He considered the famous poets of his time, listed them and evaluated the relative time spent defecating, urinating, sleeping, eating and washing in comparison to the 'creative' act. His conclusion was that the body organs of the artists required an energy investment in their base functions out of all proportion to the amount of energy invested in the higher, creative acts. Organs were therefore distracting and even impeding the body from carrying out its aesthetic activities" (87). See also Nat Chard, "Architecture of Our Interior," in ibid., 77–81.

5. William L. MacDonald, *The Architecture of the Roman Empire,* vol. 2, *An Urban Appraisal,* 2nd ed. (New Haven: Yale University Press, 1986), 146.

6. Georges Teyssot, "Frammenti per un discorso funebre: L'architettura come lavoro di lutto = Fragments of a Funerary Discourse: Architecture as a Work of Mourning," *Lotus International,* no. 38 (1983): 7.

7. Franz Schulze, *Mies van der Rohe: A Critical Biography* (Chicago: University of Chicago Press, 1985), 156.

8. Robin Evans, *Translations from Drawing to Building and Other Essays* (Cambridge, Mass.: MIT Press, 1997), 256.

9. Bernard Cache, *Earth Moves: The Furnishing of Territories,* trans. Anne Boyman, ed. Michael Speaks (Cambridge, Mass.: MIT Press, 1995), 51–52.

10. Greg Lynn, "Architectural Curvilinearity: The Folded, the Pliant, and the Supple," *Architectural Design,* no. 102 (1993): 8–9.

11. See the exhibition catalogue by Yve-Alain Bois and Rosalind Krauss, *Formless: A User's Guide* (New York: Zone Books, 1997). Also see the exhibition catalogue by Craig Houser, Leslie C. Jones, Simon Taylor, and Jack Ben-Levi, *Abject Art: Repulsion and Desire in American Art,* Isp Papers, no. 3 (New York: Whitney Museum of Art, 1993).

12. Daniel Cottom, "Orifices Extended in Space," in *Cannibals and Philosophers: Bodies of Enlightenment* (Baltimore: Johns Hopkins University Press, 2001), 37.

13. Ibid., 62.

14. Jean-Paul Sartre, "The Hole," in *Existentialism and Human Emotions* (New York: Wisdom Library, dist. by Citadel Press, 1957), 89.

15. Ibid., 87. Also see my essay "Devouring Architecture: Ruskin's Insatiable Grotesque," *Assemblage,* no. 32 (April 1997): 108–125.

16. Sartre, "The Hole," 84.

17. Robert Smithson, "Quasi-Infinities and the Waning of Space," in *Slow Space,* ed. Michael Bell and Sze Tsung Leong (New York: Monacelli Press, 1998), 72.

18. Ibid., 73.

19. Louis Marin, *Food for Thought,* trans. Metter Hjort (Baltimore: Johns Hopkins University Press, 1989), 107.

20. Ibid., 108. According to Marin, the Abbey of Thélème is an architectural body and Pantagruel's body/mouth is a world and a part of the cosmos.

21. Jacques Derrida, "Fors/Foreward" to Nicolas Abraham and Maria Torok, *The Wolfman's Magic Word: A Cryptonymy,* trans. Nicholas Rand (Minneapolis: University of Minnesota Press, 1986), xxxvii.

22. Ibid., xxxv, xxxviii.

23. Allen S. Weiss, "Edible Architecture, Cannibal Architecture," in *Eating Culture,* ed. Ron Scapp and Brian Seitz (Albany: State University of New York Press, 1998), 161–168.

24. Roger Caillois, "Mimicry and Legendary Psychasthenia," *October,* no. 31 (winter 1984), as cited by Hal Foster in *The Return of the Real: The Avant-garde at the Turn of the Century* (Cambridge, Mass.: MIT Press, 1996), 165. Also see Caillois's observation in *The Writing of Stones:* "A piece of marble can suggest a river flowing among hills; the clouds and lighting flashes of a storm; thunderbolts and the grandiose plume of frost; a hero fighting a dragon; or a great sea full of fleeting galleys" ([Charlottesville: University Press of Virginia, 1985], 8).

25. Evans, *Translations from Drawing to Building,* 256.

26. Mark Wigley, *The Architecture of Deconstruction: Derrida's Haunt* (Cambridge, Mass.: MIT Press, 1993), 125.

27. Julia Kristeva, *Powers of Horror: An Essay on Abjection,* trans. Leon S. Roudiez (New York: Columbia University Press, 1982), 2, 14, 15.

28. Victor Burgin, "Geometry and Abjection," in *In/different Spaces: Place and Memory in Visual Culture* (Berkeley: University of California Press, 1996), 52.

29. Ibid., 40–41, 56, 51, 44.

30. Ibid., 43, 44.

31. Georges Bataille, *Visions of Excess: Selected Writings, 1927–1939,* ed. and trans. Allan Stoekl (Minneapolis: University of Minnesota Press, 1985), 31. Bataille writes:

   Formless

   A dictionary begins when it no longer gives the meaning of words, but their tasks. Thus formless is not only an adjective having a given meaning, but a term that serves to bring things down in the world, generally requiring that each new thing have its form. What it designates has no rights in any sense and gets itself squashed everywhere, like a spider or an earthworm. In fact, for academic men to be happy, the universe would have to take shape. All of philosophy has no other goal: it is a matter of giving a frock coat to what is, a mathematical frock coat. On the other hand, affirming that the universe resembles nothing and is only formless amounts to saying that the universe is something like a spider or spit.

32. For Rem Koolhaas's interest in Dalí's soft forms, see "Dalí and Le Corbusier: The Paranoid Critical Method," *AD Profiles: Surrealism* 11, nos. 2–3 (1978): 152–163. In this essay Koolhaas also speculates on the value of concrete as a "mouse-grey liquid" that is poured into "empty speculative counterforms to give them permanent life on earth" (156).

33. For the correspondences between these forms, see Georges Bataille, *Story of the Eye, by Lord Auch,* trans. Joachim Neugroschel (New York: Urizen Books, 1977).

34. Yves-Alain Bois considers Bataille's transgressive position regarding the informe: "In Bataille it is more like a *crachat dans la soupe.* It always has a situational quality" (Bois, with Benjamin Buchloh, Hal Foster, Denis Hollier, Rosalind Krauss, and Helen Molesworth, "The Politics of the Signifier II: A Conversation on the *Informe* and the Abject," *October,* no. 70 [winter 1994]: 20). On "rot" and "eroticism," see Bernard Tschumi, *Architecture and Disjunction* (Cambridge, Mass.: MIT Press, 1996), 70. On Tschumi and Bataille, see Denis Hollier, *Against Architecture: The Writings of Georges Bataille,* trans. Betsy Wing (Cambridge, Mass.: MIT Press, 1989), 70.

35. Benjamin Buchloh, "The Politics of the Signifier II," 8.

36. Hal Foster, "The Politics of the Signifier II," 14.

CONTRIBUTORS

Alex T. Anderson is Assistant Professor of Architecture at the University of Washington.

Architecture Urbanism Design Collaborative is a nonprofit founded by Kazys Varnelis, who is on the faculty at the Southern California Institute of Architecture, and Robert Sumrell, who teaches in the Architecture Department at Woodbury University.

Phyllis Pray Bober was Professor of the Humanities at Bryn Mawr College. A scholar of Renaissance art and modern culinary history, she was the author of *Art, Culture, and Cuisine: Ancient and Medieval Gastronomy* (1999). She died on May 30, 2002, at the age of 81.

Clare Cardinal-Pett is Associate Professor and Director of Graduate Education in the Department of Architecture at Iowa State University. She teaches studios, American architectural history, and travel seminars in Cuba.

Annie Chu is principal of Chu + Gooding Architects in Los Angeles and project designer for Israel Callas Shortridge on the Fine Arts Building at the University of California, Riverside.

Gina Ferrari works in landscape, sculpture, and video and has been exhibited widely, including at the Radcliffe Institute for Advanced Study at Harvard University.

Marco Frascari is G. Truman Ward Professor of Architecture at the Washington Alexandria Architectural Center at Virginia Tech University, Alexandria.

Daniel S. Friedman is director of the School of Architecture at the University of Illinois at Chicago.

Mark Hamin is Instructor and Director of the Master's of Regional Planning Program in the Department of Landscape Architecture and Regional Planning, University of Massachusetts Amherst.

Dorita Hannah is Associate Professor in the College of Design, Fine Arts and Music, Massey University, Wellington, New Zealand.

Susan Herrington is Associate Professor of Landscape Architecture at the University of British Columbia, Vancouver, a licensed landscape architect in the United States, and author of *Schoolyard Park: 13-Acres International Design Competition* (2002).

Jamie Horwitz is Associate Professor of Architecture at Iowa State University.

Rachel Hurst and Jane Lawrence lecture in architecture and interior architecture at the University of South Australia.

Rodolphe el-Khoury is an architect, critic, and historian. He is the principal of ReK Productions and chair of Architecture at the California College of the Arts in San Francisco.

Carisima Koenig is an architect at Swanke Hayden Connell Architects, New York City.

Donald Kunze teaches architecture and general arts at Pennsylvania State University. He is the author of *Thought and Place* (1987), on the philosophy of Giambattista Vico.

David Leatherbarrow is Professor of Architecture at the University of Pennsylvania. He is author of *Uncommon Ground: Architecture, Technology, and Topography* (2000) and *The Roots of Architectural Invention: Site, Enclosure, Materials* (1993), and coauthor with Mohsen Mostafavi of *Surface Architecture* (2002) and *On Weathering: The Life of Buildings in Time* (1993).

Laura Letinsky is Associate Professor at the University of Chicago and Director of the Graduate Program for the Committee on Visual Arts. She has exhibited her color photographs at the Museum of Modern Art, New York, and Copia, Napa Valley, and is represented by the Edwynn Houk Gallery, New York.

Greg Lynn is principal of Greg Lynn FORM and a studio professor at the University of California, Los Angeles. His architectural designs have received numerous awards and his work is regularly exhibited internationally in both architecture and art museums. He is the author of *Folds, Bodies and Blobs: Collected Essays* (1998), *Animate Form* (1999), and *Embryological House* (forthcoming from Princeton Architectural Press).

Barbara L. Miller teaches art history at Western Washington University and writes on contemporary art, new media, and film.

Patricia Morton is Chair of the Art History Department and Associate Professor of Architectural History at the University of California, Riverside. She is the author of *Hybrid Modernities: Architecture and Representation at the 1913 Colonial Exposition, Paris* (2000).

Mikesch Muecke is Associate Professor of Architecture at Iowa State University.

Mark Robbins bridges the fields of art and architecture in work exhibited widely and is represented in the permanent collection of the San Francisco Museum of Modern Art.

Paulette Singley is Associate Professor in the Department of Architecture at Woodbury University in Los Angeles.

Mitchell Squire is Assistant Professor of Architecture at Iowa State University.

Studio Works principals Robert Mangurian and Mary-Ann Ray both teach at the Southern California Institute of Architecture. They have documented Hadrian's villa at Tivoli for 15 years and produce TIBVRTINI Extra Virgin Olive Oil from the villa's trees.

Natalija Subotincic is Associate Professor of Architecture at the University of Manitoba. She is collaborating with the Museum of Jurassic Technology on the design of an extension to the museum's facilities in Culver City, California.

Ferruccio Trabalzi works and teaches in Los Angeles as a regional and urban planner.

Urban Rock Design is a partnership between architect Jeanine Centuori, Director of Woodbury University's Hollywood Center for Community Research and Design, and artist Russell Rock, who teaches architecture at Pasadena City College.

Allen S. Weiss teaches in the departments of Performance Studies and Cinema Studies at New York University. He is the author, most recently, of *Feast and Folly: Cuisine, Intoxication, and the Poetics of the Sublime* (2002) and *Breathless: Sound Recording, Disembodiment, and the Transformation of Lyrical Nostalgia* (2002).

John C. Welchman is Professor of Modern and Contemporary Art History/Theory at the University of California, San Diego. He is the author most recently of *Art after Appropriation: Essays on Art in the 1990s* (2001); the editor of *Rethinking Borders* (1996) and of the collected writings of Mike Kelley (2003–2004); and coauthor, with culinary historian Anya von Bremzen, of *Please to the Table: The Russian Cookbook* (1990).

INDEX